Colonial Central America

A Bibliography

Colonial Central America

A Bibliography

Including materials on art and architecture, cultural, economic, and social history, ethnohistory, geography, government, indigenous writings, maps and plans, urbanization, bibliographic and archival documentary sources.

Compiled and Annotated

by

Sidney David Markman

DUKE UNIVERSITY

Published by
Center for Latin American Studies
Arizona State University
Tempe

Library of Congress Cataloging in Publication Data

Markman, Sidney David, 1911-
  Colonial Central America.

  Includes indexes.
  1. Central America—Bibliography. I. Title.
Z1437.M37   [F1428] 016.9728   76-23299
ISBN 0–87918–023–4

Published in the United States of America

Printed by Land O'Sun Printers, Inc.
Typeset by Text Craft, Inc.
Bookbinding by Roswell Bookbinding

Bureau of Publications • 5670

CONTENTS

INTRODUCTION

The title of this bibliography should more properly read *Reino de Guatemala,* thereby obviating the need for the qualifying word "colonial." In fact, during most of the colonial period, the greater part of present-day Central America was included within its boundaries. It was administered as the Audiencia de Guatemala and also, divided into provinces, as the Capitanía General de Guatemala. After independence from Spain, these formed the basis for the modern political divisions—the republics of Guatemala, Honduras, El Salvador, Nicaragua, Costa Rica and the Mexican state of Chiapas. During the three centuries of Spanish rule, these areas shared a common history, a history reflected in the stylistic development of the art and architecture of the period.

It was primarily the investigations into the architecture of Guatemala, the most populous and most important province of colonial Central America, that led to the eventual accumulation over a period of about twenty-five years of this bibliography. Though primarily interested in but one particular facet of Central American history, the art monuments, it soon became apparent that these were largely undocumented and undated, making art historical interpretation and stylistic analyses almost impossible. Matters seemingly far afield from the physical study of the monuments themselves had to be considered before the art-historical investigations as such could be undertaken. In order to place the art monuments within an historical context, more than a casual perusal was necessary of long-winded monkish chronicles, travel accounts, geographical descriptions, works on population and demography, maps and plans for the location and identification of colonial towns and their monuments and, most important of all, the reading of what seemed like countless numbers of documents in the Archivo General del Gobierno in Guatemala City and to a lesser extent in the Archivo General de Indias in Seville. Not only documents dealing directly with architectural matters alone were thus found, but many others of indirect import yet pertinent for the art historian, such as: *reales cédulas; cabildos* of the Ayuntamiento of Santiago de los Caballeros de Guatemala (Antigua Guatemala and the capital of the Reino before 1773); *relaciones geográficas;* reports dealing with the founding of towns; conversion of the native population; historical accounts of the monastic orders; and sundry topics as well, all seemingly remote from the original purpose, the study of the art monuments, but actually essential for their documentation. Thus, bibliographical data was accumulated which served not only the needs of art historians, but also investigators of ecclesiastic, social, economic, urban and political history, as well as a host of other disciplines, especially ethnohistory and cultural and social anthropology.

The materials have been divided into eight separate sections. In a few cases titles are listed more than once to provide completeness within each section. Section I contains works written during the sixteenth, seventeenth and eighteenth centuries and may, therefore, be considered as primary sources for investigations in most of the fields mentioned above. Included in this section are also works of broader scope, the whole of Hispano-America, but in which some reference is made to Central America, as for example: ACOSTA, 1792, 1880, 1940; VASQUEZ DE ESPINOSA, 1942, also 1943 and 1944; PONCE, 1873; LOPEZ DE VELASCO, 1894; TORQUEMADA, 1613; and LOPEZ DE GOMERA, 1554, who is of especial interest since DIAZ DEL CASTILLO, 1933, 1937, wrote his own version of the conquest of New Spain, including Chiapas and Guatemala, to correct the errors of López de Gomera, who had never been in the New World, let alone a participant in the actual conquest as had Díaz.

An impressive list of works by writers from the colonial period dealing specifically with the history of the Reino de Guatemala has been published over the past thirty years or so by the Sociedad de Geografía e Historia de Guatemala in Guatemala City. Some of these works were generally unknown except to a few specialists, since they had remained in manuscript until mid-twentieth century, as for example CORTEZ Y LARRAZ, 1958. Others, also of primary importance and in some cases published elsewhere previously were brought out once again in Guatemala City, as for example: FUENTES Y GUZMAN, 1932-33; GARCIA DE LA CONCEPCION, 1956; JUARROS, 1936; REMESAL, 1932; VASQUEZ, 1937-44; VILLAGUTIERRE Y SOTOMAYOR, 1933; XIMENEZ, 1929-31. A Spanish translation of GAGE, 1677, was also published by the Sociedad in 1946.

In addition to works of historical import, Section I also contains some early architectural handbooks which doubtlessly circulated in Hispano-America (see Section III, TORRE REVELLO, 1932) and in the Reino de Guatemala in particular, as for example: DIEZ, 1932; LOPEZ DE ARENAS, 1633; SAGREDO, 1526; and SAN NICOLAS, 1796.

Section II contains works written in the nineteenth and twentieth centuries and may be considered as secondary sources being based in large part on materials listed in Secaion I. The subjects included in Section II range through history, travel accounts, economic geography, urbanization, mestization, social and legal institutions and sundry matters. Also included are oral indigenous literature of Pre-Columbian origin committed to writing in both transliterated versions and in Spanish translation in the colonial period, and published in the nineteenth and twentieth centuries. Some of the eitles in Section II, however, like those in Section I, may also be considered as primary sources, especially those written early in the nineteenth century and being largely accounts of travel and descriptions of the country, as for example: BAILY, 1850; BETETA, 1803; DUNN, 1828; GALINDO, 1836; HALE, 1826; IRISARRI, 1847 and 1960; HAEFKENS, 1827-28, 1832 and 1969; MARURE, 1837; MONTGOMERY, 1839; PINEDA, 1845; ROBERTS, 1827; SCHERZER, 1857; SQUIER, 1852 and 1855; STEPHENS, 1841; STOLL, 1886; TEMPSKY, 1858; THOMPSON, 1829; and WELLS, 1857, all of which have descriptions of the country and frequently include observations on the architecture, particularly colonial churches, as well as discussions on the habits, customs and traditions of the people. These are, therefore, also of interest for ethnohistorians and anthropologists in general.

More recent studies especially worthy of note are: BARON CASTRO, 1942; BATRES JAUREGUI, 1915, 1920, 1949; CHINCHILLA AGUILAR, 1961; GAMEZ, 1889, is in some respects out of date; GARCIA PELAEZ, 1943-44, written between 1833-41 in the style of an eighteenth-century chronicle, summarizes the works of his colonial predecessors; and MUYBRIDGE, 1876, an album of photographs, not only important for the history of photography, but also as a visual account of the physical appearance of many towns, buildings and the countryside of Central America in the third quarter of the nineteenth century. Otḫer recent histories are: GOMEZ CARILLO and MILLA, 1892, 1897, 1905; LANNING, 1955 and 1956; MILLA, 1879–81; SALAZAR, 1897; TRENS, 1957a and 1957b; and VILLACORTA, 1942.

Section III is not as extensive as the first two and deals wholly with art historical materials of a more general nature containing items on town planning and urban development, architectural style, painting, sculpture, problems of indigenous influence, stylistic connections with Spanish art and architecture, and matters of like import but not specifically with colonial Central America alone. Especially worthy of note are ANGULO, 1933–39, containing plans of many colonial buildings in Hispano-America and Central America as well; also ANGULO, 1945, 1950, 1956, being the basic handbook for the art of colonial Latin America. Also important are ATL, 1924–27; BORAH, 1973, for urbanization and the gridiron plan; BUSCHIAZZO, 1940, for a general history of Hispano-American architecture; CHUECA GOITIA, 1966; CHUECA GOITIA, TORRES BALBAS, and GONZALEZ GONZALEZ, 1951, for plans of towns in Hispano-America; GASPARINI, 1972, for the problem of the baroque style; HARDOY and ARANOVICH, 1967, for urbanization; also HARDOY and SCHAEDEL, 1968, for the same; KELEMEN, 1951, for a general art history; KUBLER, 1948; KUBLER and SORIA, 1959, for a general art history of Spain and the New World during the colonial period; MEIS, 1963; TORRE REVELLO, 1956; and TOUSSAINT, 1948.

Section IV deals exclusively with works on the art and architecture of the Reino de Guatemala. The material consists mainly of pamphlets, articles, including some in the daily press, guide books, popular and romantic essays and the like. Though few in number, some excellent scholarly articles as well as some monographs are worthy of mention, as for example: ANGULO, 1936 and 1966; ANNIS, 1968; BERLIN, 1942, 1952, and 1965; BONET CORREA, 1965; CARRERA STAMPA, 1945; CHINCHILLA AGUILAR, 1953 and 1963, a history of art in Guatemala; also DIAZ, 1934, a miscellany of short informative essays; GONZALEZ GALVAN, 1960; LEMOINE VILLACANA, 1961; LUJAN, JORGE, 1963; LUJAN, LUIS, 1964, 1966, and 1967; MARKMAN, 1956, 1961, 1963, the latter, a monograph on San Cristóbal de las Casas, and 1966, a monograph on the colonial architecture of Antigua Guatemala; OLVERA, 1950 and 1951; PARDO and ZAMORA, 1943; RODRIGUEZ DEL VALLE, 1958; SZECSY, 1953; TOLEDO PALOMO, 1956, 1962, 1963, 1964, and 1966; TOSCANO, 1942.

Section V comprises bibliographies pertinent to subjects covered in Sections I, II, III, and IV. Some deal with the whole of Hispano-America and include sections devoted to books printed in the Reino de Guatemala. Most pertinent to Central America are: ADAMS, 1953; BANDELIER, 1880/81; AGRUPACION, etc., 1958–60; BRASSEUR DE BOURBOURG, 1871; GROPP, 1941; GUATEMALA. TIPOGRAFIA NACIONAL, 1944; MEDINA, 1910; McMURTIRE, 1942; O'RYAN, 1897; RODRIGUEZ and PELOSO, 1968. An important work worthy of being brought up to date is SMITH and WILDER, 1948, a bibliography of the art of Latin America with sections on the Central American republics. An excellent work on books printed in colonial times in Guatemala is that of VILLACORTA, 1944, being a resumé or catalogue of four separate book exhibits in Guatemala held between 1939 and 1942.

Section VI, in a sense, is also bibliographical in character, except that it includes published transcriptions of documents in the Archivo General de Indias in Seville and the Archivo General del Gobierno de Guatemala in Guatemala City. Also included in this section are indexes or lists of documents in either or both of these two archives. To a lesser extent, materials in other archives are also listed. Some items are references to as yet unpublished documents of considerable length. Of especial interest are the following; ALTOAGUIRRE Y DUVALLE, 1923–26, an index to *CODI;* AREVALO, 1857 and 1935; CHAMBERLAIN, 1937; *Colección,* etc., *CODI;* 1864/1884, 1885/1926; *Colección de libros,* etc., 1908, containing transcriptions of documents dealing with Central America; FERNANDEZ, 1881–1907; LANNING, 1954; LARREYNAGA, 1857; OROZCO Y JIMENEZ, 1906; PARDO, 1941 and 1944; SCHAEFER, 1946–47, an index to *CODI;* and TORRES LANZAS, 1903, 1906.

One of the most troublesome problems confronting the investigator concerned with colonial Central America is the physical location of towns, especially since many were sometimes moved from one site to another. The toponymy of colonial and modern times as it appears on colonial, nineteenth century and modern maps must be correlated, a task especially necessary in the case of those studies dealing with the history of urbanization and of architecture. Published materials of this sort have been assembled in Section VII including maps and published collections of building plans drawn in colonial times.

Section VIII is an index of some of the more important documents of colonial date that exist in the Archivo General del Gobierno. It should be stated at the outset, however, that the list covers a mere fraction of the thousands of documents housed there. The titles and call numbers given are, in almost all cases, direct quotations of those written by the former director, the late Joaquín Pardo, for the card catalogue in the reading room of the archives building in Guatemala City. Due to the dedication and indefatigable efforts of this one man, the documentary treasures of Archivo General del Gobierno de Guatemala are today as readily available to the investigator as are published works in a well-organized library. The classification system of the documents in Section VIII follows Pardo's (see PARDO, 1945, Section VI). However, some defy being categorized other than under very general headings such as *reales cédulas, relaciones geográficas,* etc. Immediately after the classification number, the date of the document is given in parenthesis. Then follows the *expediente* number and finally the *legajo* number, and in the case of bound tomes, the folio, thus; A 1.10.3 (1728) 18.805–2448, fol. 2. Some of the more interesting documents, especially many *relaciones geográficas,* were paleographed and transcribed by Pardo which he published in the *Boletín del Archivo General del Gobierno de Guatemala.* References to published texts in *BAGG* are given under the descriptive title. In order that these documents may be somewhat more readily useful, proper and place names are included in the general index following the bibliography as a whole.

The mechanics of this bibliography have been kept as simple as possible. Authors' names appear in capital letters followed by the date of publication. In Section I the *floruit* of the author, when known, has been added. Also, where it is known that the item is in the Library of Congress, Washington, D.C., or in the Duke University Library, Durham, N.C., the call number is given after the bibliographical data, preceded by the abbreviation LC/ or DUL/, respectively. Other abbreviations employed are listed below. The general index includes not only names of persons and places, but also subject categories.

The accumulation of the bibliographical material in Washington, D.C., Guatemala and Spain would have been impossible without the constant moral and frequent financial support over many years from the Duke University Research Council. Also, research grants from the American Philosophical Society made possible two rather extended visits, one to Spain and the other to Central America for a study of the architectural monuments as well as work in the Biblioteca Nacional in Guatemala, the Archivo General del Gobierno (Archivo General de Centro America) in that same city, the Archivo General de Indias in Seville, and the Biblioteca Nacional in Madrid.

ABBREVIATIONS

AGG ....*Archivo General del Gobierno.* The colonial archives in Guatemala City. Document numbers have four parts thus: (1) Classification, (2) date, (3) expediente, (4) legajo. For example, A 1.10.3 (1743) 31.322–4048. The name of this important archive has been changed twice. See GUATEMALA. ARCHIVO GENERAL DEL GOBIERNO, Sect. VI, for details.

AGI or AI ....*Archivo de Indias.* Sevilla. Document numbers do not follow a standard form and are given as referred to in other works cited. When read directly in the archives, the most recent catalogue number is given. Name was originally Archivo de Indias and is referred to as such in older publications. More recent name is Archivo General de Indias and is referred to as *AGI.*

AIAA ....*Anales del Instituto de Arte Americano e Investigaciones Estéticas.* Buenos Aires: Facultad de Arquitectura y Urbanismo, Universidad de Buenos Aires. 1948–.

AHG.................*Antropología e historia.* Guatemala: Instituto de Antropología e Historia de Guatemala, Ministerio de Educación Pública. 1949–.

AIAA ....*Anales del Instituto de Arte Americano e Investigaciones Estéticas.* Buenos Aires: Facultad de Arquitectura y Urbanismo, Universidad de Buenos Aires. 1948–1971.

AIIE ....*Anales del Instituto de Investigaciones Estéticas.* México: Universidad Autónoma Nacional de México. 1937–.

ANUARIO EA.......*Anuario de Estudios Americanos.* Sevilla: Escuela de Estudios Hispano Americanos, Consejo Superior de Investigaciones Científicas, 1944–.

ASGH ....*Anales de la Sociedad de Geografía e Historia.* Guatemala. 1924–.

BAGG ....*Boletín del Archivo General del Gobierno de Guatemala.* Guatemala. 1935.

BCIHE ....*Boletín del Centro de Investigaciones Históricas y Estéticas.* Caracas: Facultad de Arquitectura y Urbanismo, Universidad Central de Caracas. 1964–.

BPAU ....*Bulletin of the Pan-American Union.* Washington, D.C.

CODI.................*Colección de documentos inéditos relativos al descubrimiento, conquista y organización de las antiguas posesiones españolas de América y Oceanía, sacados de los Archivos del Reino, y muy especialmente del de Indias. Primera Serie.* Editada por Joaquín Francisco Pacheco, Francisco de Cárdenas y Luis Torres Mendoza (42 vols., Madrid, 1864/84). *Segunda Serie,* publicada por la Real Academia de la Historia (19 vols., Madrid, 1885/1926). See SCHAFER, *Indice,* below, for index of same.

COLD ....*Colección de libros y documentos referentes á la historia de América.* Manuel Serrano Sanz, ed. (Madrid, 1908). v. 8, *Relaciones históricas y geográficas de América Central.*

DUL ....Duke University Library.

DUL/Div. S. ....Duke University, Divinity School Library.

DUL/WCL ....Duke University, Women's College Library.

HAHR................*Hispanic-American Historical Review.* Durham, N.C. Feb. 1918–.

HLAS ....*Handbook of Latin American Studies.* Cambridge: Harvard University Press, Gainesville, Fla. University of Florida Press, 1936–.

HMAI ....*Handbook of Middle American Indians.* Robert Wauchope, general editor. Austin, Texas: University of Texas Press, 1964–.

JSAH................*Journal of the Society of Architectural Historians.* Louisville, Ken. Jan. 1941–.

LC ....Library of Congress.

RI....................*Revista de Indias.* Madrid: Instituto "Fernanadez de Olvedo," Consejo Superior de Investigaciones Científicas. 1940–.

RUSC ....*Revista. Universidad de San Carlos.* Guatemala. 1945–.

Section I

THE COLONIAL PERIOD

Authors of sixteenth, seventeenth, eighteenth and early nineteenth centuries.

Chronicles, histories, missionary activities, geographical reports, travel accounts, etc.

Primary sources: art and architectural history; ethnohistory; social, political and economic history; sundry topics.

1 ACOSTA, JOSE DE (fl. 1539–1600). 1792.

Historia natural y moral de las Indias, en que se tratan las cosas notables del cielo, elementos, metales, plantas y animales de ellas; y los ritos, ceremonias, leyes, gobierno y guerras de los Indios. Madrid: P. Aznar.

DUL/918.A185HA

A sixteenth-century chronicle. Was a Jesuit who spent most of his time while in the New World in Peru. In Book III, ch. 26 he speaks of the earthquakes in Guatemala. The first edition was published in Sevilla in 1590. Other editions appeared in Madrid in 1894 and 1962.

2 ACOSTA, JOSE DE (fl. 1539–1600). 1880.

The natural and moral history of the Indies. Reprinted from the edition of Edward Grimstone, 1604. Edited with notes and an introduction by C.R. Markham. London: Hakluyt Society.

Reprinted by Lennox Hill Publishing Corp. New York, 1973.

3 ACOSTA, JOSE DE. 1940.

Historia natural y moral de las Indias. México: Fondo de Cultura Económica.

See next item.

4 ACOSTA, JOSE DE. 1962.

Historia natural y moral de las Indias en que se tratan de las cosas notables del cielo, elementos, metales, plantas y animales dellas, y los ritos, y ceremonias, leyes y gobierno de los indios. 2a ed. México: Fondo de Cultura Económica, Biblioteca Americana.

This edition is annotated by Edmundo O'Gorman who also wrote a prologue, three appendices as well as the index. First published in this series in 1940. Specific references to Guatemala are to be found on pp. 134, 181, 267, 294 and 353; to Chiapas, p. 190; volcano in El Salvador, 329. Still another edition appeared in 1965, published by the Fondo de Cultura Económica.

5 AGIA, FRAY MIGUEL (fl. after 1563). 1946.

Servidumbres personales de indios. Sevilla: Escuela de Estudios Hispano-Americanos.

DUL/980.5 A267S

A contemporary MS edited by F.J. de Ayala on a special phase of the encomienda system. Spent some years in Guatemala before going to Peru.

5a *Ajpop Huitzitzil Tzuman.*

See GALL, 1963, Section II, below.

6 ALCEDO, ANTONIO DE (fl. 1736–1812). 1789–89.

Diccionario geográfico-histórico de las Indias Occidentales ó América. Madrid: En la Imprenta de B. Cano.

LC/E14.A35

Very general. Little on Central America for the art or architectural historian, but valuable for other disciplines.

7 ALCEDO, ANTONIO DE. 1812–15.

The Geographical and Historical Dictionary of America and the West Indies. Trans. by G.A. Thompson. London: J. Carpenter. 5 vols.

LC/E14.A36

An English translation of the item immediately above.

8 ALDANA, CRISTOBAL DE (fl. 18th. century). ca. 1770.

Compendio histórico chronológico de el establecimiento y progressos de la provincia de la Visitación de Nueva España del Real y Militar Orden de N.S. de la Merced. Extraído de la chrónica que dexó manuscripta el M.R.P.M.F. Francisco Pareja. México: Privately printed by José Gómez, O. Merced.

A facsimile edition, edited by Federico Gómez de Orózco, México. Sociedad de Bibliófilos Mexicanos, 1929. And a reprint of the latter, México, 1953, with an introduction and notes by José Gurría Lacroix.

See PAREJA, FRANCISCO DE. 1882–1883, below, for the history of the Mercedarian order from which this work was extracted.

9 ALVARADO, GONZALO DE (fl. 16th century). 1967.

Probanzas del capitán Gonzalo de Alvarado, conquistador que fue de las Provincias de Guatemala. *ASGH,* 40: 192–228.

Transcribed by Francis Gall. A document in the Archivo General de Indias, Seville.

The brother of Pedro de Alvarado. Founder of Gracias a Dios, Honduras.

9a ALVARADO, PEDRO DE.

see *Cartas barias-antiguas* below.

10 ALVARADO, PEDRO DE (fl. 1485–1541). 1749.

Dos relaciones hechas al mismo Hernán Cortes por Pedro de Alvarado. In Andrés|González Barcía, *Historiadores primitivos de las Indias occidentales.* (Madrid, 1749) 1, 157–166.

LC/E141.B4

11 ALVARADO, PEDRO DE. 1847.

Proceso de residencia contra Pedro de Alvarado. Illustrado con estampas sacadas de los antiguos códices mexicanos, y notas y noticias biográficas, críticas y arqueológicas por D. José Fernando Ramírez. Lo publica paleografiado del MS. original el Lic. Ignacio L. Rayón. Mexico: Impreso por Valdés y Redondas.

See RAMIREZ and RAYON in Section II, for the same in *ASGH.* 7 (1930/31); 95–122; 210–239; 360–387; 513–528.

12 ALVARADO; PEDRO DE (fl. 1485–1541). 1924.

An Account of the Conquest of Guatemala. Edited by S.J. Mackie, with a facsimile of the Spanish original, 1525. New York: Cortes Society.

Reprint, New York: Kraus Reprint Co., 1969.

LC/F1437.A466   DUL/980.08 C828

Two letters with an account of the conquest of Guatemala. First published as an appendix to the fourth letter of relation of Cortés, Toledo, 1525.

13 ALVARADO, PEDRO DE. 1925–26.

Las cartas relaciones de don Pedro de Alvarado. *ASGH,* 2: 215–226. by J. Antonio Villacorta.

A critical essay on Alvarado's letters from Guatemala. Includes facsimiles.

See also VILLACORTA CALDERON, 1925–26 and RIVEREND, n.d. in Section II, below.

14 ALVARADO, PEDRO DE. 1930–31, 1931–32, 1932–33.

Proceso de residencia contra Pedro de Alvarado. *ASGH,* 7: 95–122, 210–239, 360–387, 513–528; 8: 254–267; 392–397; 521–534; 9: 121–129; 256–264.

Transcription of the documents of the case against Alvarado. See also RAMIREZ and RAYON, 1847, Section II, for the original publication.

15 ALVARADO, PEDRO DE. 1936–1937.

Provanca del adelantado don Pedro de Alvarado y Doña Leonor de Alvarado su hija. *ASGH,* 13: 475–487.

Transcription of the original documents.

16 ALVARADO, PEDRO DE. 1934.

Libro viejo de la fundación de Guatemala y papeles relativos a D. Pedro Alvarado. Guatemala: Sociedad de geografía e Historia, Bibliotica "Goathemala," vol. XII. See *Libro viejo* etc. below for complete title.

Alvarado's letters are published along with other historical documents relative to the early years of the Spanish conquest and settlement of Guatemala.

17 ALVARADO, PEDRO DE. 1951.

Muerte de Pedro de Alvarado: Crónica de Michoacán; Cronista Mota Padilla; Cartas de relación de Alvarado a Hernán Cortés; cartas antiguas a la ciudad de Goathemala. Guatemala: Biblioteca de Cultura Popular. Editorial del Ministerio de Educación Pública.

Collection of contemporary documents. Some previously published.

18 ALVARADO, PEDRO DE. 1954.

Relación hecha por Pedro de Alvarado a Hernando Cortés, en que se refieren a las guerras y batallas para pacificar las provincias del antiguo reino de Goathemala. México: Porrúa Hermanos.

Another edition of the letters of Alvarado describing the conquest of Guatemala and the first Spanish town founded there.

19 ALVARADO, PEDRO DE. 1972.

An Account of the Conquest of Guatemala in 1524. Edited by Sedley J. Mackie. Boston: Milford House.

Gives a facsimile of the original letter to Cortés. A reprint of the 1924 edition.

20 ALVARADO, PEDRO DE. n.d.

Relación hecha por Pedro de Albarado a Hernando Cortés, en que se refieren a la conquista de muchas ciudades, las guerras, batallas, traiciones y rebeliones que sucedieron, y la población que hizo de una ciudad; de dos Volcances, uno que exhalaba fuego, y otro humo; de un río hirviendo, y otro frio, y como quedó Albarado herido de un flechazo. In *Cartas de la conquista de América.* Edited and revised by Julio Le Riverend (México: Editorial Nueva España), Vol. 1: 604–616.

See RIVEREND, n.d., sect II.

21 ALVARADO, PEDRO DE. n.d.

Relación hecha por Pedro de Albarado a Hernando Cortés, en que se refieren a las guerras y batallas para pacificar las provincias de

Chapotulan, Checialtenango y Utlatan, la Quema de su cacique, y nombramiento de sus hijos para sucederle, y de tres sierras de acije, azufre y alumbre. In *Cartas de la conquista de América.* Edited and revised by Julio de Riverend (México: Editorial Nueva España), 1:595-603.

See RIVEREND, n.d., sect. II and the foregoing three items.

21a *Anales de los Cakchiqueles. Memorial de Tecpán Atitlan.*

See TELETOR, 1946, sect II, for a translation.

22 ANDAGOYA, PASCUAL DE (fl. 1498–1548). 1825-37.

Relación de los sucesos de Pedrarias Dávila en las provincias de Tierra Firme ó Castilla del Oro, y de lo ocurrido en el descubrimiento de la mar del Sur y costas del Perú y Nicaragua escrita por el Adelantado. . . . In NAVARRETE, 1837, below, *Colección,* 3: 393–456.

23 ANDAGOYA, PASCUAL DE (d. 1548). 1865.

Narrative of the proceedings of Pedrarias Davila in the provinces of Tierra Firme or Castilla del Oro, and of the discovery of the South Sea and the coasts of Peru and Nicaragua. Translated and edited with notes and an introduction by C.R. Markham. London: Hakluyt Society.

A translation of the foregoing item.

ANGHIERA, PIETRO MARTIRE D' (fl. 1455–1526).

See MARTIR DE ANGLERIA, PEDRO.

24 ANTIGUA GUATEMALA, EARTHQUAKE. 1718.

Breve y verdadera historia del incendio del volcán (de fuego) y terremotos de la ciudad (de Guatemala) 27 de septiembre de 1717.

AGG: A1.18.6 (1718) 1400-2021.

Dramatic eyewitness account of the earthquake of 1717. Lots of information on condition of architecture.

25 ANTIGUA GUATEMALA, CATHEDRAL. (1708–43). 1943.

Erección de la santa iglesia catedral en metropolitana; gestiones de los autoridades civiles y eclesiásticos del reino de Guatemala 1708–43; bula de S.S. Benedicto XIV. Guatemala: Tipografía Nacional.

LC/BX4415.G8E7

The documents of the proceedings to raise the cathedral of Antigua Guatemala to the rank of the seat of an archbishopric. Published on the second centennial anniversary. Has some data on the actual building, too.

26 ARANA, TOMAS IGNACIO DE (fl. early 18th century). 1717.

Relación de los estragos y ruinas, que a padecido la ciudad de Santiago de Guathemala por terremotos, y fuego de sus volcanes en este año de 1717. Guatemala (Antigua): Antonio de Pineda Ybarra. Reprint: *ASGH,* 17, 2 (1941/42): 148–160, 232–243.

LC/F1461.S67

A poignant and factual account of the 1717 earthquake in Antigua Guatemala. XIMENEZ, see below, 3:343, Bk. VI, ch. 85 ff., quotes Arana and differs with him regarding the extent of the damage to the city.

A second edition was published in Guatemala City in 1876, Imprenta "El Progreso," Calle de Guadalupe.

27 AROCHENA, FRAY ANTONIO.

Catalogo y noticia de los escritores del órden de San Francisco de la Provincia de Guatemala.

This work, probably a manuscript, is apparently lost. According to BANDELIER (for title see section V, No. 1266) p. 107, he had notice of it though he never saw it. BATRES JAUREGUI (see section II, No. 357) *América Central,* 2:513, also mentions this work, referring to it as *escritos* of Fr. Antonio Arochena, but did not know where it was to be found at the time.

28 ATITLAN, GUATEMALA. 1571.

Relación de los caciques principales del pueblo de Atitlán, 1°de febrero de 1571. *ASGH,* 26 (1952): 437–438. Ecclesiastical and other matters of an Indian town on Lake Atitlán, Guatemala.

29 AVILES, FRAY ESTEVAN (fl. 17th century). 1663.

Historia de Guatemala desde los tiempos de los Indios, hasta la fundación de la provincia de los franciscanos; población de aquellas tierras, propagación, de los Indios, sus ritos, ceremonias, policía y gobierno. According to BANDELIER, Section V, No. 1266, p. 107, published in Guatemala, 1663, by José Pineda Ybarra.

VASQUEZ, writing c.1690, (see below for title), v. 4, 294, speaks of Aviles as ". . . antecesor mío en el ministerio de Cronista de esta Sta. Provincia." BANDELIER *(op. cit.)* mentions this work saying it was said to have been published in 1663 (in Antigua Guatemala), though he did not see it. BATRES JAUREGUI (see section II, No. 357), *América Central,* 2:524, says that this book was lost. SERRANO Y SANZ, *COLD,* Section VI, No. 1398, p. x, note 2, says he never saw it although it is mentioned by O'RYAN (see section VI, No. 1310). A search in the Biblioteca Nacional de Guatemala proved fruitless.

30 AYALA, MANUEL JOSE DE (fl. 1726–1805). 1945.

Notas a la Recopilación de Indias. Madrid: Ediciones Cultura Hispánica.

DUL/349.46 qA973N

See LEYES DE LAS INDIAS, below.

31 BENZONI, GIROLAMO (fl. 1519–1570). 1857.

History of The New World . . . Showing his travels in America from A.D. 1541 to 1556. London: Hakluyt Society.

DUL/910.6 H1516 no.21

Benzoni came to America in 1541, spending fourteen years there, for the most part in Mexico. Not directly pertinent to Central America, except for the early part of the sixteenth century when Guatemala was under the administration of Mexico (Nueva España). Was first published in Latin in 1565 and in Italian in Venice in 1572. See LC/ E141. B42 for this edition, the same on which the Hakluyt translation is based. A facsimile of the Italian edition of 1572 was published in Graz, Austria in 1962 by the Akademische Druk- und Verlagsanstalt.

32 BETANZOS Y QUINONES, GERONIMO (fl. late 17th century). 1961.

Historia sucinta de la construcción de la catedral de Guatemala. Escrita en 1677 por don Gerónimo de Betanzos y Quiñones. *Boletín del Archivo General de la Nación* [México], no. 3:405–430.

The construction history of the cathedral in Antigua Guatemala. See also Section IV, LEMOINE Y VILLACANA.

33 BODEGA Y MOLLINEDO, MANUEL DE LA (fl. late 18th century). 1789.

Dictamen que dio en asesoria el sr. dr. dn. Manuel de la Bodega, del consejo de Su Magestad, oidor de la Real audiencia de la Nueva Guatemala, y superintendente de la real casa de moneda en el pleyto del venerable dean y cabildo de la Santa Iglesia metropolitana de la misma ciudad con el real fisco, en que pretende no deberse comprender las rentas devengadas y no distribuidas en lo resuelto en la real cédula del 23 de agosto de 1786, que establece un nuevo plan de distribución de los diezmos en las iglesias de América, y que al mismo tiempo se obedezca y no se cumpla hasta que informado S.M. de las particulares circunstancias de esta iglesia se sirva resolver lo que estime conveniente. Lo da a luz el ilmo sr. dr. Cagetano Francos y Monroy. Guatemala: Impreso con superior permiso en la Oficina de las benditas ánimas, que dirge don Alexo Mariano Bracamonte.

LC/microfilm AC-2 reel 181, no. 21

The action taken in the controversy between the royal treasurer and cathedral regarding the distribution of tithes.

Located in the Medina Collection, Biblioteca Nacional, Santiago, Chile.

34 BRIZGUZ Y BRU, ATHANASIO GENARO (pseudonym for Zaragoza y Ebri, Agustín Bruno). 1738.

Escuela de arquitectura civil en que se contienen las órdenes de arquitectura, la distribución de los planos de los templos, y casas, y el conocimiento de los materiales. Valencia: En la oficina de J.T. Lucas.

LC/NB 082.3575   DUL/720.9 B898E

An architect's and builder's manual based on seventeenth-century forerunners, especially Fr. LORENZO DE SAN NICOLAS, see below.

35 CADENA, FRAY FELIPE (fl. 18th century). 1774a.

Breve descripción de la noble ciudad de Santiago de los Caballeros de

Guatemala y puntual noticia de su lamentable ruina ocasionada de un violento terremoto el día veintinueve de Julio de 1773. Escrita por Fray Felipe Cadena. Impreso con Superior permiso en la oficina de Don Antonio Sánchez Cubillas en el Pueblo de Mixco en la casa que llaman de Comunidad de Santo Domingo. Republished by El Museo Guatemalteco. Guatemala: Imprenta de Luna, 1858.

A moving and factual description of the ruin of Antigua Guatemala in 1773. A pamphlet of 56 pp. A copy is in the Biblioteca Nacional de Guatemala. Cited by MEDINA (see Section V), 169, no. 382.

36   CADENA, FELIPE. 1774b.

Breve descripción de la noble ciudad de Santiago de los Caballeros de Guatemala, y puntual noticia de su lamentable ruina ocasionada de un violento terremoto el día veinte y nueve de julio de mil setecientos setenta y tres. Mixco, Guatemala: A. Sánchez Cubillas.

A factual account of the damage to the city of Antigua Guatemala as a result of the earthquake of 1773. Very important descriptions of the architecture. Slightly different version of the foregoing item.

37   CADENA, FRAY FELIPE. 1865–66.

Descripción de la ciudad y reino de Guatemala. *La Semana* [Guatemala], nos. 78–85.

Probably a transcription of the item immediately above. Judging by the title as given by BATRES JAUREGUI, *América Central,* 39, seems to have included material besides the description of the ruin of 1773. See Section II below for BATRES JAUREGUI, 1915, 1920, 1949.

38   *Calendario manual y guía de forasteros.* 1792–1813.

Guatemala: Published by Ignacio Beteta.

Name is not always consistent in various editions. *Kalendario y guía de forasteros de Guatemala y sus provincias para el año de 1806.* Other editions are dated Guatemala 1792, 1806, and 1813, all published by the printer Ignacio Beteta.

See BETETA, 1803, Sect. II.

Is mentioned by SALAZAR, *Desenvolvimiento,* 392 (see Section II) and another edition is supposedly in the "Middle American Research Library: of Tulane University, New Orleans, La.

Apparently was an annual publication. It includes descriptions of colonial church architecture and sundry matters of interest to the traveler.

See RODRIGUEZ BETETA, VIRGILIO, below for an article on this publication.

39   CANO, FRAY AGUSTIN. (fl. 17th century).

Historia de la provincia de Predicadores de Chiapa y Guatemala.

A MS, the title of which as given by Beristain de Souza, see Section V, is *Historia de la provincia de San Vicente de Chiapa y Guatemala del órden de*

Santo Domingo. It is also mentioned by Bandelier, 97, see Section V below, who says it is a fragment of a larger MS then, c.1880, in the library of the Museo Nacional in Guatemala City. On page 106 he says that this MS was possibly written by Cano, but he is not certain. It is also mentioned by Salazar, *Desenvolvimiento,* 353, see Section II below.

May possibly be part of Molina's MS. See below for bibliographical data.

40 CANO, FRAY AGUSTIN. 1942–43.

> Informe dado al Rey por el Padre Fray Agustín Cano sobre la entrada que por la parte de la Verapaz se hizo al Petén en el año de 1695, y un fragmento de una carta al mismo, sobre el propio asunto. *ASGH,* 18:65–79.

This may quite possibly be the same MS mentioned by Bandelier, see item immediately above. According to Villacorta, *Historia Capitanía General,* 69, note 7, see section II below, this MS was published by the Sociedad Económica in Guatemala City in 1875. The same material is treated by XIMENEZ, see below, 2:433 ff., also 2:458 ff. dealing with an expedition to the Choles Indians in Verapaz c. 1683–1686, see also 3:7 ff. Ximénez also cites two letters of Cano, v. 3, 85 ff. The same theme is treated through page 135. He does not mention the letter published in the above item.

41 CARRANDI MENAN, FRANCO ANTONIO (fl. 18th century). 1738.

> *Viaje del gobernador Carrandí Menán al Valle de Matina.* San José, C.R.: Imprenta Nacional.

A brief description of a region in Costa Rica, 22 pages. In the Latin American Collection, University of Texas Library.

42 CARTAJENA, FRAY JUAN DE. 1747.

> *La Santa Iglesia de Guatemala, madre fecundísima de hijos ilustrísimos.* México.

Mentioned by Rodríguez Beteta, *ASGH,* v. 2 (1925/26), 91, and also listed by BANDELIER, 1880 109. See Section V below.

43 *Cartas barias-antiguas.* Early 16th century.

> *Libro rotulado: cartas barias-antiguas.* Este volumen contiene: cartas del Adelantado don Pedro de Alvarado, del Obispo Francisco Márroguin, del obispo Fray Bartolome de las Casas y otras personas.

AGG: A1.2.5(1534)15760–2202.

A bound volume of unpublished documents. See Section VIII, below.

Cartas de Indias.

See SPAIN. MINISTERIO DE FOMENTO. 1877. Sect. VI, below.

44 CASAS, BARTOLOME DE LAS (fl. 1474–1566). 1646.

> *Brevíssima relación de la destruyción de las Indias; y otros tratados.* Barcelona: Antonio Lacavellería.

45 CASAS, BARTOLOME DE LAS. 1875–76.

Historia de las Indias. Escrita por Fray Bartolomé de las Casas, obispo de Chiapa ahora por primera vez dada a luz por el marqués de la Fuensanta del Valle y d. José Sancho Rayón. Madrid: Imprenta de M. Ginesta. 5 vols.

46 CASAS, BARTOLOME DE LAS. 1909.

Apologética historia de las Indias. Ed. by Manuel Serrano Sanz. Madrid: Bailly, Bailliere é hijos.

47 CASAS, BARTOLOME DE LAS. 1951.

Historia de las Indias. Estudio preliminar de Lewis Hanke. Edición e índice analítico de A. Millares Carlo. México: Fondo de Cultura Económica. 3 vols.

DUL/972.8 C335HB A65

48 CASAS, BARTOLOME DE LAS 1965.

Tratados. México: Fondo de Cultura Económica. DUL/980.5 033STR 1966

49 CAXICA Y RADA, AGUSTIN DE LA (fl. 1700–1755) 1914.

Breve relación de el lamentable estrago, que padeció esta ciudad de Santiago de Guatemala, con el terremoto de el día quatro de Marzo, de este año de 1751. *Revista chilena de historia geografía.* 12, 16:154–169.

Also published in the same year in Mexico. The MS is in the Biblioteca Nacional de Chile. See MEDINA, 113, no. 225, section V below. Critical essay in addition to the text of the MS which was originally published as a broadside of four pages.

50 CERDA, JOSE DE LA (fl. 17th century).

Mentioned by Vásquez.

No author of this name appears in the bibliographies of works either in MS or published during the colonial period in Guatemala. VASQUEZ 1937–44, 4:147 ff., see below, mentions Cerda as layman and a writer, yet further on, 364, he refers to him as "el religioso."

51 LIC. CERRATO. (fl. mid-16th century).

His full name was Lic. Alonso López de Cerrato.

Though there are no works listed under his name, he appears time and time again in the contemporary chronicles in the mid-sixteenth century since he was responsible for seeing that the law prohibiting the enslavement of the Indians was complied with.

52 CERVANTES DE SALAZAR, FRANCISCO (fl. c.1514–c.1575). 1914, 1936.

Crónica de Nueva España. v.1, Madrid: Hausery Menet. 3 vols.

LC/F1230.C38   DUL/972 P214 t.1–3

Some reference to Chiapas and Guatemala as part of vice-royalty of New Spain. Vols. 2 and 3, México: Talleres gráficos de Arqueología y Etnografía, 1936. Another edition, M. Magallón, editor. Madrid: Hispanic Society of America, 1914. Also another Madrid: Ediciones Atlas, 1971, with preliminary notes by Agustín Millares Carlo.

53 CERVANTES DE SALAZAR, FRANCISCO 1939.

México en 1554. Tres diálogos latinos traducidos por Joaquín García Icazbalceta. México: Universidad Nacional Autónoma.

Description of Mexico City in mid-sixteenth century.

54 CEVALLOS, FRAY BERNARDO PATRICIO (fl. 1750). 1935/36.

Visión de Paz. Nueva Yerusalén. *ASGH,* 12:463–485.

Deals with the settlement and the *reducción* of Verapaz in mid-sixteenth century. Based on a transcription done in 1750. Original report written by Fr. JUAN DE RIVERA, see Section VIII for complete title of the document.

AGG: A1.18.4 (1650)38.300–4501.

55 CHIAPAS. CATHEDRAL. 1790.

Ordenanzas de la Santa Iglesia Catedral de Chiapas. Guatemala: Alejo Mariano Bracamonte y Lerín.

56 CHIAPAS. COLEGIO SEMINARIO DE NUESTRA SENORA DE LA CONCEPCION. 1779.

Erección, establecimiento, y constituciones del Colegio seminario de nuestra Señora de la Concepción, de Ciudad Real de Chiapa. Nueva Guatemala: Reimpreso de A. Sánchez Cubillas.

35 page pamphlet on the founding of the Seminario in San Cristóbal de las Casas.

Located in the Latin American Collection, University of Texas Library.

57 CHILTON, JOHN (fl. 16th century). 1809–1812.

A notable discourse of M. John Chilton, touching the people, manners, mines, cities, riches, forces, and other memorable things of New Spaine and other provinces in the West Indies, 1568–1586. In Richard Hakluyt, *Collections of the Early Voyages, Travels and Discoveries of the English Nation.* (London: R.H. Evans. 5 vols.) 3:541–588.

LC/G210.H146 v.3   DUL/910.4 qH156C

He began his travels in 1568, mainly in Mexico. Just a few words in passing on Guatemala.

58 *La ciudad martir.* 1923.

A reprint of CADENA, *Breve descripción,* see above, and GONZALEZ BUSTILLO, *Razón puntual,* see below. First published in serial form in *Diario de Centro América.* Guatemala, C.A.

Description of ruin of Antigua Guatemala after the earthquake of 1773.

59   CIUDAD REAL, ANTONIO DE (fl. late 16th century). 1873.

Relación breve y verdadera de algunas cosas de las muchas que sucedieron al Padre Fray Alonso Ponce en las provincias de la Nueva España . . . escrita por dos religiosos, sus compañeros. Madrid. 2 vols. In *Colección de documentos inéditos para la historia de España.* (Madrid 1842–1895), vols. 57–58.

See PONCE, 1873, below.

60   CIUDAD VIEJA (SANTIAGO DE LOS CABALLEROS DE GUATE-MALA).

Fundación de la ciudad de Guatemala en Almolonga–1527. *ASGH, 4 (1927–28):95–106. Libro Viejo.*

A document in Archivo de la Municipalidad de Guatemala; the contents of which are included in *Libro Viejo,* see below.

61   CLAVIJERO, FRANCISCO JAVIER (fl. 1731–1787). 1826.

Historia antigua de Mégico: sacada de los mejores historiadores, y de los manuscritos, y de las pinturas antiguas de los Indios; dividida en diez libros . . . con disertaciones sobre la tierra, los animales, y los habitantes de Mégico. Londres and Mégico: R. Ackerman. 2 vols.

LC/F1219.C624

This work has appeared in many editions and interestingly enough in English translation both in England and in the United States. The title given here is not of the first edition which was possibly published for the first time in 1780–1781, *Storia antica del Messico* Venice: Cesena. 4 vols.

The History of Mexico. Translated from the original Italian (sic) by Charles Cullen. London: G.G.J. and J. Robinson. 1787. 2 vols.

Other English editions appeared in Philadelphia, 1804; Richmond, Va., 1807; London, 1807; Philadelphia, 1817.

Mexican editions date from 1844, 1853, 1861–62, 1868, 1883, 1917, 1944, 1945 and 1948.

The inclusion of some of the "pinturas" from the Relaciones Geográficas is of interest to the art historian.

62   CLAVIJERO, FRANCISCO JAVIER. 1807.

The History of Mexico. 2nd. ed. London: J. Johnson.

LC/F1219.C622

The second edition of the item immediately above. For other editions in English see LC/F1219.C621–LC/F1219.C623.

63   COBO, BERNABE (fl. 1582–1657). 1890–95.

História del Nuevo Mundo. Sevilla: E. Rasco.

LC/F1411.C65

Though written in 1653, the MS remained unpublished until the end of the nineteenth century. It deals mainly with Peru. But he apparently spent some time in Guatemala. VASQUEZ DE ESPINOZA, *Descripción,* 194 ff., see below, cites some letters of Cobo, a member of the Companía de Jesús, with descriptions of a journey made from Guatemala to Oaxaca in the early seventeenth century.

64 COBO, BERNABE. 1956.

Obras del P. Bernabé Cobo de la Compañia de Jesús. Estudio preliminar y edición del P. Francisco Mateos. Madrid: Biblioteca de Autores Españoles, vols. 91–92.

Contains the foregoing as well as his letters and other writings.

65 COCKBURN, JOHN, *mariner.* 1735.

A Journey Over Land, from the Gulf of Honduras to the Great South Sea. London: C. Rivington.

LC/1431.C66   DUL/TR 972.8 C665

Appended to title is the following: *To which is added . . . A Brief Discovery of some Things best worth Noteing in the Travels of Nicholas Withington, a Factor in the East Indiase . . . As also an account of the manner, customs, and behaviour of the Indians.*

In 1730 the ship Cockburn was on was overwhelmed by pirates and he and about five Englishmen made their way from the Atlantic coast of Honduras to the Pacific, avoiding towns. The Englishmen were killed or died en route.

See MELENDEZ CHAVERRI, 1962b, section II for a recent treatment of Cockburn's travels in Costa Rica.

66 CONTRERAS GUEBARA, ALONSO (fl. late 16th century). 1946.

Relación hecha a su magestad por el gobernador de Honduras de todos los pueblos de dicha gobernación. Año de 1582. *BAGG,* 11:5–19.

A report in compliance with a royal order. Written in Valladolid de Comayagua, Honduras, 20 April 1592. Gives in detail the number of Spanish towns and their population. Also lists the Indian towns and the number of *tributarios* in each. The document is written on eight sheets of paper and located in *AGG.* Document number is not given in the published version cited here.

67 CONCEPCION, FRAY MIGUEL DE LA. 1956.

Historia Belemítica. Vida ejemplar y admirable del venerable siervo de Dios y Padre Pedro de San José Betancur. Guatemala: Sociedad de Geografía e Historia.

A detailed history chronicling the establishment of the Bethlemite order in Guatemala and beyond including a biography of Betancur, the first member of the order.

68   CONVENTOS, FRANCISCAN. 1689.

Descripción de los conventos de la provincia del nombre de Jesús de Guatemala, hecha el año de 1689. *Archivo Arzobispal.* Guatemala, C.A. A 4.5–2(1689). Transcribed in VASQUEZ, 4:33–67.

The editor of VASQUEZ, see below, Lázaro Lamadrid, transcribes this important document with a description of all the Franciscan monastic establishments in Chiapas, Guatemala, Honduras and El Salvador. Data on the number of friars in residence in each is also given. Of invaluable help in locating and dating buildings. This document may have also been used by FUENTES Y GUZMAN, see below, since many of his factual information data seem to have been extracted from it.

69   CORDOVA, FRAY MATIAS DE (d. 1828). 1798.

Utilidades de que todos los indios y ladinos se vistan y calcen a la española y medios de consequirlo sin violencia, coacción ni mandato. Guatemala: En la Imprenta de d. Ignacio Beteta. Memoria premiada por la real Sociedad Económica de Guatemala. Reprinted in *ASGH*, (1937–38):211–222.

He won the prize for this short work 13 December 1797. A Dominican, who was "Maestro de Estudiantes en su Convento de Santo Domingo de la Capital." This work is cited and praised by GARCIA PELAEZ, v. 3, 202 ff., see Section II below, in the nineteenth century and more recently by VILLACORTA CALDERON, 182, note 16, see Section II below.

70   CORTES, HERNANDO. (fl. 1485–1547). 1868.

The Fifth Letter of Hernando Cortes to the Emperor Charles V., Containing an Account of his Expedition to Honduras. Translated from the original Spanish by Don Pascual de Gayangos. London: Hakluyt Society.

See following item.

71   CORTES, HERNAN. 1942.

Cartas de relación de la conquista de Méjico. Madrid: Espasa-Calpe. 5a ed. 2 vols.

Contains the fifth letter with an account of the expedition to Honduras. Has an illustration, p. 227, from the *Lienzo de Tlaxcala,* plate 79 dealing with Alvarado's expedition to Guatemala. Also mentions Alvarado in Utatlán and his military operations there, p. 226 ff.

72   CORTES, HERNAN. 1971.

Hernan Cortes: Letters from Mexico. Trans. and ed. by A.R. Pagden. Introduction by J.H. Elliot. New York: Grossman Publishers.

73   CORTES Y LARRAZ, PEDRO DE (fl. 1711–1786).

Descripción geográfico-moral de la diócesis de Goathemala hecha por su Arzobispo el Ilmo. Sr. dn. Pedro Cortés y Larraz del Consejo de S.M. en el tiempo que visitó y fue desde el día 3 de Noviembre de 1768 hasta el día 5 de Julio de 1719 desde el día 22 de Noviembre de 1769 hasta el día 9 de Febrero de 1770. MS. AGI, Aud. Guat. 948. 3 tomos en pergamino.

A remarkable work on conditions in Guatemala and El Salvador in the third quarter of the eighteenth century. Gives statistics on character of population, economy, religion, society, and sundry matters on the tens of towns he visited. Also vivid factual descriptions of road conditions and local scenery. Includes 112 beautifully done maps, bird's-eye views, so that topography is clear and even domestic, civil and religious buildings, especially churches, are depicted.

The report was sent to Spain in 1771 and may still be seen in the Archivo de Indias, Seville.

74 CORTES Y LARRAZ, PEDRO DE. 1958.

Descripción geográfico-moral de la diócesis de Goathemala. Guatemala: Sociedad de Geografía e Historia de Guatemala, Tipografía Nacional. Biblioteca "Goathemala," v. 20.

DUL/972.81 qB582

The preceding item published for the first time. Unfortunately it is printed on a poor quality paper so that the maps are unclear.

BANDELIER, 108, knew of the existence of this MS, see Section V, and it is also listed by TORRES LANZAS, *Relación,* no. 74 ff., see section VII below, who gives the former number used for documents, AGI 103-Cajón 1, Legajo 14, 1768–1770. Descripción etc.

75 CORTES Y LARRAZ, PEDRO DE. 1921.

Descripción geográfico-moral de la provincia de San Salvador en la diocesis de Goathemala. *Colección de documentos importantes relativos a la República de El Salvador* (San Salvador: Imprenta Nacional), pp. 45–294.

The parts dealing with El Salvador extracted from the MS in the Archivo de Indias. The maps are not reproduced.

76 CORTES Y LARRAZ. 1925.

Expediente de visita general de la diócesis, practicada por el Arzobispo don Pedro Cortez Y Larraz, durante los años 1770 a 1778. *AGI* 103-1-14. Descripción y mapa de la parroquía de Chiquimula. *ASGH,* 2:36–42. Transcribed by Lisandro Sandoval.

See also *ASGH,* 16 (1939–40): 417, where it is listed among documents pertinent to Guatemala. The section dealing with Chiquimula, Guatemala extracted from the MS of CORTES Y LARRAZ, see above.

77 CRIADO DE CASTILLA, ALONSO (fl. 17th century). 1946.

Informe rendido ante su Magestad por el presidente de la Real Audiencia, Alonso Criado de Castillo, sobre varios asuntos y calamidades habidas en su jurisdicción. Año de 1608. *BAGG,* 11:20–44.

Transcription of a document.

78 *Crónicas de un franciscano.*

Title mentioned by V.M. Díaz (Section IV) in *La romántica ciudad colonial,*

p. 8 and elsewhere. Author is not mentioned, though presumably from the colonial period.

79 CRUZ Y MOYA, FRAY JUAN JOSE (fl. ca. 1706–ca. 1760). 1955.

Historia de la santa y apostólica Provincia de Santiago de Predicadores de México en la Nueva España. México: Librería de M. Porrúa. 2 vols.

This work was written 1756–57 and is mentioned by both BERISTAIN, no. 2027 and MEDINA, no. 4233, though neither of them probably saw it. This first printing was made from the original MS once in the possession of Joaquín García Icazabalceta.

A history of the founding of the Dominican order in New Spain. Period covered is 1527–1544.

80 DAVILA, PEDRARIAS (fl. 1525). 1946.

Carta al Emperador, refiriendo al descubrimiento de Nicaragua. Revista de la Academia de Geografía e Historia de Nicaragua [Managua], 8, 3:1–12.

A transcription of a letter, 1525, of Pedrarias Davila dealing with the discovery of Nicaragua.

81 DAVILA PADILLA, FRAY AGUSTIN (fl. 1562–1604). 1955.

Historia de la fundación y discurso de la Provincia de Santiago de México, de la Orden de Predicadores. 3a ed. México: Editorial Academia Literaria.

The first edition of this work was published in 1596 and the second sometime between 1626–1648. It deals with the time of the conquest and settlement of the Dominican province in New Spain, including Guatemala. Interesting sidelights on languages, customs, religion of the native population.

82 DAZA, FRAY PEDRO.

Memorias históricas de la fundación y predicación de los Religiosos de la Merced de la Redención de cautivos en Guatemala.

This seventeenth-century work is mentioned by Bandelier, 107, see Section V, who heard of it, but who had never seen it. An unpublished MS, supposedly a history of the Mercedarian order in Chiapas and Guatemala and possibly the rest of Central America.

83 DIAZ DEL CASTILLO, BERNAL (1492–1584). 1852–53.

Verdadera historia de los sucesos de la conquista de la Nueva España, por Bernal Díaz del Castillo. In Enrique de Vedia, editor, Historiadores primitivos de Indias (Madrid: Imprenta de M. Rivadeneyra). 2 vols. See items immediately below for some other editions and translations.

84 DIAZ DEL CASTILLO, BERNAL. 1933, 1934.

Verdadera y notable relación del descubrimiento y conquista de la Nueva España y Guatemala. Guatemala: Sociedad de Geografía e Historia de Guatemala, Tipografía Nacional. Biblioteca "Goathemala," vols. X–XI.

LC/F1230.D5363   DUL/972.81 qB582 v.10–11.

Díaz was one of the conquistadors in the forces of Pedro de Alvarado, who lived out his declining years in Antigua Guatemala where he died. His straightforward accounts are of inestimable importance not only for the history of the conquest, but also as a source of information on urbanization, Indian customs, early colonial society, and a plethora of facets of sixteenth-century Chiapas and Guatemala.

He probably finished writing in 1568, but the book was not published for many years. There are many modern editions printed in Spain, Mexico and Guatemala as well as translations in English and other languages. Two documents concerning the original MS are in the Archivo General de Gobierno de Guatemala. A1.23(1575)1513–496

The president of the Audiencia sends Diaz del Castillo's *crónica* to the king. See PARDO, *Prontuario,* 41, Section VI below, also Section VIII, A1.23 (1575) 1513–496. Receipt of same is acknowledged, A1.23 (1576) 1513–497. See PARDO, *ibid.*

85 DIAZ DEL CASTILLO, BERNAL. 1941–42.

Carta de Bernal Díaz del Castillo, dirigida a Fray Bartolomé de las Casas. *ASGH,* 17:430–432.

Transcribed from *AGI.* Simancas. Audiencia de Guatemala. Cartas y expedientes de personas seculares del distrito de dicha Audiencia, años 1526 y 1560. Díaz petitions for help for the Indians of his encomienda who have been cheated out of their land. Dated in 1558.

86 DIAZ DEL CASTILLO, BERNAL. 1943.

Historia verdadera de la conquista de la Nueva España. México: Nuevo Mundo. 2 vols.

A modernized version of the foregoing item with a prologue and notes by Ramón Iglesia.

87 DIAZ DEL CASTILLO, BERNAL. 1956.

The Bernal Díaz Chronicles; *The True Story of the Conquest of Mexico.* Translated and edited by Albert Idell. Garden City; N.Y.: Doubleday.

LC/ F1230. D5442   DUL/ 972.02 D542HA

88 DIAZ DEL CASTILLO, BERNAL (1492–1584). 1956 (1958).

The Discovery and Conquest of Mexico, 1517–1521. New York: Grove Press.

DUL/ 972.02 D542D

A translation by A.P. Maudslay. Based on a MS edited and published in México: Genaro García, 1904. Introduction by Irving A. Leonard. An abridged version published in New York: Noonday Press, 1965.

89 DIEZ, RAMON PASCUAL (fl. late 18th century). 1932.

Arte de hacer el estuco jaspeado, o de imitar jaspes a poca costa, y con la mayor propeidad. Transcribed and edited by José Gabriel Navarro, in *Archivo español de arte y de arqueología*, 8 (1932): 237–257. See Section III for a description.

90 DIEZ DE LA CALLE, JUAN (fl. 1646). 1646.

Memorial, y noticias sacras, y reales del imperio de las Indias Occidentales. Madrid.

LC/F1412 D56 (office)

See item immediately below. No publisher given. A second edition, Bibliófilos Mexicanos, México, 1932. Privately printed edition of 50 copies.

91 DIEZ DE LA CALLE, JUAN. 1648.

Memorial y compendio breve del libro intitulado Noticias sacras y reales de los imperios de la Nueva España, el Perú y sus Islas de las Indias Occidentales. Madrid.

LC/F1412 D56 (office)

Gives a description of the audiencia de Guatemala in chp. IV, 113–132 of LC copy. A microfilm of the above from the Medina Library in Santiago de Chile is in the Library of Congress: LC/microfilm, AC-2, reel 195, no. 23.

Another copy is in the Library of Congress dated 1646 with a slightly different title *Memorial, y noticias sacras, y reales de las Indias Occidentales* etc. . . . published in Madrid, 1646.

BANDELIER, 88, see Section V, gives the title as *Memorial y Resumen breve de Noticias de las Indias Occidentales,* Madrid, 1654.

Apparently FUENTES Y GUZMAN, see below, had a copy at his disposal for his mentions Diez, v. 2, 12, note 1.

92 DIEZ DE NAVARRO, LUIS (fl. 18th century). 1744.

Información rendida por el Ing. Luis Diez de Navarro de su viaje por las provincias de Guatemala. Año de 1744. AGG: A1.17.3 (1744) 17.508–2335.

Diez was a Spanish military engineer and architect who worked in Guatemala during the third quarter of the eighteenth century and who had an important influence on the architecture of Antigua Guatemala. He apparently made an inspection trip of the Reino de Guatemala of which this document is his report.

It is possibly the same as that mentioned by SERRANO SANZ, see Section VI, *COLD,* page xxix, note who says it is in the Biblioteca Real, Miscelánea de Ayala, tomo 3, folios 298–305. He gives the title as "Descripción de Guatemala, 1745." BATRES JAUREGUI, *ASGH,* 5 (1928–29): 384, mentions this item, but does not say if it was in MS or in published form. He may, however, have been referring to *Relación sobre el Antiguo Reyno de Guatemala, hecha por el Ingeniero don Luís Diez de Navarro en 1745,* published by Imprenta Nueva de L. Luna, Guatemala, 1850. See below.

The title of the foregoing is also given as *Extracto de una relación* etc. also published by Imprenta Luna, Guatemala, 1850. See below.

93 DIEZ DE NAVARRO, LUIS. 1850a.

Extracto de una relación sobre el Antiguo Reyno, hecha por el Ingeniero Don Luis Diez Navarro en 1745. Guatemala: Imprenta de Luna.

See the item immediately above.

94 DIEZ DE NAVARRO, LUIS. 1850b.

Relación sobre el Antiguo Reyno de Guatemala, hecha por el Ingeniero don Luis Diez de Navarro en 1745. Guatemala: Imprenta Nueva de L. Luna.

See the two items immediately above.

95 DIEZ DE NAVARRO, LUIS. 1939.

Informe sobre la Provincia de Costa Rica presentado por el Ingeniero Don Luis Diez de Navarro al Capitán General de Guatemala Don Tomás de Rivera y Santa Cruz, año de 1744. *Revista de los Archivos Nacionales, Costa Rica,* 3:579-600.

The same as the foregoing, *AGG* A1.17.3 (1744) 17.508-2335.

96 DURAN, PADRE FRAY DIEGO (fl. 16th century). 1867-80.

Historia Indias de Nueva España y Islas de Tierra Firme. México: Imprenta de J.M. Andrade y F. Escalante. 2 vols.

The first edition. Vol. 2 was published in 1880 including an atlas. Some plates are hand colored.

Mainly on Mexico.

97 DURAN, FRAY DIEGO. 1967.

Historia de las Indias de Nueva España e Islas de la Tierra Firme. México: Editorial Porrúa Hermanos. 2 vols.

LC/F1219. D944 1967

See item immediately above. Another edition, México: Imprenta Nacional, 1951.

98 ECHEVERZ, FERNANDO DE. 1742.

Ensayos mercantiles para adelantar por medio de el establecimiento de una compañia el comercio de los fructos de el reyno de Guatemala. A beneficio de el publico, real haver, y diezmos ecclesiásticos. Guatemala: Sebastián de Arebalo.

LC/microfilm AC-2, reel 178, no. 21

A plan for economic development. According to GARCIA PELAEZ (Section II), it was written c.1741-1742. A microfilm copy is in the Library of Congress.

99   Efemérides de Guatemala desde su fundación hasta la ruina de 1773.

This MS is noted by BANDELIER, 108, see Section V below. He gives no details as to its contents. Apparently it is lost now.

100   ENCINAS, DIEGO DE (fl. 16th century). 1945–1946.

Cedulario indiano. Facsimile edition, A. García Gallo, ed. Madrid: Instituto de Cultura Hispánica.

DUL/ 349.72 fM611C

See ENCINAS . . . 1945, sec. VI for a description.

101   ESCUINTLA, GUATEMALA. 1779.

Varias noticias del reyno de Guatemala. 1779. Folio 16 hojas. In *Biblioteca del Depósito Hidrográfico de Madrid.* Virreinato de México, tomo 4, doc. 70.

Description of a journey from Guatemala City to Escuintla.

102   ESPINO, FRAY FERNANDO. 1674a.

Historia de la reducción y conversión de la provincia de Tegusgalpa con la vida, virtudes y pródigos de tres mártires. Guatemala: José Pineda Ibarra.

An account of missionary activity in a still non-pacified region of Honduras in the seventeenth century. A slight variation in spelling and in the title is given by BANDELIER, 105, see Section V below, *Historia de la reducción y conversión de la provincia de Taguzgalpa* etc. He did not know if it still existed at the time, (1880).

This may be the same work as that published in *COLD,* 329–373, see Section VI below, with a longer title and another variant spelling of the region missionized. See item immediately below.

103   ESPINO, FRAY FERNANDO. 1674b.

Relación verdadera de la reducción de los Indios infieles de la provincia de Taguisgalpa, llamados Xicaques, cuyos operarios han salido, y salen desta provincia del SS. nombre de Iesús de Goatemala, desde el año 1612 hasta el presente de 1674 . . . Guatemala: Joseph de Pineda Ybarra.

LC/1401.C68, vol. 8

Probably the same as the item immediately above. Published in *COLD,* 329–374.

104   ESPINOSA, FRAY ISIDORO FELIX DE (fl. 1679–1755). 1737.

Nuevas espresas del peregrino Americano-Septentrional Atlante, descubiertas en lo que hizo cuando vivía, y aún despues de su muerte manifestado el V.R.P. Antonio Márgil de Jesús. México: Imprenta Real del superior gobierno, y del Nuevo Rezado de Doña María de Rivera.

LC/BX4705.M3252

The missionary activity of the convento of La Recolección, Colegio de Propaganda Fide, in Antigua Guatemala. A biography of an outstanding missionary. Data on the establishment of conventos, gathering of Indians into towns, construction of churches, and other data.

Published also with a slightly different title, *El peregrino* . . . México: Impresa por Joseph Bernado de Hogal, 1737.

See the following two items for a history of Franciscan missionary activity in Mexico and especially in Guatemala.

105 ESPINOSA, ISIDRO FELIX DE. 1746.

Chrónica apostólica y seráphica de todos los colegios de Propaganda Fide de esta Nueva España de misioneros franciscanos observantes, erigidos con autoridad pontificia y regia, para la reformación de los fieles y conversión de los gentiles . . . México.

Contains detailed information on Franciscan houses in Guatemala. For a recent, updated edition with notes, see item immediately below.

106 ESPINOSA, FRAY ISIDRO FELIX DE. 1964.

Crónica de los Colegios de Propaganda Fide de la Nueva España. Washington, D.C.: American Academy of Franciscan History.

DUL/271.3 qF896

An important source for missionary activity in colonial Mexico and Central America as well as data on the construction of the monastic establishments of the order of La Recolección whose principal house was located in Antigua Guatemala.

The edition was prepared by Lino G. Canedo, O.F.M. who also annotated the text.

107 ESTRADA, JUAN DE (fl. 1579). 1955.

Descripción de la provincia de Zapotitlán y Suchitepéquez. Año de 1579. Por su Alcalde Mayor, capitán Juan de Estrada y el escribano Fernando de Niebla. *ASGH*, 28:68–84.

A *relación* on a region in Guatemala. Data on geography, native and Spanish inhabitants. See also Suchitepéquez, 1579, Section VII, below.

108 ESTRADA DE RAVAGO, JUAN. 6 May 1572.

Descripción de las Provincias de Costa Rica, Guatemala, Honduras, Nicaragua y Tierra-Firme y Cartagena.

A geographical relation. BANDELIER, 104, see Section V, saw it and says it was a MS belonging to E.G. Squier.

109 EXQUEMELIN, ALEXANDRE OLIVIER (fl. late 17th century). 1891.

The Buccaneers and Marooned of America: Being an Account of the Famous Adventures and Daring Deeds of Certain Notorious Freebooters of the Spanish Main. Edited by Howard Pyle. London: T. Fisher and Unwin; New York: Macmillan and Co.

LC/F2161.E Newberry Library.

Part I deals with Exquemelin's account; Part II with later pirate activity. The first English edition was published in London in 1684, being a translation from the Dutch which appeared in 1678. Piratical activity on the coasts of Central America and in the West Indies.

F2161.G9355, Buenos Aires, 1945; F2161. E84, London, 1951, includes reproductions of original engravings of the 1684 edition; and F2161.E717, Ciudad Trujillo, 1953.

110 EXQUEMELIN, ALEXANDRE OLIVIER. 1926.

Die amerikanischen Seeräuber: ein Filibustierbuch aus dem 17. Jahrhundert. Erlangen.

Pirate activity in the seventeenth century. Also some illustrations and three maps.

A German translation of the foregoing item, Part I.

111 FERIA PEDRO DE (fl. 16th century). 1899.

Relación que hace el obispo de Chiapa sobre la reincidencia en sus idolatrías de los indios de aquel país después de treinta años de cristianos. *Anales del Museo Nacional de México,* 6:481–487.

A brief account of the persistence of pagan rites and beliefs in mid-sixteenth-century Chiapas.

112 FLORENCIA, FRANCISCO DE. 1694.

História de la provincia de la compañia de Jesús de Nueva España. México: L. Guillena Carrascoso.

LC/BX3712.A1F6

Mainly on Mexico. Has information on artists and craftsmen in Mexico.

113 FLORENCIA, FRANCISCO DE. 1755.

Zodíaco mariano. Juan Antonio de Oviedo, editor. México: Colegio de San Idélfonso.

LC/BT650.F6

Gives a survey of the ecclesiastical establishments in New Spain. Refers to artists in Guatemala. See next item.

114 FLORENCIA, FRANCISCO DE. 1924–25.

Nobles artes en Guatemala. Famosas esculturas hechas en Guatemala y llevadas a México por el obispo de Yucatán, el celebre Padre Fray Diego de Landa. *ASGH,* 1:188–189.

Extracted from his *Zodiaco Mariano.* See item immediately above.

115 FRANCOS Y MONROY, CAYETANO (fl. 18th century). 1956.

Carta del Obispo Cayetano Francos y Monroy a su Majestad Carlos III informándole sobre asuntos de su arquidiócesis. *AHG,* 8, 2:16–23.

Was archbishop of Guatemala from 1779 to his death in 1792. Deals with some ecclesiastical problems. Letter dated 20 June 1786. Transcription of *AGG* A1.23 (1786) 1532–10087, folios 27–36, 1784.

116   FUENTES Y GUZMAN, FRANCISCO ANTONIO DE (fl. 17th century). 1882–83.

Historia de Guatemala, o recordación florida. Madrid: L. Navarro. Biblioteca de Americanistas. 2 vols.

LC/F1466.F95

The first edition of this extremely important history and chronicle by a layman of the Reino de Guatemala. Of importance for the history and identification of towns, demography, economic-geography, art and architecture. Was completed c.1690. On October 29, 1689, he asked permission of the Ayuntamiento (of Antigua Guatemala) to be allowed to use the public and secret archives in order to obtain information for his *crónicas.* He repeats this request on November 4, 1689. Apparently he was not given permission very readily. See PARDO, *Efémerides,* 108 ff., see Section VI, below.

117   FUENTES Y GUZMAN, FRANCISCO ANTONIO DE. 1932–33.

Recordación florida: discurso historial y demonstración natural, material, militar y política del Reyno de Guatemala. Guatemala: Sociedad de Geografía e Historia. 3 vols. Biblioteca "Goathemala," Vols. VI, VII, VIII.

See item immediately above. This edition has some chapters not published in the Madrid edition of 1882–1883. But it lacks some of the maps reprodued in the latter. The original MS is in Madrid, Real Palacio and has the following maps.

folio 26v-city of ":Goathemala"

folio 71v-Guatemala showing both oceans

folio 111v-Milpas Altas (a town near Antigua)

folio 209(or 200?)v-Tecpán showing the wall and moat and two gates in tandem, closing a break in the *foso* (moat).

118   FUENTES Y GUZMAN, FRANCISCO ANTONIO DE. 1969.

Obras históricas de Francisco Antonio de Fuentes y Guzmán. Edición y estudio preliminar de Carmelo Sáenz de Santa María. Madrid: Biblioteca de Autores Españoles, Vol. 230.

A new edition of the foregoing item.

119   GAGE, THOMAS (fl. 1603?–1656). 1677.

A New Survey of the West Indies, or, the English American, his travel by sea and land: containing a journal of three thousand and three hundred miles within the main land of America. London: Printed by A. Clark and to be sold by John Martyn, Robert Horn and Walter Kettiby.

The title continues thus: "wherin is set forth his voyage from Spain to S. John Ullua; and thence to Xalapa, to Tlaxalla, the city of Angels, and forward to Mexico: with the description of that Great City as it was in former times, and also at present. Likewise his journey from Mexico through the Provinces of Guaxaca, Chiapa, Guatemala, Vera Paz, Truxillo, Comayagua, especially in the Indian towns of Mixco, Pinola, Petapa, Amatitlan, etc."

This is a most remarkable book despite the bias of the author, an apostate Dominican friar. Valuable information on architecture among a host of other subjects.

This is actually the third edition of Gage's experiences in Guatemala between the years c.1620–1637.

120   GAGE, THOMAS. 1946a.

The English-American. A New Survey of the West Indies, 1648. Edited with an introduction by A.P. Newton. Guatemala City: El Patio. First published, London: George Routledge and Sons, 1928.

121   GAGE TOMAS. 1946b.

Nueva relación que contiene los viajes de Tomás Gage en la Nueva España. Guatemala: Sociedad de Geografía e Historia de Guatemala.

A Spanish translation of the two foregoing items.

122   GAGE, THOMAS. 1958.

Travels in the New World. Edited with an introduction by J. Eric S. Thompson. Norman, Oklahoma: University of Oklahoma Press.

LC/F1211. G13 1958

123   GARCIA CALEL TEZUMPAN, FRANCISCO.

Mentioned as an Indian author who describes conquest of stronghold of Xelajú. See FUENTES Y GUZMAN, 1932–33, above, v. 3, 47, note 1 (part 2, book 8, chapter 2).

Xelajú is the colonial and modern city of Quetzaltenango, Guatemala.

124   GARCIA DE LA CONCEPCION, FRAY JOSEPH. 1723.

Historia bethlehemita. Vida exemplar, y admirable del venerable siervo de Dios, y padre Pedro de San Joseph Betancur, fundador de el Regular Instituto de Bethlehén en las Indias Occidentales. Sevilla: J. de la Puerta, Impresor.

LC/BX4705.B45G3

A copy of this book is in the Biblioteca Nacional de Guatemala, Guatemala City, no. 100–50.

A modern edition was published by the Sociedad de Geografía e Historia de Guatemala: Biblioteca "Goathemala," vol. 17, in 1956. See immediately below.

A history of the Bethlemite Order and a biography of Betancur.

125   GARCIA DE LA CONCEPCION, FRAY JOSEPH. 1956.

Historia bethlemita; vida ejemplar y admirable del venerable siervo de Dios, y padre Pedro de San José Betancur, fundador de el regular Instituto de Belén en las Indias Occidentales; frutos singulares de su fecundo espíritu, y sucesos varios de esta religion. 2a ed. Guatemala: Sociedad de Geografia e Historia de Guatemala Biblioteca "Goathemala", v. 19.

126   GARCIA DE PALACIO, LIC. DIEGO (fl. 1576–1587). 1860.

Carta dirijida al rey de España, por el licenciado Dr. Don Diego García de Palacio . . . año 1576. In E.G. Squier, ed., *Collection of Rare and Original Documents and Relations* . . . No. 1 (Albany: J. Munsell).

LC/F1411.S77

A description of the provinces of Guazacapán, Izalco, Cuscutlán (in El Salvador) and Chiquimula (in Guatemala) by the *Oidor* of the Audiencia de Guatemala. Vivid descriptions of the countryside and the Indian population. Original text and English translation in SQUIER, see Section VI below.

127   GARCIA DE PALACIO, DIEGO. 1873.

San Salvador und Honduras im Jahre 1576. Translated by A. von Frantzius. Berlin: D. Roimer; New York: B. Westermann and Co.

128   GARCIA DE PALACIO, DIEGO. 1881.

San Salvador y Honduras el año 1576. San José, C.R.: Imprenta Nacional.

LC/ F1546. F36

Two documents in FERNANDEZ, LEON, *Colección. . . . históricos . . . estadísticos,* v.1, 1–52. See Section VI below. "Informe oficial del licenciado Diego García de Palacio al rey de España sobre las Provincias Centro-Americanas de San Salvador y Honduras el año de 1576.

"Relación hecha por el Licenciado Palacio al Rey D. Felipe II en la que describe la provincia de Guatemala, las costumbres de los indios y otras cosas notables." He takes the above from *Colección Muñoz*, vol. XXXIX. This item is the same as the two immediately above.

129   GARCIA DE PALACIO, DIEGO. 1890.

Carta dirijida al rey de España, por el licenciado Dr. Don Diego García de Palacio, oydor de la Real audiencia de Guatemala, año 1576; being a description of the ancient provinces of Guatemala, Izalco, Cuscatlan and Chiauimula, in the Audiencia of Guatemala; with an account of the languages, customs and religion of their aboriginal inhabitants, and a description of the ruins of Copán. New York: Charles B. Norton.

Spanish text and English translation on opposite pages.

130   GARCIA DE PALACIO, LIC. DIEGO 1927/28.

Relación hecha por el licenciado Palacio al Rey D. Felipe II, en a que describe la provincia de Guatemala, las costumbres de los indios y otras cosas notables. *ASGH,* 4:71–92.

Reprinted from TORRES DE MENDOZA, *CODI,* 6:5–40. Also in FERNANDEZ, LEON, *Colección.* . . . El Salvador, 13–43. See Section VI below for both of the above. See also item immediately below.

This relación was used by HERRERA Y TORDESILLAS, see below, in writing Década VI, libro VIII, being the history of Guatemala. But he used only that which was convenient for his purpose.

Travels through the rest of Central America but makes no mention of any of the architecture, which at that time was largely still of non-descript character.

131 GARCIA DE PALACIO, DIEGO. 1944a.

Diálogos militares. Obra impresa en México, por Pedro de Ocharte, en 1583, y ahora editada en facsímil. Madrid: Ediciones de Cultura Hispánica.

LC/Z241.3 A1C6 v. 7.   DUL z094.1 qC691 v. 7

Military science.

132 GARCIA DE PALACIO, DIEGO. 1944b.

Instrucción náutica para navegar. Obra impresa en México por Pedro Ocharte, en 1587, y ahora editada en facsímil. Madrid: Ediciones de Cultura Hispánica.

LC/Z241.3 A1C6 v. 8.   DUL/ z0941. qC691 v. 8

Art of sailing.

133 GARCIA DE PALACIO, DIEGO. 1954.

Relación de Guatemala y de la provincia de Izalcos. México: Vargas Rea. Biblioteca de Historiadores Mexicanos.

A limited edition of 70 copies. In the Latin American Collection, University of Texas Library, and catalogued under Anonymous.

A transcription of a *relación* dated March 8, 1576, in the Archivo de Simancas. Also published in *Documentos Inéditos del Archivo de Indias* (Madrid, 1952), vol. 6, 13–27.

See GARCIA DE PALACIO, 1860, 1873, 1890, above.

134 *Gazeta de Goathemala,* or *Gaceta de Guatemala.*

First number published 1 November 1729. Continued to March 1731. Resumed 13 February 1797. Eighteen volumes in all appeared. Issues from 1729–31 in Biblioteca Nacional de Guatemala, Guatemala City. Library of Congress has vols. 2 to 14, 1798–1810. See Batres Jáuregui *America Central,* 2:513–514, who saw a complete collection in the Royal Library of London ("Biblioteca Real de Lóndres"). Claims authorities tried to suppress the journal in 1798, but were unsuccessful. Also says, eighteen vols. published in all.

LC/AP63.G3

135 GOICOECHEA, JOSE ANTONIO (fl. 1735–1814). 1797.

Memoria sobre los medios de destruir la mendicidad, y de socorrer los verdaderos pobres de esta capital. Nueva Guatemala: Por d. Ignacio Beteta.

LC/microfilm AC-2, reel 184, no. 7

Economic and social conditions at the end of the eighteenth century. For a similar work see above CORDOVA, FRAY MATIAS, *Utilidades* etc.

136 GOICOECHEA, FRAY JOSE ANTONIO 1936–37.

Relación del R.P. Dr. Fr. José Antonio Goicoechea, sobre los indios de Pacura, en el Obispado de Comayagua. *ASGH,* 13:303–315.

Problems with some groups of Indians in Honduras not yet Christianized at the very end of the eighteenth century.

GOMARA, FRANCISCO LOPEZ DE.

See LOPEZ DE GOMARA, FRANCISCO.

137 GONZALEZ BARCIA, ANDRES. 1749.

Historiadores primitivos de las Indias Occidentales. Madrid: 3 vols.

LC/E141 B4

An anthology of works of authors of the early colonial period. Volume I has some material on Guatemala, including the letters of ALVARADO, see above. A later edition, Madrid: Edición Rivadeneyra, 1855.

138 GONZALEZ BUSTILLO, JUAN. 1774a.

Demonstración de las proporciones ciertas y dudosas, o defectos que ofrece el pueblo o valle de la Hermita, según el quaderno de autos instruido con arreglo a la instrucción comunicada con fecha 13 de Agosto de 1773. Pueblo de Mixco, Guatemala: Impresa en la oficina de A. Sánchez Cubillas.

LC/F1466.G64
also LC/microfilm AC-2, reel 180, no. 4

A report on the valley where it was proposed to move the capital after the destruction of Antigua Guatemala in the earthquake of 1773. La Hermita was actually chosen and is the present-day city of Guatemala.

139 GONZALEZ BUSTILLO, JUAN. 1774b.

Demonstración de las proporciones ciertas y dudosas, o defectos que ofrece el pueblo o valle de Xalapa, según el quaderno de autos instruido con arreglo a la instrucción comunicada con fecha 13 de Agosto de 1773. Pueblo de Mixco, Guatemala: Impresa en la oficina de A. Sánchez Cubillas.

Among sites inspected but rejected for relocating the capital after the earthquake of 1773, was Jalapa.

140 GONZALEZ BUSTILLO, JUAN. 1774c.

Extracto o relación methódica y puntual de los autos de reconicimiento, practicados en virtud de comisión del señor Presidente de la real audiencia de este reino de Guatemala. Pueblo de Mixco, Guatemala: Impreso en la oficina de Antonio Sánchez Cubillas.

More of the proceedings relative to the transfer of the capital of the Reino de Guatemala from Antigua to another site.

141   GONZALEZ BUSTILLO, JUAN. 1774d.

Razón particular de los templos, casas de comunidades, y edificios públicos y por mayor del número de los vecinos de la capital Guatemala; y del deplorable estado a que se hallan reducidos por los terremotos de la tarde del veinte y nueve de Julio, trece, y catorce de Diciembre del año proximo pasado de setenta y tres. Pueblo de Mixco, Guatemala: Impresa en la oficina de Don Antonio Sánchez Cubillas.

A report on the condition of Antigua Guatemala after the earthquakes of 1773. González represented the point of view of the civil administration which wished to move. The point of view of the ecclesiastical authorities was against such a decision, and hence accused González of exaggerating the extent of the damage to buildings.

Cited by MEDINA, *Imprenta en Guatemala,* no. 6784, see Section V, below. A copy also exists (or existed) in the Biblioteca Nacional, Guatemala City, and the original document is still in the Archivo General del Gobierno de Guatemala.

AGG: A1.18(1774)38.306–4502 and also a modern transcription of the same *AGG:* A1.18.6(1904)14.001–2021

142   GONZALEZ BUSTILLO, JUAN. 1774e.

Razón puntual de los sucesos más memorables y de los estragos, y daños que ha padecido la ciudad de Guatemala, y su vecindario, desde que se fundó en el parage llamado ciudad vieja, o Almolonga, y de donde se trasladó a en que actualmente se halla. Mixco, Guatemala: Impreso en la oficina de A. Sánchez Cubillas.

LC/F1466.G64
also LC/microfilm AC-2, reel 180, no. 1

Representing the forces in favor of moving the city, he gives an account of all the earthquakes that had plagued the capital of the Reino de Guatemala since its first establishment in nearby Ciudad Vieja.

Cited by MEDINA, *Imprenta,* p. 70. A copy also in Biblioteca Nacional de Guatemala.

143   GONZALEZ DAVILA, GIL (fl. 1578–1658). 1649–1655.

Teatro ecclesiástico de la primitiva Iglesia de las Indias Occidentales. Madrid: D. Díaz de la Carrera. 2 vols.

LC/BX1425.G6 (office)

This work was known and used by Guatemalan chroniclers and authors during the colonial period. Cited by XIMENEZ, 2:244, relative to the construction of the nunnery and church of Santa Catalina in Antigua

Guatemala. FUENTES Y GUZMAN, 1:139, refers to it as *Theatro Eclesiástico.* Some material from vol. 1 on Guatemala was extracted in *ASGH,* 14 (1937–38): 111–130, and 241–252. BANDELIER, 88, see Section V below, gives the date of publication as Madrid, 1649–1655.

Vol. I, 139 ff., deals with Guatemala.

144 GONZALEZ DAVILA, GIL. 1959.

Teatro ecclesiástico de la primitiva Iglesia de las Indias Occidentales. José Porrua Turanzas, ed. Madrid: Porrúa Hermanos. "Colección Chimalistac."

A modern edition, probably the second (sic) after a lapse of 310 years.

145 GUATEMALA. AUDIENCIA (1549). 1942.

Tasaciones de los pueblos de la Provincia de Yucatán, pertenecientes a los encomenderos de la Villa de San Francisco de Campeche hechas por la Audiencia de Santiago de Guatemala en el mes de febrero de 1549. Campeche, México: Gobierno del Estado de Campeche.

List of *encomiendas* and *tributo* assessments in Campeche at the time the Audiencia was located in Guatemala and which included Yucatan.

Transcription of a document in Archivo de Indias, Seville. Papeles de Simancas. Est. 64.-caj. G.- leg. 1.

146 GUATEMALA. INSTITUTO DE ANTROPOLOGIA E HISTORIA. 1953.

El Ayuntamiento de Guatemala desde sus orígines hasta nuestros días. Guatemala.

An anthology of selected documents arranged in chronological order of *cabildos* and other matters of the City Council of the capital of the Reino de Guatemala.

147 GUATEMALA-MONTERREY. 1779.

Varias noticias del reyno de Guatemala y Monterrey, y la distancia de unos pueblos a otros. 1779. En folio 19 hojas. *Biblioteca del Depósito Hidrográfico de Madrid.* Virreinato de México, tomo 4. See *COLD,* page xxx.

148 GUTIERREZ Y ULLOA, ANTONIO (fl. late 18th—early 19th century). 1926.

Estado general de la provincia de San Salvador: Reyno de Guatemala, año de 1807. San Salvador: Imprenta Nacional, Ediciones de la Biblioteca Nacional.

LC/F1487. G8

See next item.

149 GUTIERREZ Y ULLOA, ANTONIO. 1962.

Estado general de la Provincia de San Salvador: Reyno de Guatemala, año de 1807. 2a ed. San Salvador: Ministerio de Educación, Dirección de Publicaciones.

Information on the province of San Salvador just prior to the independence. Population, government, geography and economy.

Originally published in Guatemala in 1807, a copy of which exists in the
Biblioteca Nacional de Guatemala, no. 59–46.

Published in San Salvador, 1926 as a first edition of this item.

150 GUTIERREZ Y ULLOA, ANTONIO. 1968(1969).

La Provincia de San Salvador, Reyno de Guatemala, año de 1807. An un-
paginated reprint from *Cultura. Revista del Ministerio de Educación* [San
Salvador].

Geographical description of San Salvador, the capital city as well as the
whole province.

An abridged version of the foregoing item.

151 HERRERA Y TORDESILLAS, ANTONIO DE (fl. 1559–1625). 1601.

*Descripción de las Indias Occidentales de Ant. de Herrera y Tordesillas, cor-
onista mayor de Su Magestad de las Indias y su coronista de Castilla.*
Madrid: En la Oficina Real de Nicolás Rodríguez Franco.

LC/E141.H57

This item is Vol. I of the item immediately below, *Historia general* etc., and
was published first in 1601. Chp. X, 83 ff., "Audiencia de Guatemala,"
contains descriptions of Guatemala, Chiapas, Verapaz, Honduras,
Nicaragua, the Soconusco, etc.

He seems to lift this information directly and without credit, from LOPEZ
DE VELASCO, see below.

152 HERRERA Y TORDESILLAS, ANTONIO DE. 1601, 1615.

*Historia general de los hechos de los castellanos en las islas y tierra firme del
mar oceano, que llaman Indias Occidentales.* Madrid: Imprenta Real de
Nicolás Rodríguez Franco. 4 vols.

LC/E141.H585 and E141.H586

Vol. I is the same as the item immediately above, *Descripción* etc.

The last three volumes were published in 1615, and deal with the rest of
Spanish America.

There are a number of other editions: Madrid, 1726, 1730; Antwerp, 1728;
and in recent years, Madrid, 1934–35, edited by A. Ballesteros, 5 vols., and
in Asunción, 1944–47, 10 vols.

153 HIDALGO, JOSEPH DOMINGO (fl. late 18th century). 1952.

Memoria para hacer una descripción puntual del Reino de Guatemala.
ASGH, 26:383–413. Originally published in *Gazeta de Guatemala,* 2a
época, 1 & 2 (1797–98).

This was to be part of a larger work, never written, on the whole Reino de
Guatemala by various authors. Hidalgo's section was submitted first. In it

he describes the provinces of Quetzaltenango and Totonicapán. Full of detailed information on demography, customs, economic activity, etc.

154 HINCAPIE MELENDEZ, CRISTOBAL (fl. early 18th century). 1727.

Relación de la ruina de la ciudad de Santiago de los Caballeros en Goathemala por el terremoto y quatro volcanes el dia 17 de Agosto de 1717. Guatemala: Imprenta de Antonio Velasco.

A pamphlet describing the effects of the earthquake of 1717 in Antigua Guatemala. Was first published in 1727, and written in verse. Cited by MEDINA, *La Imprenta,* 60, no. 110, see Section V below.

See item immediately below.

155 HINCAPIE MELENDEZ, CRISTOBAL DE. 1964.

Breve relación del fuego, temblores y ruina de la Muy Noble y Leal Ciudad de Caballeros de Santiago de Guatemala, año 1717. *ASGH,* 38:150–157.

A reprint of the item immediately above.

156 HONDURAS. (1538). 1930–1931.

Real Cédula mandando que los conquistadores de la provincia de Honduras gasten la décima parte de sus haciendas en beneficio de ella y de su población, 29 de enero de 1538. *Revista del Archivo y Biblioteca Nacionales* [Tegucigalpa]. 9:65–67.

157 HUMBOLDT, ALEXANDER FREIHERR VON (1769–1859). 1811.

Political Essay on the Kingdom of New Spain. Trans. by John Black. New York: I. Riley, 2 vols.

LC/F1211.H921

English translation of *Essai politique* etc. below.

158 HUMBOLDT, ALEXANDER FREIHERR VON. 1811–1812.

Essai politique sur le royaume de la Nouvelle–Espagne. Paris: 2 vols. F. Schoell.

LC/F2216.H903 DUL/972 fH919v

Deals with Mexico.

See *Political Essay* etc. above for an English translation.

159 HUMBOLDT, ALEXANDER FREIHERR VON and AIME BONPLAND. 1814–1829.

Personal Narrative of Travels to the Equinoctial Regions of the New Continent, during the years 1799–1804. Translated by Helen Maria Williams. London: Longman, Hurst, Rees, Orme, and Brown. 7 vols. in 9.

Data on Reino de Guatemala in vol. 6, ch. 26.

160 ISAGOGE HISTORICA . . . 1892.

Isagoge histórica apologetica general de todas las Indias y especial de la provincia de San Vicente Ferrer de Chiapa y Goathemala de el orden de Predicadores; libro inédito hasta ahora, que, con motivo de la celebración del cuarto centenario del descubrimiento de América, ha mandado publicar el gobierno de la República de Guatemala. Madrid: Tip. de T. Minuesa de los Rios.

LC/F1434. I74

See next item.

161 ISAGOGE HISTORICA . . . 1935.

Isagoge histórica apologética de las Indias occidentales y especial de la Provincia de San Vicente de Chiapa y Guatemala, de la orden de Predicadores. Guatemala: Tipografía Nacional. Biblioteca Goathemala, v. 13.

DUL/972.81 qB582 v. 13   LC/F1437.I75

Written by an anonymous author, most likely a Dominican friar, between 1700–1711. Was first published in an incomplete text in Guatemala City in 1892 from a copy in the Biblioteca Nacional transcribed by Juan Gavarrete in 1875.

The first part is quite medieval in point of view regarding the history of the New World. But the latter part is replete with information, especially on Dominican activities, of the Reino de Guatemala. The author depended on writings of authors such as Remesal, Bernal Díaz del Castillo and others. Appended to the present edition, 229–437, are the texts of a number of contemporary archival documents all important for the colonial history of Central America.

162 ITURBIDE, DON MIGUEL MARIANO (fl. 1775). 1927–28.

"Número 175." Informe detallado y curioso sobre la situación religiosa de la Provincia de Verapaz que el Alcalde Mayor y Teniente de Capitán General de ella D. Miguel Mariano Iturbide da al Arzobispo Larraz en 1775. *ASGH,* 4:178–289.

A report on conditions in Verapaz including data on Indians, towns and political administration of the territory still not entirely pacified.

JIMENEZ, FRANCISCO DE.

See XIMENEZ, FRANCISCO DE.

163 JUARROS, DOMINGO. 1823.

A Statistical and Commercial History of the Kingdom of Guatemala, in Spanish America: Containing Important Particulars Relative to its Productions, Manufactures, Customs, etc. Trans. by J. Baily, London: J. Hearne.

An English translation of the item below. The title continues "with an account of its conquest by the Spaniards, and a Narrative of the Principal Events Down to the Present Time: From original records in the Archives; Actual Observation, and other Authentic Sources."

This edition has two folding maps, one of which is of "The Kingdom of Guatemala."

•

164 JUARROS, DOMINGO (fl. 1752–1820). 1936.

Compendio de la historia de la ciudad de Guatemala. 3a ed. Guatemala: Tipografía Nacional. Biblioteca "Payo de Rivera," Folletín del Diario de Centro-América. 2 vols.

Juarros is by far the most important historical source for the colonial history of Central America. His data is frequently corroborated by archival documents still to be found in *AGG* and of which he obviously made use. His geographical index of towns, including statistics on population, is of fundamental importance in tracing the history of church building activity and the number of churches standing in his day. There is also much information on historical matters, both civil and ecclesiastical, demography, economic activity and a host of other subjects.

This work was first published in Guatemala City between 1808 and 1818, by Ignacio Beteta. Salazar, *Desenvolvimiento,* 392, see Section II, gives the date of publication as 1809. Another edition was published in Guatemala City in 1857. An English translation appeared in 1823, see items immediately above and below.

165 JUARROS, DOMINGO. 1971.

A Statistical and Commercial History of the Kingdom of Guatemala. Translated by J. Baily. New York: AMS Press.

A reprint of the London, John Hearne, edition of 1823.

166 LANDIVAR, RAFAEL (1731–1793). 1782.

Raphaelis Landivar Rusticatio Mexicana. Editio altera auctior, et emendatior . . . Bononiae: ex typographia S. Thomae Aquinatis.

DUL/868.11 L257RA

An epic poem by a Guatemalan Jesuit extolling his homeland. Descriptions of Mexico and Guatemala.

This is the second edition in Latin.

See next item for description.

167 LANDIVAR, RAFAEL. 1924.

Rusticación mejicana, de Rafael Landívar. Translated by Ignacio Loureda. México: Sociedad de Edición y Librería Franco Americana.

LC/PA8540. L4A75   DUL/868.11 L257R

Parallel texts with the original Latin and a Spanish translation based on the second edition published in Bologna.

A native-born Guatemalan Jesuit who left when the order was expelled in the mid-eighteenth century.

See foregoing item.

168 LANDIVAR, RAFAEL. 1948.

Rusticatio mexicana (Mexican Country scenes). New Orleans: Tulane

University, Middle American Research Institute. *Publications,* 1, 5: 156–312.

LC/ PM3001.T8 v.1   DUL/ 497 qT917 v.1, no. 5.

The Latin text with an English prose translation by Graydon W. Regenos.

See LANDIVAR, 1782, above.

169 LARRAZABAL, ANTONIO (fl. early 19th century). 1953/54a.

Apuntamientos sobre agricultura y comercio del Reyno de Guatemala, que el Dr. Antonio Larrazabal, diputado en las cortes extraordinarias de la nación por la misma ciudad, pidió al Real Consulado en junta de Gobierno de 20 octubre de 1810. Nueva Guatemala. *ASGH,* 27:87–109.

A brief report on commerce and agriculture as part of a petition for certain regulations in favor of same in Guatemala.

170 LARRAZABAL, ANTONIO 1953/54b.

Bosquejo estadístico del Arzobispado de Goatemala y Obispados sufráganeos. *ASGH,* 27:113–125. Taken from *Memoria documentada que al Ilmo. Señor Arzobispo Coadjutor de esta Santa Iglesia, Doctor Francisco Garcia Peláez, presenta el Doctor Antonio Larrazábal, Canónigo Pentenciario, al cesar en el cargo de Vicario Capitular Gobernador de este Arzobispado. Año de 1844.* Guatemala: Imprenta del Exército.

Data on greater part of Central America, the archbishopric of Guatemala, in the early nineteenth century, before the independence.

171 LARRAZABAL, ANTONIO 1953/54c.

Discurso que el Sr. Diputado en Cortes (de Cádiz) por la Provincia de Guatemala don Antonio Larrazábal dijo en la sesión del 29 de marzo de 1813, abogando por la libertad de comercio en las colonias de España. *ASGH,* 27:79–86.

A plea for freedom of direct trade between the Reino de Guatemala and the rest of Hispano-America and Spain.

172 LEON PINELO, ANTONIO RODRIGUEZ DE (d. 1660). 1629.

Epitome de la biblioteca oriental i occidental, náutica i geográfica. Madrid: I. González.

LC/Z1601.L55, 1629b

A geography of the New World. Very little data on Central America.

173 LEON PINELO, ANTONIO RODRIGUEZ DE 1958.

Relación sobre la pacificación y población del Manché y Lacandón. 2a ed. Madrid: José Porrúa Turanzas.

The same as the item immediately below and included in SCHOLES and ADAMS, *Relación* etc. See Section II below.

174 LEON PINELO, ANTONIO RODRIGUEZ DE. 1960.

Relación que en el Consejo Real de las Indias hizo sobre la pacificación y población de las provincias del Manché y Lacandón, el Licenciado Antonio León Pinelo. France B. Scholes, and Eleanor B. Adams, paleographers and editors. Guatemala: Editorial Universitaria.

See SCHOLES and ADAMS, *Relaciones histórico-descriptivas,* 254–272, Section II, below. Both this item and that by TOVILLA, *Relación, see below, are published in the same volume.*

A history of the editions on this work is on p. 17.

175 LEYES DE INDIAS, 1542–43 [1893, 1968].

The New Laws for the Government of the Indies and for the Preservation of the Indians, 1542–1543. Amsterdam: N. Israel, 1968. Reprint of the facsimile edition, London, 1893.

DUL/349.46 S733LNA

See below.

176 LEYES DE INDIAS, 1542–43 [1893, 1971].

The New Laws of the Indies. Leyes y ordenanzas nuevas hechas por su Magestad, 1542–1543. Literal translation into English and a historical introduction by H.S. Vermont and F.W. Lucas. London: Privately printed at the Chiswick Press. Reprinted, New York: AMS Press, 1971.

177 LEYES DE INDIAS, 1542–43 [1961].

Las leyes nuevas de 1542–1543. 2a ed. Sevilla: Escuela de Estudios Hispano Americanos.

Introductory study and notes by Antonio Muro Orejón. 59 pages of facsimiles.

178 LEYES DE INDIAS, 1791 [1943].

Recopilación de leyes de los reynos de las Indias (Edición facsimilar de la cuarta impresión, hecha en Madrid en año 1791). Madrid: Ediciones de Cultura Hispánica. 4 vols.

179 *Libro de Actas del Ayuntamiento de la ciudad de Santiago de Guatemala desde la fundación de la misma ciudad en 1524 hasta 1530.* Guatemala. 1856.

DUL/972.81 G9182

See AREVALO, 1856 and 1932, Section II, below.

Titles continues "Copiado literalmente por Rafael Arévalo, secretario de la municipalidad de la Nueva Guatemala. Año de 1856.

180 *Libro viejo de la fundación de Guatemala y papeles relativos a D. Pedro de Alvarado.* Guatemala: Sociedad de Geografía e Historia. Biblioteca "Goathemala," vol. XII. 1934.

Miscellaneous documents of the early history of Guatemala. Includes Libro de actas, immediately above.

181   LIENDO Y GOICOECHEA, JOSE (fl. late 18th—early 19th centuries). 1969.

Relación sobre los indios gentiles de Pacura, Departamento de Olancho en el Obispado de Comayagua: Año de 1808. *Anales del Archivo Nacional* [Tegucigalpa]. 5:5–14.

An account of conditions and missionary activity in early nineteenth-century Honduras.

182   LLAGUNO Y AMIROLA, EUGENIO (d. 1799). 1829.

Noticias de los arquitectos y arquitectura de España desde su restauración. Madrid: En la Imprenta Real. 4 vols.

LC/NA1312.L8

In volumes 3 and 4 he gives the biographies of Spanish and Italian architects who worked in the Americas.

183   LOBO, R.P. MANUEL (fl. 17th century). 1667.

Relación de la vida y virtudes del V. Hermano Pedro de San José Betancurt, de la Tercera Orden de penitencia de N. Seráfico P. San Francisco [Antigua Guatemala].

This work may be lost. VASQUEZ, 4:466 ff., (Bk. V, Trat. 3, chp. 16) says this book was written not very long after the death of Hermano Pedro. It consisted of "76 fojas de cuartilla pequeña que contienen 28 capítulos." He goes on to say it was published in (Antigua) Guatemala in 1667, and that Juan Francisco Blas, in 1673 published another edition in Seville, with about the same number of pages as the original.

JUARROS, 1:244, see above, repeats the same information but gives the publication date of the Seville edition as 1683, and that Lobo was a Jesuit.

184   LOBO, FRAY MARTIN (fl. 18th century).

Arbitrios para que en el Reino de Guatemala se cojan todos los frutos, yerbas y plantas de Europa y de todo el mundo.

A pamphlet mentioned by BATRES JAUREGUI, *América Central,* 3:520. See Section II below.

185   LOBO, FRAY MARTIN.

Medios y modos de juntar el Mar del Norte con el del Sur, para el paso de los galeones de España hasta el Callao de Lima, sin necesidad de buscar el estrecho de Magallanes.

A work mentioned by BATRES JAUREGUI, *América Central,* 3:520, see Section II below.

186   LOPEZ DE ARENAS, DIEGO (b.ca. 1579). 1633.

Breve compendio de la carpinteria de lo blanco y tratado de alarifes con la conclusion de la regla de Nicolas Tartaglia, y otras cosas tocantes a la ieometria, y puntas del compas. Sevilla: Luis Estupiñan.

An architects' and builders' handbook probably known and employed in colonial Central America. Traditional carpentry methods of *mudéjar* origin especially for the construction of *alfarjes* and *artesonados*.

A second edition, Sevilla, 1727, and a third, Madrid, 1867.

187 LOPEZ DE ARENAS, DIEGO. 1867.

Carpintería de lo blanco y tratado de alarifes. 3. ed. Madrid. Impr. de M. Galiano.

LC/TH5603.L6 1867

Third edition of the item immediately above.

188 LOPEZ DE GOMARA, FRANCISCO (fl. 1510/11–1560). 1552–53.

Crónica de la Nueva España con la conquista de México. Çaragoça: A. Millan, a costa de M. Capila, mercader de libros.

GONZALEZ BARCIA, vol. 2, see above, reproduces this work under the title *Historia de las Indias: Crónica etc.*, and says it was first published in 1552.

BANDELIER, 101, see Section V below, mentions this work too. DIAZ DEL CASTILLO, see above, insisted that López de Gomara's account of the conquest of Mexico was inaccurate, and to correct the errors he wrote the "true" history of the conquest of Mexico. Second part deals with the conquest of Mexico.

189 LOPEZ DE GOMARA, FRANCISCO. 1554.

Historia general de las Indias, y todo lo acaescido enellas dende que se ganaron hasta agora. Antwerp: M. Nucio.

Another edition with a slightly different title published in Antwerp.

190 LOPEZ DE GOMARA, FRANCISCO. 1912.

Historia general de las Indias, etc. *Annals of the Emperor Charles V by Fs. L. de G.* Spanish text and English translation edited with an introduction by Roger Bigelow Merriman. Oxford.

LC/DD178.9G6

Based on the 1554 Antwerp edition.

191 LOPEZ DE GOMARA, FRANCISCO. 1932.

Historia general de las Indias. Madrid: Espasa-Calpe. 2 vols.

A reprint of the edition published in Zaragoza, 1552–53.

192 LOPEZ DE GOMARA, FRANCISCO. 1941.

Historia general de las indias. México: Espasa-Calpe. 2 vols.

DUL/980L 864H

A popular edition.

193 LOPEZ DE GOMARA, FRANCISCO. 1954.

Historia general de Indias. Barcelona: Editorial Iberia.

The second part deals with the conquest of Mexico. Text modernized by Pilar Guibelalde. Preliminary notes by Emiliano M. Aguilera.

194 LOPEZ DE GOMARA, FRANCISCO. 1966.

Cortés. The Life of the Conqueror of Mexico. Translated and edited by Lesley Bird Simpson. Berkeley: University of California Press.

This is a translation of the second part of his *Historia general* etc. dealing with the conquest of Mexico and the exploits of Cortés.

Paperback edition.

195 LOPEZ DE VELASCO, JUAN (fl. 16th century). 1894.

Geografía y descripción universal de las Indias. Recopilado por el cosmó-grafo-cronista . . . desde el año de 1571–1574, publicada por primera vez en el Boletín de la Sociedad de Geografía de Madrid, con adiciones e ilus-traciones, por Don Justo Zaragoza. Madrid.

LC/E141 L86

This work remained unpublished for more than 300 years. It is an in-valuable source of information on urbanization, demography and general geography not only for Central America, but also for the whole of Spanish America in the latter part of the sixteenth century.

196 MARROQUIN, FRANCISCO (d. 1563). 1932.

Testamento e Codicilios del Ilmo. D. Francisco Marroquín, primer Obispo de Guatemala, 1563. *ASGH,* 11, 2:165–185.

The last will and testament of Marroquín. Important data on ecclesiastical history and evangelization during the early sixteenth century.

A transcription of the original.

197 MARROQUIN, FRANCISCO (fl. 16th century). 1938–39.

Carta del obispo de Guatemala al Principe don Felipe, pidiendo más religiosos, para el aumento y conservación de la Fé Católica y exponiendo los abusos que habían que evitar y necesidades que satisfacer en aquella provincia. Guatemala. 20 de setiembre de 1547. *ASGH,* 15:466–470.

Describes shortages of priests (regular clergy, members of religious orders).

198 MARROQUIN, FRANCISCO DE. 1963.

Cartas y testamento: homenaje al primer obispo de Guatemala en el IV centenario de su muerte. Guatemala: Ministerio de Educación Pública. Biblioteca Guatemalteca de Cultura Popular, v. 61.

A biography of the first bishop of Guatemala. A brief bibliography is given, pp. xxxv–xxxvi.

199 MARROQUIN, FRANCISCO DE. 1968.

El licenciado Francisco Marroquín y una descripción de El Salvador, año de 1532. *ASGH*, 41:199–232.

Transcription of a document with description of early El Salvador. Also a few facsimiles of parts of the original.

200 MARTINEZ DE PEREDA, GUILLERMO (fl. c.1740). 1935–36.

Relación geográfica del Valle de Guatemala. Por. G.M. de P. *AGG* A1.17.1(1740)5002–210. In *BAGG*, 1:7–8.

201 MARTIR DE ANGLERIA, PEDRO (fl. 1455–1526). 1912.

De orbe novo, the eight Decades of Peter Martyr d'Anghera. Translated by F.A. MacNutt. New York and London: G.P. Putnam's Sons. 2 vols.

LC/E141 A604

A work that exists in numerous editions. An early geographical account of the recently discovered New World. As is to be expected at that early date, very little on Central America.

202 MARTIR DE ANGLERIA, PEDRO. 1944.

Décadas del Nuevo Mundo. Buenos Aires: Editorial Bajel.

203 MARTIR DE ANGLERIA, PEDRO. 1972.

Décadas del Nuevo Mundo. México: Porrúa. 2 vols.

MARTYR D'ANGHIERA PETER (fl. 1455–1526).
See MARTIR DE ANGLERIA, PEDRO.

MARTYR, PETRUS (fl. 1455–1526).
See MARTIR DE ANGLERIA, PEDRO.

204 MENDEZ, JOSE MARIANO. 1889.

Memoria del estado político y ecclesiástico de la capitanía general de Guatemala, presentado a las cortes el día 17 de Mayo de 1821. Madrid: Tipografía de Manuel G. Hernandez.

An account of Central America in the early nineteenth century. A copy is in the Biblioteca Nacional de Guatemala, no. 1–42.

204a MENDIETA, FRAY GERONIMO DE (fl. 1525–1604). 1973.

Historia ecclesiástica indiana. Madrid: Real Academia de la Historia, Biblioteca de Autores Españoles, vol. CCLX.

A preliminary essay by Francisco de Solano Pérez-Lila. Deals mainly with the activities of the Franciscan order in Mexico and in part in the Reino de Guatemala for the years 1574–1576. See also, Joaquín García Icazbalceta, editor, *Nueva colección de documentos para la historia de México.* México, 1892. 2 vols., for Códice Mendieta, documentos franciscanos del siglo XVI y XVII.

205 MEXICO, FOUNDING OF TOWNS. 16th century.

Fundación de pueblos en el siglo XVI. *Boletín, Archivo General de la Nación* [México] 6, 3, (1935): 321–360.

Documents relative to the founding of towns in Mexico, including Chiapas and elsewhere in Central America.

206 MOLINA, ANTONIO DE (d. l683), AGUSTIN CANO, and FRANCISCO XIMENEZ. l943.

Antigua Guatemala; memorias del m.r.p. maestro Fray Antonio de Molina continuadas y marginadas por Fray Agustín Cano y Fray Francisco Ximénez, de la Orden de Santo Domingo. Transcripción paleográfica, prólogo, y notas por Jorge del Valle Matheu. Guatemala: Unión Tipográfica.

LC/Fl466 M68

A continuation of PONCE, see below. Covers the years 1628–1678. Was important source XIMENEZ, 1929–31, below.

207 MOLINA, FRAY ANTONIO DE (d. 1683).

Cronología de los sucesos de la provincia de San Vicente de Chiapa.

A MS in *AGG* according to SALAZAR, *Desenvolvimiento,* see Section II below. Not located. Apparently the same person who accompanied PONCE, see below and also item immediately above.

208 MOLINA, FRAY ANTONIO DE.

Vidas de varios padres de la provincia de Chiapa y Guatemala del Orden de Predicadores.

BANDELIER, 106, see Section V below, saw this seventeenth-century MS in 1880 and says it is in the library of the Museo Nacional de Guatemala.

This is probably the same man as in the two items immediately above.

209 MOLINA, FRAY ANTONIO DE.

Vida de los ilustres hijos de la provincia de Chiapa, del orden de Santo Domingo Fray Andrés del Valle y Fray Pedro de Santa María.

This may be the same MS as in the preceding item. Mentioned by SALAZAR, *Desenvolvimiento,* see Section II below, as a MS in *AGG.* Unlocated.

210 MONROY, JOSE (fl. 1651–1673). 1667.

Estado del Convento de Goatemala del orden de Nuestra Señora de la Merced; relación verdadera de los aumentos que en temporal y espiritual han tenido, desde el año de sesenta y cinco, hasta el de sesenta y siete. Guatemala: J. Pineda Ybarra.

A brief pamphlet of 12 pages on the Mercedarian order in Guatemala. Convent building and church in Antigua are mentioned briefly. Mentioned by BANDELIER, 108, see Section V, below.

211 MONTALVO, FRANCISCO ANTONIO DE (fl. 17th century). 1683.

Vida admirable y muerte preciosa del V. Hermano Pedro de San José Betancur. Rome.

Mentioned by VASQUEZ, 4:381 (bk. V, Trat. 2, ch. 36) as having written a biography of Hermano Pedro. Cites him with regard to the cost of construction of the church of Belén in Antigua. Gives the title as appears here, and says it deals with matters as late as 1687.

212 MONTANUS, ARNOLDUS (fl. 1525?–1683). 1671.

De Nieuwe en onbekende weereld: of Beschryving van America en 't zuidland, etc. t'Amsterdam: J. Meurs.

LC/E143 M76

Contains a beautiful map entitled "Yucatan . . . Guatemala" between 258–259, including Southern Mexico and Central America to Western Panamá.

213 MONTANUS, ARNOLDUS. 1673.

Die unbekante neue Welt oder Beschreibung des Welteils Amerika, und des Sudlandes. Amsterdam: Jacob von Meurs.

LC/E143.M77 office

A German translation of the foregoing item.

A copy exists in the library of the Historical Society of Pennsylvania, Philadelphia, Pa.

214 MONTEJO, FRANCISCO DE (fl. 16th century). 1935.

Carta a S. M. acerca del Estado de su gobernación (1539). *Revista del Archivo y Biblioteca Nacionales* [Tegucigalpa]. 13:545–547, 611–614.

Deals with matters in Chiapas and Honduras.

215 MONTERO DE MIRANDA, FRANCISCO (fl. 1575). 1953/54.

Relación dirigida al Illmo. Señor Palacio . . . sobre la provincia de la Verapaz ó Tierra de Guerra. Reprinted in ASGH, 27:342–358 Transcription of a MS in the library of the University of Texas: Latin American Section, XX, Central America, no. 3, "Descripción de la provincia de la Verapaz por Fray Francisco Montero de Miranda."

A vivid description of Verapaz, still an unsettled frontier with Indians not yet Christianized.

216 MONTOYA, FRAY LOPE DE (fl. 17th century). 1880.

Suma de los capitulos generales y principales, ordenaciones etc. de la Provincia de Predicadores de Chiapa y Guatemala.

A MS noted by BANDELIER, 106, see Section V below, in the library of the Museo Nacional de Guatemala, c. 1880.

The whereabouts of this MS is unknown today, but it may very well be in the AGG.

From the title it seems to be a record of the official meetings *(capítulos)* of the Dominican order in Guatemala in the seventeenth century.

217 MOREL DE SANTA CRUZ, PEDRO AGUSTIN (fl. 1751).

An eighteenth century bishop of Nicaragua. BARQUERO, *Centros* etc., see section II, refers to a letter he wrote to the king with data on León and Granada.

The whereabouts of this letter has not been ascertained, though it may very well still be filed among the papers of the Audiencia de Guatemala in the Archivo de Indias, Sevilla.

218 MORERA, FRAY JOSE (fl. 17th century).

Noticias de la provincia de Guatemala, con un tratado de la mision y martirio de los P.P. Misioneros, Verdelete y Montragudo.

A MS which BANDELIER, 107, see Section V, did not actually see but believed was in Guatemala City. See VERDELETE below, the subject of this item.

219 MOTOLINIA, FRAY TORIBIO DE BENAVENTE (d. 1568). 1914.

Historia de los indios de la Nueva España. Daniel Sánchez García, editor. Barcelona: Herederos de J. Gili.

LC/F1219.M92

Nothing on Guatemala specifically, but important for customs, beliefs, etc. of Indians of Mexico.

220 MOTOLINIA, FRAY TORIBIO DE BENAVENTE 1950.

History of the Indians of New Spain. E. A. Foster, editor. Berkeley: Cortés Society.

An English translation of the foregoing.

221 MUNOZ, JUAN BAUTISTA (fl. 1745–1799). 1793.

Historia del Nuevo Mundo. Madrid: Por la viuda de Ibarra. Books 1–6 (to 1500).

LC/F1411 M961

Only one volume actually published. General history based on previously published accounts.

222 NAUIO BOLANOS, ANTONIO DE (fl. 17th century).

A MS of 284 folios being a report on the *pueblos,* and the *tributo* derived from them, in Nicaragua for the years 1662–1692. A microfilm copy is in the library of the University of Texas, Austin, Texas.

See Section VI below.

223 NAVARRETE, MARTIN FERNANDEZ DE (fl. 1764–1844). 1825–1837.

Colección de los viajes y descubrimientos que hicieron por mar los españoles desde fines del siglo XVI. Madrid: Imprenta Real. 5 vols.

LC/E123. N51

See sect. VI for description of contents.

224 NAVARRETE, MARTIN FERNANDEZ DE. 1954.

Colección de los viajes que hicieron por mar los españoles desde fines del siglo XV. Madrid: Ediciones Atlas.

A modern edition of the foregoing item.

225 NICARAGUA. 1791–1804.

Varias noticias del Río de San Juan, yslas adyacentes de la costa de los Mosquitos, provincias y partidos que tiene el Reyno de Goatemala: Descripzión del Puerto de Blufliers idem de la provincia de Nicaragua. Años 1791 a 1804. In *COLD,* 289–328.

226 NOMINA Y LISTA. 1690.

Nómina y lista y relación jurada del número de religiosos que tiene esta Santa Provincia del Santísimo Nombre de Jesús de Guatemala, con distinción de parcialidades, calidad de sujetos, y otras noticias conciernientes al perfecto conocimiento que se pretende, hecha este año de 1690.

A MS transcribed by Fray Lázaro Lamadrid, the editor of VASQUEZ, 4:12–33, see below, from *Guide to Latin American Manuscripts in the University of Texas Library,* 21, and catalogued "Central America-Guatemala. 275-G19-8 pages."

This is a most important source on activities of the Franciscan order c.1690 with data on *pueblos de indios,* conventual establishments, including churches, number of Indians under the ecclesiastical jurisdiction of the friars and sundry matters.

227 NUIX Y PERPINA, JUAN (fl. 1740–1783). 1780.

Riflessioni imparziali sopra l'umanita degli Spagnuoli nell'Indie, etc. Venezia.

LC/F1411.N96

An eighteenth century refutation of LAS CASAS', *Brevísima,* see above, indictment of the Spaniards' treatment of the Indians. For Spanish translation with additions, see immediately below.

228 NUIX Y PERPINA, JUAN. 1782.

Reflexiones imparciales sobre la humanidad de los Españoles en las Indias, contra los predendidos filósofos y políticos . . . traducidas con algunas notas por D. Pedro Varela y Ulloa. . . . Madrid: J. Ibarra.

A contemporary Spanish translation of the item immediately above. Another edition with additions by the author was published in Cervera, 1783.

229 NUIX Y PERPINA, JUAN. 1944

La humanidad de los españoles en las Indias. Madrid: Ediciones Atlas. 2 vols.

LC/F1411.N983

A modern edition of the foregoing item. Preliminary notes by C. Pérez Bustamante.

229a NUNEZ DE LA VEGA, FRANCISCO. 1702

Constituciones diocesanos del obispado de Chiappa, por Su Señoria Ilustriss. el Señor Maestro Francisco Núñez de la Vega, de la Orden de Predicadores, obispo de Ciudad Real de Chiappa, y Soconusco, del Consejo de su Magestad. Año de MDCXCII. En Roma, año de MDCCII: En la Nueva Imprenta, y Formación de caracteres de Caietano Zonobi, entallador de Nuestro Señor Papa Clemente XI, en la gran curia Inocenciana. Con licencia de los superiores.

An extremely rare work full of information of interest to investigators in divers disciplines, especially ethnohistorians, anthropologists, historians, demographers, art and urban historians and others as well dealing with the colonial period in Chiapas. Is a report of the author written after personal visits to all parts of his diocese which comprised the whole of the present state of Chiapas including the Pacific litoral, that is, the Soconusco. The official documents relative to this inspection trip still exist in AGG. See for example: AGG, A 1.30.19 (1690) 1423 – 19, "Autos de la visita general practicada a los pueblos de la provincia de Chiapas por el oidor Lic. José de Scals y por el obispo de Chiapas, Fr. Francsco Núñez de la Vega." This document is contained in one notebook of some 39 folios. The second volume, A 1.30.19(1690)–1424–183, with the same title except that it is preceded by the phrase "Segundo quaderno de la visita etc." is also some 20 folios in length.

The receipt of the original manuscript still exists in AGG, see A 1.24 (1711) 10.222–1578, fol. 290, "4 de septiembre de 1711. R. P. Agradeciendo al obispo de Chiapas, Dr. Fr. Juan Bautista Alvarez de Toledo, la remisión de las Constituciones Disocesanas formuladas por su antecesor Maestro Fr. Francisco Núñez de la Vega, en dos tomos manuscritos."

It would seem that the report was written soon after 1690, perhaps 1692 being the date of completion, and was published in Rome in 1702 judging by the Xerox copy that I saw in the library of Sr. D. Prudencio Moscoso in San Cristóbal de las Casas, Chiapas in March, 1975, the title page of which bore the date 1702. The manuscript, or a copy, was turned over to the civil authorities in 1711, and hopefully, may still exist in the archives in Guatemala City.

230 OCANA, M.R.P. FRAY DIEGO DE (fl. 17th century). 1932–33.

Descripción de la Laguna de Atitlán. *ASGH,* 9:297–302.

231 OVIEDO Y VALDES, GONZALO FERNANDEZ DE (fl. 1478–1557). 1749.

Relación sumaria de la historia natural de las Indias, compuesta, y dirigida al emperador Carlos V, por el capitán Gonzalo Fernandez de Oviedo. Madrid. First published, Sevilla, 1535–1557. Some charming stories and descriptions of the fauna and flora of the islands of the West Indies as well as Panama. Some descriptions of the first Spanish towns in the New World.

Published in many editions, some of the principal ones of which are listed immediately below.

232   OVIEDO Y VALDES, GONZALO FERNANDEZ DE. 1840.

Histoire du Nicaragua. Paris: A. Bertrand.

A translation of chapters 1–18 of his *Historia general.* In H. Ternaux-Compans, *Voyages,* t. 14. See TERNAUX-COMPANS, 1837–41, Section II below.

233   OVIEDO Y VALDES, GONZALO FERNANDEZ DE. 1851–55.

História general y natural de las Indias, Islas y Tierra-Firme del Mar Océano. Madrid: Impreso por Francisco Fernández de Cordova, Imprenta de la Real Academia de la Historca, 4 vols.

The first complete edition including all 50 books.

234   OVIEDO Y VALDES, GONZALO FERNANDEZ DE. 1950.

Sumario de la natural história de las Indias. México: Fondo de Cultura Económica. Biblioteca Americana, Serie de Cronistas de Indias.

235   PADILLA, JUAN JOSEPH DE. 1732.

Noticia breve de todas las reglas más principales de la arithmética práctica, con que se puede desatar, no solo las demandas ordinarias, sino también muchas dificultosas, que de otra suerte solo por la algebra se respondieran. Guathemala: En la Imprenta de Ignacio Jacobo de Beteta; a cuya costa se Imprime.

A method of arithmetic.

Is in the Biblioteca Nacional de Guatemala, 117–136 and another copy, 119–30.

236   PAEZ BETANCOR, ALONSO and FRAY PEDRO DE ARBOLEDA. 1964.

Relación de Santiago Atitlán, año de 1585, por Alonso Paez Betancor y Fray Pedro de Arboleda. *ASGH,* 37:87–106.

A MS in the library of the Sociedad de Geografía e Historia de Guatemala, in Guatemala City. Not published in its entirety. The remainder of the MS exists in the University of Texas Library, *Collection Joaquín García Icazabalceta,* no. 65. JGI, folio 292.

A report on conditions in an Indian town on Lake Atitlán, Guatemala.

See also Atitlán, Guatemala. 1571, above, for an earlier report.

PALACIO, LIC.

His full name was LIC. DIEGO GARCIA DE PALACIO, oidor de la

Audiencia de Guatemala. (fl. ca. 1579). He is rarely referred to by his complete name by authors of the colonial period.

See above for some items by him.

237   PAREJA, FRANCISCO DE (fl. 17th century). 1882–1883.

Crónica de la Provincia de la Visitación de Ntra. Sra. de la Merced, redención de cautivos de la Nueva, España. . . . Escrita en 1688. México. Imprenta de J.R. Barbedillo. 2 vols.

A history of the Mercedarian order including the conventos in Guatemala and Central America. Has some appendices with documents pertaining to the activities of the order up to 1844. See ALDANA, ca. 1770, above for a history of the Mercedarian order.

238   PAZ, NICOLAS DE. 1771.

Novena y bosquejo de los milagros y maravillas, que ha obrado la santísima imagen de Cristo crucificado de Esquipulas. Guatemala (Antigua): Joaquín Arevalo.

The statue revered in the basilica in Esquipulas, Guatemala, a pilgrimage town of importance even today. Information in passing on the sculpture itself and the church building.

239   PAZ Y SALGADO, ANTONIO DE (d. 1757). 1747.

Las luces del cielo de la iglesia, difundidas en el emisphério de Guathemala . . . en que se comprehende una breve relación histórica de el estado de esta iglesia hasta su feliz exaltación. México: Ma. de Ribera.

LC/microfilm AC-2, reel 29, no. 9

A panegyric exhalting the raising of the cathedral of Antigua Guatemala to the rank of that of the seat of an archbishopric. Some data on the Palacio Arzobispal adjacent to the cathedral.

A pamphlet of 9 folios.

240   PEDRAZA, CRISTOBAL DE (fl. mid-16th century). 1916.

Relación de varios sucesos ocurridos en Honduras, y del estado en que se hallaba esta provincia Gracias a Dios, 18 de Mayo de 1539. In *Relaciones históricas de América. Primera mitad del siglo XVI* (Madrid: Published by Sociedad de Bibliófilos Españoles), pp. 136–180.

An account, 1539, of the early history of Honduras before the total pacification and settlement of the country.

241   PENA, P. DE LA. 1661.

Breve tratado de todo género de bóvedas, así regulares como irregulares. Madrid: Juan de Torija.

See PENA, P. DE in Section III below.

242   PINEDA, JUAN DE (fl. late 16th century). 1924.

Descripción de la provincia de Guatemala. Año de 1594. *ASGH*, 1: 327–363.

LC/1401.C68   DUL/980 C697C

An invaluable source of information on general conditions in mid-sixteenth century Central America especially with regard to urbanization, demography. On p. 363, in discussing Cartago, Costa Rica says the region was conquered thirty-five years before the time he was writing, 1594, that is, c.1560. On p. 332 mentions an event as occurring in 1557.

Reprinted from *COLD*, 415–471 from a MS in AI, Est. 58, Caj. 6, Leg. 28.

PINELO, ANTONIO DE LEON.

See LEON PINELO, ANTONIO DE.

242a PONCE, ALONSO (fl. c. 1586). 1873.

Relación breve y verdadera de algunas cosas de las muchas que sucedieron al Padre Fray Alonso Ponce en las provincias de Nueva España. Madrid. In *Colección de documentos inéditos para la historia de España,* vols. 57–58.

LC/ F12131. A45

The same as SAN JUAN and CIUDAD REAL, Nos. 59, 261a.

An invaluable account dealing with conditions in Central America after 1574 to about 1586.

VASQUEZ, 1:240 (Bk. II, chp. l3), see below, says that Ponce, Comisario General, arrived in 1574 to settle some disputes then raging in the Franciscan province of Central America. He travelled from Nicaragua to Mexico and passed through Guatemala in 1586. The account was actually written by SAN JUAN and CIUDAD REAL.

He gives important information concerning the appearance of the towns and their architecture as well as descriptions of the Franciscan conventual establishments.

243 PONCE, ALONSO. 1947.

Viaje a Nueva España. In Andrés Henestrosa, editor, *Biblioteca enciclopedia popular* (México: Secretaría de Educación Pública), 2a. epoca, 184.

An excerpt from the foregoing item dealing with the sections on Mexico.

244 PONCE, FRAY ALONSO. 1948

Viaje a Chiapas. *Cuadernos de Chiapas,* no.14 [Tuxtla Gutiérrez, Chiapas. Depto. de Bibliotecas.]

An excerpt from PONCE, above, dealing with the section on the present Mexican state of Chiapas.

245 PORTA, ANTONIO. 1792.

Descripción del Río Motagua. Guatemala: Ignacio Beteta.

This work is mentioned by BATRES JAUREGUI, 2:512, see Section II below. This item could not be located, but may still exist in the Biblioteca Nacional de Guatemala.

246   REBULLIDA, FRAY PABLO. 1697.

Informe a la audiencia de Guatemala sobre el estado actual de la Cristianidad de la provincia de Talamanca.

A MS noted by BANDELIER, 107, see Section V. Judging by the title it deals with seventeenth-century Costa Rica.

247   *Reglamento general de Artesanos de la Nueva Guatemala que la Junta comisionada para su formación propone a la general de la Real Sociedad.* Por. D. Ignacio Beteta en la Nueva Guatemala, año 1798.

See MEDINA, *La Imprenta,* 355, no. 951, Section V, below.

Regulations concerning crafts practices, including wages, morality of workers, training and apprenticeship etc. as proposed by the Sociedad Económica.

248   REMESAL, FRAY ANTONIO DE (fl. early 17th century). 1932.

Historia general de las Indias Occidentales, y particular de la gobernación de Chiapa y Guatemala. 2a. ed. Guatemala: Tipografía Nacional. Sociedad de Geografía e Historia, Biblioteca "Goathemala," vols. 4 and 5.

LC/F1466 R383

One of the most important sources for the history of Central America. Remesal was a Dominican friar who doubtlessly had at his disposal archival materials as well as literary sources of the time. The work was probably written not long before Remesal died in the early seventeenth century. It was published for the first time, Madrid, 1619 and 1620. The above is the second edition.

Gives vivid accounts of the problems of gathering the Indians of Chiapas, and elsewhere, into towns as well as the hardships of the Dominican missionaries.

Another edition, Madrid, 1966, see immediately below.

249   REMESAL, ANTONIO DE (d. 1619). 1964–1966.

Historia de las Indias occidentales y particular de la gobernación de Chiapa y Guatemala. Edición y estudio preliminar del P. Carmelo Sáenz de Santa María. Madrid: Ediciones Atlas. 2 vols.

LC/PQ6171. A2B6 t. 175.

A modern edition with a study of the work of Remesal. See REMESAL, 1932, above.

The editor gives Remesal's *floruit* as 1593–1613, when he was supposedly engaged in writing his chronicle.

250   REYES, FRAY DOMINGO.

Apuntes históricos.

No work by this author has been found. DIAZ, *Romántica ciudad,* 106, see Section IV below, says Reyes wrote a work with the above title.

251 ROBLEDO, FRANCISCO. 1791.

Descripción de cuarteles y barrios de Guatemala. Guatemala: Ignacio Beteta.

The new capital of the Reino de Guatemala, less than twenty years after its removal from the ruined site at Antigua Guatemala.

City lay-out and municipal ordinances.

Reprinted, *ASGH*, 2 (1925):159–178.

252 ROBLES DOMINGUEZ DE MAZARIEGOS, MARIANO. 1813.

Memoria histórica de la provincia de Chiapa, una de las de Guatemala, presentada al augusto congreso por . . . Cádiz: Imp. Tormentaria, á cargo de D.J.D. Villegas.

LC/3-33128

Chiapas just before the independence from Spain.

253 RODIGUEZ, JUAN. 1541.

Relación del espatable terremoto que agora nuevamenta ha acontecido en la ciudad de Guatemala. México: Juan Cromberger.

LC/1476.G92R6 1542 (a photostat)

A pamphlet of 4 pp. describing the earthquake and avalanche that destroyed Ciudad Vieja, the town founded by Jorge de Alvarado in 1527 and the capital of Guatemala before its removal to Antigua.

Gives descriptions of houses and churches.

For a photograph of the title page, see *ASGH*, 17 (1941–42):319. Also printed in *ASGH*, 23 (1948):92–97.

254 RODRIGUEZ, JUAN. 1543.

Relación del espantable terremoto que agora nuevamente ha acontecido en las Indias en una ciudad llamada Guatimala. Toledo.

An edition with a slightly different title published two years later in Toledo, Spain.

255 RODRIGUEZ BETETA, VIRGILIO. 1925/26.

Primera guía de forasteros. Guatemala. *ASGH*, 2:92.

See *Calendario, manual y guía* 1792–1813, above for complete title. Published by Ignacio Beteta beginning in 1792.

256 RODRIGUEZ CAMPAS, ANTONIO. (fl. 18th cent).

Diario histórico de Guatemala.

This work is mentioned by SALAZAR, *Historia del desenvolvimiento*, see Section II below. It does not exist in the Library of Congress. It may possibly be in the Biblioteca Nacional in Guatemala City.

257 SAGREDO, DIEGO LOPEZ DE (fl. 16th century). 1526.

*Medidas del romano; necessarias alos oficiales que quieren seguir las for-
maciones delas Basas, Columnas, Capiteles y otras pieças delos edificios antiguos.* Toledo.

One of the earliest Spanish architects' handbooks or manuals that had an
influence on later architectural theorists and consequently on the building
tradition, not only in Spain, but also in the New World. See also Section
III below.

Another edition, Lisbon, 1541, with a slightly different title, with some new
material added. Colophon, ". . . Imprimido por Luis Rodriguez, libero del
Reyno Señor, 1541."

258 SALAZAR, FRAY JUAN JOSE (fl. mid-18th century). 1754a.

*Piedra fundamental del templo del Sacrosanto Cuerpo de Christo, Señor S.
Joseph. En cuyo día celebró . . . los sumptuosos reparos, a que se restituyó su
templo de Guathemala de las ruinas, que causó el temblor del año 1751.*
Guatemala (Antigua): Imprenta de Sebastián Arévalo.

A sermon giving an account of the repairs to the church of San José, Antigua Guatemala, after the earthquake of 1751.

259 SALAZAR, FRAY JUAN JOSE. 1754b.

*Relación descriptiva de el estado, y ruynas que padeció el templo de N.S.P.S.
Francisco,* etc.

Mentioned by MEDINA, *Imprenta,* 123, no. 246, Section V. A description
of the damage to the church of San Francisco in Antigua Guatemala.

260 SAN CARLOS, UNIVERSIDAD DE. 1686.

*Constituciones de la Real Universidad de San Carlos de Guatemala. 1686.
Aprobados por la Magestad del Señor Rey Don Carlos II.* Madrid: Por
Julián de Paredes, Impresor de Libros.

This is a transcript of the title page published as an illustration in JUAR-
ROS, I:119, see No. 164.

261 SANCHEZ DE LEON, JOSE (fl. 18th century).

Apuntaciones para la historia de Guatemala.

A MS mentioned by BANDELIER, 108, see Section V below. BATRES
JAUREGUI, *América Central,* 1:35, Section II, dates it 1724. Later on in
an article which appeared post-humously, *ASGH,* 5(1928–29):384, he says
that he owns it.

According to Rodriguez Beteta, *ASGH,* 2(1925–26):92, the MS was finally
published in the GACETA DE GUATEMALA, see above, in 1797, and
again in the nineteenth century by Francisco Gavarrete who also added
some notes.

In a footnote to HIDALGO, see above, *ASGH,* 26(1952):391, note 5, the
editor gives some further information: SANCHEZ, a native of Guatemala

died in 1783 (sic); the original MS in the hand of SANCHEZ DE LEON was dated and signed 28 June 1779; that it is not a regular type of history nor a complete description of the whole of Guatemala; and finally, that the MS is now in the hands of editor of the Sociedad de Geografía e Historia.

Presumably it is still there.

261a SAN JUAN, ALONSO, and ANTONIO DE CIUDAD REAL (fl. late 16th century). 1873.

Relación breve y verdadera de algunas cosas de las muchas que sucedieron al Padre Fray Alonso Ponce en las provincias de la Nueva España, siendo Comisario General de aquellas partes. Madrid. 2 vols. In *Colección de documentos inéditos para la historia de España.* Madrid: Real Academia de Historia, vols. 57–58.

See PONCE, 1873, and CIUDAD REAL, 1873, above, for the same item.

262 SAN NICOLAS, Fray LORENZO DE (fl. 1596?–1679?). 1796.

Arte y uso de la arquitectura, con el primer libro de Euclides traducido en castellano. 4a ed. Madrid: Por d. Placido Barco Lopez. 2 vols.

A popular and widely known handbook for architects and builders. First published in Madrid, 1633, vol. I only. Vol. 2 appeared as a second edition, Madrid, 1667. A third edition, 2 vols., was published in Madrid, 1736. The above item is the fourth edition.

263 SANTO DOMINGO, ORDER OF. 1563 and 1741.

See SAN SALVADOR, 1961–1962a and 1961–1962b, Section II, for two documents pertaining to the Dominican *convento* in San Salvador.

264 SPAIN. CONSEJO SUPERIOR DE INVESTIGACIONES CIENTIFI-CAS. INSTITUTO HISTORICO DE MARINA. 1943–47.

Colección de diarios y relaciones para la historia de los viajes y descubrimientos. Madrid: Instituto Histórico de Marina. CSIC. 5 vols.

DUL/910.8 S733C

An anthology of voyages of discovery, many relating to Mexico and Central America.

265 SCHLESINGER, A. (translator). 1930.

Viaje por la Capitania General de Guatemala. Guatemala.

Translation of an account by an anonymous German traveller from some time in the seventeenth century. General description of towns and country.

Pamphlet, 28 pages.

266 SOCIEDAD ECONOMICA DE GUATEMALA. 1815–1816.

Periódico de la Sociedad Económica de Guatemala.

Only 24 nos. published, 1 May 1815–15 April 1816. See BANDELIER, 112, Section V below.

267 SOTOMAYOR, FRAY PEDRO.

Información de los varones ilustres del Orden de San Francisco del Reino de Guatemala.

BANDELIER, 107, see Section V below, had heard of it, but did not see it. Was either a MS or a book. Seems to have dealt with the Franciscan order in Central America.

268 SUAREZ DE PERALTA, JUAN (b. 1536). 1878.

Noticias históricas de la Nueva España. First publication of a MS dating from 1589 . . . "Tratado del descubrimiento de las Indias y su conquista, y los ritos y sacrificios y costumbres de los yndios; . . ." Madrid: Imprenta de M. G. Hernández.

DUL/972.02 qS939N

Deals mainly with Mexico.

269 TECUN UMAN (fl. early 16th century). 1963.

La muerte de Tecún Umán. Estudio crítico de la conquista del altiplano occidental de Guatemala. Guatemala: Editorial del Ejército.

LC/F1466.4.M8

The conquest of highland Guatemala. A modern study, author's name not given.

270 TORQUEMADA, FRAY JUAN DE (fl. 17th century). 1723.

Primera (segunda, tercera) parte de los veinte i un libros rituales y monarchia indiana, con el origen y guerras de los Indios occidentales. 2a ed., Madrid: N. Rodriguez Franco. 3 vols.

LC/F1219.T68-1725.   LC/F1219.T68-1723a

A Franciscan friar. In vol. 1, chp. 34, "De la fundación de la ciudad de Quauhtemalan;" chps. 35, 36, an account of the earthquake and great tempest that destroyed that city (Ciudad Vieja, Guatemala) in 1541, see RODRIGUEZ, above; chp. 37, an account of some towns in Guatemala and the fertility of the land.

The above chapters are reprinted in *ASGH,* 12 (1935–36): 330 ff.

The first edition, Madrid, 1613. A third edition, México, 1943.

271 TORQUEMADA, FRAY JUAN DE (fl. 17th century). 1943.

Monarquía indiana. 3a edition. México: Porrúa y Cía.

See foregoing item.

272 TORRE, TOMAS DE LA (d. 1567). 1945.

Desde Salamanca España hasta Ciudad Real, Chiapas; diario de viaje 1544–1545. Frans Blom, ed. México: Editora Central.

Extracted from XIMENEZ, see No. 304, who quotes DE LA TORRE verbatim. The text edited by Blom includes those parts dealing with Chiapas as well as the sea voyage from Spain. VASQUEZ, 1:119, (Bk. I, chp. 24) refers to DE LA TORRE as a MS "de a cuartilla, de volumen de 286 fojas, que escribió fray Tomás de la Torre . . . cuyo título es: *Historia de la Venida de los Religiosos a la Provincia de Chiapa"* . . . etc. Says that it still existed, early eighteenth century, in the convento of Santo Domingo in Antigua Guatemala.

Prologue and notes by Franz Blom.

273 TORRE, FRAY TOMAS.

Historia de los principios de la Provincia de Chiapas y Guatemala, del Orden de Santo Domingo.

This may be the MS referred to immediately above. According to BANDELIER, 104, see Section V below, it was written before 1567. He did not know if it still existed at the time he was writing, 1880.

274 TOVILLA, MARTIN ALONSO (fl. ca. 1635). 1960.

Relación histórica descriptiva de las provincias de la Verapaz y de la del Manché. Paleografía por France V. Scholes y Eleanor B. Adams. Guatemala: Editorial Universitaria. Also contains León de Pinelo, Antonio, *Relación que en el Consejo Real de las Indias hizo sobre la pacificación y población de las provincias del Manché y Lacandón,* pp. 254–272.

LC/F1466.4.T68

An account of early seventeenth century Verapaz, Guatemala. See LEON PINELO, above. Also SCHOLES and ADAMS, Section II below, for description.

275 TOVILLA, FRAY PEDRO (b. 1576). 1633.

Representación apologética, sobre la aptitud de los religiosos nacidos en indias, para obtener y desempeñar todas las dignidades y prelácias.

A MS mentioned by SALAZAR, *Desenvolvimiento,* see Section II below, who says the author was born in San Cristóbal de las Casas, Chiapas (Ciudad Real).

This petition was presented to the General Chapter of the Franciscan Order held in Toledo, Spain in 1633.

276 URTIAGA, FRAY PEDRO DE. 1694.

Diario del viaje de los cinco misioneros desde Querétaro hasta Guatemala. Guatemala.

Mentioned by BANDELIER, 107, see Section V below.

277 VASQUEZ, FRANCISCO (fl. 1647-ca. 1714). 1937–1944.

Crónica de la provincia del Santísimo Nombre de Jesús de Guatemala de la orden de n. seráfico padre San Francisco en el reino de la Nueva España. 2a ed. Guatemala: Sociedad de Geografía e Historia, Tipografía Nacional. Biblioteca "Goathemala", v. 14–17. 4 vols.

Along with REMESAL, FUENTES Y GUZMAN, XIMENEZ, and
JUARROS, the principal chroniclers of the colonial history of Central
America, his chronicle is of primary importance for events up to the time
he completed it in the first decade or so of the eighteenth century. He was a
contemporary of FUENTES Y GUZMAN, who was asked his opinion
concerning Vasquez' chronicle, see PARDO, *Efém,* 116, see Section VI
below.

In the *Nomina* . . . 1690, see No. 226, Vásquez, 4:13, he states that he was a
criollo, that is native born, that he took the habit in 1663 and that he was
the "cronista" of the Franciscan province.

His chronicle was first published in 1714–1716 in Madrid, by Joseph González, O.F.M. in two volumes.

278 VASQUEZ DE CORONADO, JUAN (fl. 1523?–1565). 1882.

Descubrimientos de Juan Vázquez de Coronado. *Boletín de la Sociedad
Geográfica de Madrid.* v. 13.

DUL/Pam. Coll. 33304

An article on the conquest of Costa Rica with some treatment of the
colonial period to 1821. A pamphlet in DUL.

See next two items.

279 VASQUEZ DE CORONADO, JUAN. 1908.

*Cartas de Juan Vásquez de Coronado, nuevamente publicados por D. Ricardo
Fernández Guardia.* Barcelona.

Treats of the conquest of Costa Rica and sundry matters.

280 VASQUEZ DE CORONADO, JUAN (fl. 1563). 1961.

*Ensayo geográfico histórico de la primera expedición de Juan Vásquez de
Coronado al sur del país, enero 27-abril 18, 1563.* Mario Barrantes Ferrero,
ed. San José: Instituto Geográfico de Costa Rica.

LC/F1437.V432

An historical treatment of the expedition of a sixteenth–century conquistador to the Pacific side of Costa Rica.

281 VASQUEZ DE CORONADO, JUAN. 1908. 1964a.

Cartas de Juan Vázquez de Coronado, conquistador de Costa Rica. Nuevamente publicados por Ricardo Fernández Guardia. Barcelona: Imprenta
de la Vda. de L. Tasso.

LC/F1437.V43

Reprinted, San José, C.R.: Academia de Geografía e Historia de Costa
Rica, 1964.

282 VASQUEZ DE CORONADO, JUAN. 1964b.

Cartas de relación sobre la conquista de Costa Rica. San José, C.R.:
Academia de Geografía e Historia de Costa Rica.

DUL/Pam. Coll. 37269

Letters and reports of the conquest of Costa Rica. Reprint of the Barcelona, 1908 edition.

283 VAZQUEZ DE ESPINOSA, ANTONIO (d. 1630). 1623.

Tratado verdadero del viaje y navegación deste año de seiscientos y veinte y dos, que hizo la flota de Nueva España, y Honduras, general della Fernando de Sosa, y almirante don Antonio de Liri. Malaga: Imprenta de I Regne.

LC/microfilm F-18

284 VAZQUEZ DE ESPINOSA, ANTONIO. 1942.

Compendium and Description of the West Indies. Trans. by Charles Upson Clark. Washington, D.C.: Smithsonian Institution.

Book V of the first part deals with Central America.

285 VAZQUEZ DE ESPINOSA, ANTONIO. 1943.

La audiencia de Guatemala. Primera parte. Libro quinto del compendio y descripción de las Indias Occidentales, por Antonio Vázquez de Espinosa, año de 1629. Guatemala: La Tipografía Sánchez y De Guise.

LC/F1464.V3   DUL/917.281 V393A

Book V extracted from the *Compendio,* etc. an English translation of which is listed in item immediately above.

286 VAZQUEZ DE ESPINOSA, PADRE FRAY ANTONIO. 1944.

Descripción de la Nueva España en el siglo XVII por el Padre Fray Ant. V. de Esp. y otros documentos del siglo XVII. México: Editorial Patria.

He cites some letters, 199 ff., of COBO, see above.

Also 180 ff., chp. X, "De Ciudad Real y su distrito y diócecis," dealing with highland Chiapas and San Cristóbal de las Casas.

287 VEITIA LINAJE, JOSE (d. 1688). 1672.

Norte de la contratación de las Indias Occidentales. . . . Pór D. Ioseph de Veita Linage. . . . Sevilla: I.F. de Blas, 1672.

LC/HF3688.W5V35   DUL/Tr. Rm.

The regulations concerning commerce and immigration to the Spanish colonies.

Only of general interest for Central America.

288 VEITIA LINAJE, JOSE. 1945.

Norte de la contratación de las Indias occidentales. Buenos Aires: Comisión Argentino de Fomento Interamericano.

LC/HF3688. W5V35 1945   DUL/382.0946 V431N

A recent version, modernized orthography, of the first edition, the foregoing item.

289 VELASQUEZ DE GUZMAN, FERNANDO (fl. 18th century).

Relación de los Obispos de Guatemala.

BANDELIER, 108, see Section V below, mentions this work but gives no details.

290 VERDELETE, FRAY ESTEVAN. 1593-1612.

Noticias de la Provincia de Teguzigalpa.

BANDELIER, 107, see Section V below, says this work was written between 1593 and 1612. He had heard of it but had never seen it. Probably dealt with Honduras and Nicaragua.

VASQUEZ, 1:293, 294, 295, 308, gives his name as P. Fr. Esteban Verdelet, a Franciscan who arrived in Guatemala in 1593 and who then went to Nicaragua. See *ibid.,* 3:40, 60, 87, 88, 111, 160, 161, 163, 169, 279, 318, for mentions of Verdelete.

291 VIANA, FRAY FRANCISCO DE, PRIOR, FRAY LUCAS GALLEGO, AND FRAY GUILLERMO CADENA. 1955.

Relación de la provincia de la Verapaz hecha por los religiosos de Santo Domingo de Cobán, 7 de diciembre de 1574. *ASGH,* 28: 18-31.

BANDELIER, 104, see Section V below, knew this MS which he said belonged to E.G. Squier. It is now in the library of the University of Texas, from which this item was transcribed.

An account of three Dominicans from Cobán of conditions in Verapaz in the latter part of the sixteenth century.

292 VICO, FRAY DOMINGO (fl. 16th century).

Historia de los Indios, sus fábulas, supersticiones, costumbres, etc.

BANDELIER, 96, see Section V below, believed it still existed in his day, c.1880. He is mentioned in connection with CEVALLOS, see above, and apparently died in 1553.

ASGH, 12(1935-36):472 ff., for a biographical note.

293 VILAPLANA, HERMENGILDO DE. 1775.

Vida portentosa del americano septentrional apostal, el v. p. fr. Antonio Margil de Jesús, etc. Madrid: Juan de St. Martín.

LC/BX 4705 M3252V5

A biography of a Franciscan friar, 1657-1726, who carried on, among other activities, missionary work in Nicaragua and Costa Rica, see JUARROS, 1:218-222, who gives a brief biographical account probably based on VILAPLANA'S.

294 VILLAGUTIERRE Y SOTOMAYOR, JUAN DE. 1701.

Historia de la conquista . . . y Reducciones de los Itzaes y Lacandones . . . en la América Septentrional. Madrid: Imprenta de L.A. de Bedmar, y Narváez.

LC/F1466.V72

A history of the conquest and Christianization of the Petén, Guatemala.
XIMENEZ, 3:9 (Bk. IV, chp. 3), see No. 304, says that Villagutierre's book is inaccurate, that he exaggerates the size of the population of the Petén so that it is greater than that of the whole Reino de Guatemala.

JUARROS, 2:105, note 1, see No. 164, says that the work of Villagutierre served him as a direct source for all he writes about the history of the region.

295 VILLAGUTIERRE SOTOMAYOR, JUAN DE (fl. 1701). 1933.

Historia de la conquista de la provincia de el Itza etc. Guatemala: Sociedad de Geografia e Historia de Guatemala, Tipografía Nacional. Biblioteca "Goathemala," vol. IX.

LC/F1466.V722

A modern edition of the item immediately above.

296 VILLAR, JAIME (fl. 1744). 1958.

La tierra templada en la America Central. *ASGH,* 31:68–70.

The transcription of a contemporary document being a report by the author, a Venezuelan, on a journey through Guatemala in 1744. Some description of principal towns, buildings, as well as comments on economic matters.

297 VILLASENOR Y SANCHEZ, JOSE ANTONIO DE. 1746–48.

Theatro Americano. México: Imprenta de la viuda de D.J. Bernardo de Hogal. 2 vols.

LC/F1211.V72

Deals with a description of Nueva Espana.

298 WAFER, LIONEL (fl. 1660?–1705?). 1699.

A New Voyage and Description of the Isthmus of America, etc. London: J. Knapton.

LC/F1564.W13.

Cited by BANDELIER, 105, see Section V below. Very little reference to Reino de Guatemala except coasts.

Also published in Paris, 1706, as *Les voyages de Lionel Waffer.*

299 WAFER, LIONEL. 1903.

A New Voyage and Description of the Isthmus of America. Reprinted from original edition of 1699. Cleveland: The Burrows Brothers Co.

LC/F1564.W15

A modern edition of the foregoing item.

300 WAFER, LIONEL. 1934.

A New Voyage and Description of the Isthmus of America, by Lionel Wafer . . . with Wafer's Secret Report (1698) and Davis's Expedition to the Gold Mines (1704). Edited, with introduction, notes and appendices, by L.E. Elliott Joyce. Oxford: Hakluyt Society.

First published in 1699. Bibliography 203–206.

301 WAFER, LIONEL. 1960.

Viajes de Lionel Wafer al Istmo de Darién (cuatro meses entre los indios). Translated and annotated by Vicente Restrepo. Panamá: Publicación de la Revista Latina, no. 14.

This is a version of the 1888 translation of the 1706 French version, revised from the original of 1699 in English.

Deals with Wafer's voyage to the Darien in present-day Panama.

302 XIMENA, PEDRO. 1796.

Oración fúnebre en las solemnas exequias, que el dia 28 de abril de 1795, celebró en su santa Iglesia catedral el ilmo. y venerable sr. dean, y cabildo de León de Nicaragua, por el ilmo. sr. dean Esteban Lorenzo Tristán, dignísimo obispo de León, Durango, y Guadalaxara. Guatemala: Impreso de Ignacio Beteta.

LC/microfilm AC2-reel 183, no. 29

A grandeloquent oration with details of the work of the bishop of León, Nicaragua. Has a coat-of-arms engraved by Pedro Garci-Aguirre.

303 XIMENEZ, FRANCISCO (fl. 1666–ca.1722). 1857.

Las historias del origen de los indios de esta provincia de Guatemala, traducidas de la lengua Quiché al castellano para más comodidad de los ministros del S. Evangelio . . . Exactamente según el texto español en la biblioteca de la Universidad de Guatemala, publicado por primera vez, y aumentado con una introducción y anotaciones por . . . C. Scherzer . . . Vienna: C. Gerold é Hijo.

DUL/980.3 X7H

This is the Scherzer edition of Ximenez, 1964, *Escolios,* No. 305, being the *Popul Vuh.* See SCHERZER, 1857a, Section II, No. 800.

SERRANO SANZ, *COLD,* p. x, note 3, see Section VI, below, says the work was originally written ca. 1721, which would be just prior to the time Ximenez died. BATRES JAUREGUI, *ASGH,* 4(1927–28):27, note 1, says the original MS is in the library of the Universidad de San Carlos, which was augmented by Scherzer in the Vienna edition of 1857. He cites the existence of another edition, "Ediciones de la Biblioteca Nacional, San Salvador," San Salvador, 1926.

304 XIMENEZ, FRANCISCO (fl. 1666–ca.1722).

Historia de la provincia de San Vicente de Chiapa y Guatemala de la Orden de Predicadores. Guatemala: Sociedad de Geografía e Historia de Guatemala, Tipografía Nacional. Biblioteca "Goathemala." 3 vols.

A Dominican and a contemporary of FUENTES Y GUZMAN, and VASQUEZ, see above, carries on the chronicles beyond the period covered by REMESAL, see above, his correligionist. Ximénez used both documentary and literary sources. For some biographical data see RODRIGUEZ CABAL, Section II below, *ASGH,* 12:209–228, 348–367.

305 XIMENEZ, FRANCISCO (fl. 1666–ca.1722). 1964.

Escolios a las historias del origen de los indios; Escoliados por el R.P.R. Francisco Ximénez, cura Doctrinero por el Real Patronato del pueblo de Santo Tomás Chichisastenango, de la Sagrado Orden de Predicadores. *ASGH,* 38:242–274.

The *Popol Vuh.* First published by SCHERZER, Section II below and Ximenez, 1857 above. A most important document containing the myths and legends of Precolumbian origin of the Indians of highland Guatemala. Ximénez translated these oral traditions from the Quiché into Spanish. For a modern edition of the *Popol Vuh,* see Adrián Recinos, *Popol Vuh: las antiguas historias del Quiché,* (México: 1947); and also Rafael Girard, *El Popol-Vuh, fuente histórico: Tomo I, El Popol-Vuh* como fundamento de la historia maya-quiché (Guatemala: Editorial del Ministerio de Educación Pública, 1952).

306 XIMENEZ, FRANCISCO. 1966.

Biographical data in *ASGH,* 39:386–443. See also RODRIGUEZ CABAL, 1935, Section II.

307 XIMENEZ, FRANCISCO. 1967.

Historia natural del Reino de Guatemala: compuesta por el Reverendo Padre Predicador General, Fray Francisco Ximénez, de la Orden de Predicadores. Escrita en el pueblo de Sacapulas en el año de 1722. Primera edición. Guatemala: Sociedad de Geografia e Historia de Guatemala, Editorial "José de Pineda Ibarra."

DUL/917.281 X7H

The fauna and flora of Guatemala. Of interest for the historiography of natural science.

Paleography by Julio Roberto Herrera S. who owned the MS and donated it to the Sociedad de Geografía e Historia in 1932. It had been in his family for years.

Forward by Ernesto Chinchilla Aguilar. Prologue by Julio Roberto Herrera S., and notes by Francis Gall.

ZARAGOZA Y EBRI, AGUSTIN BRUNO.

See BRIZGUZ Y BRU, ATHANASID GENARD.

308   ZAMORA, JOSE MARIA. 1807.

Recopilación sumaria de los autos acordados de la Real Audiencia de este Reyno de Guatemala, providencias y bandos de su Superior Gobierno, que han podido recogerse desde el año de 1561 hasta el presente de 1807, dispuesta en orden alfabético por don José Maria Zamora de orden del mismo Tribunal de la Real Audiencia, compuesto de los SS. Ministros D. Francisco Camacho y D. Antonio Rodriguez de Cárdenas. Nueva Guatemala.

AGG: A1.25 (1807) 10357–1702, 278 folios. See Section VIII, No. 2197a.

A compilation of laws and regulations.

308a   ZURITA, ALONSO DE (fl. early 16th century). 1941.

Breve y sumaria relación de los señores y maneras y diferencias que habia de ellos en la Nueva España. México: Editorial Salvador Chavez Hayoe.

For a translation by Benjamin Keen see the item immediately below.

309   ZURITA, ALONSO DE. 1963.

Life and Labor in Ancient Mexico. The Brief Summary Relation of the Lords of New Spain. New Brunswick, N.J.: Rutgers University Press.

LC/F1219.Z943   DUL/972.02 Z96L

Some material of ethnohistorical import, mainly for Mexico.

Section II

THE MODERN PERIOD

Authors of the nineteenth and twentieth centuries.

History, travel accounts, economic-geography, urbanization, *mestizaje*, social and legal institutions, etc.

Some primary sources for the nineteenth century. Mainly secondary sources comprising published works, the primary sources of which are among the items in Section I—as well as in archival documents, some of which have been published and which are listed in Section VI.

310 ACADEMIA SALVADORENA DE LA HISTORIA. 1962.

Biografías de vicentinos ilustres. 2a ed. San Salvador: Imprenta Nacional. LC/1496.S3A–1962

Local history of town of San Vicente and some of its outstanding citizens. Not documented.

311 ADAMS, RICHARD N. 1964.

La mestización cultural en Centro-américa. *RI,* 24, 95–96:137–151, 153–176.

A general essay on the blending of indigenous and European culture and the formation of Hispano-American society.

312 ADAMS, RICHARD N. 1967.

Nationalization. *HMAI,* 6:469–487.

Gives some estimated figures for the size of the population. Treats the problem of the emergence of the national states in the nineteenth century from pre-Columbian times through the colonial period.

313 AGIA, FRAY MIGUEL (fl. 1563–1604). 1946.

Servidumbres personales de indios. Sevilla: Universidad de Sevilla, Escuela de Estudios Hispano Americanos, Consejo Superior de Investigaciones Científicas.

DUL/980.5 A267S

See Section I. Edited by F.J. Ayala.

314 AGUILAR, ARTURO. 1929.

Reseña histórica de la diócesis de Nicaragua. León, Nicaragua: Tipografía Hospicio San Juan de Dios.

LC/4BX Cath. 1602

A brief, undocumented history of León, Nicaragua. Miscellaneous information useful for the construction history of some of the churches.

315 AGUIRRE CINTA, RAFAEL. 1898.

Lecciones de historia general de Guatemala, desde los tiempos primitivos hasta nuestros días, arregladas para uso de las escuelas primarias y secundarias. Guatemala: Impreso en la Tipografía Nacional.

LC/F1466.A28

Secondary school text book based on secondary works.

316 ALONSO, ANTONINO. 1932.

Monografía de Mixco. Guatemala: Talleres Tipográficos.

LC/F1476.M6A5

Pamphlet; popular account of the small village of Mixco near Guatemala City. Some mention of local church building.

317 ALONSO, ISIDORO. 1962.

La iglesia en América Central y el Caribe. Madrid: Estudios Socio-Religiosos Latino Americanos, 4. Friburgo, Suiza; Oficina Internacional de Investigaciones Sociales de Feres.

LC/BX1426.2A36   DUL/DIV S. 261.808 E82

An ecclesiastical history. Does not deal with church architecture or art monuments.

318 ALONSO DE RODRIGUEZ, JOSEFINA. 1972.

El Ilustrisimo doctor don Luis de Peñalver y Cárdenas, sexto arzobispo de Guatemala. El hombre, el sacerdote y su tiempo. Guatemala: Tipografía Nacional.

A biography as well as an historical account, both ecclesiastical and civil, of the early nineteenth century. Was actually the twenty-second bishop and sixth archbishop. He came to Guatemala from Louisiana in 1800 and left in 1806. See JUARROS, 1936, 1:212, for a brief biographical statement.

319 ALTOLAGUIRRE Y DUVALE, ANGEL. 1927.

Don Pedro de Alvarado, Conquistador del Reino de Guatemala. Madrid: Real Academia de Historia. Colección de Manuales Hispania. v. 4, series A.

A biography of Pedro Alvarado from the point of view of a Spanish historian.

320 ALVARADO GARCIA, ERNESTO. 1936.

La discutida personalidad de don Pedro de Alvarado, y la fundación de San Pedro Sula. Tegucigalpa: Imprenta Calderón.

LC/F1437.A482

An essay on the character of Pedro Alvarado and his connection with the founding of San Pedro Sula, based in part on documentary sources.

321 ALVARADO GARCIA, ERNESTO. 1938.

Los forjadores de la Honduras Colonial. La conquista pacífica de Honduras: héroes y mártires. Tegucigalpa: Talleres Tipográficos Nacionales.

A brief history of Honduras and its founding fathers. Largely undocumented.

322 ALVARADO GARCIA, ERNESTO. 1938-39.

La conquista de Honduras. *Revista del Archivo y Biblioteca Nacionales.* [Tegucigalpa], 17:675-680.

323 ALVAREZ RUBIANO, PABLO. 1944.

Pedrarias Dávila; contribución al estudio de la figura del "Gran justador," gobernador de Castilla del Oro y Nicaragua. Madrid: C.S.I.C., Instituto "Gonzalo Fernández de Oviedo."

Based on documentary sources. An "apologia" showing Pedrarias' good side.

An appendix of documents, 393-720. Most useful.

324 *Anales de la Sociedad de Geografía e Historia.* Guatemala, 1924-.

Appears irregularly. An invaluable source for the history and geography of Guatemala. Also numerous illustrations, frequently undocumented, from old photographs of the colonial architecture.

325 *Anales del Instituto de Investigaciones Estéticas.* México: Universidad Nacional Autónoma de México, 1937-.

DUL/WCL   706.272 M611A

An important and scholarly publication with articles by well-known authorities, including some on Chiapas and Guatemala. Principally concerned with the art of Mexico.

326 ANDERSON, CHARLES L.G. 1911 (1938, 1944).

Old Panama and Castilla del Oro. New York: North River Press.

The history of the Isthmus of Panama. Chp. XIII, 217 ff., deals with the conquest of Nicaragua and Gil González Dávila; chp. XIV, 225 ff., with Pedrarias Dávila and his seizure of Nicaragua.

327   ANDRADE, VICENTE DE PAUL. 1907.

Noticias biográficas de los Ilmos. Sres. Obispos de Chiapas. México: Imprenta Guadalupana.

LC/BX1430.C5A6

Very important source for documenting the history of the churches of San Cristóbal de las Casas. Though not cited, the author utilized documents in the archives of the cathedral of San Cristóbal.

328   ANDRADE, VICENTE DE PAUL. 1914.

Excursión a Chiapas. Guadalupe, Hidalgo, México.

Pamphlet. Short travel account on the state of Chiapas.

329   *Antropología e Historia de Guatemala.*

Guatemala: Instituto de Antropología e Historia de Guatemala, 1949–.

A scholarly journal. Range of subjects includes anthropology, archaeology, history and sundry topics.

330   *Anuario de Estudios Americanos.*

Sevilla: Escuela de Estudios Hispano Americanos, Consejo Superior de Investigaciones Científicas, 1944–.

Contains long monographic articles including many on the history of colonial Central America as well as art and architecture.

331   APARICIO Y APARICIO, EDGAR JUAN. 1961.

Conquistadores de Guatemala y fundadores de familias guatemaltecas. 2a ed., corregida y aumentada. México: Tipografía Guadalajara.

Brief biographical notes on genealogy of leading personnages from the 16th through the 19th centuries.

Short work, 81 pages.

332   APARICIO Y APARICIO, EDGAR JUAN, *et alios.* 1969.

La tradición de familia. *Revista Conservadora del Pensamiento Centroamericana.* 22:1–10, 1–33.

Genealogy of the Lacayo y Briones family of Spain, Nicaragua, and Costa Rica.

333   AREVALO, MANUEL DE. 1820–1822.

El amigo de la Patria. Guatemala: Impreso por D. Manuel de Arévalo.

Latin American Collection, University of Texas, has v. 1, nos. 1–11, 13–17, 19–24; v. 2, nos. 1–24; v. 3, nos. 1, 2, 4.

Early nineteenth-century newspaper from just after the independence from Spain. Rare.

334   AREVALO, RAFAEL. 1856.

Libro de actas del Ayuntamiento de la Ciudad de Guatemala, desde la fun-

dación de la misma ciudad en 1524 hasta 1530; copiado literalmente por Rafael de Arévalo, secretario de la municipalidad de la Nueva Guatemala. Año de 1856. Guatemala.

A transcription of some very interesting and important documents, *cabildos*, from the first ten years of the city council of the first capital of the Reino de Guatemala in Ciudad Vieja.

BANDELIER, see Section V below, saw it in the library of the Museo Nacional in Guatemala City c.1880 bound together with a copy of *Colección de documentos antiguos del Archivo del Ayuntamiento de la ciudad de Guatemala*, which he says was published in 1856–1857.

See item immediately below and *Libro de actas*, Section I.

335 AREVALO, RAFAEL. 1932.

Libro de actas del ayuntamiento de la ciudad de Santiago de Guatemala desde la fundación de la misma ciudad en 1524 hasta 1530; copiado literalmente por Rafael de Arévalo, secretario de la municipalidad de la Nueva Guatemala. Año de 1856. Guatemala: Diario de Centro América, Tipografía Nacional.

LC/F1476.G9G96   DUL/972.81 G9182

A twentieth-century reprint of the work cited by Bandelier above. See also *Libro de actas* and *Libro viejo*, Section I, Nos. 179, 180.

336 AREVALO, RAFAEL. 1935.

Consulta, representaciones e informes del Ayuntamiento de la ciudad de Santiago de Guatemala al Rey de España, coleccionados por Rafael Arévalo. Guatemala: Edición Villacorta, Tipografía Nacional.

Transcription of letters to the crown from the city council of the first capital of Central America. Similar material as in *Libro viejo*, 1934, Section I, above.

337 ARDON, JUAN RAMON. 1937

Monografía geográfica e histórica del municipio de Comayagüela. Tegucigalpa: Talleres Tipográficos Nacionales.

LC/F156.C75A8

Brief historical account of small town, a suburb now, on the other side of the river from Tegucigalpa.

338 ARGUELLO ARGUELLO, ALFONSO. 1969a.

Historia de León Viejo. León, Nicaragua: Editorial Antorcha.

A history of the first capital of Nicaragua founded in 1524, destroyed by earthquake and abandoned in 1610. Data on plan of town and principal buildings.

339 ARGUELLO ARGUELLO, ALFONSO. 1969b.

Historia de Nicaragua vieja. A lecture delivered by the author, a professor at the University of León, who excavated León Viejo. Reported in the *Spanish Cultural Index*, nos. 279–281:382–383.

340 ASTURIAS, FRANCISCO. 1943.

Recordatorio. Breve panorama histórico de la medicina. Guatemala: Tipografía Nacional.

A pamphlet. 63 pp. Brief history of medicine in Guatemala from colonial to modern times.

341 ASTURIAS, FRANCISCO. 1958.

Historia de la medicina en Guatemala. Guatemala: Editorial Universitaria.

LC/R469.G8A8

A history of medicine from the colonial period to the modern. Reprint of foregoing item.

342 AYON, TOMAS. 1882.

Historia de Nicaragua, desde los tiempos más remotas hasta el año de 1852. Granada, Nicaragua: Tipografía de "El Centroamericano."

LC/F1526.A98

A well-written history of Nicaragua seemingly based on documentary and secondary historical sources.

343 AYON, TOMAS (1821–1887). 1956.

Historia de Nicaragua desde los tiempos más remotos hasta el año de 1852. Nueva edición. Madrid: Escuela Profesional de Artes Gráficas. 3 vols.

LC/F1526.A982

A new edition of the work first published in 1882.

344 BAILY, JOHN. 1850.

Central America; describing each of the states of Guatemala, Honduras, Salvador, Nicaragua, and Costa Rica. London: T. Saunders.

LC/F1428.B16

An economic geography. Very little on cultural matters.

345 BANCROFT, HUBERT HOWE. 1876.

The Native Races of the Pacific States. New York: Prospectus. 5 vols.

An early attempt to write a history of pre-Columbian Central America. Contents: v. 1, wild tribes; v. 2, civilized nations; v. 3, myths and languages; v. 4, antiquities; v. 5, primitive history.

346 BANCROFT, HUBERT HOWE. 1890.

History of Central America. San Francisco: A.L. Bancroft and Co. 3 vols.

In v. 2, p. 735, gives a good bibliographical survey, up-to-date for that time.

347 BARBERENA, SANTIAGO IGNACIO (1851–1916). 1966–1969.

Historia de El Salvador. Epoca antigua y de la conquista. 2a ed. San Salvador: Ministerio de Educación. 2 vols.

The first edition, 1914–1917. Volume one deals with Pre-Columbian times, the conquest, and the colonial period.

348 BARON CASTRO, RODOLFO. 1942.

La población de El Salvador. Estudio acerca de su desenvolvimiento desde la época prehispánica hasta nuestros días. Madrid: Consejo Superior de Investigaciones Científicas, Instituto Gonzalo Fernández de Oviedo.

LC/44.1445   DUL/312.9 B265P

A monumental work on the history of the population of Central America including the structure of society in colonial times.

349 BARON CASTRO, RODOLFO. 1943.

Pedro de Alvarado. Madrid: Ediciones Atlas.

A biography of Pedro de Alvarado, conqueror of Guatemala.

350 BARON CASTRO, RODOLFO. 1950.

Reseña histórica de la villa de El Salvador desde su fundación en 1525, hasta que recibe el titulo de ciudad en 1546. Madrid: Ediciones Cultura Hispánica.

DUL/972.8403 B265R

A detailed scholarly study of the early history of San Salvador.

351 BARON CASTRO, RODOLFO. 1962.

José Matías Delgado y el movimiento insurgente de 1811. San Salvador: Ministerio de Educación.

LC/F1487.D4B37

Revolutionary activities prior to the independence.

352 BARQUERO, SARA LUISA. 1939.

Centros de interés de la república de Nicaragua, Managua, León y Granada. Managua: Talleres Nacionales de Imprenta y Encuadernación.

A brief tourist guide with some scant reference to the architectural monuments.

353 BARRASA Y MUNOZ DE BUSTILLO, JOSE DE. 1925.

La colonización española en América. Exposición histórica de la organización social de los antiguos imperios de México y el Perú, antes del descubrimiento por los españoles; estudio histórico legal del servicio personal de los indios de las colonias españolas de América durante los siglos XV al XIX. Madrid: Tipografía de la "Revista de archivos, bibliotecas y museos."

Very little data on Central America except for the period when it was under the political jurisdiction of Mexico in the sixteenth century.

354 BARRERA VASQUEZ, ALFREDO and SILVIA RENDON. 1948.

El libro de los libros de Chilam Balam. México: Fondo de Cultura Ecónomia.

Translated and annoted with an introduction. Indigenous chronicles of the Yucatec Maya.

355 BARRIENTOS CASTILLO, JOSE. 1941.

Tecúm Umán. El Baile de la conquista como elemento de investigación histórica. Guatemala: Tipografía Sánchez y de Guise.

Ethnographic study of contemporary indigenous customs as the afterlife of Pre-Columbian.

356 BATES, H.W. 1882.

Central America, the West Indies, and South America. 2nd. ed. London: E. Stanford.

LC/F1409 B32, 2nd edition.

First edition, 1878.

A geographical survey of Central America with scant mention of the art monuments. More of interest for historians, economists and political scientists.

357 BATRES JAUREGUI, ANTONIO. 1915, 1920, 1949.

La América Central ante la historia. Guatemala: Imprenta de Marroquín Hermanos, "Casa Colorada." 3 vols.

LC/F1436. B34

A good history of Central America based mainly on nineteenth-century sources.

Vol. 2, Tipografía Sánchez y de Guise, 1920. Vol. 3, Tipografía Nacional, 1949. Vol. 1, Pre-Columbian; vol. 2, colonial period; vol. 3, 1821–1921.

358 BATRES JAUREGUI, ANTONIO. 1924.

La primera capital de Guatemala. *ASGH,* 1:12–18.

Miscellaneous information on Ciudad Vieja and Antigua. Some mention of architecture.

359 BAYLE, CONSTANTINO. 1945.

El Protector de indios. Sevilla: Escuela de Estudios Hispano-Americanos.

LC/ F1411.B38   DUL/ 980.5 B358P

This also appeared in *ANUARIO EA,* no. 5.

Las Casas' work in bettering the treatment of the Indians and the ensuing legislation enacted defining their legal status.

359a BECERRA, MARCOS E. 1932.

Nombres geográficos indígenas del Estado de Chiapas. Tuxtla Gutiérrez, Chiapas.

The origin of the place names of the towns of Chiapas. Modern names of towns are listed in alphabetical order followed by the meaning in the original native language from which the name is derived. Some of his conclusions are open to question.

360 BELLY, FELIX (1816–1886). 1867.

A travers l'Amérique central. Le Nicaragua et le canal interocéanique. Paris: Librairie de la Suisse Romande. 2 vols.

LC/TC784. B45 DUL/917.28 B449A

A second edition was published in Paris in 1870. A travel account of Nicaragua and the proposed route of the interoceanic canal.

361 BENEVOLO, LEONARDO. 1968.

Las nuevas ciudades fundadas en el siglo XVI en América Latina: una experiencia decisiva para la historia de la cultura arquitectónica del cinquecento. *BCIHE*, 9:117–136.

The philosophical implications on architectural theory resulting from Spanish urbanization activities in the New World during the sixteenth century.

362 BERLIN, HEINRICH. 1950.

Fundación del Convento de Santa Clara en la Antigua. *AHG*, 2, 1:43–54.

Based on contemporary documentary sources, the founding and early history of the nunnery of Santa Clara. Important for the building history of the convent and church of Santa Clara.

363 BERLIN, HEINRICH. 1953.

La vida franciscana en la Guatemala de 1700. *AHG*, 5, 2:9–18.

A short account, well documented, of the Franciscan order in Guatemala.

364 BERMUDEZ PLATA, CRISTOBAL. 1946.

Catálogo de pasajeros a Indias durante los siglos XVI, XVII y XVIII. vol. 3, 1539–1559. Madrid: Consejo Superior de Investigaciones Científicas.

DUL/325.246 S733

A catalogue of immigrants.

365 BETETA, IGNACIO, editor.

Gazeta de Guatemala. Guatemala, 13 febrero, 1797–1810?

See *Gazeta* etc. in Section I for bibliographical data.

366 BETETA, IGNACIO. 1803.

Kalendario [sic] *y guía de forasteros de Guatemala: y sus provincias.* Guatemala: Imprenta Ignacio Beteta.

An early guide to Guatemala and Central America. Published again in 1806, according to Salazar, *Historia del desenvolvimiento,* see below. It is also mentioned by Batres Jáuregui, *La América Central,* v. 2, 512, see above.

See *Calendario* etc., 1792–1813, Section I, above.

367 *Biblioteca de la Sociedad de Antropología y Arqueología de Honduras.*
Tegucigalpa.

LC/F1501.S62A-Z

An unnumbered series; not separately catalogued. Has articles on history, archaelogy, geography and miscellaneous topics.

368 BLAIR, CALVIN P.
Social Science Research in Guatemala and the Role of U.S. Personnel, 1950–1967. Mimeographed.

A study carried out under the auspices of the Latin American Studies Association and Education and World Affairs. Deals with contemporary matters.

369 BLANCO SEGURA, RICARDO. 1967.
Historia eclesiástica de Costa Rica del descubrimiento a la erección de la diócesis, 1502–1850. 2a ed. San José, C.R.: Editorial Costa Rica.

First edition, 1960. This edition corrects some errors in the earlier one and adds new material. Important for background to architectural history.

370 BOBADILLA, PERFECTO H. 1936.
Monografía geográfica e histórica de San Pedro Sula, IV centenario de su fundación. San Pedro Sula: Talleres "Compañía de Honduras."

LC/F1516.S3B6

General information on San Pedro Sula based on secondary sources.

371 BOBADILLA, PERFECTO H. 1944.
Monografía del Departamento de Cortés. Tegucigalpa: Talleres Tipográficos Nacionales.

Geography and history of department of Cortés. Based mainly on secondary sources.

372 BODDAM-WHETHAM, J.W. 1877.
Across Central America. London: Hurst and Blackett.

Travel account. No information on art or architecture, but interesting observations and reflections on contemporary life and customs.

373 *Boletín de la Escuela Normal de Varones.* Tegucigalpa, 1920–.

Has articles of historical, geographic and economic import.

374 BONES QUIÑONEZ, ANTONIO. 1927.
Geografía e historia de Honduras. 2a ed. Choluteca, Honduras: Imprenta Portillo.

Secondary sources uncritically employed, but much miscellaneous information, some of it helpful in identifying towns.

375 BONILLA, MARCELINA. 1952.

Diccionario histórico-geográfico de las poblaciones de Honduras. 2a ed. Tegucigalpa: Imprenta Calderón.

LC/F1502.B6(1952)

A gazeteer or an index of towns in Honduras with brief statements and historical notes for each.

376 BOYLE, FREDERIK. 1868.

A ride across a continent: a personal narrative of wanderings through Nicaragua and Costa Rica. London: R. Bentley. 2 vols.

LC/F1524.B79

A personal account, patronising in attitude, revealing the biases of the English author. Deals mainly with his impression of local customs.

377 BRANAS, CESAR. 1933.

Antigua Guatemala. *La Prensa* [Buenos Aires], sección 2, 29 oct., 1 p., 9 ill.

A newspaper article of general nature with some photographs of colonial architecture and local scenery.

378 BRASSEUR DE BOURBOURG, CHARLES ETIENNE. 1857–1859.

Histoire des nations civilisées du Mexique et de l'Amérique-Centrale, durant les siécles antérieures a Christofe Colomb. Paris: A. Bertrand. 4 vols.

LC/F1219.B82 DUL/972.02 B823H

An early account of the pre-Columbian civilizations of Mexico and Guatemala. Of interest for the historiography of pre-Columbian archaeology.

379 BRASSEUR DE BOURBOURG, CHARLES ETIENNE. 1861.

Voyage sur l'isthme de Tehuantepec, dans l'état de Chiapas et la république de Guatemala, exécuté dans les années 1859 et 1860. Paris: A Bertrand.

LC/F1359.B82

Vivid descriptions of countryside, inhabitants and their customs.

380 BRASSEUR DE BOURBOURG, CHARLES ETIENNE. 1945–1946.

De Guatemala a Rabinal: Episodio de un viaje en la América del Centro en los años de 1855 y 1856. *ASGH,* 20:113–118, 232–235, 296–299; 21:67–113, 157–170. Reprinted from the *Gaceta de Guatemala,* 11, 69–81.

An extremely interesting account of local customs, descriptions of the countryside and some brief mention in passing on architecture.

381 BRASSEUR DE BOURBOURG, CHARLES ETIENNE. 1947.

Antigüedades guatemaltecas (carta escrita en Rabinal el 9 de Julio de 1855). *ASGH,* 22:1–2; 99–104. Reprinted from *Gaceta de Guatemala,* 7 (20, 27 de julio, 1855).

382 BRIGHAM, WILLIAM T. 1965.

Guatemala. The Land of the Quetzal. A Sketch. Gainesville, Fla.: University of Florida Press.

LC/F1464.B85

This is a facsimile of the 1887 edition. An introduction by Wilson Popenoe. A travel book with descriptions of the country, towns and people in the late nineteenth century.

383 BURRUS, ERNEST J. and FELIX ZUBILLAGA. 1956–60.

Historia de la provincia de la Compañía de Jesús de Nueva España. Rome: Instituto Historicum Societatis Iesu. Bibliotheca Instituti Historici, vols. 9, 13, 16, 17. 4 vols.

An excellent history of the Jesuit order in Mexico and in part of Central America. Includes documentary appendices. Brings up-to-date and corrects errors in an earlier work on the history of the order written between 1764–1767 by Francisco Javier Alegre, S.J., same title, 3 vols. published in México, D.F.: Carlos M. Bustamante, 1841–1842.

384 BYAM, WILLIAM W. 1897.

A Sketch of the State of Chiapas, México. Los Angeles: Press of G. Rice and Sons, Inc.

LC/F1256 B992

An album or travellers guide.

385 CABRERA, VICTOR M. 1924.

Guanacaste: Libro conmemorativo del centenario de la incorporación del partido de Nicoya a Costa Rica, 1824–1924. San José, C.R.: Publicación de la Secretaría de Gobernación, Imprenta María v. de Lines.

LC/F1549.G9C6

A history of the Nicoya peninsula. Has some illustrations of the colonial churches in various towns.

386 CACERES LOPEZ, CARLOS. 1951.

Epopeya de los chiapas, tribu que dió nombre a una entidad; leyenda histórica. Tuxtla Gutiérrez, Chiapas: Departamento de Prensa y Turismo.

LC/F1221.C5C3

Pamphlet of 68 pages. Popular history and legends of the Chiapanec Indians at the time of the conquest.

387 CACERES LOPEZ, CARLOS. 1958.

Historia general del Estado de Chiapas desde la época prehispánica hasta su independencia y reincorporación a México. México: Imprenta Mexicana.

A history of Chiapas, based on published sources, mainly secondary.

388 CAIGER, STEPHEN L. 1951

British Honduras, Past and Present. London: Allen & Unwin.

389 CALDERON QUIJANO, JOSE ANTONIO. 1944.

Belice, 1663(?)-1821. Historia de los establecimientos británicos del río Valis hasta la independencia de Hispanoamérica. Sevilla: Escuela de Estudios Hispano-Americanos.

Based on documents in the Archivo de Indias, Seville, a history of British Honduras in colonial times.

390 CALDERON QUIJANO, JOSE ANTONIO. 1971.

Población y raza en Hispano-América. Sevilla: Escuela de Estudios Hispano-Americanos.

The development of the racial character of the population of Hispano-America in the colonial period.

390a CALNEK, EDWARD E. 1961

Distribution and Location of the Tzeltal and Tzotzil Pueblos in the Highlands of Chiapas from Earliest Times to the Present. Chicago: University of Chicago, Department of Anthropology. (Hectographed).

Important for ethnohistorical investigations as well as for studies in urbanization and settlement patterns in Chiapas during the colonial period.

391 CALNEK, EDWARD E. 1970.

Los pueblos indígenas de las tierras altas. In *Ensayos de antropología en la zona central de Chiapas,* compiled by Norman and Julian Pitt-Rivers (México, D.F.: Instituto Nacional Indigenista), pp. 105-133.

Tzotzil- and Tzeltal-speaking *pueblos de indios* in highland Chiapas during the colonial period. Includes a map of the region dated c. 1580.

392 CALVO, JOAQUIN BERNARDO. 1887.

Apuntamientos geográficos, estadísticos é históricos. San José de Costa Rica: Imprenta Nacional.

LC/F1543.C16

At the head of the title: Administración Soto, República de Costa Rica.

Deals mainly with nineteenth-century economic-geographical data of Costa Rica as well as history.

393 CALVO, JOAQUIN BERNARDO (fl. 1857-1915). 1890.

The Republic of Costa Rica. Chicago: Rand, McNally & Co.

An English translation of the Spanish edition published in San José in 1887. See item immediately above.

394 CARLES, RUBEN DARIO. 1959.

220 años del período colonial en Panamá. 2a ed. Panamá: Departamento de Bellas Artes y Publicaciones.

A history of Panamá. Originally a series of lectures first published in 1949. No bibliography given. Citations lack complete bibliographical information. Based in part on some primary sources in archival materials.

A 3rd edition, Panamá: Talleres Gráficos de la Escuela de Artes y Oficios "Melchor Lasso de Vega," 1969.

394a CARMACK, ROBERT M. 1973.

Quichean Civilization. The Ethnohistoric, Ethnographic, and Archaeological Sources. Berkeley and Los Angeles: University of California Press.

An extensive treatment of published and manuscript sources of the Quiché Indians of Guatemala from Pre-Columbian times to the present, including the colonial period. A critical study of the materials. Important historiographical synthesis.

395 CARRANZA, JESUS E. 1897.

Un pueblo de los Altos. Totonicapán, Guatemala: Establecimiento Tipográfico "Popular."

LC/F1469.T7C3

A history of Totonicapán, Guatemala of popular character.

396 CARRENO, ALBERTO MARIA. 1924.

Fray Domingo de Betanzos, O.P. Fundador en la Nueva, España de la venerable orden Domínica. México: Imprenta Victoria.

A detailed history of the early years of the Dominican order in New Spain (Mexico).

397 CASTANEDA, FRANCISCO. 1907.

Una ciudad histórica: Antigua Guatemala, su pasado y su presente. Guatemala: Imprenta "La República."

A popular history of Antigua with some reference to the colonial architecture.

397a CASTANEDA BATRES, OSCAR. 1959.

Los nombres de Honduras. Tegucigalpa, Honduras: Ministerio de Educación Pública, Colección Rómulo E. Durón.

Survival of indigenous toponymy of Honduras.

398 CASTANEDA PAGANINI, RICARDO. 1947.

Historia de la Real y Pontificia Universidad de San Carlos de Guatemala. Guatemala: Tipografía Nacional.

A short history of the University in Guatemala City from its beginnings in Antigua Guatemala. Sources for data rarely stated.

399 CASTRO SEOANE, JOSE. 1945.

La expansión de la Merced en la América colonial. *ASGH*, 20:39-47.

A scholarly article on the Mercedarian order. Gives lists of *conventos*, dates of founding and other pertinent data of use in dating architecture.

400 CASTRO Y TOSSI, NORBERTO DE. 1964.

La población de la ciudad de Cartago en los siglos XVII y XVIII. *Revista del Archivo Nacional* [San José, C.R.], 2. semestre, 28:151-176.

The population by castes in Cartago, and the rest of Costa Rica.

401 *Centro América.*

Revista mensual publicada por los ex-alumnos del colegio "Centro América" del Sagrado Corazón de Jesús. Granada, Nicaragua. 1922-.

Miscellaneous articles on various subjects including history.

402 CEREZO D., HUGO. 1951.

El indígena en un documento del siglo XVIII: notas preliminares. *AHG*, 3, 2:37-40.

A short note based on the then still unpublished MS of CORTES Y LARRAZ, *Descripción* etc. See Section I for complete title.

403 CERWIN, HERBERT. 1963.

Bernal Díaz, Historian of The Conquest. Norman, Okla.: University of Oklahoma Press.

LC/F1230.D5712   DUL/923.546 D542CE

A biography of Díaz, 1496-1584. See DIAZ DEL CASTILLO, in Section I, Nos. 83-88, for various editions of his work.

404 CHAMBERLAIN, ROBERT S. 1945.

Ensayo sobre el adelantado Francisco de Montejo y sus proyectos para el desarrollo económico de la provincia de Honduras y Higueras. *ASGH*, 20:209-216.

Short article with some perceptive ideas, but not documented.

405 CHAMBERLAIN, ROBERT S. 1946.

The Founding of the City of Gracias a Díos, First Seat of the Audiencia de los Confines. *HAHR*, 26:2-18.

The same in Spanish translation, *ASGH*, 22, 1-2(1947):55-68. Based on documents in the Archivo de Indias, Seville.

406 CHAMBERLAIN, ROBERT S. 1947.

The Early Years of San Miguel de la Frontera. *HAHR*, 27:623-646.

Based on various *probanzas de méritos* and other documents. Town in El Salvador. Founding date discussed. Claimed by governors of Honduras and Nicaragua.

407   CHAMBERLAIN, ROBERT S. 1948a.

The Conquest and Colonization of Yucatan, 1517–1550. Washington, D.C.: Carnegie Institution of Washington.

DUL/972.6 C443C

Extensive bibliography, pp. 347–365. Ethno-historical material included. Colonial life and institutions.

408   CHAMBERLAIN, ROBERT S. 1948b.

The Governorship of the Adelantado Francisco de Montejo in Chiapas, 1539–1544. In *Contributions to American Anthropology and History* (Washington, D.C.: Carnegie Institution of Washington), 9, 46:165–207.

The career of Montejo as governor of Chiapas. Political and governmental matters. Well documented study.

409   CHAMBERLAIN, ROBERT S. 1953.

The Conquest and Colonization of Honduras, 1502–1550. Washington, D.C.: Carnegie Institution. Publication no. 598.

DUL/972.83C443C

A well-documented scholarly monograph on the early history of Honduras. Excellent bibliography.

A reprint was issued in 1966.

410   CHAMORRO, PEDRO J. 1941.

Límites de Nicaragua; su formación histórico-geográfica durante la conquista y el período colonial, 1502–1821. 2a ed. Managua: Editorial La Prensa.

LC/F1529.B7A3

The political boundaries of Nicaragua traced back to the colonial period.

411   CHAUNU, HUGUETTE and PIERRE CHAUNU. 1955–1959.

Séville et l'Atlantique, 1504–1650. Paris: A. Colin. 8 vols.

LC/HE860.C5

8 tomes in 10 volumes. Data on shipping.

Tables and lists, year by year, of vessels to and from America.

Material specifically of interest to Central America scattered throughout. Based on archival sources, which are cited. A mine of information.

412   CHARLES, CECIL. 1890.

Honduras: The Land of Great Depths. Chicago and New York: Rand, McNally and Co.

LC/F1504.C47

An economic geography with some historical material.

413 CHARNAY, DESIRE. 1863.

Le Mexique: souvenirs et impressions de voyage. Paris: E. Dentu.

LC/F1213.C45

Chapter 15, 363 ff. dealing with various towns in Chiapas, especially San Cristóbal de las Casas, appeared in a Spanish translation in *Ateneo* [Tuxtla Gutiérrez, Chiapas], 6, (mayo, 1956):125-148. *Ateneo* was published at irregular intervals.

414 CHARNAY, DESIRE. 1885.

Les anciennes villes du Nouveau monde: Voyages d'explorations au Mexique et dans l'Amérique Centrale, 1857-1882. Paris: Hachette & Co.

LC/F1219.C48

Description of some pre-Columbian sites. Also some interesting anecdotal material on local customs in small villages, especially in San Cristóbal de las Casas, Chiapas, page 437.

415 CHARNAY, DESIRE. 1887.

The Ancient Cities of the New World: Being Voyages and Explorations in Mexico and Central America from 1857-1882. New York: Harper and Bros.

LC/F1219.C49   DUL/972.01 C483

An English translation of the French edition of 1885. See preceding item.

416 CHARNAY, DESIRE. 1974.

The Ancient Cities of the New World: Being Voyages and Explorations in Mexico and Central America from 1857-1882. New York: Lennox Hill Publishers.

A reprint of the foregoing item.

417 CHEVALIER, FRANCOIS. 1944.

Les municipalités indiennes en Nouvelle Espagne, 1520-1620. *Anuario de Historia del Derecho Español* [Madrid]. 15:352-386.

Indian towns (Pueblos de Indios) in Mexico in the light of the Spanish urbanization process. See also Markman, Section IV, Nos. 1203, 1204.

418 CHEVALIER, FRANCOIS. 1970.

Land and Society in Colonial Mexico. Berkeley: University of California Press.

Of interest to the history of Central America by analogy, especially the chapter, pp. 11 ff., dealing with the church estates. Detailed material on the Jesuit establishments.

419 CHINCHILLA AGUILAR, ERNESTO. 1953.

La Inquisición en Guatemala. Guatemala: Editorial del Ministerio de Educación Pública.

LC/F1740.G8C45   DUL/272. C5391

Was presented as a thesis for the degree of "Maestro en Historia" at the Universidad Nacional Autónoma de México. Is a well written account of the activities of the Holy Office (Inquisition) in Guatemala during the colonial period. Has some data on judaising.

420 CHINCHILLA AGUILAR, ERNESTO. 1961a.

El ayuntamiento colonial de la ciudad de Guatemala. Guatemala: Editorial Universitaria.

LC/JS2179.G8C47

A history of the city of Antigua Guatemala. Based on secondary sources, not always cited.

421 CHINCHILLA AGUILAR, ERNESTO. 1961b.

Historia y tradiciones de la ciudad de Amatitlán. Guatemala: Editorial del Ministerio de Educación Pública "José de Pineda Ibarra." Biblioteca Guatemalteca de Cultura Popular.

A history of the town on Lake Amatitlán, Guatemala with some discussion of the church.

422 CHINCHILLA AGUILAR, ERNESTO. 1962.

El licenciado don Francisco Marroquín, primer obispo de Guatemala. *AGH,* 15, 2:57–65.

A brief biographical sketch of Marroquín.

423 CHINCHILLA AGUILAR, ERNESTO. 1963.

La danza del sacrificio y otros estudios. Guatemala: Ministerio de Educación Pública, Centro Editorial "José de Pineda Ibarra."

Eleven essays on ethnohistorical and archaeological subjects dealing with native Guatemalan highland Indian culture. Traits are traceable back to the colonial and Pre-Columbian periods.

424 CHINCHILLA AGUILAR, ERNESTO. 1965.

Francisco de Fuentes y Guzmán. *RUSC,* 66:161–169.

A short biographical sketch of an important colonial author. See Section I for bibliographical data on Fuentes y Guzmán.

425 CID FERNANDEZ, ENRIQUE DEL. 1959.

Don Gabino Gainzu y otros estudios. Guatemala: Imprenta Universitaria. Colección de autores guatemalenses "Carlos Wyld Ospina," v. 4.

LC/F1466.4 G32C5

A series of short studies, the first of which is on de Gainzu, 1766–1824, a Spanish general, who had been in Chile and Peru prior to his arrival in Guatemala in 1820 as Capitán General. He was instrumental in procuring the annexation of Central America to Mexico.

Other studies of colonial interest included deal with the coinage at the time of the conquest, artillery used by the conquistadors, some aspects of the Reino de Guatemala and other miscellaneous writings.

426 CID FERNANDEZ, ENRIQUE DEL. 1960.

Del retrato de don Pedro de Alvarado Contreras. Guatemala: Universidad de San Carlos de Guatemala.

LC/N7628.A6C5

See CID, 1960, Section IV, below, for a note.

427 CIGNOLI, FRANCISCO. 1954.

Médicos y cirujanos de corsarios y bucaneros. *La Escuela de Farmacia* [Guatemala]. 15, 193–195:33–36; 15, 196–198:29–36.

An interesting essay on medicine in the seventeenth century. Based on secondary sources.

428 CLINE, HOWARD F. 1964.

The 'Relaciones Geográficas' of the Spanish Indies. *HAHR,* 44:341–374.

Important for early urbanism in Mexico and Guatemala.

429 CONDOR, JOSIAH (1789–1855). 1825.

Mexico and Guatimala. London: Printed for J. Duncan. 2 vols.

A travel account from the period soon after the Independence in the early nineteenth century.

Another edition published, London: J. Duncan and T. Tegg and Son, 1830. Slightly different title, *A Popular Description of Mexico . . .*

Both are in the Latin American Collection, University of Texas Library.

430 CONTRERAS R., J. DANIEL. 1951.

Breve historia de Guatemala. Guatemala: Ministerio de Educación Pública.

LC/F1466.C748

A short, popular history of Guatemala. Includes a map showing archaeological sites.

A second edition, 1961, "Biblioteca de Cultura Popular," v. 15.

431 CONVERS FONNEGRA, CARLOS. 1936–1937.

Cuidades fundadas en Tierre Firme de 1525 a 1550. *Boletín de Historia y Antigüedades* [Bogotá, Colombia]. 23:347–355, 459–468, 735–743; 24:103–105, 237–240, 299–302.

Urbanization in the early sixteenth century.

431a COOK, SHERBURNE F. and WOODROW BORAH. 1971, 1973.

Essays in Population History. Berkeley, California: University of California Press. 2 vols.

Essays on the demographic history of Mexico from Aztec to modern times. Though material does not deal with Central America, it serves, nevertheless, as a useful model for similar investigations in Central America. The material for the early colonial period, however, is relevant for Guatemala.

432 CORONADO, J. ADRIAN. 1953.

Monografía del Departamento de Sacatepéquez. Guatemala: Editorial del Ministerio de Educación Pública.

LC/ F1469.S13C6   DUL/ 917.281 C822M

History and geography of Sacatepéquez, Guatemala where Antigua Guatemala and Ciudad Vieja are located.

433 CORONEL URTECHO, JOSE. 1962.

Reflexiones sobre la historia de Nicaragua; I; Alrededor de la Independencia. León, Nicaragua: Tipografía de la "Editorial Hospicio."

Early nineteenth-century Nicaragua.

434 CORZO, ANGEL M. 1944.

Historia de Chiapas. México: Editorial "Protos."

LC/F1256.C85

A history text book for secondary schools.

435 COSTA RICA. ACADEMIA DE LA HISTORIA DE COSTA RICA. 1961.

IV Centenario de la entrada de Cavallón a Costa Rica. San José, C.R.: Imprenta Nacional.

The conquest of Costa Rica and the first Spanish settlements.

435a *Cuadernos de Chiapas.*

Tuxtla Gutiérrez, Chiapas: Gobierno Constitucional del Estado, Departamento de Bibliotecas, 1946–?

Articles of historical interest, from previously published materials. Also literary matter.

Ceased publication soon after 1946.

436 CULEBRO, C. ALBERTO. 1932.

Historia de Chiapas. Huixtla, Chiapas, México: Imprenta Huixtla.

LC/4F Mexico-25

A superficial pamphlet based on secondary sources which are not cited.

437 CUNNINGHAM, EUGENE. 1922.

Gypsying through Central America. London: T.F. Unwin, Ltd.

LC/ F1432.C97, F1432 C97 1922

A modern travel account with some reference to towns and colonial monuments. Illustrated with photographs by Norman Hartman. Published at the same time in New York by E.P. Dutton.

438 CURTIS, WILLIAM ELEROY. 1888.

The Capitals of Spanish America. New York: Harper and Brothers.

An extract, "Managua, la capital de Nicaragua," was published in *ASGH*, 26, (1952):414–429.

439 DANTIN CERECEDA, JUAN. 1934 (1964).

Exploradores y conquistadores de Indias; relatos geográficos. Selección, notas y mapas por Juan Dantín Cereceda, dibujos F. Marco. Madrid: Instituto-Escuela.

Reprinted, Madrid: Consejo Superior de Investigaciones Científicas, 1964.

Has accounts written by Pedro de ALVARADO on his expedition to Guatemala, LOPEZ DE GOMERA'S description of the volcano Masaya in Nicaragua, as well as letters of CORTES, sections from the works of DIAZ DEL CASTILLO, OVIEDO and others.

440 DAVIS, KINGSLEY. 1960.

Colonial Expansion and Urban Diffusion in the Americas. *International Journal of Comparative Sociology.* 1, 1:43–66.

General treatment of colonial urbanization process in Latin America as well as in the English colonies. Some mention of Central America.

441 *Diario de Centro América.* 2. época. Guatemala. 1931–.

LC/J5.G73(37c2)

A daily newspaper. Official government publication. Serial articles of historical content. Sundry subjects in serial form pertinent to the colonial period.

Issued in two sections, the official, and another with "informaciones diversas."

441a DIAZ, VICTOR MANUEL. 1930(?).

Comociones terrestres en la América Central. Guatemala: Tipografía Nacional.

A history of the earthquakes in Guatemala. Rather popular account apparently based on published and documentary sources which are not cited.

442 DIAZ DURAN, J.C. 1942–1943.

Historia de la Casa de Moneda de Guatemala. *ASGH*, 18:191–224.

An informative essay on the mint in colonial Guatemala. Some references to the Capitanía in Antigua where the mint was located.

443 DIAZ VASCONCELOS, LUIS ANTONIO. 1942a.

Apuntes para la historia de la literatura guatemalteca. Guatemala: Tipografía Nacional.

A second edition, 1950.

Deals with pre-conquest and colonial literature.

444 DIAZ VASCONCELOS, LUIS ANTONIO. 1942b.

Apuntamientos para la historia de la literatura guatemalteca. Epoca indígena y colonial. Guatemala: Tipografía Nacional.

General survey of indigenous chronicles and colonial authors. Useful for bibliographical sources for history of the Reino de Guatemala.

445 DIFFIE, BAYLE W. 1966.

Guatemala y el Real Decreto sobre enajenación de bienes de fundaciones piadosas en 1804. In *XXXVI Congreso Internacional de Americanistas, España, 1964.* (Sevilla), 4:637.

A short note on the expropriation of real property held by religious organizations. No citations.

445a DOBSON, NARDA. 1973.

A History of Belize. Port-of-Spain, Trinidad: Longman Caribbean.

British Honduras history.

446 DOMINGUEZ, WENCESLAO. 1937.

Fundación de la ciudad de San Cristóbal, según Fray Antonio Remesal. *Boletín de la Cámara de Comercio e Industria de Ciudad Las Casas* [San Cristóbal de las Casas, Chiapas]. 1, 1:1–10.

Recapitulates data from Remesal.

447 DUENAS VAN SEVEREN, J. RICARDO. 1958.

La invasión filibustera de Nicaragua y la guerra nacional. San José, C.R.: Imprenta Nacional.

LC/ F1526.27.D8   DUL/ 972.8504 9D8521

The name of the author is a pseudonym for Justo Nonualco. A short monograph on the Walker invasion of Nicaragua. Also appeared in another edition in 1959 in San Salvador published by the Secretaría de la Organización de Estados Centro-Americanos, and again in 1962.

Has a short bibliography on the subject.

448 DU LAMERCIER (pseudonym). 1933.

Corinto a través de la historia. Corinto, Nicaragua: Tipografía Saballos.

LC/F1536.C6D6

The history of the port since the sixteenth century. Realejo was the more important port during most of the colonial period.

449 DUNLOP, ROBERT GLASGOW. 1847.

Travels in Central America. London: Longman, Brown, Green, and Longmans.

LC/1431.D92

General description of Central America at mid-nineteenth century. Also has a description of Antigua Guatemala and Guatemalan houses.

450 DUNN, HENRY (fl. 1800–1878). 1828.

Guatimala, or the United Provinces of Central America, in 1827–1828. New York: G. and C. Carvill.

DUL/917.281 D923

An English traveller in Guatemala soon after the independence from Spain. Very observant of local customs. Very little on architectural monuments.

451 DUNN, HENRY. n.d.

El libro verde. Colección de impresos. 3 tomos. Document: Legajo 4148, *AGG.*

I did not see this work said to be filed in the Archivo General del Gobierno de Guatemala, Guatemala City. Probably contains the same material, if not the very same book, noted immediately above.

452 DURON Y GAMERO, ROMULO ERNESTO. 1927.

Bosquejo histórico de Honduras, 1502–1921. San Pedro Sula, Honduras: Tipografía del Comercio.

A well-written history of Honduras from the time of the discovery by Columbus to the early twentieth century. Reprinted in a second edition, Tegucigalpa: Ministerio de Educación Pública, 1956.

453 ELLIOT, L.E. (MRS. LILLIAN ELWYN JOYCE). 1924.

Central America: New Paths in Ancient Lands. London: Methuen and Co.

DUL/972.8J89C

Impressions of a traveler. Has some photographs of architectural monuments in Antigua and elsewhere.

454 ELORZA Y RADA, FRANCISCO. 1930.

A Narrative of the Conquest of the Province of the Ytzas. Trans. P.A. Means. Paris: Les Editions Genet. 2 vols.

455 ENCINAS, DIEGO DE (fl. 16th century). 1945–1946.

Cedulario indiano. Madrid: Instituto de Cultura Hispánica.

See Sect. VI for a description.

456 ESTEVA FABREGAT, CLAUDIO. 1964.

El mestizaje en Iberoamérica. *RI,* 95–96:279–354.

The problem of race mixture, *mestizaje.*

457 ESTEVA FRABREGAT, CLAUDIO. 1968.

El mestizaje en América. In José Manuel Gómez-Tabanera, ed., *Las raíces de América.* Madrid: Instituto Español de Antropología Aplicada.

Essentially the same data, somewhat expanded, as in the foregoing item.

458 ESTRADA MOLINA, LIGIA MARIA. 1964.

La investigación histórica y los Archivos Nacionales. San José, C.R.

LC/CD3743.E8

See ESTRADA MOLINA, 1964, Section VI.

459 FALLAS, MARCO ANTONIO. 1972.

La factoría de tabacos de Costa Rica. San José, C.R.: Editorial Costa Rica.

An economic history of the tobacco industry during the colonial period and later. The role of tobacco growing in the agricultural economy of the country.

460 FEGUSSON, ERNA. 1937.

Guatemala. New York: A.A. Knopf.

DUL/917.281 F354

A book on impressions and travel in Guatemala. Very little on history or art, except arts and crafts.

461 FERNANDEZ DEL CASTILLO, FRANCISCO. 1945.

Don Pedro de Alvarado. México: Sociedad Mexicana de Geografía y Estadística.

A facsimile limited edition of an earlier work. A biography of Alvarado, including his letters.

462 FERNANDEZ GUARDIA, LEON, editor. 1881–1907.

Colección de documentos para la historia de Costa Rica. San José de Costa Rica: Imprenta Nacional. 10 vols.

LC/F1546.F36

Documents of colonial dates of historical import are in v. 1. See also Section VI, below.

463 FERNANDEZ GUARDIA, LEON. 1889.

Historia de Costa Rica durante la dominación española, 1502–1821. Madrid: Tipografía de M. Ginés Hernández.

A long book, about 650 pages, on the colonial history of Costa Rica.

464 FERNANDEZ GUARDIA, RICARDO. 1905.

Historia de Costa Rica: el descubrimiento y la conquista. San José: Imprenta de Avelino Alsina.

A well documented history of the early colonial period of Costa Rica and

Central America. Based on archival sources in Archivo de Indias, Seville. Also an English translation in 1913. See below.

465 FERNANDEZ GUARDIA, RICARDO. 1913.

History of the Discovery and Conquest of Costa Rica. Trans. by Harry Weston. New York: Crowell.

A translation of the original Spanish edition of 1905, see above.

466 FERNANDEZ GUARDIA, RICARDO. n.d. [1929?].

Costà Rica en el siglo XIX: antología de viajeros. San José, C.R.: Librería Lehmann.

Anthology of accounts of nineteenth-century travellers.

467 FERNANDEZ GUARDIA, RICARDO. 1937 [1967].

Crónicas coloniales de Costa Rica. San José, C.R.: Trejos Hermanos.

Historical accounts of colonial Costa Rica. Contains 76 plates with illustrations as well as some maps.

A second edition, a reprint, appeared in 1967. Has some data on Rodrigo de Arias, Marqués de Talmananca who as Fray Rodrigo de la Cruz founded the Bethlemite order in Antigua Guatemala.

See V.M., Díaz, *ASGH* 3, (1925–26):321.

468 FERNANDEZ GUARDIA, RICARDO. 1941a.

Historia de Costa Rica: el descubrimiento y conquista. San José, C.R.: Librería Lehmann.

The early history of colonial Costa Rica. A re-issue of the edition of 1905 above.

469 FERNANDEZ GUARDIA, RICARDO. 1941b.

Historia de Costa Rica: la independencia. 2a ed. San José, C.R.: Librería Lehmann y Cía.

The history of nineteenth century Costa Rica.

470 FERNANDEZ GUARDIA, RICARDO. 1970.

Costa Rica en el siglo XIX. Antología de viajeros. 2a ed. San José, C.R.: Editorial Gutenberg.

Data on nineteenth-century Costa Rica of economic-geographical interest. A re-issue of the n.d. [1929?] edition above.

471 FERNANDEZ HALL, FRANCISCO. 1921.

La catedral de Guatemala; estudio histórico. Guatemala: Imprenta "La Patria."

Small pamphlet, 15 pages, deals with the history of cathedral in Nueva Guatemala (Guatemala City).

472 FERRARI DE HARTLING, GUADALUPE. 1953.

Recuerdos de mi vieja Tegucigalpa. Comayagüela, Honduras: Imprenta Libertad.

LC/F1516.T4F4

A popular travel book. Little of historical or art historical import.

473 FERRUS ROIG, FRANCISCO. 1965.

Relación cronológica de los castellanos gobernadores del Castillo de San Felipe del Golfo (años 1650–1820), con síntesis de los hechos más descollantes de su historia. *ASGH,* 38:150–196.

A lengthy and well-illustrated article on the history of the defense of the north coast of Guatemala. Based on documentation in Spanish archives. Relevant for history of military architecture in Central America.

474 FIALLOS GIL, MARIANO. 1958.

León de Nicaragua: campanario de Rubén. León, Nicaragua: Imprenta Hospicio.

LC/F1536.L4F5

Short literary sketches. Also some stories of local personalities.

475 FLEMION, PHILIO F. 1972.

Historical Dictionary of El Salvador. Metuchen, N.J.: Scarecrow Press.

DUL/972.84003 F598H

Short-entry references with geographical and historical data.

476 FLORES, CARLOS Z. 1909.

Departamento de Las Casas del Estado de Chiapas. Monografía. San Cristóbal de las Casas, Chiapas: Tipografía Flores.

A geography of Chiapas based on secondary sources.

477 FLORES M., ROSA. 1952.

Chiquimula en la historia. Chiquimula: Imprenta "La Cultura."

LC/F1476.C485FS

A history of Chiquimula, Guatemala, including data on architecture as well as sundry topics.

478 FLORES RUIZ, EDUARDO. 1943.

Ciudad Real, su principio y evolución. *Boletín de la Sociedad de Arte y Literatura de San Cristóbal las Casas* [San Cristóbal de las Casas, Chiapas]. 1, 6:11–16.

Short sketch of the founding of San Cristóbal de las Casas.

479 FLORES RUIZ, EDUARDO. 1954. 1957.

El Sumidero. La leyenda de los Chiapas ante la historia. *Abside,* 18, 4 (1954). Also, *Abside,* 21, 1 (1957):73–86.

The legend of the Chiapaneco Indians who chose to hurl themselves into the Grijalva River, near Chiapa de Corzo, at the site of the Sumidero, rather than submit to the conquistador Diego de Mazariegos.

480 FLORES RUIZ, EDUARDO. 1964.

Rincones de historia: la Calle de las Monjas en Ciudad Real. *Abside,* 27, 4:5–23.

An historical account of the nunnery, church and tower of El Carmen in San Cristóbal de las Casas, Chiapas. Based on documentary materials which are not cited. See Section IV, below.

481 FLOYD, TROY S. 1961.

The Guatemalan Merchants, the Government and the *Provincianos. HAHR,* 41:90–110.

Legal and economic aspects of trade and commerce in the Reino de Guatemala.

482 FORTIER, ALCEE, AND JOHN ROSE FICKLEN. 1907.

Central America and Mexico. Philadelphia: G. Barrie and Sons. The History of North America, v. 9.

Contains a reproduction, 16, of the map of the Reino de Guatemala taken from the MS of Fuentes y Guzmán's *Recordación florida . . . ,* in the Biblioteca Nacional, Madrid.

483 FOSTER, GEORGE McCLELLAND. 1960.

Culture and Conquest: America's Spanish Heritage. New York: Wenner-Gren Foundation for Anthropological Research.

Important insights into the persistence of Iberian customs in the New World.

484 FRAENKEL, MICHAEL. 1946.

Land of the Quetzal. Yonkers, N.Y.: Baradinsky.

Excerpts from the journal *The Mexican Years, 1940–1944.*

Personal impressions of modern Guatemala.

485 FRIEDE, JUAN, AND BENJAMIN KEEN, editors. 1971.

Bartolomé de las Casas in History: Toward an Understanding of the Man and His Work. DeKalb, Illinois: Illinois University Press.

DUL/922.2 C335BR

A bibliography by Raymond Marcus, pp. 601–616.

486 FUENTE, JULIAN. 1929.

Los heraldos de la civilización centro-americana; reseña histórica de la Provincia Dominicana de San Vicente de Chiapa y Guatemala. Vergara: Tipografía de "El Santísimo Rosario".

LC/F1437.F84

A history in praise of the Dominican order in Central America by a Dominican friar. Based on secondary sources.

487   GALICH, MANUEL. 1949.

La historia a escena; 3 evocaciones en un acto. Guatemala: Ministerio de Educación Pública, El Libro de Guatemala. Colección contemporaneos, 13.

Popular sketches from Guatemalan history.

488   GALINDO, JUAN. 1836

On Central America. *Journal of the Royal Geographical Society of London.* 6:116–136.

LC/F1432.G15

Contains a description of the country and especially an account of contemporary Costa Rica.

489   GALINDO Y GALINDO, BERNARDO, editor. 1933.

Monografía del departamento de Choluteca. Tegucigalpa: Biblioteca de la Sociedad de Geografía e Historia de Honduras.

LC/F1501.S652S6

An economic geography of the province of Choluteca with some historical data. Catalogued under Sociedad Pedagógica Choluteca.

490   GALL, FRANCIS. 1961a.

Estudio sobre nombres geográficos de Guatemala. Rio de Janeiro: Pan American Institute of Geography and History. Publication No. 219.

The origin and transformations of place names in Guatemala. Useful in locating towns mentioned in the colonial literature and documents.

491   GALL, FRANCIS. 1961b.

Quetzaltenango Quiché. *ASGH,* 34, 1–4:175–200.

Ethnohistorical material as well as conquest of western Guatemala in 1524 by Pedro de Alvarado.

492   GALL, FRANCIS. 1962.

Soconusco (hasta la época de la Independencia). *ASGH,* 35, 1–4:155–168.

General geographical matters including native cultures, and an account of the conquest. Uses documentary sources.

493   GALL, FRANCIS. 1963.

Título de Ajpop Huitzitzil Tzumán: probanza de méritos de los León y Cardona. Guatemala: Ministerio de Educación Pública, Centro Editorial "José de Pineda Ibarra."

LC/F1469.Q5G35

Paleography of two documents in Newberry Library, Ayer Collection, Chicago. MSS nos. 1030, 1119.

Conquest of Xelahuh (Quetzaltenango, Guatemala).

The first, an eighteenth-century copy of an original of 1567, deals with Alvarado's conquest in 1524 and the native leader Tecún Umán.

The second, dating from 1794 but a copy of an older version, deals with the proof of services of an important family descended from a conquistador.

494 GALL, FRANCIS. 1966.

Conquista de El Salvador y fundación del primigenio San Salvador. *AHG*, 18, 1: 23–41.

Route of Alvarado to Cuzcatlán. Foundation of San Salvador by Diego de Alvarado in 1542.

495 GAMEZ, JOSE DOLORES. 1889.

Historia de Nicaragua, desde los tiempos prehistóricos hasta 1860, en sus relaciones con España, México y Centro-América. Managua: Tipografía de "El País".

LC/F1526.G19 DUL/972.85 G186

A history of Nicaragua. The material on the colonial period is more acceptable than that dealing with the pre-Columbian. He gives credence to the theory that the Indians are descendants of the "Lost Tribes of Israel".

496 GAMEZ, JOSE DOLORES. 1900.

Catecismo de historia de Centro América. Managua: Tipografía Nacional.

A school textbook of the history of Nicaragua.

497 GAMEZ, JOSE DOLORES. 1907.

Compendio de historia de Centro América, escrita para la enseñanza superior de Nicaragua. Managua: Compañía Tipográfica Internacional.

Only one volume published. A high school history textbook.

498 GAMEZ, JOSE DOLORES. 1909.

Viajes marítimos o sean nociones elementales acerca de los viajes marítimos por medio de los cuales se han hecho descubrimientos geográficos. Managua: Tipografía y Encuadernación Internacional.

A recounting of the famous voyages of discovery including those pertaining to Central America.

499 GAMEZ, JOSE DOLORES. 1915–1939.

Historia de la costa de Mosquitos (hasta 1894) en ralación con la conquista española, los piratas y corsarios en las costas centro-americanas, los avances y protectorado del gobierno inglés en la misma costa y la famosa cuestión inglesa con Nicaragua, Honduras y el Salvador. Managua: Talleres Nacionales.

LC/F1529. M9G3.

A history of the Mosquito coast from the colonial period through the nineteenth century.

An extra chapter written by H.A. Castellón.

500 GARCIA, J. LUIS. 1940.

Esquipulas: resena historica del culto del Señor Crucificado que se venera en el Santuario. Jalapa, Guatemala: Editorial "Oriental".

The history of the church the Black Christ at Esquipulas, Guatemala. Scant information on the construction history. Some illustrations of church building.

501 GARCIA BAUER, JOSE. 1968.

El repartimiento de tierras en los albores del derecho indiano-guatemalte-co. *ASGH*, 41: 387–422.

Land grants, *encomiendas* during the conquest with specific reference to this practice in Guatemala.

502 GARCIA PELAEZ, FRANCISCO DE PAULA (fl. 1785–1867). 1943–1944.

Memorias para la historia del antiguo reyno de Guatemala. 2a ed. Guatemala: Biblioteca "Payo de Rivera", Tipografía Nacional. 4 vols.

An important source for the colonial history of Central America, the Reino de Guatemala. His sources are the well-known colonial authors such as Remesal, Fuentes y Guzmán, Ximénez and Juarros. He also had the archives of the archbishopric of Guatemala at his disposal.

Was first published in 1851, by L. Luna. He had started writing this history in 1833 and completed the work in 1841.

503 GARCIA SOTO, J. MARIO. 1970.

Geografía general de Chiapas, con etimologías de los nombres indígenas. México: Porrúa Hermanos.

The geography of Chiapas and the origin of place names. Useful for tracing location of towns established during colonial period.

504 GARCIA Y ARTOLA, C.M.V. 1930.

Vida del venerable siervo de Dios Pedro de San José Betancur. Hermano Pedro. Guatemala: Tipografía Sánchez y de Guise.

A biography of the founder of the Bethlehemite order in Guatemala in the seventeenth century.

505 GARZA CANTU, ARTURO. 1938.

Por tierras de Chiapas y Guatemala. Guatemala.

LC/F1256.G3

An interesting travel account with some perceptive insights into local customs, especially violent in the Soconusco. Speaking of Tuxtla Chico, near Tapachula, Chiapas, p. 27, he says "Se registran varias muertes semanalmente, y como la población es pequeña, las reses que se sacrifican también semanalmente para el abasto de la ciudad, siempre es menor que el número de hombres que pasan a mejor vida . . ."

506 GAVARRETE, FRANCISCO. 1860.

Catecismo de la geografía de Guatemala. Guatemala.

No publisher given. See following item for 2nd. and 3rd. editions.

507 GAVARRETE, FRANCISCO. 1868 and 1874.

Geografía de la República de Guatemala. 2a ed. Guatemala: Imprenta de Paz C. de Guadalupe.

Includes a brief historical survey from Pre-Columbian times to mid-nineteenth century. A secondary-school textbook. A third edition, Librería y papelaría de Emilio Goubaud, 1874. Same title and contents.

508 GERHARD, PETER. 1972.

Colonial New Spain, 1519–1786; Historical Notes on the Evolution of Minor Political Jurisdictions. *HMAI,* 12: 63–137.

Sections XVI–XXII deal with Guatemala, Chiapa, Soconusco, Honduras, Nicaragua, Costa Rica and El Salvador. See CLINE, 1972, 1973, Section V, below.

509 GETINO, LUIS ALONSO, O.P. 1945.

Influencia de los dominicos en las Leyes Nuevas. Sevilla: Escuela de Estudios Hispano-Americanos de la Universidad de Sevilla.

510 GIRARD, RAFAEL. 1952.

El Popol-Vuh, fuente histórico. Guatemala: Editorial del Ministerio de Educación Pública.

On Vol. 1, sub-titled *El Popol Vuh como fundamento de la historia maya-quiché.* An analysis of the text and a reconstruction of the history of the Maya-Quiché people of Guatemala before the Conquest. A long book which he summarizes pp. 413–439. Included is an interesting chart detailing the basic diagnostic characteristics of the four cycles of Maya-Quiché history.

511 GOMEZ CARRILLO, AGUSTIN. 1916.

Compendio de historia de la América Central. 4a ed. Barcelona: Sobrinos de López Robert.

See item immediately below.

512 GOMEZ CARRILLO, AGUSTIN, and JOSE MILLA. 1892, 1897, 1905.

Historia de la América Central desde el descubrimiento del país por los españoles (1502) hasta su independencia de España (1821). Guatemala: Tipografía Nacional. 3 vols.

A continuation of José Milla's two-volume work of the same name first published in 1879–1882, see below.

513 GOMEZ HOYOS, RAFAEL. 1961. 1964.

La iglesia de América en las Leyes de Indias. Madrid: Instituto de Cultura Hispánica de Bogotá.

DUL/262.9 G633I

514 GONGORA, MARIO. 1962.

Los grupos de conquistadores en Tierra Firme (1509–1530): fisonomía histórico-social de un tipo de conquista. Santiago, Chile: Universidad de Chile, Centro de Historia Colonial.

Includes data on the conquest and settlement of Costa Rica.

515 GONZALEZ, DARIO. 1925(?).

Estudio Histórico de la Republica de El Salvador. San Salvador: Tipografía "La Union" de Dutriz Hermanos.

A primary and secondary school textbook.

516 GONZALEZ, LUIS FELIPE. 1943.

Origen y desarrollo de las poblaciones de Heredia, San José y Alajuela durante el regimen colonial. San José, C.R.: Imprenta "La Tribuna".

A popular account of the urban history of three cities in Costa Rica.

517 GONZALEZ, LUIS FELIPE. 1945.

Historia del desarrollo de la instrucción pública en Costa Rica. Tomo I, *La Colonia.* San José: Imprenta Nacional.

518 GONZALEZ GALVAN, MANUEL. 1968.

De Guatemala a Nicaragua; diario del viaje de un estudiante de arte. México: Instituto de Investigaciones Estéticas, Universidad Nacional Autónoma de México.

The diary of an art history student written during an overland journey from Guatemala to Nicaragua. Takes note of the architectural monuments.

519 GONZALEZ ORELLANA, CARLOS. 1970.

Historia de la educación en Guatemala. 2a ed. Guatemala: Editorial "José de Pineda Ibarra."

Intellectual history from Pre-Columbian to modern times, divided into six periods.

Includes a bibliography.

520 GONZALEZ SOL, RAFAEL. 1948.

Indice geográfico de la república de El Salvador. San Salvador: Universidad Autónoma de El Salvador.

A useful book for locating towns. Also some discussion on antiquities, description of country, etc.

521 GONZALEZ VIQUEZ, CLETO. 1920.

San José y sus comienzos. *Revista de Costa Rica,* 2: 2–3.

Short article on the founding of San José, Costa Rica.

522 GONZALEZ VIQUEZ, CLETO. 1958.

Obras históricas. San José, C.R.: A. Lehmann.

Post-colonial, nineteenth-century history.

523 GREENE, RICHARD LAURENCE. 1937.

The Filibuster. The Career of William Walker. Indianapolis and New York: Bobbs-Merrill, Co.

LC/ F1526.W226

The life of William Walker, 1824–1860 and the Filibuster War in Nicaragua, 1855–1860.

524 GREENLEAF, RICHARD E., editor. 1971.

The Roman Catholic Church in Colonial Latin America. New York: Alfred A. Knopf.

525 GRIFFITH, WILLIAM JOYCE. 1965.

Empires in the Wilderness. Foreign Colonization and Development in Guatemala, 1834–1844. Chapel Hill, N.C.: University of North Carolina Press.

LC/F1466.4.G7x

Economic history of the early post-colonial period.

526 GUATEMALA. COMITE PRO-HOMENAJE AL OBISPO LIC. FRANCISCO MARROQUIN. 1963.

4° Centenario del fallecimiento del Lic. Dn. Francisco Marroquin. 1r obispo de Guatemala, 18 de abril de 1563–18 de abril de 1963. Guatemala: Editorial del Ejército.

A small pamphlet with a brief biography of Marroquín.

527 GUATEMALA. DIRECCION GENERAL DE CARTOGRAFIA. 1961–1962.

Diccionario geográfico de Guatemala. Guatemala: Tipografía Nacional. 2 vols.

The toponymy of Guatemala. Important for locating towns. Also linguistic and historical data on major political divisions.

528 GUATEMALA. DIRECCION GENERAL DE ESTADISTICA. 1952.

Seminario de crédito agrícola. Síntesis estadística de Guatemala. Guatemala: Tipografía Nacional.

A statistical survey of agricultural production c.1950. Useful for locating towns of colonial origin, as well as traditional agricultural practices in transition.

529 GUATEMALA. INSTITUTO GEOGRAFICO NACIONAL. 1968.

Suplemento del diccionario geográfico de Guatemala de 1961–1964. Guatemala: Tipografía Nacional. 2 vols.

A supplement to GUATEMALA. DIRECCION GENERAL DE CARTOGRAFIA, 1961–1962.

GUATEMALA. INSTITUTO INDIGENISTA NACIONAL. 1948. See No. 553 below.

530 GUATEMALA. PALACE HOTEL. 1925.

Guatemala. La tierra de promisión. Guatemala.

A popular book for tourists.

531 GUERRA, FRANCISCO. 1966.

The Influence on Race, Logistics and Colonization in the Antilles. *Journal of Tropical Medicine and Hygiene,* 69, 2:23–35.

Includes some pertinent quantitative information on the pre-Columbian, colonial and present day population.

532 GUERRA BORGES, ALFREDO. 1969.

Geografía económica de Guatemala. 1a ed. Guatemala: Editorial Universitaria.

A modern scientific treatment of the economic-geography of Guatemala. Of use to economists and political scientists.

533 GUNN, JUDITH AND WENDELL GUNN. 1966.

Tegucigalpa, Honduras: Its Legends and Landmarks. Tegucigalpa: Instituto Hondureño de Cultura Interamericana.

LC/F1516.T4G8

An enthusiastic but overly popular guide book including data on the architectural monuments of Tegucigalpa.

534 HAEFKENS, JACOBO (fl. 1789–1858). 1827–28.

Reize naar Guatemala. 's Gravenage: Bij W.K. Mandemaker.

Vol. 1, 1827; Vol. 2, 1828.

See HAEFKENS . . . 1969 below.

535 HAEFKENS, JACOBO. 1832.

Central Amerika. Dordrecht (Netherlands): Bij Blussé en van Braam.

See HAEFKENS . . . 1969, below.

536 HAEFKENS, JACOBO. 1969.

Viaje a Guatemala y Centroamérica. Guatemala: Editorial Universitaria. 2 vols. in 1.

A Spanish translation from the Dutch by Theodora J.M. van Lottum, of the two foregoing items which had been originally published separately. Haefkens was in Guatemala from 1826 to 1829.

Vol. 1, *Reize,* deals with his impressions on the voyage from Holland to Guatemala City. Gives a plan of same on page 41.

Vol. 2, *Central Amerika,* deals with El Salvador and reports on the history and commerce of Central America.

537 HALE, J. 1826.

Six Months' Residence and Travels in Central America through the Free States of Nicaragua, and particularly Costa Rica, giving an interesting account of that beautiful country. New York: W. Borrodaile.

Very interesting account of Central America including descriptions of the countryside and local customs, as well as some passing comments on towns and churches.

538 HANCOCK, RALPH. 1947.

The Rainbow Republics, Central America. New York: Coward-McCann.

A popular travel book.

539 HANKE, LEWIS. 1952.

Bartolomé de Las Casas, Historian. Gainesville: University of Florida Press.

540 HANSON, EARL PARKER, editor. 1945.

The New World Guides to the Latin American Republics. New York: Duell, Sloan, and Pearce. 3 vols.

DUL/R918 H251N

Some data on the history, geography, and art monuments. Meant to serve as guides for travelers and others.

541 HELBIG, KARL M. 1964a.

La cuenca superior del Río Grijalva. Tuxtla Gutiérrez, Chiapas, Mexico: Instituto de Ciéncias y Artes de Chiapas.

An excellent economic geography of the larger part of highland Chiapas. Some historical material is also included. Excellent maps. Translated from the German edition Published in Hamburg in 1961.

542 HELBIG, KARL. 1964b.

El Soconusco y su zona cafetalera en Chiapas. Tuxtla Gutiérrez, Chiapas, México: Instituto de Ciéncias y Artes de Chiapas.

An excellent economic geography of the Soconusco, the Pacific littoral of Chiapas. Has some historical data as well as excellent maps. Translated from the German edition published in Hamburg in 1961.

543 HERNANDEZ DE LEON, FEDERICO. 1925, 1929, 1930.

El libro de las efemérides. Guatemala: Tipografía Sánchez y de Guise. 3 vols.

LC/F1436.H55

Belles letres. Historical events are embellished with a florid literary style and presented in no particular order. No index.

544 HERRERA S., JULIO ROBERTO. 1942–1943.

Anotaciones y documentos para la historia de los hospitales de la ciudad de Santiago de los Caballeros de Guatemala. *ASGH*, 18: 225–272.

A brief account of the history of the hospitals in Antigua Guatemala during the colonial period. Documentary and literary sources indicated.

545 *Hispanic-American Historical Review.* Durham, N. C. 1918 –.

A journal devoted to Latin American topics. Rich materials including articles on Central America. For an index up to 1950. see BUTLER, 1950, section V.

546 HOLLERAN, MARY PATRICIA. 1949.

Church and State in Guatemala. New York: Columbia University Press.

Ecclesiastical history. Nothing on church building activity. Reprinted, New York: Octagon Books, 1974.

547 HONDURAS. BIBLIOTECA NACIONAL. 1939–

Boletín de la Biblioteca y Archivo Nacionales. Tegucigalpa: Talleres Tipográficos Nacionales.

A bi-annual publication. Still current. Bibliographical and archival materials.

548 HONDURAS. SOCIEDAD DE GEOGRAFIA E HISTORIA. 1904–.

Revista. Tegucigalpa.

LC/F1501. R45

Suspended in 1910. Reinstated in 1927. Articles on history, geography, economy, and sundry subjects.

549 *Humanidades.* Guatemala: Facultad de Humanidades, Universidad de San Carlos. 1958–.

Published in fascicules at irregular intervals.

550 HUMPHREYS, RICHARD A. 1961.

The Diplomatic History of British Honduras, 1638–1901. London and New York: Oxford University Press.

LC/F1449.B7H8 DUL/972.82 H927D

The history of the controversy between Guatemala and Britain over British Honduras (Belice). Traces the affair back to the colonial period. Documentary sources cited.

551 HUNTINGTON, H. 1825.

A View of South America and Mexico, Comprising the Political Condition, Geography, Agriculture, Commerce, etc. of the Republics of Mexico, Guatemala, Colombia, Peru, the United Provinces of South America and Chíle, with a Complete History of the Revolution in Each of These Independent States. 2 vols. in one. Reprinted, New York: Lenox Hill Publishing Co., 1972.

552 HURTADO CHAMORRO, ALEJANDRO. 1965.

William Walker: Ideales y propósitos. Granada, Nicaragua: Editorial Unión.

DUL/923.973 W186H

William Walker's role in the history of Nicaragua, especially the Filibuster War, 1855-1860. An apologia for Walker. Based on secondary sources.

553 INSTITUTO INDIGENISTA NACIONAL, GUATEMALA. 1948.

Parramos, síntesis socio-económico de una comunidad indígena guatemalteca. Guatemala.

LC/F1476.P315

A study of a contemporary Indian town near Antigua Guatemala. Some data on town layout and church.

554 INTERNATIONAL BUREAU OF THE AMERICAN REPUBLICS. 1892.

Guatemala, a Handbook. Washington, D.C.: Government Printing Office.

DUL/917.281 B952G

A survey of late nineteenth-century Guatemala including data on laws, tarrifs and sundry economic matters.

555 IRISARRI, ANTONIO JOSE DE (pseud., ROMULALDO DE VILLA-PEDROSA). 1931-33, 1933-34, 1934-35.

El cristiano errante. *ASGH,* 9:101-109; 249-155; 354-363; 492-501; 10: 245-262; 381-397; 517-529; 11:224-241; 367-385; 497-512.

First published in Bogota in 1847 and again in Santiago de Chile in 1924.

A mid-nineteenth century account of an overland journey from Guatemala to Mexico. Full of miscellaneous information of local customs as well as comments on art and architecture.

556 IRISARRI, ANTONIO JOSE (pseud., BR. HILARION DE ALTA-GUMEA). 1935-36, 1936-37.

Historia del Perínclito Epaminondas del Cauca. *ASGH,* 12:101-124; 229-253; 369-376; 497-517; 13:119-137; 231-257; 344-376; 488-514.

First published in New York in 1863.

An interesting travel account with much of the same material in the item immediately above.

557 IRISARRI, JOSE ANTONIO. 1951.

Historia del perínclito Epaminondas del cauca. Editorial del Ministerio de Educación Pública. Biblioteca de Cultura Popular, vols. 14, 16.

A reissue of the foregoing item.

558 IRISARRI, ANTONIO JOSE. 1960.

El cristiano errante (novela que tiene mucho de historia). Guatemala: Editorial del Ministerio de Educación Pública "José de Pineda Ibarra." Biblioteca Guatemalteca de Cultura Popular, vols. 31, 32, 33, in one.

Reprint of 1847 edition, above.

559 JAMES, PRESTON EVERETT. 1942.

Latin America. New York: The Odyssey Press.

A well-written and informative geography of Latin America. Also includes historical information. Chapters on Central America very useful.

560 JENSEN, AMY E. 1955.

Guatemala: A Historical Survey. New York: Exposition Press.

561 JONES, CHESTER LLOYD. 1935.

Costa Rica and Civilization in the Caribbean. Madison, Wisc.: University of Wisconsin Press.

LC/ F1543.J66   DUL/304W8115 no. 23

Economic and cultural matters of the early part of the 20th century. Some historical data.

562 JONES, CHESTER LLOYD. 1940.

Guatemala, Past and Present. Minneapolis: University of Minnesota Press.

LC/ F1466.J67   DUL/ 972.81 J76G

Some history, but mainly concerned with economic and social conditions.

563 JONES, CHESTER LLOYD. 1966.

Guatemala, Past and Present. New York: Russell and Russell.

LC/F1466.J67

A reprint of the 1940 edition. Economic history.

564 JONES, CHESTER LLOYD. 1967.

Costa Rica and Civilization in the Caribbean. New York: Russell and Russell.

LC/F1543.J66

The same as University of Wisconsin Studies in Social Science and History, no. 23.

A reprint of the 1935 edition.

565 *Journal of Interamerican Studies.* Gainesville, Florida: University of Florida Press. 1959–.

Articles range in date from the colonial through the modern period. Subject matter varies, mainly historical, political and economic topics. Also, a few on art and architecture.

566 KELLY, JOHN EOGHAN. 1932.

Pedro de Alvarado, conquistador. Princeton: Princeton University Press.

LC/F1437 A485

567 KELSEY, VERA and LILLY DE JONGH OSBORNE. 1939.

Four Keys to Guatemala. New York: Funk and Wagnalls Co.

A well-written popular treatment of the history, landscape, native population and art of Guatemala. Material on contemporary Indian arts and crafts.

568 KOEBEL, WILLIAM HENRY. 1914.

Central America: Guatemala, Nicaragua, Costa Rica, Honduras, Panama and Salvador. New York: C. Scribner's Sons.

A travel account of early twentieth-century Central America. See immediately below for a later printing in London.

569 KOEBEL, WILLIAM HENRY. 1917. 1919.

Central America: Guatemala, Nicaragua, Costa Rica, Honduras, Panama and Salvador. London: Unwin.

570 KOMOR, HUGO F. 1930.

Apuntes de viaje por los departamentos de El Paraíso, Olancho y Yoro. Tegucigalpa: Tipo-litografía Nacional.

LC/F1504 K82

Deals with economic matters in three regions of Honduras.

571 KONETZKE, RICHARD. 1946.

El mestizaje y su importancia en el desarrollo de la población hispanoamericana durante la época colonial. *RI,* 23–24:7–14, 215–237.

Race mixture, mestization, useful study of problem of indigenous influences on art.

572 KONETZKE, RICHARD. 1948.

Las fuentes para la historia demográfica de Hispanoamerica durante la época colonial. *Anuario EA,* 5:267–324.

A critical study of the sources by means of which the size of the population of Hispano-America may be determined. Well documented.

573 KROEBER, A.L. 1934.

Native American Populations. *American Anthropologist,* 36:1–25.

An early study of the population in pre-Columbian and later times.

574 KUBLER, GEORGE. 1942.

Population Movements in Mexico, 1520–1600. *HAHR,* 22: 606–643.

An essay on the demography of colonial Mexico. Some estimates of numbers.

575 LAMADRID, FRAY LAZARO. 1942–1943.

Los estudios franciscanos en la Antigua Guatemala. *ASGH,* 18:279–305.

A well-annotated essay on the schools established by the Franciscan order and others in Antigua Guatemala. Important for the history of education in the colonial period.

576 LAMADRID, FRAY LAZARO. 1948.

Una figura centroamericana, Dr. Fr. José Liendo y Goicoechea, O.F.M. Guatemala: Tipografía "La Union".

A biography of a progressive thinker of the late eighteenth century. See GOICOECHEA, 1797, Section I above.

577 LANNING, JOHN TATE. 1940.

Academic Culture in the Spanish Colonies. New York: Oxford University Press.

A well-written history of university education in Latin America, including material on the universities of Central America.

578 LANNING, JOHN TATE. 1942.

The Reception of the Enlightenment in Latin America. In A.P. Whitaker, editor, *Latin America and the Enlightenment* (New York. Appleton-Century), pp. 71–94.

Of general interest and indirect import to the Reino de Guatemala.

579 LANNING, JOHN TATE. 1944.

A Reconsideration of Spanish Colonial Culture. *The Americas* 1:166–178.

Relevant to colonial Central America.

580 LANNING, JOHN TATE. 1946.

La recepción en la América española con especial referencia a Guatemala, de la ilustración del siglo XVIII. *ASGH,* 21, 3–4:190–199.

A Spanish version of LANNING, 1942.

581 LANNING, JOHN TATE. 1954.

Reales cédulas de la Real y Pontificia Universidad de San Carlos de Guatemala. Guatemala: Editorial Universitaria.

A transcription of all the *reales cédulas* of the University of San Carlos, Guatemala.

582 LANNING, JOHN TATE. 1955.

The University in the Kingdom of Guatemala. Ithaca, N.Y.: Cornell University Press.

583 LANNING, JOHN TATE. 1956.

The Eighteenth-Century Enlightenment in the University of San Carlos de Guatemala. Ithaca, N.Y.: Cornell University Press.

584 LARDE Y ARTHES, E. 1929.

Historia de Centro América. 3a ed. San Salvador: Tipografía "La Unión."

A secondary-school textbook.

585 LARDE Y LARIN, JORGE. 1925.

Orígenes de San Salvador Cuzcatlán, hoy capital de El Salvador. Boletín Municipal, número extraordinario. San Salvador, Imprenta Nacional, pp. 108–181.

LC/F1496.S2L32

Identifies the first establishment of San Salvador at the ruined site of La Bermuda. Describes the facade of the ruined church. Some of the material from the ruins was used to build the hacienda of La Bermuda.

Baron Castro, *La población . . . ,* see above, quotes Lardé, p. 302, note 1.

586 LARDE Y LARIN, JORGE. 1943, 1944.

Orígenes de San Salvador. Cuscatlán. *Ateneo* [San Salvador], 3a. época, 31,158:13–21; 159:3–16; 160:22–27; 161:13–21; 162:3–10; 163:8–12; 164:6–11; 4a época, 32, 165:8–12; 166:12–17.

Reprint of the foregoing item.

587 LARDE Y LARIN, JORGE. 1946.

Orígenes de la villa de Choluteca. *Revista del Archivo y Biblioteca Nacionales* [Tegucigalpa] 24, 11–12:482–499.

Data on the founding of the city of Choluteca in Honduras. Also known as Xerez de la Frontera.

588 LARDE Y LARIN, JORGE. 1950a.

El Salvador antiguo. San Salvador: Ediciones del Ministerio de Cultura.

LC/F1485.L34

A treatment of the Indian population of the region before the Conquest, as well as sundry matters of historical import for the colonial period.

589 LARDE Y LARIN, JORGE. 1950b.

Orígenes de la villa de la Santísima Trinidad de Sonsonate. *Anales del Museo Nacional "David J. Guzman,"* [San Salvador]. 1, 2:45–59.

Founding of Sonsonate, El Salvador.

590 LARDE Y LARIN, JORGE. 1952.

Guía histórica de El Salvador. San Salvador: Ministerio de Cultura.

LC/F1486. L3

A popular history of El Salvador.

591 LARDE Y LARIN, JORGE. 1957.

El Salvador. Historia de sus pueblos, villas y ciudades. San Salvador: Ministerio de Cultura.

LC/F1496. A123

A gazeteer of cities and towns of El Salvador. Includes some historical data on each.

592 LARDE Y LARIN, JORGE. 1958.

Guía histórica de El Salvador. 2a ed. San Salvador: Ministerio de Cultura.

LC/F1486. L3 1958

The same as LARDE Y LARIN, 1952, above.

593 LA RENAUDIERE, PHILIPPE FRANÇOIS DE (fl. 1781–1845). 1843.

Mexique et Guatemala. L'Univers pittoresque, v. 4. Paris. Firmin Didot Freres.

A travel account with some attractive illustrations.

594 LEHMANN, WALTER. 1920.

Zentral-Amerika. Berlin: D. Reimer. 2 vols.

A geography.

595 LEMALE, CARLOS. 1881.

Guía geográfica descriptiva de los centros de población de la República de Guatemala. Ciudades, villas, pueblos. Guatemala: Imprenta del "Diaro de Centro-América."

LC/ Geological Survey 506(381) L54

Lists towns in Guatemala with data on population, economic matters, etc. A gazeteer.

596 LEMUS, MANUEL and H.G. BOURGEOIS. 1897.

Breve noticia sobre Honduras. Datos geográficos, estadísticos e informaciones prácticas. Tegucigalpa: Tipografía Nacional.

LC/F1503.L56

A geography including economic matters from the latter part of the nineteenth century.

597 LIPSCHUTZ, ALEJANDRO. 1963.

El problema racial en la conquista de América y el mestizaje. Santiago de Chile: Editorial Austral.

A well-written study on the problem of race-mixture in the New World. Gives documentary sources and on p. 16, a bibliography on the subject.

A second edition has appeared, Santiago de Chile: Editorial Andrés Bello, 1967.

598 LIPSCHUTZ, ALEJANDRO. 1966.

La despoblación de las Indias después de la conquista. *América Indígena.* 26, 3:229–247.

A recent and more up-to-date treatment of the effect on the native populations during the sixteenth century.

599 LIPSCHUTZ, ALEJANDRO. 1967.

El problema social en la conquista de América y el mestizaje. 2a ed. Santiago de Chile: Editorial Andrés Bello.

Race mixture and the development of the social classes.

600 LOZOYA, JUAN CONTRERAS and LOPEZ DE AYALA, MARQUES DE. 1920.

Vida del segoviano Rodrigo de Contreras, gobernador de Nicaragua (1534–1544). Toledo: Imprenta de la Editorial Católica Toledana.

A biography of Rodrigo Contreras, 1502–1588, and his term in office in Nicaragua.

601 LUJAN MUNOZ, JORGE. 1968.

Inicios del dominio español en Indias. Guatemala: Universidad de San Carlos de Guatemala.

LC/F1466.4.L8

A selection of writings and documents on the beginnings of Spanish colonial history.

602 LUNARDI, FEDERICO. 1945a.

Choluteca, ensayo histórico-etnográfico. Tegucigalpa: Sociedad de Antropología e Historia de Honduras.

A short account of the history of the department of Choluteca, Honduras. Data on establishment of churches and religious orders useful for dating architectural monuments.

603 LUNARDI, FEDERICO. 1945b.

Iglesia y convento de San Francisco: El Valle de Comayagua. Documentos para la História; no. 3. Tegucigalpa: Sociedad de Antropología e Historia de Honduras.

LC/F1501.S62L89, vol. 3

Important historical data for tracing the history of the construction of the church and convento of San Francisco in Comayagua, Honduras.

604 LUNARDI, FEDERICO. 1945c.

El Valle de Comayagua, documentos para la historia. Tegucigalpa: Sociedad de Antropología e Historia de Honduras.

LC/F1501.S62L89

The history of Comayagua, Honduras. Cites documentary sources important for the construction history of various churches and monastic establishments.

605 LUNARDI, FEDERICO. 1946a.

La fundación de la ciudad de Gracias a Dios y de las primeras villas y ciudades de Honduras. Tegucigalpa: Sociedad de Antropología e Historia de Honduras.

LC/F1516.G7L8

A short historical account with useful data for dating the founding of Gracias a Dios and other early towns in Honduras.

606 LUNARDI, FEDERICO. 1946b.

El Tenguax y la primera iglesia de Comayagua. Tegucigalpa: Sociedad de Antropología e Historia de Honduras.

LC/1501.S62 L89, vol. 1

Data on the history of the cathedral of Comayagua, Honduras.

606a LUQUE ALCAIDE, ELISA. 1962.

La Sociedad Económica de Amigos del País de Guatemala. Sevilla: Escuela de Estudios Hispano-Americanos.

A study of the organization founded toward the end of the colonial period for the purpose of incrementing and fometing commercial and economic activities in Guatemala. Based on archival documents.

607 MACKIE, SEDELY J., editor. 1924.

An Account of the Conquest of Guatemala in 1524 by Pedro de Alvarado. New York: The Cortez Society.

Contains the letters of Alvarado in English translation.

608 MACLEOD, MURDO J. 1970.

Las Casas, Guatemala, and the Sad but Inevitable Case of Antonio de Remesal. In *Latin American Studies, Occasional Papers, No. 5.* Pittsburgh: University of Pittsburgh.

Reprinted from *A Journal of Liberal Arts,* (1970); 53–64.

The difficulties that REMESAL, see Section I above, had with the creole Spaniards, the origin of which harked back to the controversies of Las Casas.

609 MACLEOD, MURDO J. 1973.

Spanish Central America: A Socioeconomic History, 1520–1720. Berkeley: University of California Press.

Economic and demographic history of the first 200 years of Central American history.

610 MACNUTT, FRANCIS A. 1909.

Bartholomew de las Casas; His Life, His Apostolate, and His Writings. New York and London: G.P. Putnam's Sons.

611 MARINAS OTERO, LUIS. 1963.

Honduras. Madrid: Ediciones Cultura Hispánica.

LC/F1503.M36

A popular geography and travel book on present day Honduras.

612 MARROQUIN, ALEJANDRO DAGOBERTO. 1959.

Panchimalco; investigación sociológica. San Salvador: Editorial Universitaria.

LC/F1496.P3M3

A study of the local population. Ethnological. Nothing on church building.

613 MARROQUIN A., J. EMILIO. 1937.

Monografía elemental del departamento de San Marcos. Guatemala: Litografía B. Zadik y Cia.

LC/F1469.S173M3

The geography and history of the department of San Marios, Guatemala. Some data on towns, but nothing on church architecture.

614 MARROQUIN ROJAS, CLEMENTE. 1950.

La catedral de Chiapa. *La Hora Dominical,* 27 de agosto de 1950, 9–16. [Guatemala].

An article in a weekly newspaper on the founding of Chiapa de Corzo and San Cristóbal de las Casas, Chiapas. Very informative, though sources not cited.

615 MARTIN, PERCY FALCKE. 1911.

Salvador of the Twentieth Century. London: Edward Arnold.

An early twentieth century travel book.

616 MARTIN, ROBERT M. (fl. 1803?–1868). 1836–37.

History of the West Indies. London: Whittaker and Co. 2 vols.

Descriptions and other material on early nineteenth-century Honduras in chp. 1.

617 MARTINEZ CASTILLO, MARIO FELIPE. 1968.

Capítulos sobre el Colegio Tridentino de Comayagua y la educación colonial en Honduras. Tegucigalpa: Publicaciones del 120 aniversario de la fundación de la universidad.

Only the very beginning of the book actually deals with education in the colonial period.

618 MARTINEZ DURAN, CARLOS. 1942.

Las ciencias médicas en Guatemala. Origen y evolución. Guatemala: Tipografía Sánchez y De Guise.

Based on uncited documentary sources. Largest section of book deals with university medical education, 1682–1820.

619 MARTINEZ LOPEZ, EDUARDO. 1907.

Historia de Centro-América. Tegucigalpa: Tipografía Nacional.

LC/F1436.M35

A popular history of Central America based on secondary sources which are not cited.

620 MARTINEZ PEREZ, FELIPE and JOSE AZNAR LOPEZ. 1958.

Los estudios de medicina, cirugía y farmacia en la Universidad de Guatemala durante los siglos XVII y XVIII. *Medicamenta* [Madrid]. 16, 319:127–128.

Brief note.

621 MARURE, ALEJANDRO. 1837.

Bosquejo histórico de las revoluciones de Centro América desde 1811 hasta 1834 escrito por A.M., catedrático de Historia y Geografía en la N. Academia de Estudios del Estado de Guatemala, y uno de los comisionados por el G.S., Dr. Mariano Gálvez, para la formación del Atlas de mismo estado, de que forma parte esta obra. Tomo primero. Año de 1837. Guatemala: Imprenta de la N. Academia de Estudios.

A photograph of the title page appears in *ASGH*, 13 (1936–37): 397.

A second edition, see immediately below, appeared in 1877, and still another in 1913.

Has an atlas of maps of Guatemala.

See MARURE, 1832, also Atlas, 1835, Section VII, Nos. 1414, 1428.

622 MARURE, ALEJANDRO. 1877, 1913.

Bosquejo histórico de las revoluciones de Centro América . . . 2a ed. 1877. Tipografía "El Progreso". Another edition, México, D.F. and Paris, 1913.

See item immediately above.

622a MATA GAVIDIA, JOSE. 1943.

La influencia de España en la formación de la nacionalidad centroamericana.
Guatemala. Tipografía Nacional.

A study of the juridical basis beginning with Spanish legislation during the
colonial period for the formation of the Central American republics, especially Guatemala.

623 MATA GAVIDIA, JOSE. 1948.

Panorama filosófico de la Universidad de San Carlos al fin del siglo XVIII.
Guatemala: Universidad de San Carlos de Guatemala.

DUL/ Pam. Coll. 40568

A pamphlet of 38 pages on the study and teaching of philosophy in
Guatemala in the colonial period.

624 MATA GAVIDIA, JOSE. 1949.

*Temas de filosofía moderna sustentados en 1785 en la Universidad de San
Carlos de Guatemala.*

LC/ LE11.G8K   DUL/ Pam. Coll. 16251

Pamphlet of 63 pages. Latin text, Spanish translation including notes.
Intellectual history. Higher education in colonial Guatemala.

625 MATA GAVIDIA, JOSE. 1950.

Rafael Landívar, el poeta de Guatemala. Guatemala: Ministerio de Educación Pública.

DUL/ 868.11 L257RL

A popular study of the eighteenth-century Guatemalan poet. Some excerpts from his *Rusticatio mexicana.* See LANDIVAR . . . 1782, 1924,
1948, Section I, Nos. 166–168.

626 MATA GAVIDIA, JOSE. 1951.

El Colegio de Santo Tomás. *AHG,* 3, 2:21–36.

Deals with the school founded in Antigua Guatemala by Bishop Marroquín and the Dominicans in the sixteenth century which was later incor-
porated into the Universidad de San Carlos.

627 MATA GAVIDIA, JOSE. 1954.

Fundación de la Universidad en Guatemala, 1548–1688. Guatemala: Editorial Universitaria.

LC/LE11.G82M3

Based on documents in *AGG.*

628 MATA GAVIDIA, JOSE. 1969.

Anotaciones de historia patria centroamericana. Guatemala: Editorial
Universitaria.

LC/ F1436.M38   DUL/ 972.8 M425A

A history of Central America, especially of the colonial period. Has a good bibliography pp. 395–402. Also some facsimile illustrations of colonial import as well as maps.

629　McBRYDE, FELIX WEBSTER. 1947.

Cultural and Historical Geography of Southwest Guatemala. Washington, D.C.: Smithsonian Institution.

Social anthropology of local population, mainly Indian, in the highlands west of Guatemala City. Well illustrated. Also has good maps.

630　McBRYDE, FELIX WEBSTER. 1969.

Geografía cultural e histórica del suroeste de Guatemala. Guatemala: Seminario de Integración Social Guatemalteca.

Spanish translation of foregoing item.

630a　McVICKER, DONALD E. 1974.

Variation in Protohistoric Maya Settlement Pattern. *American Antiquity,* 39, 4:546–556.

A theoretical essay in which he re-examines the question of ethnographic analogy as a basis for investigations in highland Chiapas.

631　MEDINA, ALBERTO. 1945.

Efemérides nicaragüenses, 1502–1941. Managua: Editorial La Nueva Prensa.

A history of Nicaragua, from the colonial through the modern period.

632　MEJIA, MEDARDO. 1969.

Historia de Honduras. Tegucigalpa: Editorial Andrade.

LC/F1506.M43

A school textbook.

633　MELENDEZ CHAVERRI, CARLOS. 1962a.

La ciudad del lodo, 1564–1572; estudio acerca del primitivo asiento de la ciudad de Cartago en el Valle del Guarco. San José, C.R.: R. Facio.

LC/F1556.C3M4

A monograph of 46 pages on the location of the first city of Cartago. Has a bibliography of his sources. Inconclusive.

634　MELENDEZ CHAVERRI, CARLOS. 1962b.

Los viajes de Cockburn y Lievre por Costa Rica. San José, C.R.: Editorial Costa Rica. Biblioteca de Autores Costarricenses, t. 9.

LC/F1544.V5

Excerpts from COCKBURN, 1735, Section I, No. 65, and from a nineteenth-century traveller.

Has some maps and photographs.

635   MELENDEZ CHAVERRI, CARLOS. 1966a.

Datos históricos y etnográficos sobre los indios térrabas y chánguenes de Talamanca, Costa Rica, durante el régimen colonial. In *XXXVI Congreso Internacional de Americanistas, España, 1964* (Sevilla), 3:155–164.

Ethnohistory of two groups of Costa Rican Indians from the period of "contact" to the present.

636   MELENDEZ CHAVERRI, CARLOS. 1966b.

Los orígenes de los esclavos africanos en Costa Rica. In *XXXVI Congreso Internacional de Americanistas, España, 1964* (Sevilla), 4:387–391.

The numbers of Negroes imported to Costa Rica. Negroes were there from the very first in the sixteenth century. Some data and discussion on race mixture during the rest of the colonial period. Regions in Africa whence Negroes of Costa Rica originated.

637   MELENDEZ CHAVERRI, CARLOS. 1969.

Los orígenes de la propiedad territorial en el Valle Central de Costa Rica durante el siglo XVI. *Revista de la Universidad de Costa Rica* [San Jose]. 27: 53–71.

Land distribution in Costa Rica c. 1584. Transcriptions of some important contemporary documents appended.

638   MELENDEZ CHAVERRI, CARLOS. 1970.

La ilustración en el antiguo reino de Guatemala. San José, C.R.: Editorial Universitaria Centroamericana.

LC/F1463.M54

A history of the "enlightenment" in colonial Central America.

639   MEMBRENO, ALBERTO. 1901.

Nombres geográficos indígenas de la República de Honduras. Tegucigalpa: Tipografía Nacional.

LC/F1502.M53

Toponymy of Honduras. Survival of indigenous place names.

640   MEMBRENO, ALBERTO. 1908.

Nombres geográficos de la República de El Salvador. México: Imprenta de I. Escalante.

LC/F1482.M53

Toponymy of El Salvador. A pamphlet, 53 pages.

641   MENCOS FRANCO, AGUSTIN. 1894.

Crónicas de la Antigua Guatemala. Guatemala: Tipografía Nacional.

Popular legends, stories and history of Antigua Guatemala.

642   MENCOS FRANCO, AGUSTIN. 1937.

Literatura guatemalteca en el período de la colonia. Guatemala: Tipografía Nacional.

LC/PQ7490.M4

Survey of colonial authors, chroniclers, and ecclesiastics.

642a   MENCOS FRANCO, AGUSTIN. 1959.

Estudios históricos sobre Centroamérica. Guerras contra los ingleses y administración de don Matías de Gálvez. Guatemala. Tipografía Nacional.

A general history of the conflicts during the eighteenth century with the English along the north coasts of Central America and the part played in bringing the issue to a successful end under the leadership of Matías de Galvez.

643   MENDIZABAL, MIGUEL O. DE. 1943.

La conquista espiritual de la 'Tierra de Guerra' y su obstruccion por los conquistadores y pobladores. ASGH 29, 2:132–140.

The evangelization of Vera Paz, Guatemala, in the sixteenth century.

644   MENDOZA, JUAN MANUEL. 1920.

Historia de Diriamba, Ciudad del departamento de Carazo, república de Nicaragua. Guatemala: Imprenta "Electra", G.M. Staebler.

LC/F1536.D5M4

Short undocumented account of Diriamba, Nicaragua. No information on local church architecture.

645   MENOCAL, A.G. 1886.

Report of the U.S. Nicaragua Surveying Party 1885. Washington, D.C.: General Printing Office. Senate Ex. Doc. No. 99, 49th Congress, 1st Session. (55 pp, 11 folding maps, 6 plates).

Excellent route maps, views of countryside and other descriptive material.

646   MEYER, HARVEY K. 1972.

Historical Dictionary of Nicaragua. Metuchen, N.J.: Scarecrow Press.

LC/F1522.M4   DUL/917.285 M612H

Useful for locating towns mentioned in colonial literature and archival documents.

Geographical and historical matters. Has a bibliography, 483–503.

646a   MILES, S.W. 1957.

The Sixteenth-Century Pokom-Maya: A Documentary Analysis of Social Structure and Archaeological Setting. Philadelphia: American Philosophical Society.

Published in *Transactions of the APS,* vol. 47, part 4. Important for social anthropologists, ethnohistorians as well as for those interested in the history of urbanization and settlement patterns.

647   MILLA, JOSE (1827–1882). 1879–1882.

Historia de la América Central. Guatemala: Tipografía "El Progreso." 2 vols.

The first edition. See GOMEZ CARRILLO, 1892, 1897, 1905, above, for the last 3 vols. See next item for a more recent edition.

648   MILLA, JOSE. 1937.

Historia de la América Central. 2a ed. Guatemala: Tipografía Nacional. 2 vols.

LC/F1437.M642

A history of the colonial period from 1502–1821. Also an introductory section on the Indians of Pre-Conquest times.

649   MIRO, RODRIGO. 1950.

La cultura colonial en Panamá. Mexico.

Pamphlet. Journalistic, literary style. Colonial education. Early theatre.

650   MOE, ALFRED K. 1904.

Honduras: Geographical Sketch, Natural Resources, Laws, Economic Conditions, Actual Development, Prospects. Washington, D.C.: Government Printing Office.

LC/F1503.I6

A geographical work on the natural resources, laws, economic conditions and prospects for development. Has good maps and statistical charts.

651   MOLINA ARGUELLO, CARLOS. 1949.

El gobernador de Nicaragua en el siglo XVI. Sevilla: Escuela de Estudios Hispano-Americanos.

DUL/972.85 M722G

The development of the royal administration in Nicaragua in the sixteenth century. Has a bibliography.

652   MONTALBAN, LEONARDO. 1931.

Historia de la literatura de la América Central. San Salvador: Talleres Tipográficos del Ministerio de Instrucción Pública.

DUL/868.09 M762H

Deals with Pre-Columbian chronicles, colonial works as well as those of the modern period.

653   MONTERO BARRANTES, FRANCISCO. 1892.

Geografía de Costa Rica. Barcelona: Tipografía Literatura de J. Cunill Sala.

LC/F1543.M75

A geography of Costa Rica. Helpful in locating and identifying towns founded in colonial times.

Also published as *Compendio de la geografía de Costa Rica*. San José: Tipografía Lehmann, 1914.

654 MONTERO BARRANTES, FRANCISCO. 1892–94.

Elementos de historia de Costa Rica. San José, C.R.: Tipografía Nacional.

Deals with the colonial period but major emphasis is on the period of the independence to the last decade of the nineteenth century.

655 MONTGOMERY, GEORGE WASHINGTON. 1839.

Narrative of a Journey to Guatemala, in Central America in 1838. New York: Wiley and Putnam

DUL/917.281 M787N

A very entertaining travel book including observations on local customs as well as some references to churches.

656 MONTUFUR Y RIVERA MAESTRE, LORENZO (fl. 1824–1898). 1878–1887.

Reseña histórica de Centro-América. Guatemala: Tipografía de "El Progreso". 7 vols.

LC/F1436.M81, vol. 1, office.

A detailed history of Central America, based on many literary sources of the colonial period still unpublished at the time he was writing.

657 MONTUFAR Y RIVERA MAESTRE, LORENZO. 1887.

Walker en Centro-América. Guatemala: Reprinted, New York: Lenox Hill Publishing Co., 1972.

658 MOORE, RICHARD E. 1973.

Historical Dictionary of Guatemala. Revised edition. Metuchen, N.J.: Scarecrow Press.

DUL/R972.81003 M823HA

Useful short-entry reference for both geographical and historical data.

659 MORELET, ARTHUR. 1857.

Voyage dans l'Amérique Centrale, l'île de Cuba et le Yucatan. Paris: Gide et J. Baudry. 2 vols.

LC/F1432.M83

Describes mid-nineteenth century Guatemala City, in v. 2, chp. 20, 185 ff.

660 MORELET, ARTHUR. 1871.

Travels in Central America. Trans. by M. F. Squier. New York: Leypoldt, Holt & Williams.

LC/F1432.M84

First published in French in 1857, see immediately above. Describes the architecture of Antigua Guatemala in chapter 12.

661 MORENO, JOSE. 1962.

La Pax Hispánica y los desplazamientos de los pueblos indígenas. *Cuadernos americanos* [Mexico]. 6:186–190.

Pre-Columbian settlements in the light of the urbanization of the Indians in the sixteenth century. Mainly on Mexico with some references to Central America and elsewhere.

662 MORENO NAVARRO, ISIDORO. 1969.

Un aspecto del mestizaje americano. El problema de terminología. *Revista española de antropología americana.* 4:201–218.

The problem of race-mixture.

663 MORNER, MAGNUS. 1960.

El mestizaje en la historia de Iberoamérica. Stockholm: Latinamerikanska-institutet.

The history of race-mixture.

664 MORNER, MAGNUS. 1964.

La politica de segregación y el mestizaje en la Andiencia de Guatemala. *RI,* 24, 95–96:137–152.

The caste system in Central America. See also BARON CASTRO, *La población,* No. 348.

665 MORNER, MAGNUS, editor. 1967a.

The Expulsion of the Jesuits from Latin America. New York: Knopf Borzoi Books.

666 MORNER, MAGNUS. 1967b.

Race Mixture in the History of Latin America. Boston: Little Brown and Co.

See 1960, *El mestizaje,* above, for the original study. This is essentially the same but expanded and brought up to date.

667 MORNER, MAGNUS. 1969.

La política de segregación y el mestizaje en la Audiencia de Guatemala. *Revista Conservadora de Pensamiento Centròamericano* [Managua]. 21: 41–47.

Brief resumé of colonial legislation with regard to the separation of the castes and race mixture. Reprint of MORNER, 1964, above.

668 MORNER, MAGNUS, editor. 1970a.

Conference on Race and Class in Latin America, New York, 1965. New York: Columbia University Press.

Twelve essays by various authors on several aspects of racial mixing, the caste system of colonial times as well as modern subjects such as immigration and the abolition of slavery and their effects.

669   MORNER, MAGNUS. 1970b.

La corona española y los foráneos en los pueblos de indios de América. Stockholm: Latinamerikanska-institutet, Almqvist and Wiksell.

LC/F1410.M78   DUL/325.346 M694C

A general history of the transformation of the ethnic character of *pueblos de indios* during the course of the colonial period. Central American examples.

670   MUNOZ, JOAQUIN. 1952.

Guatemala, From Where the Rainbow Takes Its Colors. 3a ed. Guatemala: Tipografía Nacional.

Some maps and illustrations. A guide book for the tourist.

671   MUNOZ, JOAQUIN and ANNA BELL WARD. 1940.

Guatemala, Ancient and Modern. New York: The Pyramid Press.

History—ancient, colonial and modern. A background book for the traveller.

672   MUNRO, DANA G. 1918.

The Five Republics of Central America: Their Political and Economic Development and Their Relation to the U.S. Edited by David Kinley. New York: Oxford University Press.

Has a good bibliography up to date for the time.

673   MUYBRIDGE, EADWEARD (fl. 1830–1904). 1876.

The Pacific Coast of Central America and Mexico; the Isthmus of Panama; and the cultivation and shipment of coffee. San Francisco.

An unpublished album of 144 mounted photographs. There were five copies originally. Two no longer exist. One set may be seen in LC/A21–1239.

Extremely interesting photographs of Guatemala and Central America including views of inhabitants, towns and cities, local scenery, coffee plantations and coffee processing, as well as views of colonial and nineteenth-century architecture.

Another copy is in the Art Gallery and Museum of Stanford University, and a third is owned privately. The latter set is unmounted.

These photographs are also important for the history of photography.

674   NAVARRETE, CARLOS. 1966.

The Chiapanec History and Culture. Provo, Utah: Papers of the New World Archaeological Foundation. Publication No. 16.

An excellent monograph on the pre-Columbian and colonial history of Chiapa de Corzo, Chiapas, Mexico. Includes data on layout of town and other data obliquely pertinent for the urban and architectural history of one of the first towns established in Central America.

675 NERI FERNANDEZ, FELIPE. 1926.

Geografía de la América Central. 2a ed. Guatemala: Tipografía Nacional.

Descriptions of the landscape as well as statistics on trade, population, industry and sundry economic matters of the time.

676 NICAISE, AUGUSTE. 1861.

Les filibustiers américains; Walker et l'Amérique Centrale. Le tueur de jaguars. Paris. Reprinted, New York: Lenox Hill Publishing Co. 1972.

677 NICARAGUA. JUNTA NACIONAL DE TURISMO. 1937.

Tourist Guide of Nicaragua. Managua: "Junta Nacional de Turismo de Nicaragua."

LC/F1524.N54

Pamphlet, 10 pages.

678 NICARAGUA. UNIVERSIDAD CENTRAL, MANAGUA. 1941.

Memoria de su fundación, 15 de septiembre de 1941. Managua: Talleres Nacionales.

DUL/378.7285 N583M

A commemorative essay on the history of the city of Managua.

679 NIEDERLEIN, GUSTAVO. 1898.

The Republic of Guatemala. Philadelphia: The Philadelphia Commercial Museum.

A pamphlet 63 pages with a map of Guatemala. General economic and tourist information.

680 NORIEGA, FELIX F. 1904.

Diccionario geográfico de Costa Rica. San José: Imprenta de A. Alsina.

LC/F1542.N84

A gazetteer with brief commentaries on the towns of Costa Rica. Important for locating and identifying towns of colonial origin.

681 NORIEGA, FELIX F. 1923.

Diccionario geográfico de Costa Rica. 2a ed. San José, C.R.: Imprenta Nacional.

On pages 269–274, he gives a list of the governors of Costa Rica from the time of its discovery and conquest to the twentieth century.

682 NOVAL, JOAQUIN. 1952.

Algunas modalidades del trabajo indígena de Guatemala. *AHG,* 4:47–51.

Classification and description of the present day Indian population of Guatemala.

683 OAKES, MAUD. 1951.

The Two Crosses of Todos Santos. New York: Pantheon Books.

A study of the afterlife of pre-Columbian religious rites among the Indians of Todos los Santos, Guatemala.

684 OSBORNE, LILLY DE JONGH. 1956.

Four Keys to El Salvador. New York: Funk and Wagnalls.

LC/F1484.2.08

A general description designed for the traveller.

685 OSBORNE, LILLY DE JONGH, 1965.

Folklore, supersticiones y leyendas de Guatemala. Guatemala: Tipografía Nacional.

Pamphlet, 70 pages. Folklore and popular legends, some of remote origin.

686 PALM, ERWIN W. 1951.

Los orígenes del urbanismo imperial en América. México: Instituto Panamericano de Geografia e Historia, Comisión de Historia.

An important study of the origins of town layout in colonial Hispano-America and the problem of pre-Columbian influences.

686a PALM, ERWIN WALTER. 1973.

Rasgos humanistas en la cartografía de las relaciones geográficas de 1579–1881. *Comunicaciones, Proyecto Puebla-Tlaxcala* [Puebla, México], 7:109–112.

Some interesting observations with regard to the influence of humanistic studies in the compiling and rendering up of the maps accompanying the relaciones geográficas.

687 PALMA S., ALVARO ENRIQUE. 1959.

Monografía mínima del Departamento de Jutiapa. Guatemala: Imprenta Real.

LC/F1469.J8P3

A brief geographical survey of the department of Jutiapa, Guatemala with some information on founding of towns.

688 PANIAGUA, FLAVIO ANTONIO. 1876.

Catecismo elemental de historia y estadística de Chiapas. San Cristóbal Las Casas: Imprenta del "Porvenir" a cargo de M.M. Trujillo.

LC/F1256.P19

A history of Chiapas and San Cristóbal de las Casas in the form of question-and-answer. Contains information on church construction history.

689 PARKER, FRANKLIN D. 1951.

The Histories and Historians of Central America to 1850. Ann Arbor: University Microfilms. Publication No. 2738.

LC/MIC#A51-479

An historiography of colonial Central America.

690 PARKER, FRANKLIN D. 1970.

Travels in Central America, 1821–1840. Gainesville, Florida: University of Florida Press.

An historical interpretation of travel accounts from the early national period.

691 PAZ SOLORZANO, JUAN. 1914.

Historia del Señor Crucificado de Esquipulas. Guatemala.

A history of the veneration of the Black Christ of Esquipulas with some details concerning the building history of the church.

692 PAZ SOLORZANO, JUAN. 1949.

Historia del Santo Cristo de Esquipulas. 2a ed. Guatemala: Unión Tipográfica Castañeda, Avila y Cía.

693 PERALTA, MANUEL MARIA. 1883.

Costa Rica, Nicaragua y Panamá en el siglo XVI. Madrid: M. Murillo.

LC/F1437.P42

Information of conquest and establishment of first towns in Costa Rica, Nicaragua and Panama. Some treatment of racial elements including Spaniards, Indians, and Negroes.

694 PERALTA, MANUEL MARIA. 1887.

El canal interoceánico de Nicaragua y Costa Rica en 1620 y en 1887. Relaciones de Diego de Mercado y Thos. C. Reynolds. Brussels: Imprenta de A. Mertens.

LC/TC784.P42

Also includes some pertinent documents on the subject.

695 PEREZ, FRAY PEDRO NOLASCO. 1923.

Religiosos de la Merced que pasaron a la América española. Sevilla: Tipografía Zarzuela. 2 vols.

LC/BX3800.P4

A study of the friars of the order of La Merced in Latin America, especially in Chiapas, Guatemala and other Central American countries.

696   PEREZ ESTRADA, ALVARO, editor. 1936.

Homenaje a la ciudad de Gracias a Dios en el CD aniversario de su fundación 1536–1936. San Pedro Sula: Tipografía Pérez Estrada.

LC/F1516.G7P5

The history of the founding and development of Gracias a Dios, Honduras.

697   PEREZ VALENZUELA, PEDRO. 1934.

La Nueva Guatemala de la Asunción. Guatemala: Tipografía Nacional.

DUL/972.81 P438N

A history of the transfer of the capital of the Reino de Guatemala from Antigua to Guatemala City after 1773. Based on documentary sources in *AGG.*

698   PEREZ VALENZUELA, PEDRO. 1936.

Historia de piratas. Los aventureros del mar en la América Central. Guatemala: Tipografía Nacional.

LC/F2161.P47   DUL/972.8 P438H

Gives a short list of his sources on pages 141–142. A history of pirates, buccaneers, and freebooters on the Spanish Main.

699   PEREZ VALENZUELA, PEDRO. 1937.

Estampas del pasado; crónicas de la época colonial. Guatemala: Tipografía Nacional.

DUL/972.81 P438E

Short literary sketches of the colonial period in Guatemala.

700   PEREZ VALENZUELA, PEDRO. 1943.

Los recolectos, apuntes para la historia de las misiones en la América Central. Guatemala: Tipografía Nacional.

LC/BV2840.P4

A study of the missionary activity of the order of Los Recolectos. Data on founding of conventos, pacification and evangelization of Indians.

701   PEREZ VALENZUELA, PEDRO. 1956.

Santo Tomás de Castilla: apuntes para la historia de las colonizaciones en la costa atlántica. Guatemala: Tipografía Nacional.

LC/F1469.S2P45

History of English and Belgian abortive settlements in Guatemala between 1824 and 1850.

702 PEREZ VALENZUELA, PEDRO. 1960.

Ciudad Vieja. Guatemala: Imprenta Universitaria.

A history of the first Spanish city in colonial Central America, 1524–1543. Based on secondary sources.

703 PEREZ VALENZUELA, PEDRO. 1964.

La nueva Guatemala de la Asunción. Terremoto de Santa Marta: fundación en el Llano de la Virgen. 2a ed. Guatemala: Centro Editorial "José de Pineda Ibarra", Ministerio de Educación Pública.

LC/F1476.G9P47

Well-documented account of the transfer of the capital of the Reino de Guatemala to its present location. Events of 1775–1780.

Re-issue of the 1934 edition.

704 PEREZ VALENZUELA, PEDRO. 1970.

Memoria de los trabajos del M. N. Ayuntamiento de la Nueva Guatemala de la Asunción en el año MDCCLXXVI, conforme a las actas de su escribano D. Joseph Manuel Laparte. Guatemala: Imprenta Municipal.

LC/F1476.G9P46

The cabildos celebrated by the city council of Guatemala City in 1776, the year the transfer of the capital from Antigua was finally effected after its destruction by earthquake in 1773.

705 PEREZ VALLE, EDUARDO. 1960.

El desaguadero de la Mar Dulce; historia de su descubrimiento. Managua: Ministorio de Educación Pública.

LC/F1526.25.P4

Scholarly work on discovery and explorations of San Juan River. Good sketch maps. Also bibliography.

706 PERINGY, MAURICE DE. 1914(?).

Les cinq républics de l'Amérique Centrale. Costa Rica, Guatemala, Honduras, Nicaragua, Salvador. Paris: P. Roger et Cie.

Economic geography, mainly of the modern period. Some historical data.

707 PERRET, FERDINAND. 1959.

Indice del ensayo de la Perret-Enciclopedia del arte hispano-americano de la época colonial en las Américas y en las Islas Filipinas. México: Litográfica y Tipográfica Yolva, S.A.

Reviewed by Ricardo Toledo Palomo, *AHG,* 11, 1, (1959):74–75.

Has some data on Guatemala.

708 PINEDA, EMETERIO. 1845.

Descripción geográfica del departamento de Chiapas y Soconusco. México, D.F.: Cumplido.

A geography of Chiapas. Interesting for early period immediately after the Independence.

For the same, see *Boletin de la Sociedad de Geografia y Estadistica* [Mexico], 3.

709 PINEDA, VICENTE. 1888.

Historia de las sublevaciones indígenas habidas en el estado de Chiapas. Chiapas: Tipografía del Gobierno.

Indian insurrections in the eighteenth century and later.

710 POESSY, RODOLFO, editor. 1939–1940.

Guia ilustrada de Granada; anuario de información general. Granada.

LC/F1536.G72G8

A guide book of Granada, Nicaragua. Some reference to colonial architecture.

711 POPENOE, DOROTHY. 1933 (1935).

Santiago de los Caballeros de Guatemala. Cambridge: Harvard University Press.

LC/F1476.G92P7   DUL/972.81 P826

See POPENOE . . . 1933, Section IV, No. 1221a, for a description.

712 PRADO, ELADIO. 1926.

Monografía del santuario de Nuestra Señora de los Angeles de Cartago. San José, C.R.: Imprenta Lehmann.

The history of the principal church in Cartago, Costa Rica.

713 PRADO, ELADIO. 1942.

Breve compendio de la história de la milagrosa imagen de Nuestra Señora de Los Angeles, que se venera en la ciudad de Cartago, Costa Rica. San José: Imprenta Lehmann.

LC/BT660.A5P,7

Pamphlet.

714 PRADO, ELADIO. n.d.

Historia de Orosí y la ruina de Ojaras renovado en el año de 1925.

A small pamphlet with some data on the little church of Orosí, Costa Rica. No date or place of publication, probably soon after 1925 and in San José.

715 QUINTANA OROZCO, OFSMAN. 1968.

Apuntes de historia de Nicaragua. 4a ed. Managua: Editora Mundial.

LC/F1526.Q5

A history textbook.

716 RADELL, DAVID R. and JAMES J. PARSONS. 1971.
Realejo: Forgotten Colonial Port and Shipbuilding Center in Nicaragua. *HAHR,* 51:205–312.

An economic history of the principal port of Nicaragua until the middle of the nineteenth century.

717 RAMIREZ, JOSE FERNANDO and IGNACIO L. RAYON. 1847.
Proceso de residencia contra Pedro de Alvarado. México: Impreso por Valdés y Redondas.

Reprinted in *ASGH,* 7 (1930–31): 95–122; 210–239; 360–387; 513–528; 8 (1931–32): 254–267; 392–397; 521–534; 9 (1932–33): 121–129; 256–264. See *ALVARADO, Proceso.* Section I.

Taken from a MS in the Archivo General (de México) and also illustrated from some native codices.

718 RAMOS, MIGUEL ANGEL. 1956.
Reseña histórica de Nicaragua desde el descubrimiento hasta la invasión de Walker. Combate de San Jacinto. Tegucigalpa: Imprenta Calderón.

LC/F1526.R2

Only the first part deals with the colonial period.

719 RECINOS, ADRIAN. 1913, 1954.
Monografía del departamento de Huehuetenango. Guatemala: Tipografía Sánchez y DeGuise.

DUL/972.81 R297M

History and geography of Huehuetenango, Guatemala. Appeared as articles in the *Diario de Centro-América* during the year of 1912.

A second edition. Guatemala: Editorial del Ministerio de Educación Pública, 1954.

720 RECINOS, ADRIAN. 1947.
Popol vuh; las antiguas historias del Quiché. México: Fondo de Cultura Económica.

LC/F1465.P828   DUL/913.7281 P829P

Translated from the Quiché into Spanish and annotated by the author. Deals with the religion, mythology and oral history of the Quiches of highland Guatemala. Important ethnohistorical source. An excellent introduction giving a survey of native literature including a detailed account of the history of this manuscript.

Also a second edition, 1953.

721   RECINOS, ADRIAN. 1949.

La ciudad de Guatemala, 1524–1773. *AHG*, 1, 1:57–62

Very brief but perceptive article on the founding of the first Spanish town in Guatemala.

722   RECINOS, ADRIAN. 1950a.

Popol vuh; the Sacred Book of the Ancient Quiché Maya. Norman, Okla.: University of Oklahoma Press.

LC/F1465.P814   DUL/Div.Sch.913.7281 P829PA

An English translation of RECINOS' Spanish version by Delia Goetz and Sylvanus G. Morley. See RECINOS, 1947, above.

723   RECINOS, ADRIAN. 1950b.

Memorial de Sololá. Anales de los Cakchiqueles. México: Fondo de Cultura Económica.

Indigenous literature of Guatemala. Source for religion, beliefs, customs of the Cakchiquels preserved in the oral tradition, probably based on a mid-seventeenth-century transcription of an original of earlier date.

This is a new translation by Recinos who also gives an extensive introduction including a history of the manuscript and its contents. Added to this edition is a shorter native work, *Titulo de los señores de Totonicapán,* translated from the original Quiché by Dionisio José Chonay, and possibly dating from 1554.

724   RECINOS, ADRIAN. 1950c.

Título de los señores de Totonicapán. México: Fondo de Cultura Económica.

Included in RECINOS 1950b, *Memorial de Sololá. Anales de los Cakchiqueles.* See the foregoing item.

725   RECINOS, ADRIAN. 1952.

Pedro Alvarado, conquistador de México y Guatemala. México: Fondo de Cultura Económica.

Critical biography of Pedro Alvarado based on primary sources.

726   RECINOS, ADRIAN. 1953.

The Annals of the Cakchiquels. Translated from the Cakchiquel Maya by Adrian Recinos and Delia Goetz. *Title of the Lords of Totonicapán.* Translated from the Quiché into Spanish by Dionisio José Chonay: English version by Delia Goetz. Norman, Okla.: University of Oklahoma Press.

DUL/970.3 A613A

See RECINOS 1950b, 1950c, above.

727   RECINOS, ADRIAN. 1957.

Crónicas indígenas de Guatemala. Guatemala: Editorial Universitaria.

Transcribes a number of shorter indigenous accounts which corroborate the data given in the *Popol-Vuh* and in the *Memorial Cakchiquel de Sololá.* Pre-Columbian history, the oral tradition. Five such short accounts are included.

Parallel pages with original language and Spanish translation. See RECINOS. 1947, 1950b, 1953.

728 RECINOS, ADRIAN. 1958.

Doña Leonor de Alvarado y otros estudios. Guatemala: Editorial Universitaria.

LC/F1461.6.R4   DUL/872.81 R297D

Essays and lectures by Recinos and a study of the life of the daughter of Pedro de Alvarado, born in 1520.

729 REICHARDT, C.F. 1854.

Nicaragua. Nach eigener Anschauung in Jahre 1852 und mit besonderer Beziehung auf die Auswanderung nach den heissen Zonen Amerikas. Braunschweig: F. Vieweg und Sohn.

Deals in part with Germans in Nicaragua. Economic opportunities for immigrants.

730 REINA, RUBEN F. 1966.

The Law of the Saints; a Pokoman Pueblo and its Community Culture. Indianapolis: Bobbs-Merrill Co.

LC/F1465.2 P6R4

An ethnographic and social anthropological study of the village of Chinautla near Guatemala City.

731 REINA VALENZUELA, JOSE. 1968.

Comayagua antañona: 1537–1821. Tegucigalpa: Biblioteca de la Academia de Geografía e Historia.

Based on archival documents and contemporary literary material. Important as background to architectural history as well as political history, which it is primarily.

732 RESTREPO, VICENTE. 1888.

Viajes de Lionel Wafer al Istmo de Darién: cuatro meses entre los indios. Bogotá.

See WAFER, 1960, Section I, for a description.

733 *Revista de Indias.* Madrid: Instituto de Fernández de Oviedo, Consejo Superior de Investigaciones Científicas, 1940–.

Volume 24, 95–96 (1964) is devoted in its entirety to mestization in the New World.

734 *Revista de la Academia de Geografía e Historia de Nicaragua.* Managua. 193? –

Eleven volumes published to 1952. Appeared intermittently. Reprints of articles in other journals and also of archival documents pertinent to Nicaragua.

735 Revista: Universidad de San Carlos de Guatemala.

Guatemala, 1945–.

DUL/X Per U58SC

Not published regularly. Contains articles in various fields: humanities, social sciences, history, education, etc.

736 REYES M., JOSE LUIS. 1945.

Catálogo razonado de las leyes de Guatemala. Contiene adiciones de don Alejandro Marure, que lo dejó hasta 1850, al del Licenciado Andrés Fuentes Franco, hasta 1856, y su continuación hasta 1871. Guatemala: Tipografía Nacional.

DUL/349.7281 G918C

A list of laws of the early independence period.

737 REYES M., JOSE LUIS. 1951

Datos curiosos sobre la demarcación política de Guatemala. Guatemala.

DUL/354.7281 R457D

Data on the establishment of the departmental boundaries of Guatemala. Good index.

737a REYES-MAZZONI, ROBERTO. 1974.

El nombre de Olancho y los grupos de habla nahuat en Honduras. *Notas Antropológicas* (México: Instituto de Investigaciones Antropológicas, U.N.A.M., xeroxed), 1, 5:31–39.

Nahua place names in eastern Honduras.

738 REYNOLDS, PHILIP KEEP. 1927.

The Banana: Its History, Cultivation, and Place Among Staple Foods. Boston: Houghton Mifflin Co.

Important product of Central America. Well documented. Extensive bibliography of interest to botanists and agronomists.

739 RICARD, ROBERT. 1933.

Conquete spirituelle du Mexique, published as *Travaux et Mémoires de l'Institut d'Ethnologie,* 20, complete volume.

A germinal book. Distinguishes between the "physical" and the "spiritual" or cultural conquest. Relevant for Central America.

740 RICARD, ROBERT. 1947.

La conquista espiritual de México. Ensayo sobre el Apostolado y los métodos misioneros de las órdenes mendicantes en la Nueva España de 1523-24 a 1572. México: Colección de Estudios Históricos.

A Spanish translation of the item immediately above.

741 RICARD, ROBERT. 1966.

The Spiritual Conquest of Mexico. Trans. by Lesley Byrd Simpson. Berkeley: University of California Press.

An English translation of the two items immediately above.

Illustrated with 15 plates.

742 RIVAS, PEDRO. 1934.

Monografía geográfica e histórica de la isla de Tigre y puerto de Amapala. Tegucigalpa: Talleres Tipográficos Nacionales.

LC/F1501.S652R5

Geographical and historical study of Amapala, Honduras.

743 RIVEREND, JULIO LE. n.d.

Cartas de la conquista de América. México: Editorial Nueva España. 2 vols.

Volume 2 contains the fifth letter of Cortés relating his expedition to Honduras, as well as two letters of Pedro de Alvarado with accounts of the conquest of Guatemala. See CORTES, 1868, 1942, 1971, and see also ALVARADO, 1954, 1972, and n.d., Section I.

744 ROBERTS, ORLANDO W. 1827

Narrative of Voyages and Excursions on the East Coast and in the Interior of Central America. Edinburgh: Constable and Co.

LC/F1431.R64   DUL/917.28 R646

An interesting personal account of Nicaragua. The author was there during the time of the revolution in 1821. He depends to a great extent on Juarros, see Section I. Also cited by Squier, 1855, below, p. 390.

745 ROBERTS, ORLANDO W. 1965.

Narrative of Voyages and Excursions on the East Coast and the Interior of Central America: Describing a Journey up the River San Juan, and Passage across the Lake of Nicaragua to the City of Leon. Gainesville, Fla.: University of Florida Press.

LC/F1431.R64

A facsimile of the 1827 edition, edited with an introduction by Hugh Crags.

746 ROBERTSON, DONALD. 1959.

The 'Relaciones Geográficas' of Mexico. In *XXXIII Congreso Internacional de Americanistas; Actas y Memorias.* San Jose, C.R., vol. 2, 540–547.

747 ROCA, JULIO CESAR DE LA. 1966.

Biografía de un pueblo; síntesis monográfica de Quetzaltenango. Guatemala: Editorial "José de Pineda Ibarra".

LC/HC144.Z7Q47

An historical and geographical survey of an important city in Guatemala.

748 ROCHE, JAMES JEFFREY. 1891.

The Story of the Filibusters; To Which Is Added the Life of Colonel David Crockett. London: Unwin Co.; New York: MacMillan Co.

DUL/972.8504 R6735

Deals with activities of William Walker in Nicaragua and Central America.

749 RODAS, JAYME R. 1948.

Monografía de la ciudad de Comitán Estado de Chiapas. 2a ed. Comitán, Chiapas.

Small pamphlet of 21 pages on an important town in Highland Chiapas.

750 RODAS M., JOAQUIN. 1965.

Alma patria. Cuentos regionales y narraciones de hechos y episodios históricos sucedidos en Centro América. 2a ed. Guatemala: Centro Editorial "José de Pineda Ibarra".

LC/F1428.R6

Popular treatment of historical events from colonial through modern period.

751 RODRIGUEZ, LEOPOLDO ALEJANDRO. 1912.

Estudio geográfico, histórico, etnográfico, filológico y arqueológico de el república de El Salvador en Centro-América. México: Imprenta de Murguía.

LC/F1483.R69

A paper read before the XVII International Congress of Americanists, México, D.F., 1910.

Pre-Columbian subject matter, full of unsubstantiated conclusions.

751a RODRIGUEZ-BECERRA, SALVADOR. 1974.

Metodología y fuentes para el estudio de la población de Guatemala en el siglo XVI. *Atti del XL Congresso Internazionale degli Americanisti, Roma Genova, 1972.* Genova. 3:243–253.

Some discussion of the literary and documentary sources for the study of the population of sixteenth-century Guatemala.

752 RODRIGUEZ BETETA, VIRGILIO. 1929.

Evolución de las ideas. Paris: Editorial Paris-América.

LC/F1433.5.R65

Intellectual history of Guatemala during the colonial period.

753 RODRIGUEZ CABAL, O.P., FRAY JUAN. 1935.

Apuntes para la vida del M.R.P. Presentado y Predicador General Fr. Francisco Ximénez, O.P. *ASGH,* 12:209–28, 348–67. Also published as a monograph, Guatemala: Tipografía Nacional.

A short biographical sketch of Ximénez, see XIMENEZ, 1857, 1929–31, 1964, and 1966, section I above.

754 RODRIGUEZ CABAL, O.P., FRAY JUAN. 1965.

Don Fray Payo de Ribera y la Universidad de Guatemala. *Missionala Hispanica.* 22, 66: 17–54. Reprinted in *ASGH,* 39(1966): 36–75.

This item was reprinted once again in *RUSC,* see immediately below, in the 1967 issue which actually appeared two years later. The *ASGH,* 1966, version also includes transcriptions of the documents.

755 RODRIGUEZ CABAL, O.P. FRAY JUAN. 1967.

Don Fray Payo de Ribera y la Universidad de Guatemala. *RUSC,* 70 (enero-junio): 5–56.

A long article on the founding of the university in Guatemala. Mainly a transcription of a document of 52 folios, dated 25 October 1659. "Informe que hace al Rey Nuestro Senor el obispo de la ciudad de Santiago de Guatemala, sobre el punto de la universidad cuya fundación en la dicha ciudad se pide a Su Magestad licencia." This is preceded by a short item "Parecer del Imo. Sr. D. Fr. Payo de Ribera, obispo de Guatemala, sobre la fundación de la Universidad de Guatemala."

756 RODRIGUEZ CERNA, JOSE. 1938.

El hermano Pedro. Guatemala: Librería "Patria Grande".

LC/BX4705.B45R6

A popular biography of the founder of the Bethlemite order in Antigua Guatemala.

757 RODRIGUEZ CERNA, J. 1948.

El Hermano Pedro. Guatemala: Imprenta Hispania.

DUL/Div. Sch. 922.27281 B562R

A pamphlet of 28 pages with an appreciation of the life of the founder of the Bethlehemite order published as part of the celebrations on the second anniversary of the "Liberation," that is, the revolution of 1946. Reprinted again in 1967.

758 ROSALES, NICESIO. 1941.

Apuntes históricos del hospital de San Juan de Dios. Granada, Nicaragua. Could not be located in LC or DUL.

759 ROSENBLAT, ANGEL. 1938–39, 1939–40.

El desarrollo de la población indígena de América. *ASGH,* 15:367–379;

486–503; 16:114–131. Reprinted from *Tierra Firme*, 1, 1(1935):115–133; 1, 2(1935):117–148; 1, 3(1935):109–141.

A provocative article on the possible number of inhabitants in the New World at the time of the conquest.

760 ROSENBLAT, ANGEL. 1954.

La población indígena y el mestizaje en América. Buenos Aires: Editorial Nova. 2 vols.

He revises some of his estimates of 1935.

761 ROSENBLAT, ANGEL. 1967.

La población de América en 1492. Viejos y nuevos cálculos. Mexico: El Colegio de México.

762 ROYS, RALPH L. 1933.

The Book of Chilam Balam of Chumayel. Washington, D.C.: Carnegie Institution of Washington.

LC/F1435.C53   DUL/972.015 qC535BA

A translation of the original Maya text, from Mani, Yucatan, dating from the first half of the sixteenth century. Compiled in 1782.

Another edition, with an introduction by J. Eric S. Thompson, Norman, Okla.: University of Oklahoma Press, 1967.

762a ROYS, RALPH. 1972.

The Indian Background of Colonial Yucatan. 2nd edition. Norman, Okla: University of Oklahoma Press.

The background and the history of the conquest of Yucatan including a history of the area during the colonial period. First edition, Washington, D.C., Carnegie Institution of Washington, 1943.

763 RUBIO SANCHEZ, MANUEL. 1952.

El añil ó el xiquilate. *ASGH*, 36:313–49.

A well-documented study of the production of indigo dye in colonial Guatemala.

764 RUBIO SANCHEZ, MANUEL. 1953

Apuntes para el estudio del comercio marítimo en la Capitanía General del Reino de Guatemala durante el siglo XVI. *AHG*, 5, 2:63–74.

Bibliography and list of documents in *AGG* on the subject of overseas commerce of colonial Guatemala.

765 RUBIO SANCHEZ, MANUEL. 1958.

El cacao. *ASGH*, 31:81–106.

A study of cacao production in colonial Guatemala. Well-documented.

766 SACO, JOSE ANTONIO. 1938.

Historia de la esclavitud de la raza africana en el Nuevo Mundo y en especial de los países américo-hispanos. In *Colección de libros cubanos* (La Habana: Cultural), No. 38. 4 vols.

Volume 2 includes colonial Central America.

767 SAENZ DE SANTA MARIA, CARMELO. 1963.

El licenciado don Francisco Marroquín, primer jefe de la conquista espiritual de Guatemala (1528–1563). *RI*, 91–92; 29–97.

The work of Marroquín in Guatemala. Biographical data.

768 SAENZ DE SANTA MARIA, CARMELO. 1964.

El licenciado Francisco Marroquín, primer obispo de Guatemala (1499–1563); su vida, sus escritos: En el cuarto centenario de su muerte, 1563–1963. Madrid: Ediciones Cultura Hispánica.

LC/BX4705.M4112A3   DUL/Div.Sch.922.27281 M361

A well-documented biography of the first bishop of Guatemala. Numerous references to the building history of the cathedrals in Ciudad Vieja: pp. 133, 146, 177, 184, 192; and Antigua: pp. 190, 230, 241, 245, 248, 255, 260, 262, 278, 279, 292, 304, 324, 330, 333, 337, 339, 350–1.

Includes bibliographical footnotes. The writings of the first bishop of Guatemala. Data on the evangelization of the Indians in Central America.

769 SAENZ DE SANTA MARIA, CARMELO. 1966a

Institucionalización de los grupos indígenes en Guatemala en el siglo XVI. In *XXXVI Congreso Internacional de Americanistas España, 1964* (Sevilla), 2:195–202.

Deals with the first bishop of Guatemala, Francisco Marroquín, the urbanization of the Indians, the *ordenanzas* of García de Palacio, the *ordenanzas* of Yucatán, the *autos-da-fe* in Patinamit and Mani and other matters.

770 SAENZ DE SANTA MARIA, CARMELO. 1966b.

Remesal, la Verapaz y fray Bartolomé de las Casas. In *Estudios lascasianos: IV centenario de la muerte de fray Bartolomé de las Casas, 1566–1966* (Sevilla: Escuela de Estudios Hispano-Americanos), 329–349.

Rectification of the errors perpetuated by Remesal concerning Fray Bartolome's missionary work in Vera Paz.

771 SAENZ MAROTO, ALBERTO. 1970.

Historia agrícola de Costa Rica. San José, C.R.: Universidad de Costa Rica.

A large book of over 1000 pp. dealing with the agricultural history of Costa Rica from Pre-Columbian times to the twentieth century.

772 SAINT-LU, ANDRE. 1968.

La Vera Paz. Esprit évangéliane et colonisation. Paris: Centre de Recherches Hispaniques, Institut d'Etudes Hispaniques.

The evangelization of Verapaz in the sixteenth and seventeenth centuries.

773 SAINT-LU, ANDRE. 1970.

Condition coloniale et conscience créole: Guatemala, 1524–1821. Paris: Presses Universitaires de France, Faculté de Lettres et Sciences Humaines de Poitiers.

The history of national identity of the criollo in Guatemala and Central America. Has a good bibliography.

774 SALAS, ALBERTO M. 1960.

Crónica florida del mestizaje .de las Indias. Siglo XVI. Buenos Aires: Editorial Losada.

An account of race mixture in the sixteenth century.

775 SALAZAR, RAMON A. 1897.

Historia del desenvolvimiento intelectual de Guatemala. Tomo I: *La Colonia.* Guatemala: Tipografía Nacional.

LC/F1463.5 S26   DUL/917.281 S161H

An early and important work on the history of ideas in colonial Guatemala. No second volume ever published. Important source for education and the arts.

776 SALAZAR, RAMON. 1951.

Historia del desenvolvimiento intelectual de Guatemala. Epoca colonial. Guatemala: Editorial del Ministerio de Educación Pública. Biblioteca de Cultura Popular, vols. 11, 12, 13. 3 vols.

A reprint of the foregoing item.

777 SALGADO, FELIX. 1927.

Elementos de historia de Honduras. Tegucigalpa: Tipografía Nacional. LC/F1506.S16

A pamphlet of 76 pp. written as a textbook for secondary school students.

778 SALVATIERRA, SOFONIAS. 1939.

Contribución a la historia de Centroamérica; monografías documentales. Managua, Nicaragua: Tipografía Progreso. 2 vols.

LC/F1437.S23

A history of Central America, mainly Nicaragua. Vol. 1 begins with Columbus and continues through the colonial period. Vol. 2 deals with the latter part of colonial history up to the independence. Based principally on secondary sources.

779 SAMAYOA GUEVARA, HECTOR HUMBERTO. 1955.

El gremio de salitreros de Antigua Guatemala. *AHG,* 7, 1:25–45.

Manufacture of gunpowder. Has an appendix of relevant documents.

780 SAMAYOA GUEVARA, HECTOR HUMBERTO. 1956.

Carta del arzobispo de Guatemala don Cayetano Francos y Monroy a su Magestad Carlos III, informándole sobre asuntos de su arquidiócesis. *AHG,* 8, 2:16–23.

Interesting sidelights on conditions in Guatemala. Letter dated in 1786. Has information on churches. Text transcribed *in toto.*

781 SAMAYOA GUEVARA, HECTOR HUMBERTO. 1956b.

Condiciones del estanco de la pólvora en Guatemala. *AHG,* 8, 1:22–31.

The gunpowder monopoly in 1735 based on a document in *AGG.*

782 SAMAYOA GUEVARA, HECTOR HUMBERTO. 1957.

Historia del establecimiento de la Orden Mercedaria en el Reino de Guatemala, desde el año 1537 hasta 1632. *AHG,* 9, 2:30–42.

A history of the Mercedarian order in Guatemala based to a great extent on the article by José Castro Seoane, 1945, above.

783 SAMAYOA GUEVARA, HECTOR HUMBERTO. 1959.

Fundación de intendencias en el Reyno de Guatemala. *AHG,* 11, 2:73–80.

Brief essay on the new system of colonial administration in late eighteenth century. Gives a list of *intendencias* and the areas of their jurisdiction.

784 SAMAYOA GUEVARA, HECTOR HUMBERTO. 1960a.

Implantación del régimen de intendencias en el Reino de Guatemala. Guatemala: Editorial del Ministerio de Educación Pública, "José de Pineda Ibarra."

LC/JL1489.I553

A careful and well-documented study of the intendency system of government in late colonial Central America. Deals with the establishment of the system, its legislation, and the results engendered, especially the dismemberment of Central America.

785 SAMAYOA GUEVARA, HECTOR HUMBERTO. 1960b.

La reorganización gremial guatemalense en la segunda mitad del siglo XVIII. *AHG,* 12, 1:63–106

The legislation regulating the crafts in eighteenth-century Reino de Guatemala. Transcribes some pertinent contemporary documents.

786 SAMAYOA GUEVARA, HECTOR HUMBERTO. 1961a.

Gremios guatemalenses. Guatemala: Editorial del Ministerio de Educación "José de Pineda Ibarra". Biblioteca Guatemalteca de Cultura Popular, vol. 45.

A popular treatment of the guild system in colonial Central America.

787   SAMAYOA GUEVARA, HECTOR HUMBERTO. 1961b.

El real estanco de tintes y colores. *Humanidades* [Guatemala], 3, 5: pp. 1–6.

Small pamphlet on the monopoly of dyes for cloth in colonial Guatemala.

788   SAMAYOA GUEVARA, HECTOR HUMBERTO. 1962.

Los gremios de artesanos en la ciudad de Guatemala, 1524–1821. Guatemala: Editorial Universitaria.

An important study, well documented, on guilds and labor in colonial Guatemala.

789   SAMAYOA GUEVARA, HECTOR HUMBERTO. 1965.

El obispo Francisco Marroquín y la Junta Ecclesiástica de 1539. *AHG,* 17, 1:31–40.

A short sketch based on documentary sources, of some of the activities of bishop Marroquín.

790   SAMAYOA GUEVARA, HECTOR HUMBERTO. 1966.

El mestizo en Guatemala en el siglo XVI, a través de la legislación indiana. *AHG,* 18, 1:65–74.

The special laws and regulations enacted as a result of the mixture of Indian and Spanish elements resulting in a special caste, the mestizo.

791   SAN SALVADOR. 1961/1962a.

Relación histórica de los monasterios de San Vicente de Chiapa y de Guatemala: Convento de Santo Domingo de San Salvador. *Anales del Museo Nacional "David J. Guzmán"* [San Salvador]. 10:53–57.

An extract from a report of 1741, *AGG,* A 1.11 (1741) 5025–211, transcribed in *BAGG* 10, (1945): 162–167, being historical reports from each of the religious orders, including that of Santo Domingo.

792   SAN SALVADOR. 1961/1962b.

Otra Real Cédula sobre la obra del monasterio de San Salvador. *Anales del Museo Nacional "David J. Guzman."* [San Salvador]. 10:59–60.

A royal cedula dated in 1563 requiring the *encomenderos* to contribute to the cost of the construction of the Dominican monastery.

793   SANTIBANEZ, ENRIQUE. 1907.

Geografía regional de Chiapas. Tuxtla Gutiérrez, Chiapas: Imprenta del Gobierno del Estado.

Pamphlet of 66 pages on the geography of Chiapas. Also some description of countryside and towns.

794   SAPPER, KARL. 1924.

Die Zahl un die Volksdichte der indianischen Bevölkerung in Amerika vor der Conquista und in der Gegenwart. In *XXIst International Congress of Americanists, Netherlands.* The Hague.

Speculations on the estimated population before and after the conquest. No citations from sources on which conclusions are based.

795 SAPPER, KARL THEODOR. 1925.

El infierno de Masaya—documentos históricos publicados con una introducción. Halle, Germany: M. Niemeyer.

LC/QE524.S25

The activity of the Masaya volcano in Nicaragua.

796 SAPPER, KARL. 1936a.

Die Verapaz im 16. und 17. Jahrhundert. Ein Beitrag zur historischen Geographie und Ethnographie des nordostlichen Guatemala. In *Abhandlungen der bayerischen Akademie der Wissenschaften, matematisch-naturwissenschaftliche Abteilung* [München]. Bayerische Akademie der Wissenschaften. n.f., heft 37.

Ethnohistory of the Verapaces based on contemporary works and MS sources.

797 SAPPER, KARL T. 1936b.

Fray Bartolomé de las Casas und die Verapaz (Nordost-Guatemala). Berlin: Verlag von Dietrich Reimer/Andrews und Steiner.

The role of Las Casas in the pacification and evangelization of the Verapaces.

798 SARAVIA, MIGUEL G. 1881.

Compendio de la historia de Centro-américa. Guatemala: Editorial Reformada.

LC/F1436.S47

A secondary-school textbook.

799 SCHEIFLER, JOSE RAIMUNDO. 1949.

Riqueza de las doctrinas en el antiguo reino de Guatemala. *ASGH,* 24: 325–349.

The income and holdings of the parish churches in colonial Central America.

800 SCHERZER, CARL, ed. 1857a.

Popol Vuh: las historias del origen de los indios de esta provincia de Guatemala. Vienna: C. Gerold é hijo.

This is the translation of the Popol Vuh by Fray Francisco Ximénez, see XIMENEZ, 1857, 1964, Section I, with notes and an introduction by Scherzer.

801   SCHERZER, CARL. 1857b.

Travels in the Free States of Central America: Nicaragua, Honduras and San Salvador. London: Longman, Brown, Green, Longmans, and Roberts. 2 vols.

An excellent travel book with many detailed descriptions including church architecture.

802   SCHERZER, CARL. 1970.

Travels in the Free States of Central America: Nicaragua, Honduras and San Salvador. New York: AMS Press.

A reprint of the London, 1857 edition.

803   SCHOLES, FRANCE V. and ELEANOR B. ADAMS. 1938.

Don Diego de Quijada, alcalde mayor de Yucatán, 1561–1565; documentos sacados de los archivos de España. México: Antigua Librería Robredo de J. Porrúa e Hijos. 2 vols.

A transcription of sixteenth-century documents related to the career of Quijada, d. 1571, in Yucatan and the treatment of the Indians.

803a   SCHOLES, FRANCE V. and ELEANOR B. ADAMS, editors. 1960.

Relaciones histórico-descriptivos de la Verapaz, el Manché y Lacandón en Guatemala. Guatemala: Editorial Universitaria.

LC/F1466.4T68

Two important early seventeenth-century reports on conditions in an outlying, still largely un-Christianized area of Guatemala. See LEON PINELO and TOVILLA, Section I, for complete titles.

804   SCROGGS, WILLIAM OSCAR. 1969.

Filibusters and Financiers. The Story of William Walker and his Associates. New York: Rusell and Russell.

LC/F1526. 27W3S3 1969

A reprint of the 1916 edition.

805   SEMINARIO CENTROAMERICANO DE CREDITO AGRICOLA, GUATEMALA. 1954.

Síntesis estadística de Guatemala, 1952. México: Publicación de las Naciones Unidas.

806   SERRANO Y SANZ, MANUEL. 1911.

El Archivo de Indias y las exploraciones del istmo de Panamá en los años 1527–1534. *Anales de la Junta para Ampliación de Estudios é Investigaciónes Científicas* [Madrid], 7, memoria 2:417–475.

Pertinent documentation on the subject.

807   SHERMAN, WILLIAM L. 1971.

Indian Slavery and the Cerrato Reforms. *HAHR,* 51:25–50.

Well-documented study of Alonso López de Cerrato, who, as president of the Audiencia de Guatemala, instituted reforms protecting the Indians from enslavement.

808 SMITH, ROBERT SIDNEY. 1956.

Forced Labor in the Guatemalan Indigo Works. *HAHR,* 36:319–328.

Labor conditions in the manufacture of indigo dye in colonial Guatemala.

809 SMITH, ROBERT S. 1959.

Indigo Production and Trade in Colonial Guatemala. *HAHR,* 39: 181–211.

A survey of production and trade in indigo through the whole of the colonial period.

810 SMITH, T. LYNN. 1964.

Urbanization in Latin America. In N. Anderson, editor, *Urbanism and Urbanization: International Studies in Sociology and Anthropology* (Leiden: J. Brill) v. 2.

A theoretical and historical treatment of urbanization in Latin America. General interest.

811 SOCIEDAD DE GEOGRAFIA E HISTORIA DE HONDURAS.

Revista. Tegucigalpa, 1904–.

LC/F1501.R45

Appears irregularly. Wide range of subjects.

812 SOLANO PEREZ-LILA, FRANCISCO DE. 1969a.

Areas linguísticas y población de habla indígena de Guatemala en 1772. *Revista Española de Antropología Americana,* 4:145–200.

An exacting study based on primary documentary sources.

813 SOLANO PEREZ-LILA, FRANCISCO DE. 1969b.

La espiritualidad del indio: Guatemala, siglo XVIII. *Missionalia Hispanica* [Madrid] 27, 79:5–58.

Religious syncretism in eighteenth-century Indian towns. Cites some letters written to archbishop, 1768–1770, with interesting information on religious beliefs of the Indians.

814 SOLANO PEREZ-LILA, FRANCISCO DE. 1969c

La población indígena de Guatemala, 1492–1800. *Anuario EA,* 26:279–355.

A study based on documentary and published sources for the native population of the former Reino de Guatemala.

815 SOLANO PEREZ-LILA, FRANCISCO DE. 1970a.

Castellanización del indio y áreas del castellano en Guatemala en 1772. *Revista de la Universidad de Madrid,* 19, 72:289–340.

Well-written and fully documented study on the spread of the Spanish language among the native population of Guatemala. Charts and maps.

816 SOLANO PEREZ-LILA, FRANCISCO DE. 1970b.

Estudio histórico y socioeconómico de Guatemala durante el siglo XVIII. Madrid: Facultad de Filosofía y Letras.

LC/F1465.S74

A well-documented economic history of the Reino de Guatemala in the eighteenth century.

817 SOLANO PEREZ-LILA, FRANCISCO DE. 1970c.

Población y áreas lingüísticas en El Salvador 1772. *Revista Española de Antropología Americana* [Madrid]. 5:275–316.

Demographic study and linguistic material for late eighteenth-century El Salvador, based on documentary sources, especially a census taken 1768–1771. Gives areas where native languages as well as Spanish were spoken.

818 SOLANO PEREZ-LILA, FRANCISCO DE. 1971a.

Economía agraria de Guatemala en el siglo XVIII. *RI,* 123–124:285–327.

An economic history of agriculture in the last century of the colonial period in the Reino de Guatemala. Based on documentary and published sources.

819 SOLANO PEREZ-LILA, FRANCISCO DE. 1971b.

Tierra, comercio y sociedad: un análisis de la estructura social agraria centroamericana durante el siglo XVII. *RI,* 125–126:311–365.

A well-documented socio-economic monograph. Gives statistical data.

820 SOLANO PEREZ-LILA, FRANCISCO DE. 1972a.

Algunas consideraciones sobre demografía histórica: problemas en el cálculo de la población en la América hispánica (1492–1800). *Revista de la Universidad de Madrid* [Madrid]. 22:218–251.

A refinement of some of the hypotheses concerning the number of inhabitants in the New World prior to the European contact. See ROSENBLAT, ANGEL, 1938/40 and 1967, above, for treatment of the same question.

821 SOLANO PEREZ-LILA, FRANCISCO DE. 1972b.

Autoridades indígenas y población india en la Audiencia de Guatemala en 1572. Revista Española de Antropología Americana. [Madrid]. 7, 2: 133–150.

The role of the Pre-Conquest native rulers and other elite elements in the urbanization of the Indians in colonial Central America. Estimates of native population in the last quarter of the sixteenth century. Based on primary documentary sources and other contemporary materials.

821a SOLANO PEREZ-LILA, FRANCISCO DE. 1972c.

El conocimiento gráfico de América y el valor de Jerónimo de Mendieta como ilustrador. *Anuario EA,* 29:171-186.

The visual materials employed by MENDIETA in his *Historia ecclesiástica indiana,* see Section I, No. 204a.

822 SOLANO PEREZ-LILA, FRANCISCO DE. 1974.

Los mayas del siglo XVIII. Madrid: Ediciones de Cultura Hispánica.

Deals with the persistence and transformations of indigenous society of colonial Guatemala during the eighteenth century. Includes data on populations, linguistics, labor, commerce, religion and sundry subjects. Has some clear and well-drawn maps. Statistical data culled from archival sources.

823 SOLEY GUELL, TOMAS. 1940.

Compendio de historia económica y hacendaria de Costa Rica. San José, C.R.: Soley y Valverde.

LC/HC147.C856   DUL/330.97286 S685C

An economic history of Costa Rica. Some treatment of colonial period.

824 SOLORZANO FERNANDEZ, VALENTIN. 1947.

Historia de la evolución económica de Guatemala. Mexico: Universidad Nacional Autónoma de Mexico. Tésis para optar el título de Licenciado.

825 SOLORZANO FERNANDEZ, VALENTIN. 1963.

Evolución económica de Guatemala. Guatemala: Seminario de Integración Social Guatemalteca.

Same as foregoing item with some additions and revisions.

826 SOLTERA, MARIA. 1964.

A Lady's Ride Across Spanish Honduras. Doris Stone, ed. Gainesville, Fla.: University of Florida Press. Reprint of London, 1884, edition.

827 SOMOZA VIVAS, FERNANDO. 1905.

Guía de Honduras. Tegucigalpa: Tipografía Nacional.

LC/F1503.S69

An economic geography.

828 SOTO HALL, MAXIMO (fl. 1871-1944). 1949a.

El San Francisco de Asís americano, Pedro de San José Bethancourt. Guatemala: Ediciones del Gobierno de Guatemala, Colección Los Clásicos del Istmo.

A biography of the founder of the Bethlehemite order.

829 SOTO HALL, MAXIMO 1949b.

Pedro de San José Bethencourt, el San Francisco de Asís americano. Guatemala: Ediciones del Gobierno de Guatemala.

LC/BX4705 B45S58

A biography of the founder of the Bethlemite order in Antigua Guatemala. First published in Buenos Aires in 1935.

830 SQUIER, EPHRAIM GEORGE (fl. 1821–1888). 1852.

Nicaragua: Its People, Scenery, Monuments, Resources, Condition, and the Proposed Inter-oceanic Canal. New York: D. Appleton and Co. 2 vols. Revised edition, New York: Harper and Brothers, 1860.

LC/F1523.S77   LC/F1523.S78(1860)

Among other matters, includes some descriptions of architecture.

The 1860 edition appeared as a single volume.

831 SQUIER, EPHRAIM GEORGE. 1855.

Notes on Central America; particularly the States of Honduras and San Salvador; their geography, topography, climate, population, resources, productions, etc., and the proposed Honduras Inter-oceanic Railway. New York: Harper and Brothers.

LC/1428.S75   DUL/917.28 S773N

832 SQUIER, EPHRAIM G. 1858.

The States of Central America. New York: Harper and Brothers.

LC/F1428.S77

Apparently another edition of the item immediately above, *Notes* etc.

833 SQUIER, EPHRAIM GEORGE. 1870.

Honduras: Description, Historical and Statistical. London: Trubner and Co.

LC/F1503.S78

An economic geography.

834 SQUIER, E.G. 1965.

Waikna; or, Adventures on the Mosquito Shore. Gainesville, Fla.: University of Florida Press. Reprint of New York, 1855, edition.

835 STEPHENS, JOHN L. 1841.

Incidents of Travel in Central America, Chiapas, and Yucatan. New York: Harper and Brothers. 2 vols.

A most valuable book for information on countless small villages and towns and their churches which Stephens never fails to describe, and in some instances includes beautiful line drawings by Catherwood who accompanied him.

Has appeared in a number of reprints in recent years.

836 STOLL, OTTO. 1886.

Guatemala, Reisen und Schilderungen aus den Jahren 1878–1883. Leipzig: F.A. Brockhaus.

An excellent travel book with descriptions of architecture, scenery, local customs and sundry matters.

837 STOLL, OTTO (1849–1922). 1958.

Etnografía de Guatemala. Versión castellana de Antonio Goubaud Carrera. 2a ed. Guatemala: Editorial del Ministerio de Educación Pública.

DUL/497S 875E

A translation from the German of a pioneer work on the ethnography of the Indians of Guatemala.

838 STONE, DORIS. 1954.

Apuntes sobre la fiesta de la Virgen de Guadalupe celebrada en la ciudad de Nicoya, Costa Rica. San José: Imprenta Nacional.

LC/BT660.G82N5

A pamphlet of 31 pages. Of ethnographic interest.

839 STONE, DORIS. 1966.

Symposium: Los indios talamanqueños de Costa Rica y algunos nexos. In *XXXVI Congreso Internacional de Americanistas, España, 1964* (Sevilla), 3: 115–176.

Ethnography, physical anthropology, culture history, both modern and colonial, of a group of Indians in Costa Rica.

840 STOUT, PETER F. 1859.

Nicaragua: Past, Present and Future. A Description of its Inhabitants, Customs, Mines, Minerals, Early History, Modern Filibusterism, Proposed Inter-Oceanic Canal and Manifest Destiny. Philadelphia: J.E. Potter.

LC/F1523.S88

A nineteenth-century travel book. Description of towns, people, customs, and sundry topics.

841 SUTHERLAND, STELLA H. 1936.

Population Distribution in Colonial America. New York: Columbia University Press.

Reprinted in 1969.

A seminal work on the demography of colonial America.

842 TAPLIN, GLEN W. 1972.

Middle American Governors. Metuchin, N.J.: Scarecrow Press.

LC/F1426.T3   DUL/920.0728 T173M

Deals with biographies of the governors of colonial Central America and of Mexico as well. A short bibliography, pp. 170–171.

843 TELETOR, CELSO NARCISO. 1946.

Anales de los Cakchiqueles. Memorial de Tecpán Atitlán (última parte). Primera versión del cakchiquel al castellano. Guatemala: Tipografía Nacional.

A translation of the last part of the Annals of the Cakchiquels dealing with the period 1583–1602.

844 TELETOR, CELSO NARCISO. 1955.

Apuntes para una monografía de Rabinal, Baja Verapaz y algo de nuestro folklore. Guatemala: Tipografía Nacional.

LC/F1476.R3T4

History and geography of Rabinal in Guatemala, including some material on its folklore.

845 TELETOR, CELSO NARCISO. 1965 (1966).

Síntesis biográfica del clero de Guatemala. Guatemala: Tipografía Nacional.

LC/BX1438.T4

History of clergy since colonial period.

846 TEMPSKY, GUSTAV FERDINAND VON. 1858.

Mitla: A Narrative of Incidents and Personal Adventures . . . in Mexico, Guatemala and Salvador in the years 1853–1855. With observations on the modes of life in those countries. London: Longman, Brown, Green, Longmans, and Roberts.

LC/F1213.T28

Some material on Guatemala and El Salvador.

847 TERAN, FRANCISCO. 1970.

Sebastián de Benalcázar en tierras de Nicaragua. *Museo Histórico* [Quito]. 16, 48:195–210.

Many of the conquistadors, including Benalcázar, came from León, Nicaragua where they were active in the early years of the sixteenth century, between 1524–1533.

848 TERMER, FRANZ. 1935/1937.

La habitación rural en la America del centro, a través de los tiempos. *ASGH,* 11:391–409.

An important study of the private dwelling in contemporary Guatemala and its pre-Columbian antecedents.

849 TERNAUX-COMPANS, HENRI, ed. (1807–1864). 1837–41.

Voyages, relations et mémoires originaux pour servir a l'histoire de la découverte de l'Amérique, publiés pour la première fois en français. Paris: A. Bertrand. 20 vols.

LC/E121.T32   DUL/910.4 T321

Volume 14 has a selection from OVIEDO dealing with Nicaragua. See OVIEDO, 1840, Section I, above.

850 THIEL, BERNARDO AUGUSTO. 1902.

Monografía de la población de Costa Rica en el siglo XIX. *Revista de Costa Rica en el siglo XIX.* 1:3–52.

The racial elements in nineteenth century Costa Rica and their origins during the colonial period.

851 THIEL, A. BERNARDO. 1940.

Distribución de tierras y encomiendas de indios entre los primeros conquistadores de Costa Rica. In José Trejos, ed., *Progenitores de los costarricenses, los conquistadores* (San Jose: Lehman) pp. 189–197.

LC/F1542.7T7

The encomienda in early Costa Rica.

852 THOMPSON, GEORGE ALEXANDER. 1829.

Narrative of an Official Visit to Guatemala from Mexico. London: John Murray.

LC/1464.T47

Travel book. Many errors in his descriptions of the colonial architecture of Antigua Guatemala.

853 TOBAR CRUZ, PEDRO. 1965.

La esclavitud del negro en Guatemala. *AHG,* 17, 1:3–14.

Some documentation on Negro slavery in Central America, particularly Guatemala.

854 TOBAR CRUZ, PEDRO. 1966.

Tercer centenario del nacimineto del dominico Fray Francisco Ximénez. *AHG,* 18, 2:19–31.

A short biographical sketch and an appreciation of the early eighteenth-century chronicler of Guatemala and Chiapas.

855 TOLEDO PALOMO, RICARDO. 1965.

La ruina de la cabecera del Corregimiento de Chiquimula. *ASGH,* 38: 99–149.

A detailed account of the destruction by earthquakes in 1765 and 1773. Has an appendix with transcriptions of ten documents.

856 TRAVEN, B. 1928.

Land des Frühlings. Berlin: Büchergilde Gutenberg.

A travel book on Chiapas by the author of many adventure books about Mexico.

DUL/833.91 T779L

857 TREJOS, JOSE FRANCISCO, editor. 1940.

Progenitores de los costarricenses, los conquistadores. San José: Imprenta Lehmann.

LC/F1542.7.T7

Short essays on the early settlers and conquistadors of Costa Rica.

858 TRENS, MANUEL B. 1951.

Reseña histórica de Chiapas. Ateneo [Tuxtla Gutiérrez, Chiapas]. 2: 137–161.

Synopsis of the history of Chiapas from the colonial period to the twentieth century. Deals mainly with the colonial period.

859 TRENS, MANUEL. 1957a.

Bosquejos históricos de San Cristóbal Las Casas. México.

LC/F1391.Si85T7

Invaluable information of San Cristóbal de las Casas, Chiapas with regard to urban development, colonial architecture and sundry matters.

860 TRENS, MANUEL. 1957b.

Historia de Chiapas. México.

LC/F1256.T79

The history of the state of Chiapas, Mexico written by a competent historian. Based on contemporary documentary and literary sources. Only one volume published; deals with colonial period. An earlier edition was published in México, D.F. in 1942.

861 TRIGUEROS BADA, ROBERTO. 1956.

Las defensas estratégicas del río de San Juan de Nicaragua. Anuario EA, 11:413–513.

Summarized in TRIGUEROS and RODRIGUEZ, 1969, below. See also Section IV, No. 1249.

862 TRIGUEROS BADA, ROBERTO and MARIANA RODRIGUEZ DEL VALLE. 1969.

Defensas estratégicas de la Capitanía General de Guatemala. Revista Conservadora de Pensamiento Centroamericano [Managua]. 21.

Two articles on the defensive fortifications on the San Juan River in

Nicaragua and at San Felipe del Golfo Dulce in Guatemala, in the seventeenth and eighteenth centuries.

863 URBANO, VICTORIA. 1968.

Juan Vásquez de Coronado y su ética en la conquista de Costa Rica. Madrid: Ediciones Cultura Hispánica.

LC/F1437.U7   DUL/923.946 V393U

The role of Vásquez de Coronado, 1523–1565, in the conquest of Costa Rica. See VASQUEZ DE CORONADO, 1882, 1908, 1961, Section I, above.

864 VALENZUELA, GILBERTO. 1933.

La Imprenta en Guatemala. Guatemala:. Folletín del Diario de Centro América.

Published in the newspaper *Diario de Centro América.* The articles were re-issued as a separate work which carries the added note ". . . algunas adiciones a la obre que con este título publicó en Santiago de Chile el ilustre liberato don José Toribio Medina."

865 VALIENTE, GILBERTO and CARLOS MONTERROSA. 1931.

Metapán; monografía del distrito. San Salvador: Imprenta Nacional.

LC/F1489.M46V3

Economic geography of the town of Metapán, El Salvador and the surrounding region. Some data on church.

866 VALLE, JOSE. 1929.

Guatemala para el turista; crónicas de viaje. Guatemala: Tipografía Nacional.

DUL/917.281 V181G

A guide book.

867 VALLE, RAFAEL HELIODORO. 1948.

Cristóbal de Olid, conquistador de México y Honduras. México: Universidad Nacional Autónoma de México. Tesis.

LC/F1506.05V3

A biography.

868 VALLE, RAFAEL HELIODORO. 1950.

Cristóbal de Olid, conquistador de Honduras. México: Editorial Jus.

LC/F1506.05V3

Originally a doctoral thesis, 1948, Universidad Autónoma de México. A biography of Cristóbal de Olid, 1488–1525, and the conquest of Honduras.

Excellent scholarly apparatus, voluminous sources, mainly published materials.

869   VALLE MATHEU, JORGE. 1942-43.

Páginas inéditas de la Antigua. *ASGH,* 18:313-326.

A discussion of MOLINA, 1943, Section I, above, a work which he paleographed and edited.

870   VALLEJO, ANTONIO R. 1926.

Compendio de la historia social y política de Honduras. 2a ed. Tegucigalpa: Tipografía Nacional.

Only one volume published. A secondary-school textbook. Nineteenth-century material.

871   VASQUEZ, ANDRES CLEMENTE. 1932.

Bosquejo histórico de la agregación a México de Chiapas y Soconusco y de las negociaciones sobre límites entabladas por México con Centro América y Guatemala. México: Publicaciones de la Secretaria de Relaciones Exteriores.

LC/F1203.M585 no. 36   DUL/327.72 M533H

The boundary question between Guatemala and Mexico. Sums up the earlier work of Matías Romero, same title, of 1877. Late colonial political conditions, prior to the Independence.

872   VASQUEZ, FRANCISCO. 1931.

Cronistas de la colonia: literatura guatemalteca. *ASGH,* 7:482-512.

A brief review of some of the principal religious and secular chroniclers of the colonial period.

872a   VASQUEZ DE HERRERA, F. 1962.

Virtudes del venerable Hermano Pedro de San José de Betacur. Guatemala: Tipografía Nacional.

A laudatory biography of the founder of the Bethlehemite order in Guatemala. Betancur's floruit was in the second half of the seventeenth century.

873   VASQUEZ VASQUEZ, ELENA. 1965.

Distribución geográfica y organización de las órdenes religiosas en la Nueva España: siglo XVI. México: Universidad Nacional Autónoma de México, Instituto de Geografía.

Religious orders in Mexico and the Audiencia de Guatemala. Includes a useful bibliography.

874   VELA, DAVID. 1935.

El Hermano Pedro (en la vida y en las letras). Guatemala: Tipografía Nacional.

LC/BX4705 B45V4

A biography of the founder of the Bethlemite order in Antigua Guatemala.

875   VELA, DAVID. 1944–1948.

Literatura guatemalteca. Guatemala: 2nd ed. Unión Tipográfica. 2 vols.

LC/PQ7490.V413   DUL/868.09 V432L

A school text book including native chronicles and colonial as well as modern works.

876   VELA, DAVID. 1960.

La imprenta en la colonia. Guatemala: Editorial del Ministerio de Educación Pública "José de Pineda Ibarra".

DUL/Pam. Coll. 33130

A pamphlet giving a brief resumé of the history of the press in colonial Guatemala.

877   VERLINDEN, CHARLES, J. CRAEYBECK, and W. BRULEZ. 1958.

"Santa María la Antigua del Darien, the first Colonial town on American terra firma." *Revista de Historia de América,* 45:1–47.

878   VIDAL, MANUEL. 1957.

Nociones de historia de Centro América, especial de El Salvador. 5a ed. San Salvador: Ministerio de Cultura.

LC/F1436.V65

First edition, 1935. Largely on Central America as a whole. Secondary-school textbook.

879   VILLACORTA CALDERON, JOSE ANTONIO. 1925–26.

"Las cartas relaciones de don Pedro de Alvarado." *ASGH,* 2:215–226.

A critical essay on Alvarado's letters, these letters were originally published in Toledo in 1825. See also RIVEREND, n.d., above, and ALVARADO, 1925/26, Section I.

880   VILLACORTA CALDERON, JOSE ANTONIO. 1926.

Monografía del Departamento de Guatemala. Guatemala: Tipografía Nacional.

Economic geography of department where Guatemala City is located. Also some historical data.

880a   VILLACORTA CALDERON, JOSE ANTONIO. 1938.

Memorial de Tecpán Atitlán. Anales de los Cakchiqueles. Guatemala: Tipografía Nacional.

A new translation by the author of this important indigenous chronicle. Includes notes and explanations.

881   VILLACORTA CALDERON, JOSE ANTONIO. 1940.

Indice analítico de la historia de la capitanía general de Guatemala, 1542–1821. ASGH 16, 5:341–383.

A synoptic and analytical index of the history of the Reino de Guatemala. See VILLACORTA, 1942, below, for a history of colonial Guatemala.

882 VILLACORTA CALDERON, JOSE ANTONIO. 1942.

Historia de la Capitanía General de Guatemala. Guatemala: Tipografía Nacional.

An excellent history of colonial Central America, especially Guatemala. Is well illustrated. Includes a chapter on the architecture, but unfortunately uses an antiquated stylistic terminology no longer accepted.

883 VILLACORTA CALDERON, JOSE ANTONIO. 1960.

Historia de la República de Guatemala, 1821–1921. Guatemala: Imprenta Guatemala.

LC/F1466.45.V5

History of modern Guatemala.

884 VILLACORTA C., JOSE ANTONIO and CARLOS A. VILLACORTA. 1933.

Códices mayas. Guatemala: Tipografía Nacional.

Pre-Columbian codices illustrated with original hieroglyphic texts.

885 VINAS MEY, CARMELO. 1929.

El estatuto del obrero indígena en la colonización española. Madrid: Compañía Ibero-Americana de Publicaciones.

LC/F1410.V76

A re-hash of the legislation on Indians and Negros in the Leyes de las Indias. An apologia for the treatment of Indians and blacks by the Spaniards.

885a VOGT, EVON Z. and ALBERTO RUZ L., editors. 1971.

Desarrollo cultural de los mayas. 2a ed. México: Centro de Estudios Mayas, Universidad Nacional Autonoma de México.

Important for ethnographic materials dealing with Pre-Columbian, colonial and modern periods. First edition, 1964.

886 WAGNER, HENRY R. and HELEN RAND PARISH. 1967.

The Life and Writings of Bartolomé de las Casas. Albuquerque, N.M.: University of New Mexico.

LC/E125.C4W3

A narrative catalogue with critical estimates of the writings of Las Casas.

887 WAIBEL, LEO. 1946.

La Sierra Madre de Chiapas. Traducción del alemán por Enrique Berlin. Revisada, comentada y ampliada por Jorge A. Vivó. México: Sociedad Mexicana de Geografía y Estadística.

A good geography of the highlands of the state of Chiapas, Mexico. Translated by Heinrich Berlin, archaeologist and art historian, and emended by Jorge Vivó, an authority on the geography of Mexico.

888 WALKER, WILLIAM (1824–1860). 1860.

The War in Nicaragua. Mobile: S.H. Goetzel. Reprinted, Detroit: B. Ethridge Books. 1971.

LC/1526.27.W28(1472)

An account of the Filibuster War in Nicaragua by its chief protagonist.

889 WAUCHOPE, ROBERT, general editor. 1964–1976.

Handbook of Middle American Indians. Austin, Texas: University of Texas Press. 16 vols.

Mainly concerned with Pre-Columbian material. Vol. 6, Social Anthropology; vols. 12–15, Ethnohistorical sources; vols. 7 and 8, Ethnology. Material on colonial Central America treated in more general articles as well as in others specifically related to the area.

890 WELLS, WILLIAM VINCENT (1826–1876). 1857.

Explorations and Adventures in Honduras, Comprising Sketches of Travel in the Gold Regions of Olancho, and a Review of the History and General Resources of Central America. New York: Harper and Brothers.

LC/F1504.W45   DUL/972.83 W456

A description of mid-nineteenth-century Honduras. Customs, people, landscape and towns.

891 WELLS, WILLIAM VINCENT (1826–1876). 1960.

Exploraciones y aventuras en Honduras. Comayagüela: Banco Central de Honduras.

A Spanish translation of the foregoing item, including explanatory footnotes.

892 WHETTEN, NATHAN LASELLE. 1961.

Guatemala: The Land and the People. New Haven: Yale University Press. Yale Caribbean Series no. 6.

893 WHITE, ALASTAIR. 1973.

El Salvador. New York: Praeger Publishers.

Social system analyzed. Contemporary matters. Comprehensive study of the country. Some colonial antecedents of contemporary conditions included.

894 WILSON, JAMES. 1829.

A Brief Memoir of the Life of James Wilson. London: A. Panton; Edinburgh: J. Boyd.

A journal and correspondence of the author while he was a resident in Guatemala in the 1820's. Notes and comments on contemporary life and mores.

895 WOODWARD, RALPH LEE, JR. 1966.

Class Privilege and Economic Development. The Consulado de Comercio of Guatemala, 1793–1871. Chapel Hill, N.C.: University of North Carolina Press.

LC/F251.J28 vol. 48   DUL/975.6 J29

Well-written and documented history of the *Consulado de Comercio* and its role in the economic development of late colonial and nineteenth-century Central America.

896 YDIGORAS FUENTES, CARMEN. 1959.

Compendio de la historia de la literatura y artes de Guatemala. 5a ed. Guatemala: Editorial del Ministerio de Educación Pública "José de Pineda Ibarra".

History of literature from Pre-Columbian to modern times.

897 ZAVALA, SILVIO A. 1945.

Contribución a la historia de las instituciones coloniales en Guatemala. [México]: El Colegio de México. Centro de Estudios Sociales. *Jornadas,* no. 36, 88 pp.

Indian slavery, encomiendas and personal service. Based mainly on documents in *AGG.*

898 ZAVALA, SILVIO. 1947.

"Contribución a la historia de las instituciones coloniales en Guatemala." *ASGH,* 22:206–257.

A reprint of the foregoing item.

899 ZAVALA, SILVIO A. 1967a.

Contribución a la historia de las instituciones coloniales en Guatemala. Guatemala: Universidad de San Carlos de Guatemala.

A reprint of the foregoing.

900 ZAVALA, SILVIO. 1967b.

El mundo americano en la época colonial. México: Editorial Porrúa. 2 vols.

An excellent cultural, political, legal and social history. Mainly on Mexico and only briefly on Central America.

901 ZAVALA, SILVIO ARTURO. 1971.

Las instituciones jurídicas en la conquista de América. 2a ed., México: Editorial Porrúa.

DUL/973.16Z391

The legal basis for the conquest and the special legislation concerning the indigenous population.

902 ZAVALA URTECHO, JOAQUIN. 1969.

Huellas de una familia vascocentro-americana en cinco siglos de historia. *Revista Conservadora del Peusamiento Centroamericano* [Managua]. 23, 111:1–138.

A compilation of genealogy, articles, documents and other data on the Zavala family from Vizcaya (Spain), then in Nicaragua and Guatemala from as far back as the sixteenth century.

903 ZELEDON, MARCO TULIO. 1967.

El acta de independencia de Centro América a la luz del derecho y la razón. San José, C.R.: Instituto Cultural Costarricense Argentino.

LC/F1437.Z4

The legal and moral basis for the independence from Spain.

904 ZUNIGA CORRES, IGNACIO. 1968.

El orígen de la Orden de la Merced en Guatemala. *ASGH,* 41:432–464.

History of the Mercedarians from the 1530's through the colonial period.

904a ZUNIGA CORRES, IGNACIO. 1971.

750 aniversario de la fundación de la órden de Nuestra Señora de la Merced. Guatemala: Tipografía Nacional.

A history of the Mercedarian order in Guatemala. Reference to primary sources of colonial data as well as secondary materials.

Section III

ART AND ARCHITECTURAL HISTORY: GENERAL

Town planning, urbanization, architectural styles, sculpture, painting, problems of indigenous influence, Spanish art and architectural antecedents, etc.

904b AGUILERA ROJAS, JAVIER and LUIS MORENO REXACH. 1974.

Urbanismo español en América. Madrid.

A selection of plans and texts, transcribed. Handsomely done book with many plans in color. Same material in part as in FERNANDO CHUECA GOITIA, 1951, Sect. VII, No. 1419 below.

905 ANGULO INIGUEZ, DIEGO. 1932.

Arquitectura mudéjar sevillana de los siglos XIII, XIV y XV. Sevilla: Imprenta Gráficas Marinas.

LC/NA5809.S4A8 1932.

A most important work on the *mudéjar* style, basic for understanding the stylistic transformations that occur not only in colonial Central America, but also in the rest of Latin America.

906 ANGULO INIGUEZ, DIEGO. 1932–33.

Arquitectura mudéjar sevillana de los siglos XIII, XIV, y XV. *Boletín de la Sociedad Española de Excursiones,* 40 (1932):245–293; 41 (1933):1–35, 81–112.

The same as the foregoing item.

907 ANGULO INIGUEZ, DIEGO. 1935.

The Mudejar Style in Mexican Architecture. *Ars Islamica.* 2, pt. 2: 225–230.

DUL/709.5 A781I

A short note on the *mudéjar* style in Mexico.

908 ANGULO INIGUEZ, DIEGO. 1933–39.

Planos de monumentos arquitectónicos de América y Filipinas existentes en el Archivo de Indias. Sevilla. Madrid: Laboratorio de Arte. 4 vols.

LC/NA702.A6

A monumental work with three portfolios of facsimile reproductions. Some plans of buildings in Central America. The volumes of text include transcriptions of the verbal material on each plate as well as historical data for each written by Angulo. A basic source for the whole of Hispano-American architecture.

909 ANGULO INIGUEZ, DIEGO. 1943.

Las catedrales mejicanas del siglo XVI. *Boletín de la Real Academia de la Historia* [Madrid]. 113, 1:137–194

A stylistic analysis of Mexican cathedrals and Iberian prototypes.

910 ANGULO INIGUEZ, DIEGO. 1945–46.

"Eighteenth-Century Church Fronts in Mexico City." *JSAH*, 5:27–32.

Some Mexican examples of facades. Useful for a comparison with the type of retable-facade in Antigua and the rest of Central America.

911 ANGULO INIGUEZ, DIEGO. 1947.

El gótico y el renacimiento en las Antillas. *Anuario EA*, 4:1–102.

A perceptive study on the late medieval and early renaissance architectural style in Santo Domingo and elsewhere in the Antilles. Useful for comparison with the early architecture of Chiapas and Antigua Guatemala.

912 ANGULO INIGUEZ, DIEGO. 1945. 1950. 1956.

Historia de arte hispanoamericano. Barcelona: Salvat. 3 vols.

The basic handbook for Hispano-American Art and Architecture. Chapters on Central America including not only architecture but also painting, sculpture and retables.

913 ANGULO INIGUEZ, DIEGO, MARIO J. BUSCHIAZZO and ENRIQUE MARCO DORTA. 1966.

Symposium: Aportación indígena al arte hispanoamericano. In *XXXVI Congreso Internacional de Americanistas, España, 1964*. Sevilla. 4:245–256.

Problem of indigenous influence on Hispano-American art treated by a number of specialists.

914 ATL, DR. (GERARDO MURILLO). 1924–27.

Iglesias de México. México: Publicaciones de la Secretaría de Hacienda. 6 vols.

See TOUSSAINT, MURILLO, BENITEZ, *Iglesias,* below.

915 BAIRD, JOSEPH A. 1951.

The Eighteenth-Century Retable in the South of Spain, Portugal and Mexico. Unpublished doctoral thesis, Harvard University.

Useful for comparative study of the retables and retable-facade of the Reino de Guatemala.

916 BAIRD, JR., JOSEPH A. 1959.

Style in 18th Century Mexico. *Journal of Interamerican Studies.* 1:261–276.

917 BANKART, GEORGE PERCY. 1908.

The Art of the Plasterer. London: B.T. Batsford.

LC/NA3690.B3

A technical book on the plasterers' craft. Important for comparative purposes for study of the decoration in *argamasa* plaster so common in the colonial architecture of Central America.

917a BARBER, EDWIN A. 1908.

The Maiolica of Mexico. Philadelphia: Pennsylvania Museum and School of Industrial Art.

A handbook of use in identifying this pottery style which was also current in Central America during the time of the colony. Includes modern examples as well.

918 BEVAN, BERNARD. 1938.

History of Spanish Architecture. London: B.T. Batsford.

LC/NA1301.B4   DUL/720.946 B591H

A survey of Spanish architecture. Nothing on the New World.

919 BIALOSTOCKI, JAN. 1964.

"El barroco: estilo, epoca, actitud." *BCIHE,* 4:9–36.

An essay on the meaning of the baroque style. Comparisons between the European and Latin American examples.

920 BONET CORREA, ANTONIO. 1963.

"Antecedentes españoles de las capillas abiertas hispanoamericanas. *RI.*" 23, 91–92:269–280.

Forces some comparisons in form, not in function, of some Spanish and Italian open chapels and those of Mexico. There are practically no open chapels in Guatemala, that is for Indians.

921 BONET CORREA, ANTONIO. 1964.

Lo indígena y lo popular en la arquitectura barroca mejicana. In *XXXVI Congreso Internacional de Americanistas, España, 1964.* Sevilla. 4:181–188.

Indigenous influence on the baroque style in Mexico.

922 BONET CORREA, ANTONIO. 1971.

Integración de la cultura indigena en el arte hispanoamericano. *BCIHE,* 12:9–17.

The afterlife of indigenous traits in Hispano-American art.

923 BONET CORREA, ANTONIO and VICTOR MANUEL VILLEGAS. 1967.

El barroco en España y en México. México: Porrúa.

A comparative study of the stylistic connections between the Spanish and Mexican architecture of the eighteenth century.

924 BORAH, WOODROW. 1973.

La influencia cultural europea en la formación del primer plano para centros urbanos que perdura hasta nuestros dias. *BCIHE,* 15:55–76.

Urbanization. An interpretation on the introduction of the gridiron plan. Recapitulates the bibliography to date.

925 BOTTINEAU, YVES. 1970.

Iberian-American Baroque. New York: Grosset and Dunlap.

A survey of the baroque architecture of Spain and Latin America. Beautifully illustrated. Town planning in Spanish America, 173–76. Antigua Guatemala, 174, figs. 159–62.

925a BRIZGUZ Y BRU, ATHANASIO GENARO (pseudonym for ZARA-GOZA Y EBRI, AGUSTIN BRUNO). 1738.

Escuela de arquitectura civil.

See Section I.

925b BUENO, MIGUEL. 1966.

La estética del espacio. *AIIE,* 35:59–68.

926 BUSCHIAZZO, MARIO J. 1941.

Indigenous influences on the colonial architecture of Latin America. *BPAU,* 75, 5:257–265.

LC/F1403.B955

See also Buschiazzo, 1966, *El problema,* below and the symposium on indigenous influence, ANGULO; BUSCHIAZZO and MARCO, 1966 above.

927 BUSCHIAZZO, MARIO JOSE. 1944.

Estudios de arquitectura colonial hispano-americano. Buenos Aires. G. Kraft.

DUL/WCL 720.98 B977E

Essays. Deals with Antigua Guatemala, 44–46.

928 BUSCHIAZZO, MARIO J. 1945-46.

Exotic Influences in American Colonial Art. *JSAH,* 5:21-23.

Non-European or indigenous influences, mainly from the Far East.

929 BUSCHIAZZO, MARIO J. 1961.

Historia de la arquitectura colonial en Iberoamérica. Buenos Aires: Emecé Editores.

General survey of Latin American colonial architecture. Brief summary of the style in each country, including Guatemala.

930 BUSCHIAZZO, MARIO J. 1966.

El problema del arte mestizo: contribucion a su esclaricimiento. In *XXXVI Congreso Internacional de Americanistas, España, 1964.* Sevilla, v. 4:229-244.

Part of symposium on indigenous influence on Latin American art and architecture. See ANGULO, BUSCHIAZZO and MARCO, 1966, above.

A well-thought and carefully documented study of the problem of the blending of indigenous and Hispanic motifs in the so-called mestizo style.

931 CALDERON QUIJANO, JOSE ANTONIO. 1949.

Ingenieros militares en Nueva España. *Anuario EA,* 6:1-72.

Documentary sources examined for some of the military engineers who built forts on the Carribean.

932 CALDERON QUIJANO, JOSE ANTONIO. 1953.

Historia de las fortificaciones en Nueva España. Sevilla: Escuela de Estudios Hispano-americanos.

Based on documentary source AI. Lots of plans.

933 CALZADA Y ECHEVARRIA, ANDRES. 1933.

Historia de la arquitectura española. Barcelona: Editorial Labor.

LC/NA1301.C26   DUL/WCL 720.946 C171H

A brief history of Spanish architecture.

934 CASTAGNOLI, FERDINANDO. 1971.

Orthogonal Town Planning in Antiquity. Cambridge, Mass.: MIT Press.

LC/9085.H5C313   DUL/711.41q C346IA

The grid plan town is the most typical in Spanish America. Some ancient examples useful for comparative historical study.

935 CASTEDO, LEOPOLDO. 1969.

A History of Latin American Art and Architecture. New York: Praeger.

General history of art including pre-Columbian, colonial and modern times.

936 Cathedrals of the New World; North America. *BPAU,* 29, 4 (Oct. 1909): 726–750.

LC/F1403.B955

Brief cursory description of major cathedrals including the one in Guatemala City.

937 CHARLES, GEO. 1954.

Art baroque en Amérique Latine. Paris: Plon. Collection Psyche, 4.

DUL/709.C475A

Popular book on baroque art.

938 CHUECA GOITIA, FERNANDO. 1947.

Invariantes castizos de la arquitectura española. Madrid: Editorial Dossat.

A perceptive study of the stylistic constants underlying the history of Spanish architecture. Forms the basis for his later essay on Hispano-American architecture. See Invariantes 1966 and 1968 below.

939 CHUECA GOITIA, FERNANDO. 1965.

Historia de la arquitectura española: edad antigua y edad media. Madrid: Editorial Dossat.

DUL/WCL 720.946 C559H

A scholarly well-written and copiously illustrated history of ancient and medieval Spanish architecture with an excellent chapter on the *mudéjar.* Useful for comparative study of architecture of Ibero-America.

940 CHUECA GOITIA, FERNANDO. 1966.

Invariantes en la arquitectura hispanoamericana. *Revista de Occidente,* 4, 38:241–273.

An excellent study of the determinants and constants in the development of Hispano American architecture.

941 CHUECA GOITIA, FERNANDO. 1967a.

Invariantes en la arquitectura hispanoamericana. *BCIHE,* F:74–120.

A reprint of the foregoing item of the same title.

942 CHUECA GOITIA, FERNANDO. 1967b.

Desgracia y triunfo del barroco. *BCIHE,* 8:89–132.

Problems of terminology and development of the baroque style in architecture of Latin America.

943 CHUECA GOITIA, FERNANDO. 1968a.

Breve historia del urbanismo. Madrid: Alianza Editorial, Sección: Ciéncia y Técnica.

Brief history of urbanism in the Western world, including colonial Hispano-America.

944   CHUECA GOITIA, FERNANDO. 1968b.

El método de los invariantes. *BCIHE,* 9:44–57.

A restatement of his theory of the constants in Spanish and Hispano-American architecture. See the two similar items above. The most pervasive constant is the *mudéjar.*

945   CHUECA GOITIA, FERNANDO, L. TORRES BALBAS, and J. GON-ZALEZ GONZALEZ. 1951.

Planos de ciudades iberoamericanas y filipinas existentes en el Archivo de Indias. Madrid: Instituto de Estudios de Administración Local. 2 vols.

DUL/711.4q S733P

Facsimile reproduction of town plans with an introduction on urbanization in colonial Hispano–America.

946   COLLIER, MARGARET. 1968.

Altarpiece and Façade as Scenic Art. *JSAH,* 27:222.

An abstract of a paper given at the 21st annual meeting of the Society of Architectural Historians, 1968.

Mexican church facades being a regrouping and enlargement of European forms. Facade like an altarpiece at the end of straight streets.

947   DACOS, NICOLE. 1969.

La découverte de la Domus Aurea et la formation des grotesques a la Renaissance. London: Studies of the Warburg Institute.

The ultimate source of the "grotesque" in the plateresque style in colonial Mexico and Guatemala.

948   DONY, PAUL. 1969.

Transposición de estilos en la arquitectura hispanoamericana. *AIAA,* 22:58–71.

The problem of the stylistic origin of Hispano-American architecture. Compares it to a "transposition" such as is done in music.

949   FUENTE BENAVIDES, RAFAEL DE LA. 1968.

De lo barroco en el Perú. Lima: Universidad Nacional de San Marcos.

DUL/868.09 F956D

The baroque in Peru. Useful for comparisons with the baroque of Central America.

950   GAKENHEIMER, RALPH ALBERT. 1964.

Determinants of Physical Structure in the Peruvian Town of the Sixteenth Century. Unpublished Ph.D. dissertation, University of Pennsylvania.

951   GAKENHEIMER, RALPH A. 1973.

The Early Colonial Mining Town: Some Special Opportunities for the Study of Urban Structure. *BCIHE,* 15:41–54.

Mainly towns in Ecuador, Peru and Bolivia. Problems of urbanization.

952 GALIAY SARINANA, JOSE. 1950.

Arte mudéjar aragonés. Zaragoza: Institución "Fernando el Católico" de la Excma. Diputación Provincial.

Mudéjar architecture. Useful for comparisons with *mudéjar* traits in architecture of Guatemala and Central America.

953 GARCIA SALINERO, FERNANDO. 1964.

Contribución al estudio del vocabulario español de arquitectura y ingeniería de los siglos XVI y XVII—(Léxico de trazadores, muradores y alarifes). Madrid: Facultad de Filosofía y Letras. Tesis doctoral.

Technical terminology used in architects' handbooks of 16th and 17th-century date. Invaluable for investigations of contemporary building contracts in the Reino de Guatemala in *AGG* as well as the handbooks themselves, many of which actually circulated in Hispano-America including colonial Central America. See GUTIERREZ, 1973, below and in Section V.

954 GASPARINI, GRAZIANO. 1965a.

Análisis crítico de las definiciones de 'arquitectura popular' y "arquitectura mestiza.' *BCHIE,* 3:51–66.

Problems of terminology in Hispano-American art and indigenous influence.

955 GASPARINI, GRAZIANO. 1965b.

Significación de la arquitectura barroca en Hispanoamérica. *BCIHE,* 3: 45–50.

Meaning of Hispano-American baroque style.

956 GASPARINI, GRAZIANO. 1966.

Las influencias indígenas en la arquitectura barroca colonial de Hispanoamérica. *BCIHE,* 4:75–80.

Problem of indigenous influence. See also ANGULO, BUSCHIAZZO, MARCO, above for *Symposium* where this paper also appeared.

957 GASPARINI, GRAZIANO. 1967.

Análisis crítico de la historiografía arquitectónica del barroco en América. *BCIHE,* 7:9–29.

A controversial article criticising historians of Latin American art and architecture in their interpretation of what is and what is not baroque.

958 GASPARINI, GRAZIANO. 1968.

Formación de ciudades coloniales en Venezuela, siglo XVI. *BCIHE,* 10: 9–43.

Urbanization in Venezuela.

959   GASPARINI, GRAZIANO. 1971.

"Space, Baroque and Indians." *Americas,* 23, 4:18–21, supplement.

No Indian influence, except in architectural decoration. Not baroque architecture since it lacks spatial innovations.

960   GASPARINI, GRAZIANO. 1972.

América, barroco y arquitectura. Caracas: Ernesto Armitano Editor.

A well written and provocative interpretation of the so-called "baroque" style in America.

961   GIBSON, CHARLES. 1968.

Spanish Indian Institutions and Colonial Urbanism in New Spain. In *XXXVII Congreso Internacional de Americanistas, Argentina, 1966.* Buenos Aires, 1:225–240.

Urbanization in Mexico.

961a   GOGGIN, JOHN. 1968.

Spanish Majolica in the New World: Types of the Sixteenth to Eighteenth Centuries. New Haven: Yale University Press.

In the series *Yale University Publications in Anthropology,* No. 72, published by the Department of Anthropology of Yale University.

An excellent survey of the imported majolica wares found in the New World including Mexico and Central America. Useful not only for art historians but also for field archaeologists in dealing with colonial materials found in association with Pre-Hispanic artifacts from the century of "contact."

962   GOMEZ, MARTA INES, AND GUILLERMO ZEA. 1968.

Análisis arquitectónico y estilístico de la espadaña en el período neogranadino. In *Apuntes* [Bogotá, Colombia]. 2.2:1–148.

A monograph, 148 pages reproduced in Xerox. The arcaded belfry. Stylistic connections with Spain. Interesting for comparisons with this feature in colonial architecture of Guatemala. Well-executed drawings. Very clear despite reproduction in Xerox.

963   GONZALEZ GALVAN, MANUEL. 1966.

"El espacio en la arquitectura religiosa virreinal de México." *AIIE,* 35: 69–102.

964   GRAJALES RAMOS, GLORIA. 1953.

Influencia indígena en las artes plásticas de México colonial. *AIAA,* 6: 75–100.

Subscribes to the theory that the Mexican art style owes much to the Indian.

965   GUARDA, GABRIEL. 1965.

Santo Tomás de Aquino y las fuentes del urbanismo indiano. Santiago de Chile: Academia Chilena de la Historia, Pontificia Universidad Católica de Chile, Facultad de Arquitectura.

Some hitherto unknown and unexpected theoretical sources relative to the history of New World urbanization.

966   GUERRERO MOCTEZUMA, FRANCISCO. 1934.

Las plazas en las ciudades de la Nueva España en relación con las ordenanzas de nuevas poblaciones de Felipe II. México: Colección Terrazas.

The plaza in the town plan. See also RICARD, *La plaza mayor,* below.

967   GUIDO, ANGEL. 1925.

Fusión hispanoamericana en la arquitectura colonial. Rosario, Argentina: Editorial "La Casa del Libro".

An early interpretation of Hispano-American architectural style as being the result of the fusion of the Spanish and Indian races and mentality.

968   GUIDO, ANGEL. 1927a.

La arquitectura hispanoamericana a través de Wölfflin. Rosario, Argentina: Talleres Gráficos.

An attempt to relate the theories of Wölfflin to Hispano-American architecture. Out-of-date by now.

969   GUIDO, ANGEL. 1927b.

Diversidad barroca en el arte hispanoamericano. *La Prensa* [Buenos Aires] Sección 3, p. 1, 8 illus.

A newspaper article summarizing the foregoing items. Discusses the types of formal compositions employed in eighteenth-century architecture according to the categories of Wölfflin. The diversity of styles is due to local aboriginal styles.

970   GUIDO, ANGEL. 1928.

Diversidad barroca en el arte hispanoamericano. *Revista del Colegio de Arquitectos de la Habana,* 12, 11:7–11.

A reprint of the foregoing item above.

971   GUIDO, ANGEL. 1938.

El estilo mestizo o criollo en el arte de la colonia. Academia Nacional de la Historia, *Segundo Congreso Internacional de Historia de América, Buenos Aires, 5–14 de julio de 1937* (Buenos Aires), 3: 474–494.

Indigenous influence in colonial art and architecture. One of the first studies on the subject. Term "mestizo" style coined.

972 GUIDO, ANGEL. 1944.

Redescubrimiento de América en el arte. 3a ed. Buenos Aires: Librería y Editorial "El Ateneo".

The aesthetic principles of Hispano-American art.

973 GUSTIN, MONIQUE. 1966.

Iconographie et symbolisme de quelques façades rurales mexicaines (XVIIIe). *L'Information d'histoire de l'art,* 11:217–18.

Short note on the iconography of sculptures on some eighteenth-century Mexican churches.

974 GUTIERREZ, RAMON. 1973.

Notas para una bibliografía hispanoamericana de arquitectura, 1526–1875. Resistencia, Argentina.

See Section V for a complete description.

975 HARDOY, JORGE E. 1964a.

Centros ceremoniales y ciudades planeadas de la América precolombina. *Ciencia e investigación,* 20, 9:387–404.

Pre-Columbian urbanism.

976 HARDOY, JORGE E. 1964b.

Ciudades precolombinas. Buenos Aires: Ediciones Infinito.

Pre-Columbian urbanism and ceremonial centers.

First Spanish edition of his *Urban Planning in Pre-Columbian America.* New York: Braziller, 1968.

977 HARDOY, JORGE E. 1965.

La influencia del urbanismo indígena en la localización y trazado de las ciudades coloniales. *Ciencia e investigación,* 21, 9:386–405.

Indigenous influence in choice of town sites and plans of towns.

978 HARDOY, JORGE E. 1968a.

El modelo clásico de la ciudad colonial hispanoamericana. Buenos Aires: Instituto Torcuato di Tella.

The standard town plan in Hispano-America and its antecedents.

979 HARDOY, JORGE, coordinador. 1968b.

El proceso de urbanización en América desde sus orígenes hasta nuestros días. In *XXXVII Congreso Internacional de Americanistas, Argentina, 1966.* Buenos Aires. 1:3–359.

See HARDOY and SCHAEDEL, 1968, below.

980 HARDOY, JORGE. 1968c.

Urban Planning in Pre-Columbian America. New York: Braziller.

An English version of *Ciudades precolombinas,* 1964b, above.

981 HARDOY, JORGE E. 1972.

Las formas urbanas europeas durante los siglos XV al XVII y su utilización en América Latina. In *XXXIX Congreso Internacional de Americanistas, Lima, 1970.* Lima. v. 2, 157–190.

Standardized town plans of European origin utilized in the New World.

982 HARDOY, JORGE E. and CARMEN ARANOVICH. 1967.

Cuadro comparativo de los centros de colonización existentes en 1580 y 1630. *Desarrollo Económico,* 7, 27:349–360.

A statistical study by rank-population of all the towns in Hispano America from 1580–1630. Based mainly on LOPEZ DE VELASCO and VASQUEZ DE ESPINOZA, see Section I above.

983 HARDOY, JORGE E. and CARMEN ARANOVICH. 1968.

Escalas y funciones en América hispánica hacia el año 1600, primeras conclusiones. In *XXXVII Congreso International de Americanistas, Argentina, 1966.* Buenos Aires. 1:171–208.

Essentially the same as *Cuadro comparativo,* 1967, above.

984 HARDOY, JORGE and CARMEN ARANOVICH. 1969.

Urbanización en América hispánica entre 1580 y 1630. *BCIHE,* 2:9–89.

A reprinting of *Cuadro comparativo,* above.

985 HARDOY, JORGE E. and CARMEN ARANOVICH. 1970.

Urban Scales and Functions in Spanish America Toward the Year 1600: First Conclusions. *Latin American Research Review,* 5, 3:57–92.

An English version of *Escalas,* 1968, above.

986 HARDOY, J.E. and R.P. SCHAEDEL, editors. 1968.

El proceso de urbanización en América desde sus orígenes hasta nuestros días. 23 textos presentados al XXXVII Congreso Internacional de Americanistas, Argentina, 1966. Buenos Aires: Centro de Estudios Urbanos y Regionales.

A separate printing of all the papers presented at the first symposium on urbanization at the International Congress of Americanists held in Argentina in 1966. See HARDOY, 1968b, above.

Papers range from Pre-Columbian times through the colonial period to modern times.

987 HARDOY, J.E. and C. TOBAR, EDITORS. 1969.

La urbanización en América Latina. Buenos Aires: Editorial del Instituto Torcuato di Tella.

Seventeen essays on urbanization, some the same as in HARDOY and SCHAEDEL, 1968, above.

988 HEMPEL, EBERHARD. 1965.

Baroque Art and Architecture in Central Europe. Baltimore: Penguin Books.

General treatment of the baroque style in Bavaria and Austria. Reviewed in *JSAH,* 29(1970):195 ff.

989 HERNANDEZ DIAZ, JOSE. 1936.

Papeletas para la historia del retablo en Sevilla, durante la segunda mitad del siglo XVII. (Cristóbal de Guadix, Sebastián Rodríguez, Francisco y Baltazar de Barcelona.) *Boletín de bellas artes,* 3:3–32.

Documentary sources for the work of some important retable builders of Seville who exerted an influence in Mexico, Guatemala and elsewhere.

990 HERNANDEZ DIAZ, JOSE, ANTONIO SANCHO CORBACHO and FRANCISCO COLLANTES DE TERAN. 1939. 1943. 1951. 1955.

Catálogo arqueológico y artístico de la provincia de Sevilla. Sevilla: Diputación Provincial de Sevilla.

LC/N7109.S4H38

A catalogue of the art monuments—architecture, sculpture, painting etc.—in the province of Seville. Data on many buildings useful for tracing stylistic connections with colonial Central America.

991 HOUSTON, J.M. 1968.

The Foundation of Colonial Towns in Hispanic America. In P.R. Beckinsale, and J.M. Houston, eds., *Urbanization and its Problems.* Oxford: Oxford University Press.

992 IGUAL UBEDA, A. 1944.

El barroquismo. Barcelona: Editorial I.G. Seix y Barral. Colección Estudio, v. 28.

DUL/709.03 I24B

A study of the meaning and stylistic character of baroque art.

993 INIGUEZ ALMECH, FRANCISCO. 1937.

Torres mudejares aragoneses. *Archivo español de arte,* 13:173–189.

A study of the mudéjar towers of Aragon, mainly Teruel. Useful for comparisons with tower of El Carmen in San Cristobal de las Casas, Chiapas. Well-illustrated, 16 plates.

994 INSTITUTO PANAMERICANO DE GEOGRAFIA E HISTORIA. COMISION DE HISTORIA. 1951.

Contribuciones a la historia municipal de América. México.

Has a bibliography on colonial cities as well as other subjects relative to urbanization.

995   KELEMEN, PAL. 1951.

Baroque and Rococo in Latin America. New York: Macmillan. Reprinted, New York: Dover Publications, 1967, 2 vols.

The colonial period. He coins the term "earthquake baroque" for the architecture of Antigua Guatemala.

996   KELEMEN, PAL. 1966.

El barroco americano y la semántica de importación. *AIAA,* 19:39–44.

European sources for the baroque style in the Latin America.

997   KELEMEN, PAL. 1969.

Art of the Americas: Ancient and Hispanic. New York: Thomas Y. Crowell Company.

General history of art from pre-Columbian through colonial times.

998   KING, GEORGIANA GODDARD. 1927.

Mudéjar. Bryn Mawr, Pa.: Longman's Green, and Co.

LC/NA385.K5   DUL/378.748 B916N, v. 8

Excellent little book on the *mudéjar* architecture of Spain. Still useful though written more than forty years ago.

999   KOCHNITZKY, LEON, and MATHILDE POMES, editors. 1936.

Le Baroque américain. *Renaissance,* [Paris]. 19, 10–12 (oct–déc 1936).

LC/N2.R25

The entire volume of this journal devoted to Hispano American baroque. Contributions by various authors.

1000   KUBLER, GEORGE. 1942.

Mexican Urbanism in the Sixteenth Century. *Art Bulletin,* 24:160–171.

An early essay on Mexican urbanization. Important parallels for Central America.

1001   KUBLER, GEORGE. 1948.

Mexican Architecture of the Sixteenth Century. New Haven: Yale University Press. 2 vols.

LC/NA753.K8   DUL/WCL 720.972 K95M

Important account of sixteenth-century Mexican architecture and the role of the religious orders in its development.

1002   KUBLER, GEORGE. 1957.

Arquitectura de los siglos XVII y XVIII. Madrid: Editorial Plus-Ultra. Ars Hispaniae, Historia del Arte Hispánico, v. 14.

DUL/WCL 709.46 A781, v. 14

Baroque architecture of Spain. Useful for stylistic comparisons with colonial Guatemala.

1003 KUBLER, GEORGE. 1961.

On the Colonial Extinction of the Motifs of Pre-Columbian Art. In Samuel K. Lothrop, editor, *Essays in Pre-Columbian Art and Archaeology* (Cambridge, Mass.: Harvard University Press), 14–34.

The problem of indigenous influence on Hispano-American art is viewed not so much as a survival of forms, as their gradual extinction during the colonial period.

1004 KUBLER, GEORGE. 1964a.

Cities and Culture in the Colonial Period in America. *Diogenes* [Montreal], 47:53–62.

A facet of urban history.

1005 KUBLER, GEORGE. 1964b.

Ciudades y cultura en el período colonial de América Latina. *BCIHE*, 1: 81–90.

Urbanization. In English, *Diogenes,* 47(1964):53–62.

1006 KUBLER, GEORGE. 1965.

Indigenismo, indianismo y mestizaje en las artes visuales como tradición americana clásica y medieval. *Revista histórica* [Lima], 28:36–44.

The afterlife of medieval traditions in Hispano-American art.

1007 KUBLER, GEORGE. 1966a.

Indianismo y mestizaje. *Revista de Occidente,* 4, 38 (1966):158–165.

Related to question of indigenous influence on Hispano-American art and architecture.

1008 KUBLER, GEORGE. 1966b.

Indianismo y mestizaje como tradiciones americanas medievales y clásicas. *BCIHE*, 4:51–61.

Identifies the "primitive" character of early Hispano-American colonial art as comparable to a similar process that took place in early Christian and medieval art in Europe, aside from questions of indigenous influence and race mixing.

1009 KUBLER, GEORGE. 1966c.

The Unity of Cities in America. *Journal of World History,* 9: no. 4.

Urbanization. Origin of town plans.

1010 KUBLER, GEORGE. 1968.

The Colonial Plan of Cholula. *XXXVII Congreso Internacional de Americanistas, Argentina, 1966.* Buenos Aires: 1:209–224.

1011 KUBLER, GEORGE and MARTIN SORIA. 1959.

Art and Architecture in Spain and Portugal and their American Dominions, 1500–1800. Baltimore: Penguin Books. The Pelican History of Art, Z17.

DUL/709 P384, v. 17

General history of art of Spain and Latin America. Chapters on Central America.

1012   KUHNEL, ERNST. 1966.

Islamic Art and Architecture. London: Bell.

DUL/WCL 709.53 K951

Useful as background for *mudéjar* style in Spain and in New World.

1013   LAMPEREZ Y ROMEA, V. 1922.

La arquitectura hispanoamericana en las épocas de la colonización y de los virreinatos. Madrid.

An offprint of a lecture. Published in the magazine *Raza española*, Madrid. A copy in the British Museum library.

1014   LAMPEREZ Y ROMEA, VICENTE. 1930.

Historia de la arquitectura cristiana española en la edad media, etc. 2a ed. Madrid: Espasa-Calpe. 3 vols.

LC/NA 5803.L3   DUL/WCL 726.546 L237H

Large detailed history of Spanish architecture. First published in 1908–09.

1015   LANDOLT, HANSPETER. 1956.

El espacio en la arquitectura barroca. *AIAA*, 9:53–70.

Problem of the organization of space in baroque architecture.

1016   LEES-MILNE, JAMES. 1960.

Baroque in Spain and Portugal. London: Batsford.

LC/N7106.L4   DUL/WCL 709.033 L487B

General treatment of baroque style.

1016a   LLAGUNO Y AMIROLA, EUGENIO. 1829.

Noticias de los arquitectos y arquitectura.

See Section I.

1016b   LOPEZ DE ARENAS (b. ca. 1579) 1867.

Carpintería de lo blanco.

See Section I.

1017   LOZOYA, JUAN CONTRERAS and LOPEZ DE AYALA, MARQUES DE. 1931-1945.

Historia del arte hispánico. Barcelona: Salvat Editores. 2 vols.

LC/N7101.L6   DUL/WCL 709.46L925H

Has a few chapters on Hispano-American art and architecture based entirely on published materials; good survey of Spanish art as background for Hispano-American including Central American.

1018 MAGGIOROTTI, LEONE ANDREA. 1933–39.

Architetti militari italiani nel l'America latina. Rome: La Libreria Dello Stato. 3 vols.

LC/NA490.M3

Has biographical and other data on architects in the New World, mainly in Mexico.

1019 MARCO DORTA, ENRIQUE. 1951.

Fuentes para la historia del arte hispanoamericano. Estudios y documentos. Sevilla: Escuela de Estudios Hispano-Americanos, Instituto Diego Velázquez, Sección de Sevilla. Publicaciones, Serie 6, Colección de Documentos, no. 2.

DUL/709.8 M321F

Transcription of some documents in *AI,* mainly Peru.

1020 MARCO DORTA, ENRIQUE. 1966.

La influencia indígena en el barroco del Perú: aspectos y problemas. In *XXXVI Congreso Internacional de Americanistas, España, 1964.* Sevilla. 4: 195–211.

Indigenous influence, especially in the architecture of the Collao region of Peru.

1020a MARCO DORTA, ENRIQUE. 1974.

Arte en América y Filipinas. Madrid: Editorial Plus-Ultra.

A general survey of colonial art and architecture in Hispano-America including material on Central America. Copiously illustrated with an excellent text.

1020b MARKMAN, S.D. 1974.

Pre-Columbian Survivals in Colonial Hispano-American Art and Architecture. *BCIHE,* 19:43–56.

The question of indigenous influence in colonial architecture and art. A summary of the different conclusions of various art historians, including a bibliography.

1021 MAZA, FRANCISCO DE LA. 1944.

Mexican Colonial Retablos. *Gazette de Beaux Arts,* 25:175–186.

General article on Mexican retables, mainly of eighteenth-century date.

1022 MAZA, FRANCISCO DE LA. 1950.

Los retablos dorados de la Nueva España. In *Enciclopedia mexicana de arte.* México: Ediciones Mexicanas.

The iconography of sculptured and painted retables.

1023 MAZA, FRANCISCO DE LA. 1956.

Arquitectura de los coros de monjas en México. Mexico: Imprenta Universitaria.

DUL/WCL 706.272 M611E, v. 6

Study of nunnery choirs. Useful for comparisons of parallels in Antigua Guatemala.

1024 MAZA, FRANCISCO DE LA. 1965.

Tepotzlán en el arte de la Nueva España. *Artes de México,* 62–63:15–20.

The iconography of the architectural decoration. English, French and German summaries.

1025 MEISS, MILLARD, editor. 1963.

Studies in Western Art. Princeton: Princeton University Press. 4 vols.

Vol. 3, *Latin American Art and the Baroque Period in Europe.*

DUL/WCL 706.31-1614

Very few of the articles deal directly with Latin American art and architecture. Theoretical essays on the baroque style and its transformations in the New World.

1026 MESA, JOSE DE and TERESA GISBERT. 1962.

La arquitectura 'mestiza' en el Collao: la obra de Diego Choque y Malco Maita. *AIAA,* 15:53–65.

The authors discern the existence of a "mestizo" style.

1027 MESA, JOSE DE and TERESA GISBERT. 1965.

Renacimiento y manierismo en la arquitectura 'mestiza.' *BCIHE,* 3:9–44.

Stages of development of the "mestizo" style in highland Peru and Bolivia.

1028 MESA, JOSE DE and TERESA GISBERT. 1968a.

Determinantes del llamado estilo mestizo y sus alcances en América: breve consideración del término. In *XXXVII Congreso Internacional de Americanistas, Argentina, 1966.* Buenos Aires. 3:219–232.

The problem of indigenous influence and the emergence of a style blending Spanish and Indian influences.

1029 MESA, JOSE DE and TERESA GISBERT. 1968b.

Determinantes del llamado estilo mestizo—breves consideracciones sobre el término. *BCIHE,* 10:93–119.

A reprint of the foregoing item.

1030 MESA, JOSE DE and TERESA GISBERT. 1971.

Lo indígena en el arte hispano-americano. *BCIHE,* 12:18–31.

Indigenous influence in Hispano-American art and architecture.

1031 MOLLER, CARLOS MANUEL. 1951.

Artesanía mudéjar en Venezuela. *AIAA,* 4:69–74.

Short essay on the mudéjar style, mainly *alfarjes.* Useful for study of Central American parallels.

1032 MONTIGNANI, JOHN B. 1943.

Books on Latin America and its Art in the Metropolitan Museum of Art. New York: Metropolitan Museum of Art.

See section V.

1033 MORENO VILLA, JOSE. 1942.

La escultura colonial mexicana. México: El Colegio de México.

LC/NB253.M6   DUL/735.72 M843E

Some reference to Guatemalan colonial sculptors and sculpture.

1034 MORENO VILLA, JOSE. 1948.

Lo mexicano en las artes plásticas. México: El Colegio de México.

LC/N6550.M6   DUL/WCL 709.72 M843M

The distinctive stylistic character of Mexican colonial art.

1035 MORSE, RICHARD. 1962.

Some Characteristics of Latin American Urban History. *American Historical Review,* 67:317–338.

A review of the problems of urban research. Good bibliography. See item immediately below for up-to-date bibliography.

1036 MORSE, RICHARD M. 1965.

Recent Research on Latin American Urbanization: A Selective Survey with Commentary. *Latin American Research Review,* 1, 1:35–74.

Excellent bibliography up-to-date to 1964 for urbanization in Latin America.

1037 MORSE, RICHARD M. 1971.

Trends and Issues in Latin American Urban Research, 1965–1970. (Part I). *Latin American Research Review,* 6:3–52.

Brings the 1965 article, "Recent Research" etc. above, up-to-date.

1037a MORSE, RICHARD M. 1971b

The Urban Development of Latin America, 1750–1920. Palo Alto, Calif.: Stanford University Press, Center for Latin American Studies.

Of general interest. Does not deal directly with urbanization in colonial Central America.

1038 MORSE, RICHARD M. 1972.

Trends and Issues in Latin American Urban Research, 1965–1970. (Part II). *Latin American Research Review,* 2:19–75.

The second half of 1037.

1038a MORSE, RICHARD M. 1973.

Las ciudades latinoamericanas. México: Secretaría de Educación Pública, SepSetentas. 2 vols.

A translation of his *Urban Development,* 1971b, above. Vol. 1, *Antecedentes;* vol. 2, *Desarrollo histórico.*

1039 MOYA BLANCO, LUIS. 1947.

Bóvedas tabicadas. Madrid: Dirección General de Arquitectura.

A modern handbook for brickmasons on the technique of vault construction in brick. Useful for understanding colonial building methods.

1039a NAVARRO, J. GABRIEL, editor. 1932.

Arte de hacer el estuco, escrito en el siglo XVIII por don Ramón Pascual Diez. *Archivo español de arte y de arqueología,* 8:237–257.

An interesting eighteenth-century technical work on the plasterers' craft. Important for understanding *mudéjar* technique of making architectural decoration in plaster, common in colonial Central America. See also Section I, DIEZ, RAMON PASCUAL.

1040 NEUMEYER, ALFRED. 1948.

The Indian Contribution to Architectural Decoration in Spanish Colonial America. *Art Bulletin,* 30:104–121.

A hypothesis formulated in 1948 that there is a great deal of indigenous influence in Hispano-American architectural decoration.

1041 NUTTAL, ZELIA, translator. 1921.

Royal Ordinances for Laying Out of New Cities, Towns or Villages. *HAHR,* 5:249–254.

The section from the Recopilación de las Leyes de las Indias of 1573 dealing with the founding of towns.

1042 OLIVER, PAUL, editor. 1970.

Shelter and Society. Studies in Vernacular Architecture. New York: F.A. Praeger.

LC/GT171.04   DUL/728 048S

Interesting study of popular or vernacular architecture of today. Many ideas applicable to colonial Central America.

1043 PALM, E.W. 1951.

Origenes del urbanismo imperial en América. In *Contribuciones a la his-*

toria municipal de América (México: Instituto Panamericano de Geografía e Historia), 239–268.

Very well-written article on urban history in sixteenth century.

1044 PALM, ERWIN WALTER. 1955.

Los monumentos arquitectónicos de la Española. Ciudad Trujillo: Universidad de Santo Domingo. 2 vols.

DUL/WCL 720.97294 P171M

A definitive monograph on the architecture of Santo Domingo. Important sources of information on the transplantation of Spanish architectural styles to the New World in the sixteenth century.

1045 PALM, ERWIN WALTER. 1968a.

Elementos salomónicos en la arquitectura del barroco. *XXXVII Congreso Internacional de Americanistas, Argentina, 1966.* Buenos Aires. 3:233–240.

Deals with the cathedral of Comayagua, Honduras. Iconology of façade sculptural decoration.

1046 PALM, E.W. 1968b.

La ville espagnole au Nouveau Monde dans la première moitié du XVIe siècle. In *De Pétraque á Descartes, XVIII: Dixième Stage International d'Etudes Humanistes, Tours, 1966.* Paris. 241–251.

The first towns in Spanish America.

1047 PEACOCK, VERA L. 1959.

The Open Chapel in Mexico. *Journal of Interamerican Studies,* 1:277–280.

The *capilla de indios* in Mexico. See McAndrew, John, *The Open-Air Churches of Sixteenth-Century Mexico.* Harvard University Press. Cambridge, 1965, for a definitive study of the open chapel.

1047a PENA, P. DE LA. 1661.

Breve tratado de todo género de bóvedas, así regulares como irregulares. Madrid: Juan de Torija.

Mentioned by SCHUBERT, *Historia del barroco,* 166, see below. Copied from a MS of P. de Valdevira, *Libro de trazas de corte de piedras,* as noted by Fray LORENZO DE SAN NICOLAS, 1796, see below; also in Section I, No. 262.

1048 PRAT PUIG, FRANCISCO. 1947.

El prebarroco en Cuba; una escuela criolla de arquitectura morisca. Habana.

LC/NA 803.P7   DUL/720.97291q P912P

Some early architecture in Cuba of *mudéjar* style.

1049 PRENTICE, ANDREW NOBLE. 1893.

Renaissance Architecture and Ornament in Spain 1500–1560. London: B.T.

Batsford. Reprinted, London: Tiranti, 1970.

1893-LC/NA565.P8   1970-LC/NA1305.P7 19706

Plateresque ornament, useful for stylistic comparisons.

1050 RAFOLS, JOSE F. 1926.

Techumbres y artesonados españoles. Barcelona: Editorial Labor.

LC/NK 2119.R3

Wooden ceilings of *mudéjar* style. Useful for comparison with *alfarjes* in the Reino de Guatemala.

1051 RICARD, ROBERT. 1947.

La *Plaza Mayor* en Espagne et en Amérique Espagnole. *Annales, Econo-mie-Sociétés-Civilisations,* 2, 4(1947):433–38.

A study of the plaza in Hispano-American towns, which are essentially plazas with a grid of streets developing from them.

1052 RICARD, ROBERT. 1950.

La plaza mayor en España y en América española. *Estudios geográficos,* 11:321–327.

LC/G1.E96-XI, 1950

The Spanish version of the above.

1053 RODRIGUEZ DEMORIZI, E. 1966.

España y los comienzos de la pintura y la escultura en América. Madrid: Gráficas Reunidas.

The transplantation of Spanish painting to the New World in the sixteenth century.

Prologue by Juan Contreras López de Ayala, Marqués de Lozoya. Deals mainly with material in Santo Domingo.

1054 ROJAS RODRIGUEZ, PEDRO MARIO. 1963.

Historia general del arte mexicano: época colonial. México: Editorial Hermes.

DUL/709.72 aH673

A good general history of art in colonial Mexico. Some material on Central America as well.

1055 ROMERO DE TORREROS Y VINCENT, MANUEL. 1923.

Las artes industriales en la Nueva España. México: Librería de P. Robredo.

Arts and crafts in colonial Mexico. Some reference to Guatemala.

1056 ROYS, RALPH L. 1952.

Conquest and Subsequent Destruction of Maya Architecture in the Interior of Northern Yucatan. *Carnegie Institution of Washington: Contributions to American Anthropology and History*, 2, 54:129–182.

Deals with the *ramada* churches. Important for the conceptualization of the church plan and the function of each part of the same.

1057 SAENZ DE LA CALZADA GOROSTIZA, CONSUELO. 1956.

El retablo barroco español y su terminología artística, Sevilla. *Archivo español de arte*, 29:211–242.

Technical terminology of the retable. Same terms applied in New World.

1058 SAGREDO, DIEGO DE. (1526). 1946.

Medidas del romano; necessarias alos oficiales que quieren seguir las formaciones de las basas, colunas, capiteles y otras pieças de los edificios antiguos. Toledo, Madrid: Publicaciones de la Asociacion de Libreros y Amigos del Libro, 1946.

LC/NA210.S3 1526a   DUL/WCL 720.9 S129M

The first architects' handbook published in Spain. His ideas taken up and expanded by later architectural theorists. See Section I above, for the original edition.

1059 SANCHO CORBACHO, ANTONIO. 1947.

Dibujos arquitectónicos del siglo XVII. Una colección inéditos de 1663. Sevilla: Laboratorio de Arte, Universidad de Sevilla.

Some architectural drawings. Interesting for study of architectural rendering techniques and plan preparation.

1060 SANCHO CORBACHO, ANTONIO. 1949.

Leonardo de Figueroa y el patio de San Acasio de Sevilla. *Archivo español de arte*, 22:341–352.

An innovative early eighteenth-century architect of Seville, reflections of whose style are discerned in the Reino de Guatemala as well as Mexico and Peru.

1061 SANCHO CORBACHO, ANTONIO. 1952.

Arquitectura barroca sevillana del siglo XVIII. Madrid: Instituto "Diego Velásquez", Consejo Superior de Investigaciones Científicas.

A definitive monograph on the seventeenth and eighteenth century architecture of Seville and its province. Important for stylistic comparison.

1062 SAN MIGUEL, FRAY ANDRES DE. n.d.

Tratado de carpinteria.

A MS in the library of the University of Texas. See item immediately below.

1063   SAN MIGUEL, FRAY ANDRES DE. 1969.

Obras. Introducción, notas, version paleográfica de Eduardo Báez Macías. Mexico: Universidad Nacional Antónoma de Mexico.

A transcription of the foregoing item.

1063a   SAN NICOLAS, FRAY LORENZO DE (fl. 1596?–1697?). 1796.

Arte y uso de la arquitectura, con el primer libro de Euclides traducido en castellano. 4a ed. Madrid. 2 vols.

See Section I above for information on editions etc.

1064   SCHUBERT, OTTO. 1908.

Geschichte des Barock in Spanien. Esslingen, Germany: N.P. Neff (M. Schreiber).

LC/NA1306.S4

See item immediately below.

1065   SCHUBERT, OTTO. 1924.

Historia del barroco en España. Traducción del alemán por Manuel Hernández Alcalde. Madrid: Editorial "Saturnino Calleja".

LC/NA 1306.S43

Spanish baroque architecture. Somewhat out of date with regard to stylistic analyses.

1066   SEBASTIAN, SANTIAGO. 1967.

La influencia de los modelos ornamentales de Serlio en Hispano-américa. *BCIHE,* 7:30–67.

A discussion of the Serlio's influence on baroque architectural decoration as derived from his handbooks.

1067   SEBASTIAN, SANTIAGO. 1969.

La evolucion del soporte en la decoración arquitectónica de Santa Fe de Bogotá. *AIAA,* 22:72–83.

Non-architectonic pilaster shafts, *estípites,* mainly on retables.

1068   SERLIO, SEBASTIONO (fl. 1475–1554). 1611.

The Book of Architecture. London: R. Peake. Reprinted, with an introduction by A.E. Santaniello, New York: Benjamin Blom, 1970.

LC/NA2517.S5   DUL/WCL 720.92 S485Ta

Reprinted from the English translation of 1611. Serlio's influence on architectural decoration in Latin America is being documented more and more, also in Antigua Guatemala. See LUJAN MUNOZ, LUIS, *La pilastra,* Section IV below.

1069 SMITH, ROBERT C. 1945.

The Colonial Art of Latin America. Washington, D.C.: The Library of Congress.

LC/N6502.U5   DUL/WCL 709.8 U58C

1070 SMITH, ROBERT C. 1955.

Colonial Towns in Spanish and Portuguese America. *JSAH,* 14:1–12.

The differences between the Spanish and Portuguese concepts of town planning in the New World.

1071 SOLA, MIGUEL. 1935.

Historia del arte hispano-americano: arquitectura, escultura, pintura y artes menores en la América española durante los siglos XVI, XVII y XVIII. Barcelona: Editorial Labor.

LC/N6502.563   DUL/WCL 709.8 S684H

A very general and popular history of art. Somewhat out-of-date.

1072 SOSA GALLARDO, SANTIAGO A. 1969.

Frontones realzados con ático en la arquitectura hispanoamericana. *AIAA,* 22:47–57.

Doubled pediments or doubled raking cornices on church facades.

1073 STANISLAWSKI, DAN. 1946.

The Origin and Spread of the Grid-Pattern Town. *Geographical Review,* 36: 105–120.

Important for the history of urbanization. Problem of the introduction of the orthogonal plan.

1074 STANISLAWSKI, DAN. 1947.

Early Spanish Town Planning in the New World. *Geographical Review,* 37: 94–105.

Some examples of sixteenth-century towns.

1075 THOMPSON, LAWRENCE S. 1964/1965.

El grabado in la América colonial. *Boletín de la Biblioteca General. Universidad de Zulia* [Maracaibo], nos. 4/5–7/8:11–26.

Prints in book-illustration in the colonial period in Latin America. Some specific examples from colonial Guatemala.

1076 TOLEDO PALOMO, RICARDO. 1959.

Indice de la Perret—Enciclopedia de arte hispano-americano de la época colonial en las Américas y en las Islas Filipinas. *AHG,* 11, 1:74–75.

A book review with special reference to material from Guatemala.

1077 TORRE REVELLO, JOSE. 1932.

El gremio de plateros en las Indias Occidentales. Buenos Aires: Imprenta de la Universidad. Publicaciones del Instituto de Investigaciones Históricas, no. 61.

LC/HD6473.S744S55 and F2801.B98 no. 61

Documents dealing with silversmiths guilds in Mexico, Peru, Guatemala, Chile, Havana, and Buenos Aires.

1078 TORRE REVELLO, JOSE. 1956.

Tratados de arquitectura utilizados en Hispano-América (siglos XVI a XVIII). *Revista interamericana de bibliografía,* 6, 1:3–24.

LC/Z1007.R4317

The architects' manuals which circulated in Hispano-America in the colonial period.

1079 TORRES BALBAS, LEOPOLDO. 1949.

Arte almohade. Arte nazari. Arte mudéjar. Editorial Plus-Ultra. Madrid: Ars Hispaniae, historia universal del arte hispánico, v. 4.

DUL/WCL709.46 A781 v. 4

Spanish architecture of Moorish origin and style. Important for stylistic comparisons of *mudéjar* traits in New World.

1080 TORRES BALBAS, LEOPOLDO, et al. 1954.

Resumen histórico del urbanismo en Espãna. Madrid: Instituto de Estudios de Administración Local.

The history of Spanish urbanization.

1081 TOUSSAINT, MANUEL. 1943.

A Defense of Baroque Art in America. *In proceedings of the Inter-American Conference on Intellectual Interchange.* Austin Texas: 161–175. University of Texas, Institue of Latin American Studies.

LC/F1418.L595 1943.

An exposition of the meaning of the term "baroque" as applied to Hispano-American architecture.

1082 TOUSSAINT, MANUEL. 1946.

Arte mudéjar en América. México: Editorial Porrúa.

LC/NA388.AT6   DUL/723.3 qT734A

A general survey of *mudéjar* traits in Hispano-American architecture. Includes material on Chiapas and the rest of Central America.

1083 TOUSSAINT, MANUEL. 1948.

Arte colonial en México. México: Universidad Nacional Autónoma de México, Instituto de Investigaciones Estéticas.

LC/N6553.T68   DUL/WCL 709.72 T734A

A good general history of Mexian art. Has some material on Chiapas. An English edition brought up-to-date by Elizabeth Wilder Weissman, *Colonial Art in Mexico*. Austin, Texas: University of Texas Press, 1967.

1083a TOUSSAINT, MANUEL, GERARDO MURILLO (DR. ATL), and J.R. BENITEZ. 1924–27.

Iglesias de México México: Secretaría de Hacienda. 6 vols.

LC/NA 5250.M7

Vol. VI deals with the architecture of Puebla and the surrounding region. Important for the development of the "popular" baroque style. Material on sixteenth-century Guatemala included.

1084 VARGAS LUGO, ELISA. 1969.

Las portadas religiosas de México. México: Universidad Nacional Autónoma de México.

A study of the Mexican retable-facade.

1085 VILLEGAS, VICTOR MANUEL. 1956.

El gran signo formal del barroco: ensayo histórico del apoyo estípite. Mexico: Instituto de Investigaciones Estéticas. Imprenta Universitaria.

LC/N6553.V5   DUL/WCL 709.72 qV732G

The origin and development of the non-architectonic pilaster shaft, the *estípite*. See also LUJAN MUNOZ, LUIS, *La pilastra-estípite*. Section IV below.

1086 VIOLICH, FRANCIS. 1944.

Cities of Latin America, housing and planning to the south. New York: Reinhold Publishing Corp.

LC/NA9159.V5   DUL/711.4 V795C

Contemporary Latin American cities. Some historical material on colonial origins.

1087 WEISMANN, ELIZABETH WILDER. 1950.

Mexico in Sculpture, 1521–1821. Cambridge, Mass.: Harvard University Press.

DUL/730.972 qW428M

The sculpture of colonial Mexico with some treatment of that of Guatemala.

1087a WEISMANN, ELIZABETH WILDER. 1975.

The History of Art in Latin America, 1500–1800: Some Trends and Challenges in the Last Decade. *Latin American Research Review*, 10, 1:7–50.

An excellent article including a copious bibliography of materials published between 1964 and 1974. Publishers are not always given. Many of the items listed are also to be found in this bibliography, sections III and IV. There are one or two unfortunate errors in the listings; on page 32 under Flores Marini, Carlos, 1964, the title "Rincones de historia . . ." is actually by Eduardo Flores Ruiz, item 481 or 1147 b, and on page 38 the title listed under Luis Luján Muñoz, 1968, "El edificio circular. . . ." is actually by his brother, Jorge Luján Muñoz, item 1172 a.

1088   WETHEY, HAROLD E. 1949.

Colonial Architecture and Sculpture in Peru. Cambridge, Mass.: Harvard University Press.

DUL/WCL 720.985 W539C

Useful for stylistic parallels in Central America.

1089   WILDER, ELIZABETH, editor. 1949.

Studies in Latin American Art, proceedings of a conference held in the Museum of Modern Art, New York, 28–31 May 1945. Washington, D.C.: American Council of Learned Societies.

DUL/709.C148S

Various essays on stylistic problems of Latin American Art, especially architecture.

1090   WHITMAN, NATHAN T. 1970.

Roman Tradition and the *Aedicular* Façade. *JSAH*, 29:108–123.

Traces the influence of Vignola's rejected design for Il Gesu. Della Porta's design, the one built. Another source of the baroque style, a two-pronged development.

1091   ZAWISZA, LESZEK. 1969.

Tradición monástica europea en los conventos mexicanos del siglo XVI. *BCIHE*, 2:90–122.

Traces origin of conventual plans in Mexico. Useful for tracing parallels to development in Reino de Guatemala.

1092   ZAWISZA, LESZEK M. 1972.

Fundación de las ciudades hispanoamericanas. *BCIHE*, 13:88–128.

Some theoretical considerations on urbanization in colonial Hispano-America.

1093   ZUCKER, PAUL. 1959.

Town and Square from the agora to the village green. New York: Columbia University Press.

LC/NA9070.28   DUL/711.5 qZ94T

Important study on urban plans. Spain and the New World, 132–140.

Section IV

ART AND ARCHITECTURE: REINO DE GUATEMALA
(Colonial Central America)

Chiapas, Guatemala, Honduras, El Salvador, Nicaragua and Costa Rica.

Pamphlets, monographs, articles, guide books, etc.

1094 ABASCAL, VALENTIN. 1961.

Santiago de los Caballeros de Goathemala. Guatemala: Centro Editorial del Ministerio de Educación Pública, "José de Pineda Ibarra."

LC/F1476.A5A6   DUL/917.281 A1185

History of the former capital of the Reino de Guatemala. General description of the architecture. Has a bibliography.

1095 ACENA DURAN, RAMON (fl. 1898–1945).

Itinerario. Guatemala: Imprenta Universitaria.

Literary impressions on Antigua Guatemala. Includes some plans of the town.

1096 ADAMS, ROBERT M. 1961.

Changing Patterns of Territorial Organization in the Central Highlands of Chiapas, Mexico. *American Antiquity,* 26:341–360.

Deals with settlement patterns from pre-Columbian and colonial times to present. Important for urbanization process.

1097 AGUIRRE MATHEU, JORGE. 1936.

La metrópoli colonial centro-americana, Antigua Guatemala. Guatemala: Tipografía Nacional.

A literary evocation of the history of Antigua Guatemala.

1098 AGUIRRE MATHEU, JORGE. 1942/43.

Descripción del Valle del Panchoy. *ASGH,* 18:173–185.

The valley where Antigua Guatemala located. Some historical data on founding and urban history.

1099 ANGULO INIGUEZ, DIEGO. 1936.

Frontales de plata de Guatemala y Caracas. *Arte en América y Filipinas,* [Sevilla], 2:165–167.

LC/N6502.A7

The altar by Manuel Quesada done in Antigua Guatemala in 1730 is in Jerez de la Frontera, Spain.

1100 ANGULO INIGUEZ, DIEGO. 1941.

1100 ANGULO INIGUEZ, DIEGO. 1942.

Bautista Antonelli, las fortificaciones americanas del siglo XVI. Madrid: Real Academia de la Historia.

LC/NA0328493

Bautista Antonelli worked in Guatemala and probably did the town plan of Antigua Guatemala.

1101 ANGULO INIGUEZ, DIEGO. 1947.

Martínez Montañés y su escuela en Honduras y Guatemala. *Archivo Español de Arte* [Madrid]. 20, 80:185–291.

Stylistic parallels with a famous Spanish sculptor.

1102 ANGULO INIGUEZ, DIEGO. 1950.

Orfebrería de Guatemala en el Museo Victoria y Alberto de Londres. *.Archivo Español de Arte* [Madrid]. 23:351–354.

An eighteenth-century silver piece. Stylistic analysis.

1103 ANGULO INIGUEZ, DIEGO. 1952.

Andrés y Francisco Ocampo y las esculturas de la catedral de Comayagua, Honduras. *Arte en América y Filipinas* [Sevilla]. 2 no. 4:113–120.

Some sculptures and other religious objects by the two sculptors shipped to Honduras in 1620, based on documents in *AGI.*

1104 ANGULO INIGUEZ, DIEGO. 1966.

Orfebrería religiosa en Guatemala. In *XXXVI Congreso Internacional de Americanistas, España, 1964.* Sevilla. 4: 287–292.

Silverwork, especially on altar fronts in colonial Guatemala.

1105 ANNIS, VERLE. 1945.

Antigua, monumento nacional. *Revista de Guatemala* [Guatemala], 1, 1: 105–113.

A report on the state of preservation of the colonial buildings in Antigua Guatemala in 1945. Suggestions for the conservation and preservation of the architecture. Well-illustrated with excellent photographs by the author.

1106   ANNIS, VERLE LINCOLN. 1949.

El plano de una ciudad colonial. *AHG*, 1:48–56.

A discussion of the layout of Antigua Guatemala.

1107   ANNIS, VERLE LINCOLN. 1968.

The Architecture of Antigua Guatemala, 1543–1773. Guatemala: Universidad de San Carlos de Guatemala.

DUL/720.97281 A615A

A large volume rich with photographs and some plans. Historical data included. Little on stylistic analysis.

Also published privately by the author, Laguna Beach, California. Parallel texts in Spanish and English.

1108   ANTIGUA, GUATEMALA. CENSUS. 1604.

Becerro del asiento general y particular de las cuadras, casas y vecinos que hay en ellas, de la ciudad de Santiago de los Caballeros de la provincia de Guatemala, en que se ha de repartir la alcabala que está obligada a su Magestad.

AGG: A 1.2.6(1604)11.810-1804.

A most valuable document giving a block by block census of Antigua Guatemala in 1604.

1108a   ARMAS LARA, M. 1964.

El renacimiento de la danza guatemalteca, y el orígen de la marimba. Guatemala: Ministerio de Educación Pública.

A popular treatment of the folk dances of Guatemala and their origin. Something of the music and the marimba.

1109   ARCOS Y MORENO, ALONSO DE (fl. 1700–1760). 1759.

Relación individual de las fiestas, con que se celebró la dedicación del Calvario de Esquipulas. Guatemala: Sebastián Arévalo.

LC/NAO38.1903 Cty

A small church in Esquipulas, Guatemala. Some description and history of the building.

1110   AYCINENA, JUAN JOSE DE (fl. 1793–1865). 1860.

Consagración de la catedral de la archdiósesis de Santiago de Guatemala; descripción de su templo y altar mayor de mármol. Guatemala: L. Luna.

Small pamphlet of 7 pp. Description of cathedral in Guatemala City.

1111   BENITEZ, JOSE R. 1941.

La fuente monumental de Chiapa de Corzo. Guadalajara, Jalisco.

A pamphlet of 8 pp. The report of the condition of the fountain prior to restoration done in 1940. The drawing is totally erroneous, showing a circular plan. In fact, it is octagonal.

1112 BERLIN, HEINRICH. 1942.

El convento de Tecpatán. *AIIE*, 3, 9:5–13.

An informative account of the Dominican church and convento at Tecpatán, Chiapas, including historical data.

1113 BERLIN, HEINRICH. 1947.

El ingeniero Luis Diez de Navarro. *ASGH*, 22:89–95.

An account of the architectural activities of DIEZ DE NAVARRO, see Section I, in Guatemala in the eighteenth century.

1114 BERLIN, HEINRICH. 1950.

Fundación del convento de Santa Clara en La Antigua. *AHG*, 2, 1:43–54.

Documentary sources in the Museo Nacional de México, in the group called "Fondo Franciscano," two *expedientes* in *tomos* 102 and 114, present classification. Documents begin on *foja* 68 of *tomo* 102.

The nunnery of Santa Clara in Antigua Guatemala.

1115 BERLIN, HEINRICH. 1952a.

Historia de la imaginería colonial en Guatemala. Guatemala: Ministerio de Educación Pública.

LC/NB277.G8B4

A basic work on sculpture in colonial Guatemala based on archival sources.

1116 BERLIN, HEINRICH. 1952b.

Pintura colonial mexicana en Guatemala. *ASGH*, 26:118–128.

Some Guatemalan paintings now in Mexico. Some observations on architecture also.

1117 BERLIN, HEINRICH. 1953.

El pintor Tomás de Merlo. *AHG*, 5, 1:53–58.

The work of the colonial Guatemalan painter.

1118 BERLIN, HEINRICH. 1965.

Artistas y artesanos coloniales de Guatemala. *Cuadernos de Antropología.* [Guatemala]. 5:5–35.

A check list of building-trade craftsmen, sculptors, painters and retable-makers culled from *AGG*. Biographical data is invaluable for the art historian.

1119 BLOM, FRANS. 1955.

El retablo de Teopisca en Chiapas. *AIIE*, 6, 23:39–42.

A retable now in church of Teopisca, Chiapas, formerly in San Agustín, San Cristóbal de las Casas, Chiapas.

1120 BONET CORREA, ANTONIO. 1965.

Las iglesias barrocas en Guatemala. *Anuario EA*, 22:705–765.

. A survey of the architecture of Guatemala with some reference to Iberian antecedents.

1121 BORHEGYI, STEPHEN F. DE. 1953.

El Cristo de Esquipulas de Chimayo, Nuevo México. *AHG*, 5, 1:11–28.

A comparison between the "black" Christ of Esquipulas, Guatemala with that of New Mexico.

1122 BRANAS, CESAR. 1943.

Visión y ensueño de Esquipulas. Guatemala: Unión Tipográfica.

LC/BT 580.E75B7

Personal impressions of a visit to Esquipulas. More like a prose-poem. A small pamphlet.

1123 BUSCHIAZZO, MARIO J. 1936.

Guatemala Antigua, das Amerikanische Pompeii. *Lasso* [Buenos Aires], 3, 9:422–428.

LC/F2801.L36

A brief description of colonial Antigua Guatemala with some reference to the dating of the buildings.

1124 BUSCHIAZZO, MARIO J. 1940.

Santiago de los Caballeros de Guatemala. *La Prensa* [Buenos Aires], 14 julio 1940, sección 2, 1 p.

A brief description of Antigua Guatemala and what survived the earth-quake of 1773. A newspaper article.

1125 BUSTO, INOCENCIO DEL. 1961.

San Juan Comalapa. *AHG*, 13, 2:27–48.

A description of the colonial church and its furnishings in San Juan Comalapa, Guatemala.

1126 CAAL CHAMPNEY, RICARDO. 1962.

La catedral de Santo Domingo de Cobán. *RUSC*, 62:74–92.

The history of the Dominican church in Cobán, Guatemala.

1127   CALERON QUIJANO, JOSE ANTONIO. 1943.

El fuerte de San Fernando de Omoa: su historia e importancia en la defensa del golfo de Honduras. *RI.* 11:127–163.

A documentary study including plans, maps. For a more recent treatment see ZAPATERO, 1973, below.

1128   CARRERA STAMPA, MANUEL. 1945.

Ordenanzas del noblísimo arte de la platería para el Reino de Guatemala. 1776. *ASGH,* 20:97–102.

The silversmith's guild, based on documentary sources in AGG.

1129   CASTANEDA, FRANCISCO. 1907.

Una ciudad histórica: Antigua Guatemala, su pasado y su presente. Guatemala. Imprenta "La República".

LC/NC019537 NNPPU ICN CV-B LHHT

History of Antigua Guatemala. Literary style.

1130   CASTELLANOS, J. HUMBERTO R. 193?.

Guía del Museo Colonial de la Antigua Guatemala. Compiled by J. Humberto Castellanos and translated by Wilson Popenoe and Manuel Jonama.

A small pamphlet of 77 pp. with some data on objects in colonial museum in Antigua Guatemala.

1131   CASTELLANOS, J. HUMBERTO R. 1941.

Relación sintética del desarrollo del arte en Guatemala. *Boletín de museos y bibliotecas* [Guatemala], ep. 2, 1, 2:73–92.

A brief summary of the architecture, sculpture, painting and other arts of colonial Guatemala.

1132   CATHERWOOD, FREDERICK. 1844.

Views of Ancient Monuments in Central America, Chiapas and Yucatan. New York: Barlett and Welford.

LC/F1435. C36

A reprint, Barre, Mass., Barre Publishers, 1965.

An album of 25 plates of Pre-Columbian antiquities with a short text of some 24 pages.

Essentially the same type of illustrative material which appeared in STEPHENS, 1841, Section II.

1133   CHAVEZ Y GONZALEZ, LUIS. 1946.

Datos y apuntes importantes de la parroquia de San Jerónimo Nejapa de El Salvador. *Tzunpame* [San Salvador]. 6, 5:126–128.

Short article with data on a colonial church.

1134 CHINCHILLA AGUILAR, ERNESTO. 1953a.

Ordenanzas de escultura, carpinteros, escultores, ensambladores y violeros de la ciudad de México. *AHG,* 5, 1:29–52.

Regulations of the various craft guilds, based on documentary sources in *AGG.* Has a glossary of archaic terms. Also gives some documents from the Archivo Nacional de México, dated 1568, 1589 and 1704.

1135 CHINCHILLA AGUILAR, ERNESTO. 1953b.

El Ramo de Aguas de la ciudad de Guatemala en la época colonial. *AHG,* 5, 2:19–31.

The water supply system of Antigua Guatemala. Informative material on public services.

1136 CHINCHILLA AGUILAR, ERNESTO. 1963. 1965.

Historia del arte en Guatemala, 1524–1962. Guatemala: Centro Editorial "Jose de Pineda Ibarra", Ministerio de Educación Pública.

A survey of the art of Guatemala from the colonial period to the present. Based on secondary sources.

1137 CHINCHILLA AGUILAR, ERNESTO. 1965(1966).

La gran arquitectura de Antigua Guatemala hacia 1700. *Cultura: Revista del Ministerio de Educación* [San Salvador]. 38:75–79.

An account of the work of the architects-stone masons Joseph de Porres and Diego de Porres in Antigua Guatemala.

An extract from his book on the art history of Guatemala, above.

1137a CID FERNANDEZ, ENRIQUE DEL. 1960.

Del retrato de don Pedro de Alvarado Contreras. Guatemala: Universidad de San Carlos de Guatemala.

LC/N7628.A6C5

A careful study of the portrait of Pedro de Alvarado located in the office of the mayor (alcalde) of the Ayuntamiento in Guatemala City, painted by Juan José Rosales in 1802.

1138 CORDOY, DONALD BUSH and DOROTHY M. CORDRY. 1941.

Costumes and Weaving of the Zoque Indians of Chiapas, Mexico. Los Angeles, Calif.: The Southwest Museum.

DUL/572 L879p

Mid-twentieth century textiles and clothing of Zoques. Colonial and Pre-Columbian antecedents of design patterns.

1139 CORONADO Y PACHECO, ANGEL B. 1918.

La ruina de Guatemala, capital de Guatemala, América Central acaecida durante la noche del 25 de diciembre de 1917. Quetzaltenango, Guatemala: Tipografía Sánchez y de Guise.

A brief pamphlet of 32 pages describing the destruction of Guatemala City in 1917. Important for the architectural historian since many buildings of colonial date were damaged or ruined and were subsequently rebuilt. An aid to determining their original architectural character.

In the Latin American Collection, University of Texas Library.

1140   CRUZ, FRANCISCO SANTIAGO. 1949.

Ruinas de la iglesia de Ostuta, Chiapas.

An unpublished MS in the library of Frans Blom, Casa Na Bolom, San Cristóbal de las Casas, Chiapas. Deals with a sixteenth-century Dominican church.

1141   DIAZ, VICTOR MIGUEL. 1927.

La romántica ciudad colonial. Guatemala: Tipografía Sánchez y de Guise.

LC/F1476.G92D5

A guide book to Antigua Guatemala. Full of historical information. Sources not cited.

1142   DIAZ, VICTOR MIGUEL. 1934.

Las bellas artes en Guatemala. Guatemala: Tipografía Nacional.

LC/N6576.D5

A series of unconnected articles arranged in no particular order. Full of information, much from contemporary colonial literary and documentary sources which are never cited.

1143   DIAZ DURAN, J.C. 1942/43.

Historia de la Casa de Moneda del Reino de Guatemala, desde 1731 hasta 1773. *ASGH,* 18:191–224.

A well-written account of the mint in Antigua Guatemala, housed in the Capitanía. Well documented.

1144   ESCALONA RAMOS, ALBERTO. 1943.

Algunas construcciones de tipo colonial en Quintana Roo. *AIIE,* 3:10, 17–40.

Information on colonial buildings in this remote area, on the periphery of Central America. Photographs and plans.

1145   FERNANDEZ, JESUS. 1948.

Monografía de la Ermita del Cerro del Carmen escrita en 1894. *ASGH,* 23:72–91.

A history of an early church in Guatemala City that existed there before the capital of the Reino de Guatemala was transferred there in 1773/74.

1146   FERNANDEZ, JESUS. 1958.

Monografías de los templos de Guatemala. *ASGH,* 31:299–338.

Data on the removal of various churches from Antigua Guatemala after the ruin of 1773, and the location of their furnishings in churches of Guatemala City.

1147 FERRUS ROIG, FRANCISCO. 1961.

General Mayor de la Universidad de San Carlos en la Guatemala de la Asuncíon: Reseña histórica. Guatemala: Universidad de San Carlos de Guatemala, Imprenta Universitaria.

A history of the university building in Guatemala City from 1778 to 1961.

1147a FLORENCIA, FRANCISCO DE (fl. c. 1755). 1924–25.

Nobles artes en Guatemala. Famosas esculturas hechas en Guatemala y llevadas a México por el obispo de Yucatán, el celebre Padre Fray Diego de Landa. *ASGH,* 1:188–189.

Extracted from the author's *Zodiaco Mariano,* see Section I, No. 114.

1147b FLORES RUIZ, EDUARDO. 1964.

Rincones de historia: la calle de las monjas en Ciudad Real. *Abside* [México], 27, 4:5–23.

Historical data on the nunnery and tower of El Carmen in San Cristóbal de las Casas, Chiapas.

1148 FUSON, ROBERT H. 1964.

House Types of Central Panama. *Annals of the Association of American Geographers.* 54, 2:190–208.

Domestic architectural types as determined by environmental and historical factors. Fusion of indigenous and Spanish design and construction elements. A useful model for architectural studies elsewhere in Central America.

1149 GONZALEZ GALVAN, MANUEL. 1960.

Vignola en San Cristobal Las Casas. *AIIE,* 8, 29:15–36.

The work of a local architect and the remodelling of colonial buildings in San Cristóbal de las Casas, Chiapas in the late nineteenth and early twentieth centuries.

1150 GONZALEZ GALVAN, MANUEL. 1968.

De Guatemala a Nicaragua, diario del viaje de un estudiante de arte. México: Universidad Nacional. Instituto de Investigaciones Estéticas.

LC/NA760.G6

A journal of an art history student. Some descriptions and impressions of colonial architecture.

1151 GONZALEZ MATEOS, MARIA VICTORIA. 1949.

Marcos Ibáñez, arquitecto español en Guatemala. *ASGH,* 24:49–75. Reprinted from *Anuario EA,* 3:877–910.

The work of an architect largely responsible for the plan and construction of the cathedral of Guatemala City and at the end of the eighteenth century. Drawings included, also, some documents.

1152   GRAJEDA MENA, GUILLERMO. 1969.

Los Cristos tratados por los escultores de Guatemala. Guatemala.

Pamphlet, 15 pages, with a short essay on colonial and later sculpture.

1153   GUATEMALA. DIRECCIÓN GENERAL DE OBRAS PUBLICAS. 1967.

Análisis urbano de la ciudad de Antigua Guatemala. Guatemala.

The urban history of Antigua Guatemala. Has maps and tables.

1154   GUATEMALA. CONSULATE, BERLIN. 1934.

Album de Guatemala. Berlin: Feyl. 3 vols.

LC/F1464.A7

Complete picture book of country, including views of colonial buildings.

1155   GUERRA TRIGUEROS, ALBERTO. 1938.

The Colonial Churches of El Salvador. *BPAU,* 72:271–279.

Brief survey of the colonial churches of El Salvador. Very little historical data.

1156   HERRERA S., JULIO ROBERTO. 1942/43.

Anotaciones y documentos para la historia de los hospitales de la ciudad de Santiago de los Caballeros de Guatemala. *ASGH,* 18:225–272.

A well-documented history of the hospitals of colonial Antigua Guatemala. Includes some plans of the buildings, most of which are still in ruins. He does not cite who drew the plans or the sources of the information on which these drawings are based.

1157   HIBBITS, JOHN F. 1968.

Estado de conservación de las iglesias de Antigua Guatemala. Guatemala: Universidad de San Carlos.

A report on the physical condition of the principal colonial monuments, including sketches and photographs.

1158   HOPPENOT, HELENE. 1955.

Guatemala. Lausanne: La Guilde du Livre.

An album of 80 photographs of contemporary Guatemala with brief descriptive text in French. Some colonial buildings included.

1159   IRIARTE, AGUSTIN. 1943.

La pintura en Guatemala. *Ars* [México], 1, 5:9–20.

A survey of Guatemalan painting from Pre-Columbian to modern times. Deals with some famous colonial painters.

1160 IZAGUIRRE, CARLOS. 1952.

La catedral de Comayagua, Honduras. *La pajarita de papel* [Tegucigalpa], 4, 22–24:53–59.

Popular. Various churches in Comayagua, particularly the cathedral.

1161 JICKLING, DAVID L. 1970.

La Calle Ancha de Santo Domingo en Santiago de Guatemala, en el siglo XVIII. *Revista de la Academia Guatemalteca de Estudios Genealógicos, Heráldicos, e Históricos,* 4:437–456.

Genealogical data on the owners of houses on the Alameda de Santa Rosa in Antigua Guatemala.

1162 JIMINEZ, TOMAS FIDIAS.

El Salvador: *Monumentos históricos y arqueológicos.* México: Instituto Panamericano de Geografía e Historia, Organizacion de Estados Americanos.

1163 JUAREZ Y ARAGON, J. FERNANDO. 1950.

Esta es Guatemala: estudio histórico-geográfico. Guatemala: Imprenta Iberia.

Short literary sketches—stories, legends—and some descriptions of the architectural monuments in Antigua Guatemala and elsewhere.

1164 JUAREZ MUNOZ, J. FERNANDO. 1942-43.

Perigrinación por las ruinas de la Antigua Guatemala. *ASGH,* 18:148–156.

Personal impressions of a visit to Antigua Guatemala.

1165 KELEMEN, PAL. 1941.

Colonial Architecture in Guatemala. *BPAU,* 65, 8:437–448.

LC/F1403.B955

Brief survey of colonial architecture in Antigua Guatemala and elsewhere.

1166 KELEMEN, PAL. 1942.

Guatemala Baroque. *Magazine of Art.* 35:22–25.

Discusses Antiguan style also the church Cerro del Carmen in Guatemala City.

1167 KELEMEN, PAL. 1944.

Some Church Facades of Colonial Guatemala. *Gazette des Beaux Arts,* series 6, 25, 924:113–126.

Discusses style of some provincial churches in Guatemala.

1168 KELEMEN, PAL. 1947.

Observaciones sobre el arte colonial y precolombino en Honduras. *Honduras Maya* [Tegucigalpa] 2: (Sept.).

Brief essay on both pre-Columbian and colonial art in Honduras.

1168a LEMOINE VILLACANA, ERNESTO. 1961.

Historia sucinta de la construcción de la catedral de Guatemala. Escrita por don Gerónimo de Betanzos. Boletín del Archivo General de la Nación. Mexico, 3:405–430.

See BETANZOS QUINONES, Section I, No. 32, for description. Paleography and explanatory essay by Lemoine.

1169 LEMOS, PEDRO JOSEPH. 1940.

Colonial Days Lived Again; the Story of Art Recreation in Old Antigua. *School Arts* [Palo Alto, California. Stanford University Press], 3:87–94.

Some photographs and short description of the "House in Antigua." See POPENOE, 1933(1935), for reference to Louis Adamic's book of that name.

1170 LEMOS, PEDRO JOSEPH. 1950.

Guatemala Art Crafts. Worcester, Mass.: The Davis Press.

LC/F1465.L4   DUL/970.6745q L557G

Contemporary Indian crafts.

1171 LINES, JORGE A. and MARIA MOLINA DE LINES. 1967

Costa Rica: Monumentos históricos y arqueológicos. México: Instituto Panamericano de Geografía e Historia.

General survey of pre-Columbian and colonial monuments. Well illustrated.

1172 LUJAN MUNOZ, JORGE. 1963.

El monasterio de Nuestra Señora del Pilar de Zaragoza en la ciudad de Guatemala (1720–1874). Universidad de San Carlos de Guatemala: thesis for degree of Licenciado en Historia, Facultad de Humanidades. Mimeographed.

A monograph on the convento of Las Capuchinas in Antigua Guatemala as well as its history after removal to Guatemala City after 1773.

1172a LUJAN MUNOZ, JORGE. 1972.

El edificio circular del monasterio de Capuchinas en Antigua Guatemala. *Verhandlungen des XXXVIII internationalen Amerikanistenkongresses, Stuttgart-München, 12 bis 18 August 1968.* München. 4:201–209.

A shorter version of item 1172. The origins of this unique circular convento is discussed in greater detail.

1173 LUJAN MUNOZ, JORGE. 1966.

Permanencia de Antigua. Guatemala: Universidad de San Carlos.

An essay on the history and art of Antigua Guatemala.

1174 LUJAN MUNOZ, LUIS. 1961.

Noticia breve sobre la segunda catedral de Guatemala. *ASGH*, 34:61–82.

An account of the cathedral of Antigua Guatemala that preceded the one standing now and completed 1680.

1175 LUJAN MUNOZ, LUIS. 1963. [i.e., 1967]

Breves consideraciones arquitectónicas sobre el templo de Esquipulas. *ASGH*, 36:417–425.

The architectural style and dating of the basilica of Esquipulas, Guatemala.

1176 LUJAN MUNOZ, LUIS. 1964.

Breve panorama de la arquitectura religiosa guatemalteca durante el período colonial. *RUSC*, 63:63–90.

Resumé of church and monastic architecture in colonial Guatemala.

1177 LUJAN MUNOZ, LUIS. 1965a

Exposición de máscaras guatemaltecas en homenaje a la VIII Asamblea General del Instituto Panamericano de Geografía e Historia: 28 de junio- 5 de julio de 1965. Guatemala: Alianza Francesa.

Seven page, illustrated catalogue of masks, Pre-Columbian, colonial and modern. Reproductions poor in quality.

1178 LUJAN MUNOZ, LUIS. 1965b.

La pilastra-estípite serliana en el Reino de Guatemala. Guatemala: Universidad de San Carlos.

The non-architectonic pilaster shaft seen on the churches of Santa Clara and Escuela de Cristo in Antigua Guatemala derived from a drawing of Serlio for a fireplace.

1179 LUJAN MUNOZ, LUIS. 1966 [i.e. 1968].

Las artes plásticas guatemaltecas a mediados del siglo XVIII y en el siglo XIX. *RUSC*, 68:125–152.

A survey of painting and sculpture in Guatemala of the late colonial period.

1180 LUJAN MUNOZ, LUIS. 1967a.

La catedral y mercado de la ciudad de Guatemala hacia 1680. *RUSC*, 70: 85–100.

The main plaza of Antigua Guatemala in the late seventeenth century as depicted in a painting discovered in Mexico City showing the cathedral in construction. See also below, MOYSSEN, *Como se construía*, for another article on the same painting.

1181 LUJAN MUNOZ, LUIS. 1967b.

Nómina provisional de monumentos coloniales arquitectónicos de Guatemala. *AHG,* 19, 2:54–58.

A check list of colonial buildings, both ecclesiastical, civil and private, which should be declared national monuments, restored and preserved.

1182 LUJAN MUNOZ, LUIS. 1967c.

Protección y preservación de los bienes culturales, monumentos y lugares de interés artístico e histórico en la República de Guatemala. *AHG,* 19, 1:118–124.

A plea for a law to protect the art monuments of Guatemala.

1183 LUJAN MUNOZ, LUIS. 1968a.

La plaza mayor de Santiago de Guatemala hacia 1678. *AHG,* 20, 1:53–94.

The same material as LUJAN MUNOZ . . . 1967a, *La catedral* etc. above.

1184 LUJAN MUNOZ, LUIS. 1968b.

Síntesis de la arquitectura en Guatemala. Guatemala: Universidad de San Carlos de Guatemala.

LC/NA776.L8

A pamphlet of 31 pages. Well illustrated. Colonial architecture, mainly of Antigua.

A second edition, Colección Universitarios, 1972.

1185 LUJAN MUNOZ, LUIS. 1969.

La plaza mayor de Santiago de Guatemala hacia 1678. Guatemala: Instituto de Antropología e Historia, Publicación Especial, No. 3.

An extended treatment of the same subject as LUJAN MUNOZ, 1967a above. Transcribes some contemporary documents and includes some plans and photographs.

1186 LUJAN MUNOZ, LUIS. 1971a.

Guía de los museos de Guatemala. Guatemala: Instituto de Antropología e Historia.

Well-illustrated pamphlet outlining the history as well as the collections of all the museums in the Republic of Guatemala.

1187 LUJAN MUNOZ, LUIS. 1971b.

Notas sobre el uso de máscaras en Guatemala. *Guatemala indígena.* 6, 2/3: 129–145.

The ritual mask from Pre-Columbian times through the colonial and modern periods. Formal aspect of style of masks treated, as well as ethnological implications.

1188 LUJAN MUNOZ, LUIS. 1974.

Legislación protectora de los bienes culturales de Guatemala. Guatemala: Instituto de Antropología e Historia.

The legal instruments to protect the art, architectural and archaeological monuments of Guatemala. Contains an introduction as well as the actual texts of all the laws currently in effect.

1189 MARINAS OTERO, LUIS. 1959.

La pintura en Honduras. Tegucigalpa: Universidad Nacional Autónoma de Honduras, Departamento de Extensión Universitaria. Cuadernos universitarios, no. 1.

Pamphlet of 21 pages with a concise history of painting, mainly nineteenth and twentieth centuries.

1190 MARINAS OTERO, LUIS. 1960.

La escultura en Honduras, *Cuadernos hispanoamericanos* [Madrid], 42, 125:215–223.

A short general account of the religious sculptures of the colonial period.

1191 MARKMAN, S.D. 1951.

The Colonial Architecture of Antigua Guatemala, 1543–1773. *Archaeology,* 4:204–212.

Brief summary of the Antiguan architectural style.

1192 MARKMAN, S.D. 1956.

Santa Cruz, Antigua Guatemala and the Spanish Colonial Architecture of Central America. *JSAH,* 15:12–19.

An article on a stylistically important church of eighteenth-century date.

1193 MARKMAN, S.D. 1961a.

Las Capuchinas: an 18th century convent in Antigua Guatemala. *JSAH,* 20:27–33.

The unusual plan of one cloister, circular, of this nunnery has no Hispano-American or Iberian antecedents. See also MESA and GISBERT below for a discussion of the plan and LUJAN MUNOZ, JORGE 1963, above.

1194 MARKMAN, S.D. 1961b.

Stylistic Connections of the Architecture of Colonial Guatemala and Central America with that of Contemporary Spain. In *American Philosophical Society: Yearbook, 1960* (Philadelphia), pp. 599–600.

The results of a physical inspection of the baroque architecture of Spain in search of possible stylistic antecedents of the architecture of the Reino de Guatemala.

1195   MARKMAN, S.D. 1963.

San Cristóbal de las Casas. Sevilla: Escuela de Estudios HispanoAmericanos.

A monograph on the urban history and colonial architecture of San Cristóbal de las Casas, Chiapas, Mexico.

1196   MARKMAN, S.D. 1966a.

The Antiguan Non-Architectonic Pilaster or 'Estípite.' In *XXXVI Congreso Internacional de Americanistas, España, 1964.* Sevilla. 4:285.

The various types of non-architectonic pilaster shafts seen on Santa Clara, Escuela de Cristo, La Candelaria, Santa Isabel and La Merced in Antigua Guatemala.

1197   MARKMAN, S.D. 1966b.

The Colonial Architecture of Antigua Guatemala. Philadelphia: American Philosophical Society.

LC/NA 777A6M3

A monograph on the urban history, architecture, labor and the building trades, building activity in the Reino de Guatemala and other matters pertinent to architectural history. 220 illus., bibliography, documentary sources, index.

1198   MARKMAN, S.D. 1966c.

The Non-Spanish Labor Force in the Development of the Colonial Architecture of Guatemala. In *XXXVI Congreso Internacional de Americanistas, España, 1964.* Sevilla. 4:189–194.

Mestizos, mulattoes and *ladinos* in the building trades. Absence of indigenous influence.

Also in Spanish translation in *BCIHE*, 3, (1965):85–97.

1199   MARKMAN, SIDNEY D. 1966d.

The Plaza Mayor of Guatemala City. *JSAH,* 35:181–196.

The plan of the Plaza Mayor of the capital of the Reino de Guatemala after its removal from Antigua after 1773. The fountain, the cathedral, the Capitanía and the Portal de Comercio.

1200   MARKMAN, S.D. 1966e.

Proyecto de institución para proteger la arquitectura y el arte colonial de Guatemala. *RUSC,* 69:75–83.

A plan for the establishing of a legal body to preserve the colonial art and architecture of Guatemala.

1201   MARKMAN, S.D. 1968.

Mudéjar Traits in the Baroque Architecture of Colonial Guatemala. In *XXXVII Congreso Internacional de Americanistas, Argentina, 1966.* Buenos Aires. 3:251–258.

The afterlife of *mudéjar* craft traditions in the architecture of the Reino de Guatemala.

1202 MARKMAN, S.D. 1969.

Mudéjar Influence on the Colonial Architecture of Central America. In *American Philosophical Society: Yearbook 1968*, (Philadelphia), pp. 634–636.

A report on a physical inspection and study of the *mudéjar* architecture of Spain in search of possible antecedents for the vestiges of that style in the Reino de Guatemala.

1203 MARKMAN, S.D. 1971.

Pueblos de españoles y pueblos de indios en el Reino de Guatemala. *BCIHE*, 12:76–97.

The two types of urban centers established in the sixteenth century by the Spaniards in Central America.

A Spanish translation of the item immediately below.

1204 MARKMAN, S.D. 1973.

Pueblos de Españoles and Pueblos de Indios. In *Verhandlungen der XXXVIII Internationalem Amerikanisten Kongresess, Stuttgart-München, 1968*. München, 4:189–199.

The original English version of the item immediately above.

1205 MAZA, FRANCISCO DE LA. 1956.

Arte colonial en Chiapas. *Ateneo* [Tuxtla Gutiérrez, Chiapas], 6:59–122.

Gives data on most of the colonial buildings in San Cristóbal de las Casas, the little church of "La Quinta del Aserradero," and the fountain in Chiapa de Corzo, Chiapas.

1206 MENCOS GUAJARDO-FAJARDO, FRANCISCO XAVIER. 1950.

Arquitectos de la época colonial en Guatemala. *Anuario EA*, 7:163–209.

Some documentary material from Archivo de Indias, Seville, on architects who worked in Central America, especially Antigua Guatemala.

1207 MENCOS GUAJARDO-FAJARDO, FRANCISCO XAVIER. 1951.

La arquitectura hispano-americana en la capitanía general de Guatemala. Unpublished. Tesis doctoral, Universidad de Madrid, Facultad de Filosofía y Letras.

Based entirely on documents in Archivo de Indias. Transcribes many important ones. Very little on style, rather an historical documentation of buildings, mainly in Antigua Guatemala.

1208 MESA, JOSE DE and TERESA GISBERT. 1963.

El edificio circular de capuchinas, en Antigua Guatemala. *AIAA*, 16: 13–27.

The circular cloister may have served as a public bath house. See MARKMAN . . . 1961, *Las Capuchinas,* above. Also LUJAN MUNOZ, JORGE . . . 1963, *El monasterio,* above.

1209 METHODS OF CONSTRUCTION. 1776.

Metodo regular en formación de los cimientos. Sobre colacación de horcones. Instrucción para construir.

AGG: A1.10.3 (1776) 31.361-4049.

Three documents on building construction techniques of the late eighteenth century in Guatemala.

1210 MOYSSEN, XAVIER. 1969.

Como se construía una catedral en Indias en el siglo XVII. *Boletín Instituto Nacional de Antropología e Historia* [México], 38:1–10.

The seventeenth-century painting discovered in Mexico depicting the construction of the cathedral of Antigua Guatemala. See also above LUJAN MUNOZ, LUIS . . . 1967, *La catedral,* for the same.

1210a NAVARRETE, CARLOS. 1966.

The Chiapanec History and Culture. Provo, Utah: New World Archaeological Foundation, Brigham Young University.

LC/E51.N38

A well-documented history of the Chiapa de Corzo, Chiapas, including material on urbanism and architecture of both the Pre-Columbian and colonial periods. See Section II, above, for further details.

1211 OLVERA, JORGE. 1950.

Joyas de la arquitectura colonial de Chiapas. *Chiapas* [Tuxtla Gutiérrez, Chiapas]. 2, 13:14–17 and 29–39.

The architecture of three Dominican churches and conventos in Chiapas Mexico: Tecpatán, Copainalá, and Copanaguastla.

1212 OLVERA, JORGE. 1951.

Copanaguastla, joya del plateresco en Chiapas. *Ateneo* [Tuxtla Gutiérrez, Chiapas], 1, 2:115–136.

The history of the Dominican convento and church as well as a stylistic analysis. Has a plan of the building.

1213 OLVERA, JORGE. 1957.

El convento de Copanaguastla: otra joya de la arquitectura plateresca. *Tlatoani* [México], 2:4–13.

Recapitulates the item immediately above.

1214 O'NEALE, LILA M. 1945.

Textiles of Highland Guatemala. Washington, D.C.: Carnegie Institution.

Well-written scholarly monograph on textiles and clothing of Guatemalan highlands in first half of twentieth century. Patterns and techniques, traditional, provide important ethnographic parallels for colonial and Pre-Columbian studies of art motifs.

1215 O'NEALE, LILA M. 1965.

Tejidos de los altiplanos de Guatemala. Guatemala: Seminario de Integración Social Guatemalteca. 2 vols.

Spanish translation by Edith Recourat C. of the foregoing item.

1216 OSBORNE, LILY DE JONGH. 1945.

Arterias comerciales. *ASGH,* 20:320–325.

The production and commerce of contemporary Indian arts and crafts in Guatemala. Ethnographic parallels for colonial and Pre-Columbian trade.

1217 OSBORNE, LILY DE JONGH. 1965.

Indian Crafts of Guatemala and El Salvador. Norman, Okla.: University of Oklahoma Press.

Mainly on contemporary textiles, a tradition stemming back to colonial times and beyond. Iconology of decorative motifs, some of which stem back to colonial and Pre-Columbian times.

1218 PALM, ERWIN WALTER. 1947.

Observaciones sobre la arquitectura colonial en Honduras. *BPAU,* 71, 3: 121–134.

The colonial architecture of Comayagua and Tegucigalpa. Some stylistic observations.

1219 PARDO, J.J. and PEDRO ZAMORA CASTELLANOS. 1943.

Guía turística de las ruinas de la Antigua Guatemala. Guatemala: Sociedad de Geografía e História de Guatemala.

The best guide book to the city of Antigua Guatemala. Text was written by Pardo, late director of the Archivo General del Gobierno in Guatemala City, who had at his disposal all the contemporary documents relating to the architecture. He does not cite these documents, unfortunately, but in rare instances are the historical data in error. In fact, they are often corroborated when the documents he read are inadvertently come upon in the archives.

Has an excellent plan of the present-day city as well as one of the colonial period.

A second edition with a long essay on art and architecture of Antigua by Luis Luján Muñoz was published in 1968. See item immediately below.

1220 PARDO, J.J., PEDRO ZAMORA CASTELLANOS and LUIS LUJAN MUNOZ. 1968.

Guía de Antigua Guatemala. 2a ed. Guatemala. Editorial "José de Pineda Ibarra".

The same as the item immediately above with an introduction by Luis Luján Muñoz on the art and architecture.

1220a PAZ, NICOLAS DE. 1771.

Novena y bosquejo . . .

See Section I for complete title. Deals with the basilica of Esquipulas, Guatemala.

1221 PAZ SOLORZANO, JUAN. 1949.

Historia del Señor Crucificado de Esquipulas. 2a. ed. Guatemala: Unión Tipográfica, Castañeda, Avila y Cía.

See Section II above for description of first edition. This is a reprint.

1221a POPENOE, DOROTHY. 1933 (1935).

Santiago de los Caballeros de Guatemala. Cambridge: Harvard University Press.

LC/F1476.G92P7   DUL/972.81 P826

A romantic history of the colonial capital of Central America. Illustrated with some drawings by the author who restored an old colonial mansion which figures in *The House of Antigua* by Louis Adamic, New York, Harper and Bros., 1937.

Some data on colonial architecture culled from secondary sources.

1222 RECINOS, ADRIAN. 1949.

La ciudad de Guatemala, 1524–1773. AHG, 1, 1:57–62.

The first Spanish town in Ciudad Vieja, Guatemala. An interpretation of the act of founding by Pedro de Alvarado.

1223 REINA VALENZUELA, JOSE. 1959.

Estampas de Comayagua. Revista de la Sociedad de Geografía e Historia de Honduras [Tegucigalpa], 38, 7–9:57–63.

History of the colonial period. Some discussion of the art and architecture.

1224 REINA VALENZUELA, JOSE. 1965–66.

Construcción y organización de la Iglesia Catedral de Comayagua. *Revista de la Sociedad de Geografía e Historia de Honduras* [Tegucigalpa], 15 (agosto 1965):166; 16 (juno-julio-agosto, 1966):196.

The construccion history of the cathedral of Comayagua, Honduras.

1225 *Revista de Guatemala.* Guatemala. 1945–.

A literary and art journal edited by Luis Cardoza y Aragón. Well-written and illustrated articles on colonial and Precolumbian art and archaeology as well as poetry and short literary pieces, criticism and book reviews. Suspended in 1946(?).

1226 RIVERA Y GALVEZ, JOSE DE. 1773.

Supposedly published a plan of Antigua Guatemala in 1773 which included the elevations of the buildings. Whereabouts unknown.

1227 RODRIGUEZ DEL VALLE, MARIANA. 1958.

El castillo de San Felipe del Golfo Dulce. *Anuario EA* 17:1–103.

The architecture of a Spanish fortress on the Atlantic side of Guatemala based entirely on documents in *AGI*. Some plans and photographs by F. Francisco Ferrus Roig.

1228 RUBIN DE LA BORBOLLA, DANIEL and HUGO CEREZO. 1953.

Guatemala: monumentos históricos y arqueológicos. México: Instituto Panamericano de Geografía e Historia. Publicación núm. 144.

LC/F1401.P153   DUL/910.6 I59P no. 144

General survey of pre-Columbian and colonial monuments of Guatemala.

1229 RUBIN DE LA BORBOLLA, DANIEL F. and PEDRO RIVAS. 1953.

Honduras: monumentos históricos y arqueológicos. México: Instituto Panamericano de Geografía e Historia, Publicación núm. 146.

LC/F1401.P153   DUL/910.6 I59P no. 146

General survey of pre-Columbian and colonial monuments of Honduras.

1230 RUBIO MANE, JORGE IGNACIO. 1941.

La casa de Montejo en Mérida de Yucatán. Mérida: Imprenta Universitaria.

History of the house of the conquistador based on documentary materials. Little on architectural style or character.

1231 RUBIO Y MUNOZ-BOCANEGRA, ANGEL. 1950.

Panamá: monumentos históricos y arqueológicos. México: Instituto Panamericano de Geografía e Historia, Comisión de Historia. Publicación núm. 23.

DUL/910.6 I59P no. 109.

General survey of the pre-Columbian and colonial monuments of Panama.

1231a SALAZAR, FRAY JUAN JOSE. 1754a.

Piedra fundamental . . .

See Section I, SALAZAR, 1754a, for description. Deals with church of San José in Antigua Guatemala.

1231b SALAZAR, FRAY JUAN JOSE. 1754b.

Relación descriptiva . . .

See Section I, SALAZAR, 1754b, for a description. Deals with church of San Francisco in Antigua Guatemala.

1232   EL SALVADOR. SAN SALVADOR, 1935–40.

Has some articles on art. In the library of the Pan American Union, Washington, D.C.

1233   SALVATIERRA, SOFONIAS. 1937/38.

Los castillos en el Reino de Guatemala. *ASGH*, 14:158–170.

A survey of Spanish fortifications in Central America. History, does not treat matters of military architecture.

1234   SENN BONILLA, JORGE and DOLORES YURRITA G., editors. 1974.

Antigua Guatemala. Programa de puesta en valor. Primera fase. Guatemala: Instituto Guatemalteco de Turismo.

The first report of the investigations of the commission in charge of the restoration and preservation of the colonial city carried out under the direction of Carlos Flores Marini of the Organización de Estados Americanos and Ricardo Camacho Fahsen of the Instituto Guatemalateco de Turismo.

Included are many photographs and city plans as well as plans of some of the important colonial buildings.

1235   SZECSY, JANOS DE. 1953.

Santiago de los Caballeros de Goathemala en Almolonga. Investigaciones del año 1950. Guatemala: Editorial de Educación Pública.

LC/F1476.G92S9

A report on the excavations carried out in 1950 in Ciudad Vieja, Guatemala in which were uncovered the foundations of some early sixteenth-century buildings.

1236   TARACENA FLORES, A. 1970.

Los terremotos de Guatemala. Album gráfico conmemorativo del cincuentenario, 1917/1918–1968. Guatemala.

An album of photographs with views of Guatemala City at the time of the earthquakes of 1917. Important for views of late colonial buildings prior to their destruction and in some cases, their subsequent reconstruction.

See CORONADO Y PACHECO, 1918, above, for a pamphlet on the same subject.

1237   TERMER, FRANZ. 1929/30.

La Antigua, una ciudad encantada. *ASGH*, 6:326–332.

Literary description of Antigua Guatemala by a German geographer. Nomenclature of style and dates of buildings not sound.

1238   TERMER, FRANZ. 1934–35.

La habitación rural en la América del centro, a través de los tiempos. *ASGH*, 11:391–409.

The private dwelling of pre-Columbian and colonial times and its afterlife in the modern period.

1239 TOBAR CRUZ, PEDRO. 1966.

Fundación de la congregación de San Felipe Neri en la ciudad de Santiago de los Caballeros, por el venerable padre Bernardino Obando y Obregón. *AHG*, 18, 1:51–58.

The history of the church and convento of Escuela de Cristo in Antigua Guatemala.

1240 TOLEDO PALOMO, RICARDO. 1956.

La fuente de la Plaza Mayor de la Nueva Guatemala. *AHG*, 8, 1:32–46.

The monumental fountain, now located in the Plaza de España, of late eighteenth-century date. See also above MARKMAN . . . 1966, *The Plaza Mayor*.

1241 TOLEDO PALOMO, RICARDO. 1959.

Capilla abierta o capilla de Indios. *AHG*, 11, 1:40–43.

The problem of the origin of the open chapel. See also Section III above, BONET CORREA . . . 1963, *Antecedentes*.

1242 TOLEDO PALOMO, RICARDO. 1962.

Influencia francesa en el arte guatemalteco. *AHG*, 14, 2:66–74.

French influence on painting and sculpture in colonial and post-colonial Guatemala.

1243 TOLEDO PALOMO, RICARDO. 1963.

El templo de Esquipulas y la arquitectura antigüena. *ASGH*, 36:392–416.

An architectural study of the basilica in Esquipulas, Guatemala.

1244 TOLEDO PALOMO, RICARDO. 1964.

Apuntes en torno al barroco guatemalteco. *Revista de la Universidad de San Carlos*, 63:91–137.

The baroque architectural style in Guatemala. Problems of style and nomenclature.

1244a TOLEDO PALOMO, RICARDO. 1965.

La ruina de la cabecera del corregimiento de Chiquimula. *ASGH*, 38: 99–149.

The destruction of the town of Chiquimula in the late eighteenth century and its effect on the monuments.

1245 TOLEDO PALOMO, RICARDO. 1966.

Aportaciones del grabado europeo al arte de Guatemala. *AIIE*, 35:47–57.

European prints from the seventeenth century and later on the painting and sculpture of Guatemala.

1246   TOLEDO PALOMO, RICARDO. 1967.

Aportaciones del grabado europeo al arte de Guatemala. *AHG,* 19, 2: 94–105.

A reprint of the foregoing item.

1247   TOSCANO, SALVADOR. 1940.

La escultura colonial en Guatemala. *AIIE,* 2, 5:45–53.

LC/N16.M5

An early study of colonial sculpture in Guatemala. Has some illustrations.

1248   TOSCANO, SALVADOR. 1942.

Chiapas: su arte y su historia coloniales. *AIIE,* 2, 8:27–43.

A survey of the architecture in Chiapas, Mexico. Some treatment of sculpture. One of the first art-historical studies of the style there.

1249   TRIGUEROS BADA, ROBERTO. 1954.

Las defensas estratégicas del Río San Juan de Nicaragua. Sevilla: Escuela de Estudios Hispano Americanos.

A study of the defensive measures taken during the colonial period. Based on documentary sources. Includes plans, maps and other illustrative material.

1250   VAQUERO, JOAQUIN. 1946a.

Iglesia de Panchimalco. *RI.* 7, 23:101–106.

The colonial church. Lacks historical data. Photographs and a floor plan.

1251   VAQUERO, JOAQUIN. 1946b.

Iglesia de San Sebastián. *RI.* 7, 24:313–318.

Mudéjar traits as in Panchimalco. No historical data. Photographs.

1252   VAQUERO, JOAQUIN. 1946c.

Iglesia de Metapán. *RI.* 7, 25:575–580.

Late colonial church, 1743, photographs and a floor plan.

1253   VARONA, ESTEBAN ANTONIO DE. 1949.

Orosí. San José: Trejos Hermanos.

LC/NA 5274.07V3

The history and architecture of the little church in Orosí, Costa Rica.

1254   VIDAL, MERCEDES LUISA. 1955.

La catedral de Panamá. Buenos Aires.

Pamphlet of 65 pages. A popular account of the history of the cathedral.

1255 WAUCHOPE, ROBERT. 1938.

Modern Maya Houses: A Study of their Archaeological Significance. Washington, D.C.: Carnegie Institution of Washington. Publication no. 502.

A study of the modern domestic dwelling. Examples from various parts of highland Guatemala and from Yucatan. Of value for studies of colonial non-descript domestic architecture.

1256 YELA GUNTHER, RAFAEL. 1938/39.

Arte colonial en Guatemala. *ASGH,* 15:422–432.

A lecture given over the radio. Lots of generalities. Some good photographs.

1257 YPSILANTI DE MOLDAVIA, GEORGE. 1937.

Monografía de Comayagua, 1537–1937. Tegucigalpa: Talleres Tipográficos Nacionales.

LC/F1516.C72Y6.

Some data on the founding of the churches of Comayagua, Honduras. Sources of information not cited.

1258 YPSILANTI DE MOLDAVIA, GEORGE. 1944a.

Monografía de la parroquia del señor San Miguel de Heredia de Tegucigalpa. Tegucigalpa: Talleres Tipográficos Nacionales.

LC/BX 4165.HY6

The history of the cathedral of Tegucigalpa Hondures. Based on secondary sources which are not cited.

1259 YPSILANTI DE MOLDAVIA, GEORGE. 1944b.

El primer pintor hondureño. *Boletín de la Biblioteca y Archivo Nacionales* [Tegucigalpa]. 4, 7–8:79–81.

Brief note on Jose Manuel Gómez, born c. 1725, educated in Guatemala, worked in Honduras.

1260 ZAPATERO, JUAN MANUEL. 1973.

El fuerte de San Fernando de Omoa (Hondures) llave de la antigua Real Audiencia de Guatemala. *Asinto* [Madrid], No. 78.

Study of an important fort based on documentary materials. Reprinted *BCIHE,* 18 (1974):9–47.

Section V

BIBLIOGRAPHY

Works dealing with printed sources covered in Sections I, II, III and IV.

1261 ADAMS, ELEANOR B. 1952.

A Bio-bibliography of Franciscan authors in Colonial Central America. *Americas.* 8:431–473; 9:37–38.

See item immediately below, containing the same material.

1262 ADAMS, ELEANOR B. 1953.

A Bio-bibliography of Franciscan Authors in Colonial Central America. Washington, D.C.: Academy of American Franciscan History.

Many writers hitherto unknown, many of whose works are lost, as well as outstanding figures such as VASQUEZ and GOICOECHEA, see Section I above.

1263 AGRUPACION BIBLIOGRAFICA CUBANA JOSE TORIBIO MEDINA. 1958–60.

Bibliografía de Centroamérica y del Caribe. La Habana: Imprenta Nacional de Cuba. 3 vols.

DUL/Bibl. 015.728 B582

General bibliography.

1264 ALCINA FRANCH, JOSE and JOSEFINA PALOP MARTINEZ. 1958.

América en la época de Carlos V. Madrid: Asociación Hispano-americana de Historia.

A bibliography of works published since 1900 dealing with subject matter of sixteenth-century date. Pages 107–120, for items on Yucatan and Central America. See next item for a similar bibliography for the rest of the sixteenth and the seventeenth century.

1265 ALCINA FRANCH, JOSE and JOSEFINA PALOP MARTINEZ. 1962.

América en la época de los Austrias. Madrid: Asociación Hispano-americana de Historia.

A bibliography of works published since 1900, and completing the list assembled in the foregoing item.

A well-selected listing, but no comments or description of contents are given. Arranged by subject matter. Central American items 113–131.

1266 BANDELIER, ADOLPH FRANCIS. 1880–81.

Notes on the Bibliography of Yucatan and Central America. *In Proceedings of the American Antiquarian Society* (Worcester, Mass.), new series, vol. 1.

DUL/905 A512

A pioneer study and listing of many MSS and published books. Many of the works he saw no longer exist: some have turned up in the library of the University of Texas.

1267 BENDFELDT ROJAS, LOURDES and ALBA ROSA CALDERON DE MUNOZ. 1964.

Bibliografía filosófica de publicaciones de las Universidades de Costa Rica y San Carlos de Guatemala y de autores que exhibió la Biblioteca Nacional. Guatemala: Tipografía Nacional.

LC/Z7125.B4

A catalogue of an exhibit of books, mainly recent.

1268 BERISTAIN DE SOUZA, JOSE MARIANO (fl. 1756–1817). 1816–1821.

Biblioteca hispano americana. México: Imprenta de el Tiempo. 3 vols.

DUL/R016.98 B511

A late colonial work. Most useful in tracing editions of works printed in Mexico, Guatemala, and elsewhere. Appeared in various later editions in 1883, 1897, 1898, and 1947.

1269 BRASSEUR DE BOURBOURG, CHARLES ETIENNE. 1871.

Bibliotheque méxico-guatémalienne. Paris: Maisonneuve & Cie.

LC/Z1431.B82   DUL/Z972 qB823B

A general bibliography of printed works and MSS by an eminent anthropologist and archaeologist. Both pre-Columbian and colonial items.

1270 BROWN UNIVERSITY. 1865–1871.

The Catalogue of the John Carter Library. Books Printed 1493–1700. Providence, R.I.: Brown University Press. 3 parts in 4 vols.

See BROWN UNIVERSITY, 1919–1931, for a description of the contents.

1271 BROWN UNIVERSITY. 1875–1882.

The Catalogue of the John Carter Library. Books Printed 1482–1700. Providence, R.I.: Brown University Press.

A supplement to the 1865–1871 edition. See BROWN UNIVERSITY, 1919–1931, for a description of contents.

1271 BROWN UNIVERSITY. 1919–1931.

The Catalogue of the John Carter Library. Books Printed 1675–1700(?) Providence, R.I.: Brown University Press. 5 parts in 3 vols.

Brings the 1865–1871 edition up-to-date. Reprinted in 1973.

1,852 books, pamphlets, broadsides, and atlases in English, Spanish, French, Dutch, German, Portuguese, Italian, Swedish, Danish, and Icelandic.

Some items are of interest for Central America. Over half deal with the United States. Over fifty items deal with American Indians and Indian languages.

1273 BROWN UNIVERSITY. 1973.

The Catalogue of the John Carter Library. Short Title List of Additions—Books Printed 1471–1700. Providence, R.I.: Brown University Press.

See BROWN UNIVERSITY, 1919-1931, for a description of the contents.

1274 BURRUS, S.J., ERNEST J. 1973.

Religious Chroniclers and Historians: A Summary with Annotated Bibliography. *HMAI,* 13, part 2:138–185.

A survey of published works by religious authors during the colonial period on Mexico and Central America. Among those treated are Mercedarians, Franciscans, and Dominican chroniclers including: ESPINOSA, ISIDRO FELIX DE; XIMENEZ, FRANCISCO DE; PAREJA, FRANCISCO DE; REMESAL, ANTONIO DE; and VASQUEZ, FRANCISCO DE. See Section I for bibliographical references to the above.

1275 BUTLER, RUTH LAPHAM. 1950.

Guide to the Hispanic American Historical Review. Durham, N.C.: Duke University Press.

DUL/X Per H673AB

An index.

1276 CALIFORNIA. UNIVERSITY. LIBRARY. 1928–30.

Spain and Spanish America in the Libraries of the University of California; A Catalogue of Books. Berkeley. 2 vols.

Vol. 1, General and Departmental Libraries, comp. by Alice L. Lyser; Vol. 2, the Bancroft Library.

1277 CALIFORNIA. UNIVERSITY. BERKELEY. BANCROFT LIBRARY. 1964.

Catalog of Printed Books. Boston, Mass.: G. K. Hall and Co. 22 vols.

Excellent library for Latin America. Many original editions of colonial period.

1278 CLINE, HOWARD F. 1966.

Guide to Ethnohistorical Sources: A Progress Report. In XXXVI Congreso Internacional de Americanistas, España, 1964. Seville. 2:133–144.

A preview of the materials subsequently published in volumes 12–15 of the *Handbook of Middle American Indians.* Austin, Texas. University of Texas Press, 1972–1975.

1279 CLINE, HOWARD F., editor. 1972.

Guide to Ethnohistorical Sources, *Part One.* v. 12. *HMAI.*

See chpt. 2 for historical notes on the development of minor political jurisdictions, by GERHARD, 1972, Section II, No. 508, especially sections XVI and XXII which are concerned with colonial Central America.

Also other chapters, all dealing with *Relaciones Geograficas* in Middle America.

1280 CLINE, HOWARD F., editor. 1973.

Guide to Ethnohistorical Sources, *Part Two. HMAI.* v. 13.

Chp. 12, 42–137, by WARREN, 1973, and chp. 13, 138–185, by BURRUS, 1973, below, deal with writings and chronicles by secular and religious authors of the colonial period in Central America.

1281 DIAZ, VICTOR MIGUEL. 1930.

Historia de la imprenta en Guatemala desde los tiempos de la colonia, hasta la época actual, 1660–1930. Guatemala: Tipografía Nacional.

Written to commemorate the opening of the new building to house the Tipografía Nacional.

1282 DOLE, HENRY GRATTAN. 1935.

A Tentative Bibliography of the Belles Lettres of the Republics of Central America. Cambridge, Mass.: Harvard University Press.

A bibliographical survey of the literature in the five Central American countries. Recent works mainly.

1283 DURON, JORGE FIDEL. 1943.

Repertorio bibliográfico hondureño. Tegucigalpa: Imprenta Calderón.

A catalogue of the books in an exhibition, including materials sent from Guatemala, Chile, and the United States.

1284 GARCIA ICAZABALCETA, JOAQUIN (fl. 1825–1894). 1866.

Apuntes para un catálago de escritores en lenguas indígenas de América. México. Reprinted, New York: Lenox Hill Publishing Co., 1968.

Privately printed by the author in an edition of sixty copies. A second edition, *Obras de D. Joaquín García Icazabalceta.* México, 1896–99. v. 8, pp. 5–181. See also Section VI, below.

c

1285 GAVARRETE, JUAN. n.d.

Colección de documentos históricos.

According to BATRES JAUREGUI, *América Central*, v. 1, 36, see Section II above, he owned the collection which was put together under the direction of Gavarrete from 1865 on and which was published by the Museo Nacional. He also calls this collection *Colección histórica de la Sociedad Económica*. Part of the MS was placed in the Biblioteca Nacional and part was lost. Its whereabouts are not known today though it may still be in the Biblioteca Nacional or possibly in the library of the Sociedad de Geografía e Historia in Guatemala City.

1286 GROPP, A.E. 1941.

Guide to libraries and archives in Central America and the West Indies, Panama, Bermuda, and British Guiana. New Orleans: Middle American Research Institute, Tulane University.

LC/F1421.T95   DUL/972.01 qT917 M no. 10

1287 GROPP, AUTHUR ERIC. 1960.

Bibliografía sobre las bibliotecas nacionales de los países latino-americanos y sus publicaciones. Washington, D.C.: Unión Panamericana.

LC/Z1009.P18 no. 50.   DUL/016 P187B no. 50.

General information on library holdings, including those in Central America.

1288 GROPP, ARTHUR ERIC. 1968.

A Bibliography of Latin American Bibliographies. Metuchen, N.J.: Scarecrow Press.

LC/Z1601.A2G76

An updated version of JONES, 1942, below.

1289 GROPP, ARTHUR ERIC. 1971.

A Bibliography of Latin American Bibliographies. Supplement. Metuchen, N.J.: Scarecrow Press.

A supplement to the foregoing item.

1290 GUATEMALA. MUSEO NACIONAL DE ANTROPOLOGIA. 1948.

A collection of books pertaining to the archaeology, ethnology, and anthropology of Mexico, Guatemala, and Central America with particular reference to Guatemala, presented by Matilda Geddings Gray to the Museo Nacional de Antropología de Guatemala. San Francisco.

1291 GUATEMALA. TIPOGRAFIA NACIONAL. 1944.

Catálogo general de libros, folletos y revistos editados en la Tipografía nacional de Guatemala desde 1892 hasta 1943. Guatemala. Tipografia Nacional.

DUL/R-015.728lG918

A catalogue of all the books printed, many of which are listed in this bibliography.

1291a GUTIERREZ, RAMON. 1973.

Notas para una bibliografía hispanoamericana de arquitectura 1526–1875. Resistencia, Arg.: Universidad Nacional del Nordeste, Dirección de Bibliotecas, Departamento de Historia de la Arquitectura.

An extensive annotated listing of MSS and printed works dealing with architecture, both Spanish and Hispano-American, preceeded by a critical study of those used in Hispano America. Locations of MSS and rare books are also given, both in public libraries as well as in private collections.

Items are arranged in chronological order, so that those pertinent to the Reino de Guatemala are scattered through the text.

1292 *Handbook of Latin American Studies.* Cambridge: Harvard University Press; Gainesville, Fla.: University of Florida Press. v. 1. 1936–.

DUL/R016.98 H241H

Latin American materials in general, including humanities and social sciences: history, anthropology, economics, art history, and sundry subjects. Entries are well annotated by specialists in their respective fields.

1293 HARVARD UNIVERSITY. WIDENER LIBRARY. 1967.

Latin America. Cambridge, Mass.: Harvard University Press. 2 vols. Widener Library Shelf Lists, vols. 5–6.

A list of titles on Latin America.

1294 HELLMUTH, NICOLAS M. 1970.

Preliminary Bibliography of the Chol. Lacondon, Yucatec Lacandon, Chol, Itza, Mopan and Quejache of the Southern Maya Lowlands, 1524–1969. Greeley, *Museum, of Anthropology. Katunob Occasional Publications in Mesoamerican Anthropology,* no. 4. University of Northern Colorado, Greeley.

Mimeographed.

An annotated bibliography designed for ethnohistorical, ethnographical and archeological research. Many items of colonial import.

1295 HISPANIC SOCIETY OF AMERICA. 1962.

Catalogue of the Library of the Hispanic Society of America (New York). Boston: G.K. Hall. 10 vols.

First Supplement. Boston: G.K. Hall, 1970. 4 vols.

A card catalogue of over 100,000 entries. Numerous items relevant to Central America.

1296   JONES, CECIL KNIGHT. 1942.

A Bibliography of Latin American Bibliographies. 2nd ed. Washington, D.C.: U.S. Government Printing Office.

LC/Z1601.A2J7 1942   DUL/R061.01 J76HA

See GROPP, 1968, 1971, above for an enlarged and updated edition.

1297   LINES, JORGE A. 1967a.

Anthropological Bibliography of Aboriginal Costa Rica: Bibliografía antropológica aborigen de Costa Rica. San José, C.R.: Tropical Science Center.

LC/1208.C6L5

1298   LINES, JORGE A. 1967b.

Anthropological Bibliography of Aboriginal Guatemala, British Honduras; Bibliografía antropológica aborigen de Guatemala, Belice. San José, C.R.: Tropical Science Center.

LC/Z1208.G8L5

1299   LINES, JORGE A., EDWIN M. SHOOK and MICHAEL D. OLIEN. 1965.

Anthropological Bibliography of Aboriginal El Salvador. Bibliografía antropológica aborigen de El Salvador. San José, C.R.: Tropical Science Center.

LC/Z1208.S2L5

1300   LOPEZ SERRANO, MATILDE. 1942.

Bibliografía de arte español y americano, 1936–1940. Madrid: Instituto "Diego Velázquez", Consejo Superior de Investigaciones Científicas.

DUL/WCL 016.7 B582

1301   LOZOYA, JUAN CONTRERAS Y LOPEZ DE AYALA, MARQUEZ DE. 1920.

Biblioteca de historia hispano-americana. Madrid.

1302   MCMURTIRE, DOUGLAS C. 1942.

A Preliminary Check List of Published Materials Relating to the History of Printing in Guatemala. Chicago: Chicago Club of Printing Hand Craftsmen.

DUL/655 M168P v.4, no. 6

A pamphlet.

1303   MEDINA, J. TORIBIO (fl.1852–1930.) 1897–1907.

Biblioteca hispano-americana (1493–1810). Santiago de Chile: Impreso y Grabado en Casa del Autor. 7 vol.

LC/Z1610.M49   DUL/R–016.98 q491B

A fundamental work on colonial bibliography for all Hispano-America.

1304   MEDINA, JOSE TORIBIO 1910.

La Imprenta en Guatemala: 1660–1821. Santiago de Chile: Impreso en Casa del Autor.

LC/Z213.G9M4   DUL/015.7281 qM491G

The basic bibliography for the history of the printed book in Guatemala. Indispensable. Has illustrations of many title pages.

1305   MEDINA, JOSE TORIBIO. 1960.

La imprenta en Guatemala, 1660–1821. 2a ed. Guatemala: Tipografía Nacional de Guatemala. 2 vols.

LC/Z1461.M4 1960   DUL/015.728 qM491G

First edition, 1910. Books printed between 1660 and 1821. Long introduction includes biographies of early printers.

1306   MEDINA, JOSE TORIBIO (1852–1930). 1964.

La imprenta en Guatemala, 1660–1821. Amsterdam: N. Israel.

LC/Z1461.M4 1964

The same as the foregoing item.

1307   MOLINA ARGUELLO, CARLOS. 1969.

Bibliografía historiográfica de Nicaragua hasta 1954. *Revista conservadora de pensamiento centroamericano* [Managua]. 21:21–28.

Gives a resumé of the major works covering the history of Nicaragua.

1307a   MONTIGNANI, JOHN B. 1943.

Books on Latin America and its Art in the Metropolitan Museum Art Library. New York: Metropolitan Museum of Art.

A list of some 350 volumes covering all periods.

1308   MUNOZ, JUAN BAUTISTA. 1954. 1955. 1956.

Catálogo de la colección de Don Juan Bautista Muñoz. Madrid: Real Academia de Historia. 3 vols.

Has some materials on Central America, particularly Nicaragua.

1309   NEW YORK PUBLIC LIBRARY. 1961.

Dictionary Catalogue, History of the Americas Collection. Boston, Mass.: G.K. Hall. 28 vols.

A card catalogue.

1310   O'RYAN, JUAN ENRIQUE. 1897.

Bibliografía de la imprenta en Guatemala en los siglos XVII y XVIII. Santiago de Chile: Imprenta Elzevircana.

LC/Z1461.079

A forerunner of MEDINA, above.

1311 PAN AMERICAN UNION. COLUMBUS MEMORIAL LIBRARY. WASHINGTON, D.C. 1961, 1962.

Index to Latin American Periodicals. Boston: G.K. Hall. 2 vols.

Volume 1, 1961, volume 2, 1962. About 25,000 entries in each. A general index to published materials, mainly in the humanities and social sciences.

1312 PAN AMERICAN UNION. COLUMBUS MEMORIAL LIBRARY. WASHINGTON, D. C. 1962.

Index to Latin American Periodical Literature, 1929–1960. Boston: G.K. Hall. 8 vols.

A second series of two volumes published in 1967 covers the period 1961–65.

1312a PARRA, MANUEL GERMAN and WIGOBERTO JIMENEZ MORENO. 1954.

Bibliografía indigenista de México y Centro América. México: Instituto Nacional Indigenista, Memorias del Instituto Nacional Indigenista, vol 4.

DUL/Z970.1 P259B

An annotated bibliography useful for ethnohistorians dealing with Mexico and Guatemala and the rest of Central America.

1313 READ, BENJAMIN MAURICE. 1914.

Chronological Digest of the "Documentos inéditos del Archivo de las Indias." Albuquerque, N.M.: Albright and Anderson, Printers.

LC/DP3.C69

A chronological ordering of the vast number of documents published in 112 vols. in *Colección de documentos inéditos para la historia de España,* edited by Luis Torres de Mendoza between 1842 and 1895.

1314 REYES HERNANDEZ, MANUEL. 1971.

Catálogo del Museo del Libro Antiguo: impresos guatemaltecos de la época colonial. Guatemala: Editorial "José de Pineda Ibarra."

LC/Z213.G9A45

The catalogue of the book museum in Antigua Guatemala. A list of imprints as well as a history of the press in colonial Guatemala.

1315 REYES M., JOSE LUIS. 1960.

Bibliografía de los estudios geográficos de la República de Guatemala desde 1574 hasta nuestros días. Guatemala: Tipografía Nacional.

Material culled from published sources, mainly chroniclers and historians of the colonial period as well as more recent works.

1316 REYES M., JOSE LUIS. 1964.

Apuntes para una monografía de la Sociedad Económica de Amigos del País. Guatemala: Editorial del Ministerio de Educación Pública "José Pineda Ibarra".

A documentary source on the activities of this important society founded in 1794 and continued until the latter part of the nineteenth century, to 1881.

1317 REYES M., JOSE LUIS. 1969a.

Bibliografía de los estudios geográficos de la Republica de Guatemala desde 1574 hasta nuestros dias. Guatemala: Ministerio de Educacion Publica, "Jose de Pineda Ibarra."

LC/Z1467.G4R4

A reprint of the 1960 edition, above.

1318 REYES M., JOSE LUIS. 1969b.

Bibliografía de la imprenta en Guatemala. Adiciones de 1700–1900. Guatemala: Ministerio de Educación.

LC/Z1461.R43

1319 RODRIGUEZ, MARIO and VINCENT C. PELOSO. 1968.

A Guide for the Study of Culture in Central America. (Humanities and Social Sciences). Washington, D.C.: Pan American Union. Basic Bibliographies no. 5.

An annotated bibliography of 934 titles ranging from the colonial through the modern period.

1320 RODRIQUEZ BETETA, VIRGILIO. 1925–26.

Nuestra bibliografía colonial. *ASGH,* 2:83–98, 227–238.

A checklist with commentary on books printed in Antigua Guatemala during the seventeenth and eighteenth centuries.

1321 RODRIGUEZ CABAL, JUAN. 1961.

Catálogo de escritores dominicos en la Capitanía General de Guatemala. *ASGH.* 34:106–67.

A list of Dominican writers in Guatemala during the colonial period. Has biographical data on authors as well.

1322 SANCHEZ, ALONSO B. 1927.

Fuentes de la historia española e hispano-americana: ensayo de bibliografía sistemática de impresos y manuscritos que ilustran la historia política de España y sus antiguas provincias de ultramar. Madrid: Publicaciones de la "Revista de Filogia Española." 2 vols.

General sources for all of Hispano-America.

1323 SANCHEZ G., DANIEL. 1920.

Catalogo de los escritores franciscanos de la Provincia Seráfica del Santísimo Nombre de Jesús de Guatemala. Guatemala: Tipografía Nacional.

See ADAMS, above for a more recent and complete history of Franciscan authors.

1323a SMITH, ROBERT CHESTER and ELISABETH WILDER, editors. 1948.

A Guide to the Art of Latin America. Washington, D.C.: Hispanic Foundation, The Library of Congress.

DUL/R-016.7098 S658

An excellent source for the art history of Latin America. Materials on all the Central American countries.

1324 STREIT, ROBERT and JOHANNES DINDINGER. 1916–1939.

Bibliotheca missionum. Munster: I.W. Aachen. 11 vols.

LC/Z7838.M6S9   DUL/DNS. R-z266S915B

Vols. 1 and 3 have material on Central America.

1325 TEXAS. UNIVERSITY AT AUSTIN. LIBRARY. LATIN AMERICAN COLLECTION. 1969.

Catalogue of The Latin American Collection. Boston: G.K. Hall. 31 vols.

First Supplement. Boston: G.K. Hall, 1971. 5 vols.

1326 TORRE REVELLO, JOSE. 1940.

El libro, la imprenta y el periodismo en América durante la dominación española, con ilustraciones y apéndice documental. Buenos Aires: Universidad de Buenos Aires, Instituto de Investigaciones Históricas. 3 parts in one volume.

Comprehensive study. Has an appendix of documents as well as a bibliography. Reprinted by Lennox Hill Publishing Corp., New York, 1973.

1326a TORRE REVELLO, JOSE. 1956.

Tratados de arquitectura utilizados en Hispano-América (siglos XVI a XVIII). *Revista interamericana de bibliografía,* 6, 1:3–24.

LC/Z1007.R4317

See Section III above for description.

1327 TULANE UNIVERSITY. LATIN AMERICAN LIBRARY. 1970.

Catalogue of the Latin American Library of Tulane University (New Orleans). Boston: G.K. Hall. 9 vols.

First Supplement. Boston: G.K. Hall, 1973.

Specializes in materials dealing with Central America, both Pre-Columbian and colonial. One of the richest collections of books and periodicals on Latin America. Until 1962 was known as the Middle American Research Institute Library.

1328 VALENZUELA, GILBERTO. 1933.

La imprenta en Guatemala; algunas adiciones a la obra que con este título publicó en Santiago de Chile el ilustre literato don José Toribio Medina. Guatemala: Folletín del Diario de Centro América.

Additions arranged chronologically, 1676–1821. This book was published as an addendum to his *Biblioteca Guatemalteca* (same place, date, and publisher) covering the period from the independence to 1850.

See MEDINA, 1910, above.

Originally published in serial form in *Diario de Centro América.* This is a separate edition and has a note reading ". . . algunas adiciones a la obra que con este titulo publicó en Santiago de Chile el ilustre liberato don José Toribio Medina."

1329 VILLACORTA CALDERON, JOSE ANTONIO. 1944.

Bibliografía guatemalteca. Guatemala: Tipografía Nacional.

LC/Z1461.V5   DUL/R-015.7281 qV712B

An extensive catalogue of four exhibits of colonial Guatemala printed books held in the Museo Nacional, Guatemala City in November of 1939, 1940, 1941, and 1942. Includes some illustrations of title pages.

1330 WARREN, J. BENEDICT. 1973.

An Introductory Survey of Secular Writings in the European Tradition on Colonial Middle America. In *HMAI,* 13, part 2:45–137.

A bibliographical survey of published works on Mexico and Central America. Contains an extensive bibliography, useful for historians and ethnohistorians.

See pp. 101 ff. for data on Central America including works by PEDRO DE ALVARADO, DIEGO GARCIA DE PALACIO, MARTIN ALONSO DE TOVILLA, SEBASTIAN CALDAS, ANDRES DE AVENDANO Y LOYOLA, AGUSTIN CANO, JUAN DE VILLA-GUTIERRE Y SOTOMAYOR, FRANCISCO ANTONIO DE FUEN-TES Y GUZMAN, PEDRO CORTES Y LARRAZ and others.

Section VI

DOCUMENTARY SOURCES

Catalogues of collections of documents.

Published transcriptions of documents in the Archivo General del Gobierno de Guatemala *(AGG)* and in the Archivo de Indias *(AI* or *AGI)* as well as some unpublished documents in *AGG.*

1331 ALTOLAGUIRRE Y DUVALE, ANGEL DE. 1923–26.

Indice general de los papeles del Consejo de Indias. Madrid: Tipografía de la "Revista de Archivos, Bibliotecas y Museos". 6 vols.

An index to CODI, 2nd. series, vols. 14–19.

1332 ANGUIANO, RAMON DE. 1798.

Informe recibido por Ramón de Anguiano, gobernador intendente de la provincia de Honduras, de las zonas geográficas. Hay un mapa a colores.

AGG: A1.17.2(1798)17.514-2335

A *relación geográfica* of Honduras with an interesting map.

1333 ARCHIVO DE PROTOCOLOS. SEVILLA. 1935.

Documentos americanos del Archivo de Protocolos de Sevilla, siglo XVI. Madrid: Tipografía de Archivos.

A special publication by the organizing committee of the XXVI Congreso Internacional de Americanistas.

1334 ARCHIVO GENERAL DE INDIAS. SEVILLA. 1930, 1940.

Catálogo de pasajeros a Indias durante los siglos XVI, XVII y XVIII. Madrid. 2a ed., Sevilla: Imprenta Editorial de la Gavidia, 1940.

The second edition is an enlarged and corrected version of the first.

1335 ARCHIVO GENERAL DE INDIAS. SEVILLA. 1946.

Catálogo de pasajeros a Indias durante los siglos XVI, XVII y XVIII. Madrid. 3 vols.

DUL/325.246S733

Volume 3 covers the years 1539–59 and is pertinent for Central America. Published in various editions at different times, Madrid, 1930 and Sevilla, 1940. See foregoing item.

1336 ARCHIVO GENERAL DEL GOBIERNO. GUATEMALA. 1936.

Indice de los documentos existentes en el Archivo General de Gobierno. Guatemala. *BAGG*, 1, 2: supplement.

An index and classification scheme used to catalogue the documents in AGG by its director J. Joaquín Pardo. See below.

1337 AREVALO, RAFAEL DE. 1857.

Colección de documentos antiguos del Archivo de Guatemala. Guatemala: Imprenta de Luna.

See AREVALO, 1856, Section II above, also LIBRO DE ACTAS, Section I above, for similar material. May be the documents referred to by Batres Jauregui, *ASGH*, 5(1928–29):385 which included privileges of the city, coat-of-arms, various reports and memoranda as well as some letters of Alvarado and Marroguín.

See next item for a modern reprint.

1338 AREVALO, RAFAEL. 1935.

Colección de documentos antiguos, perrogativas y títulos concedidos a la ciudad de Guatemala, paleografiados por el Secretario del Ayuntamiento don Rafael Arevalo en 1847. Guatemala: Topografía Nacional, Edición Villacorta.

1339 ANSENSIO Y TOLEDO, JOSE MARIA, editor. 1898–1900.

Relaciones de Yucatán. Madrid: Establecimiento Typográfico "Sucesores de Rivadeneyra".

LC/E123.C70

Transcription of documents and other writings on early history of Yucatan.

1340 *Boletín: Archivo General del Estado: Documentos históricos de Chiapas.* Tuxtla Gutiérrez, Chiapas. 1953–.

Based on microfilmed copies of documents in AGG that deal with Chiapas. New name for journal after 1957 Boletín: *Archivo histórico del Estado*. Published intermittently.

1341 *Boletín del Archivo General del Gobierno.* Joaquín J. Pardo, editor. Guatemala. 1935–.

BAGG. A mine of documents transcribed by J. Joaquín Pardo. Only ten volumes published under his direction. Appears intermittently since his death.

1342 BORGES, PEDRO. 1959.

Documentación americana en el Archivo General O.F.M. de Roma. *Archivo ibero-americano* [Madrid]. 19:5–119.

A catalogue of titles, contents and description of manuscripts in the Franciscan archives in Rome dating principally from the seventeenth and eighteenth centuries. Also included are materials on the order in Guatemala.

1343 BUENOS AIRES. BIBLIOTECA NACIONAL. 1938.

Catálogo cronológico de reales cédulas, órdenes, decretos, provisiones, etc. referentes a América, 1508–1810. Buenos Aires.

1344 CALDERON QUIJANO, JOSE ANTONIO and LUIS NAVARRO GARCIA. 1961.

Guía de los documentos, mapas y planos sobre la historia de América y España moderna en la Biblioteca Nacional de Paris, Museo Británico y Public Record Office. Sevilla: Escuela de Estudios Hispano Americanos. Also, *Anuario EA,* 18.

1345 CASTRO Y TOSSI, NORBERTO DE. 1968.

Historia y vicisitudes del cabildo de Cartago: la más sureña de las ciudades del virreinato de la Nueva España: compendio de documentos publicados e inéditos. *Revista del Archivo Nacional de Costa Rica* [San José]. 32:325–347.

The history of the city government of Cartago in the colonial period. Well documented discussion.

1346 CHAMBERLAIN, ROBERT S. 1936.

A Report on Colonial Materials in the Governmental Archives of Guatemala. *HLAS.* 2:387–432.

An extensive article describing the contents of the *Archivo General del Gobierno de Guatemala.* Includes a catalogue of documents on a variety of subjects.

1347 CHIAPAS. ARCHIVO HISTORICO. 1953–.

Boletín. Documentos históricos de Chiapas. Tuxtla Gutiérrez, Chiapas.

LC/F1256.C554

Contains some transcriptions of documents from *AGG.* Appears irregularly. Some 50 numbers published to the mid-1960's.

1348 CHINCHILLA AGUILAR, ERNESTO. 1966.

Documentos existentes en el Archivo General de la Nación. *ASGH.* 39: 443–515.

An explanation of the classification system established by J. Joaquín Pardo for the Archivo General del Gobierno. He also publishes some transcriptions of colonial documents on a variety of subjects.

Archive name changed to Archivo General de Centro América, and before to Archivo General de la Nación.

1349 *Colección de documentos importantes relativos a la República de El Salvador.* San Salvador, 1921.

1350 *Colección de documentos inéditos para la historia de España.* Madrid: Real Academia de Historia, 1842–1895. 112 vols.

An uncharted sea.

1351 COSTA RICA. ARCHIVOS NACIONALES. 1893–98.

Indice general de los documentos del archivo de Cartago, anteriores al año 1850 inclusive. San José, C.R.: Imprenta Nacional.

LC/CD3747.C3AS2

1352 COSTA RICA. ARCHIVOS NACIONALES. 1902–05.

Documentos para la historia de Costa Rica. San José, C.R.: Imprenta Nacional.

Documents from the years 1605–1609. Compiled under the direction of Carlos Gagini.

1353 COSTA RICA. ARCHIVOS NACIONALES. 1904.

Indice de protocolos de Heredia, 1721–1851. San José, C.R.: Imprenta Nacional.

LC/CD3758.H4A52

1354 COSTA RICA. ARCHIVOS NACIONALES. 1905.

Indice de los protocolos de San José. San José, C.R.: Imprenta Nacional. 2 vols.

LC/CD3758.S3A5L

From 1721–1836 and 1837–1850.

1355 COSTA RICA. ARCHIVOS NACIONALES. 1908.

Indice de los protocolos de Alajuela, 1793–1850. San José, C.R.: Imprenta Nacional.

LC/CD3758A4A52

1356 COSTA RICA. ARCHIVOS NACIONALES. 1909.

Indice de los protocolos de Guanacaste, 1756–1850. San José, C.R.: Imprenta Nacional.

LC/CD3747.G8A52

1357 COSTA RICA. ARCHIVOS NACIONALES. 1909–1930.

Indice de los protocolos de Cartago. San José, C.R.: Imprenta Nacional. 6 vols.

LC/CD3747.C3517

First 5 vols., 1607–1817, vol. 6, 1818–1850.

An index of *protocolos* of the city of Cartago, Costa Rica. Reference to documents in the archives.

1358 COSTA RICA. ARCHIVOS NACIONALES. 1936–.

Revista de los Archivos Nacionales de Costa Rica.

LC/F1541.C45

1359 DESCRIPCIONES GEOGRAFICAS. 1740.

Real provisión circulada a las autoridades del Reino y RR.PP. de las Ordenes Religiosas, para que formulen descripciones geográficas e históricas.

AGG: A 1.17(1740)112-6

1359a ENCINAS, DIEGO DE. (fl. 16th century). 1945–1946.

Cedulario indiano. Madrid: Instituto de Cultura Hispánica.

DUL/349.72 M611C

A facsimile edition, edited by Alfonso García Gallo, of the compilation of *cédulas* of the vice-royalty of Mexico compiled by Diego Manuel Bringas de Manzaneda y Encinas. A preliminary study and an index by the editor.

An original is now in the John Carter Library, Brown University, catalogued: SPAIN. LAWS. STATUTES. etc.

Libro . . . de provisiones, cedulas, capitulos de ordenancas, instrucciones y cartas, libradas y despachadas en diferentes tiempos por sus magestades. . . . Madrid: En la Imprenta Real, 1596, 4 vols.

1359b ESTRADA MOLINA, LIGIA MARIA. 1964.

La investigación histórica y los Archivos Nacionales. San José, C.R.: Archivos Nacionales.

LC/CD3743.E8

Some indication of the documentary resources in the archives in San José.

1360 FERNANDEZ, LEON. 1881.

Colección de documentos históricos y estadísticos. San José, C.R.: Imprenta Nacional.

Vol. I contains among other documents, GARCIA PALACIO, see Section I above.

1360a FERNANDEZ, LEON, editor. 1881–1907.

Colección de documentos para la historia de Costa Rica. San Jose: C.R.: Imprenta Nacional. 10 vols.

LC/1546.F36

Also published in Paris and Barcelona. Documents of colonial date of historical import are in v. 1.

1361 FERNANDEZ, LEON. 1929.

Documentos relativos a los movimientos de independencia en el reino de

Guatemala. San Salvador: Talleres Tipográficos del Ministerio de Instrucción Pública.

LC/F1437.F48

Includes some documents from the colonial period.

FERNANDEZ DE NAVARETTE, MARTIN (fl. 1764–1844).
see NAVARETTE, MARTIN FERNANDEZ DE.

1362   GAGINI, CARLOS (fl. 1865–1929). 1921.

Documentos para la historia de Costa Rica. San José, C.R.: Imprenta Nacional.

DUL/972.8603 G1340

Transcribes some documents dating from 1605–1609 in *AGG.*

1363   GARCIA ICAZABALCETA, JOAQUIN (fl. 1825–1894). 1892.

Nueva colección de documentos para la historia de México. México: Andrade y Morales, Sucesores. 5 vols.

LC/F1203.G22

Has documents on Central America.

1364   GARCIA ICAZABALCETA, JOAQUIN. 1896–99.

Obras de Joaquín Garcia Icazbalceta. Mexico: Imprenta de V. Agiieros. 10 vols. Reprinted New York: Lenox Hill Publishing Co., 1968. 10 vols.

LC/1203.G24 and 1203.G25

1365   GAYANGOS Y ARCE, PASCUAL DE (fl. 1809–1897). 1875–1893.

Catalogue of Manuscripts in the Spanish Language in the British Museum. London: British Museum, Department of Manuscripts. 4 vols.

Some documents deal with Central America.

1366   GIBSON, CHARLES. 1973.

Published Collections of Documents Relating to Middle American Ethnohistory. In *HMAI,* 13, part 2:3–41.

A survey of published Central American documentary sources, p. 6.

1367   GUATEMALA. ARCHIVO DE INDIAS. 1939–40.

Indice de documentos existentes en el Archivo de Indias de Sevilla que tienen interés para Guatemala. *ASGH,* 16:401–424.

1367a   GUATEMALA. ARCHIVO GENERAL DEL GOBIERNO.

Name changed twice. First, to *Archivo General de la Nación,* and later to *Archivo General de Centro América.*

Call numbers listed for documents in Section VIII follow the system organized by the late J. Joaquín Pardo, director for many years.

Abbreviated *AGG.*

1368 GUATEMALA. AUDIENCIA. n.d.

Descripción de algunas ciudades principales que se hallan en el reyno de Guatemala.

Cited in *COLD,* xxx, footnote, supposedly this eighteenth century document in the Biblioteca del Depósito Hidrográfico de Madrid—Virreinato de México, t. IV, doc. 7.

1369 GUATEMALA. AUDIENCIA. 1581.

Relación formada por la Audiencia de Guatemala de todos los pueblos de su jurisdicción y modo de administrar en ellos justicia. *AGI,* Tomo 2, Folio 57, Est. 2, Cap. 2, Leg. 4.

See *ASGH,* 16 (1939–40):408 for text.

1370 HAMMOND, G.P., ed. 1972.

A Guide to the Manuscript Collections of the Bancroft Library. Mexican and Central American Manuscripts. Berkeley: University of California Press. Volume 2.

About 1,500 Mexican and Central American MSS listed alphabetically by author, or by subject or title. Index of topics, persons, areas.

1371 HONDURAS. ARCHIVO NACIONAL. 1901.

Nuevo índice del archivo de tierras custodiado en el Archivo Nacional, comprende los expedientes creados desde 1580 a 1901. 2a ed. Tegucigalpa: Tipografía Nacional.

LC/F1501.H77

1372 HONDURAS. ARCHIVO Y BIBLIOTECAS. 1904–.

Revista del Archivo y Bibliotecas Nacionales (Honduras). Tegucigalpa. Sociedad de Geografía e Historia.

Still current. Transcription of documents on various subjects. Also bibliographical data.

1373 KONETZKE, RICHARD. 1953–1962.

Colección de documentos para la historia de la formación social de Hispanoamérica, 1493–1810. Madrid: Consejo Superior de Investigaciones Científicas. 5 vols.

Transcription of documents in *AI* relative to formation of Hispano-American society in colonial times.

1373a LANNING, JOHN TATE. 1954.

Reales cédulas de la Real y Pontificia Universidad de San Carlos de Guatemala. Guatemala: Editorial Universitaria.

A transcription of all the reales cédulas of the university of San Carlos during the colonial period.

1374   LARREYNAGA, MIGUEL (fl. 1771–1847). 1857.

Prontuario de todas las reales cédulas, cartas acordadas y órdenes comuni-cadas a la Audiencia del Antiguo Reino de Guatemala, desde el año 1600 hasta 1818. Guatemala: Imprenta de Luna.

A check list of titles of documents in chronological order. Title page in-cludes the following: Formado por el sr. lic. don Miguel Larreynaga, y Felipe Neri y d. Rafael del Barrio etc. Guatemala: Imprenta la Luna, 1857.

1375   MOLINA ARGUELLO, CARLOS. 1957.

Misiones nicaragüenses en archivos europeos. México: Instituto Panameri-cano de Geografía e Historia, Comisión de Historia.

LC/F1401.P153 no. 223   DUL/910.6159P

An account of a search for documents of colonial date in European archives. Includes a list of documents in the first ten volumes of VEGA BOLANOS, *Colección Somoza,* see below.

1376   MONTOTO DE SEDAS, SANTIAGO, editor. 1927.

Colección de documentos inéditos para la historia de Ibero-América. Colec-ción de documentos inéditos para la historia de Hispano-América, v. 1. Madrid: Editorial Ibero-Africana-Americana.

Has some material on Central America.

1377   NAUIO BOLANOS, ANTONIO DE (fl. 1662–92). 1953.

An aquisition of the University of Texas Library. *HAHR,* 33:326.

A microfilm copy of a MS in Nicaragua of 284 folios being a report of the *oidor y visitador* B.A. de N. Bolaños. A tribute list giving in great detail a list of all the pueblos of Nicaragua and other pertinent data for the years 1662–1692.

1378   NAVARRETE, MARTIN FERNANDEZ DE, editor. 1825–37.

Colección de los viajes y descubrimientos que hicieron por mar los españoles desde fines del siglo XV, con varios documentos inéditos concernientes a la historia de la marina castellana y de los establecimientos españoles en Indias, coordinada e ilustrada por M. Fernández de Navarrete. Madrid. 5 vols. Reprinted, Lenox Hill Publishing Co., New York, 1972.

Transcription of documents with accounts of voyages, including those to the coasts of Central America.

Other editions: with a prologue by J. Natalicio González, Buenos Aires. 1954–55. 5 vols; with a preliminary study by Carlos Seco Serrano, Madrid. Biblioteca de Autores Españoles. nos. 75–77. 2 vols.

1379   NICARAGUA. 1921.

Colección de documentos referentes a la historia colonial de Nicaragua; recuerdo del centenario de la independencia nacional, 1821–1921. Managua.

Transcription of documents pertinent to colonial period.

1380 NUEVA GUATEMALA. 1775.

Traslación de la capital de Guatemala. *AGG:* A 1.2 (1775)15708-2175.

The *real cédula* with the new name of the capital dated 21 July 1775.

1381 NUEVA GUATEMALA. 1776.

Plano (cuadro) de las areas que comprenden los pueblos situados en las inmediaciones de Guatemala. *AGG:* A 1.10(1776)18.753-2445. fol. 26.

The small towns established on the outskirts of the new capital of the Reino de Guatemala. Has a plan.

1382 OROZCO Y JIMENEZ, FRANCISCO, editor. 1906.

Colección de documentos inéditos relativos a la iglesia de Chiapas. San Cristóbal Las-Casas: Imprenta de la "Sociedad Católica".

LC/BX1429.C507

Important information for dating churches of San Cristóbal de las Casas. Reprinted in 1911, see next item.

1383 OROZCO Y JIMENEZ, FRANCISCO, editor. 1911.

Colección de documentos inéditos relativos a la iglesia de Chiapas. San Cristóbal Las-Casas: Imprenta de la "Sociedad Católica".

1384 PACHECO, JOAQUIN FRANCISCO, et. al., editors. 1864-1926.

Colección de documentos inéditos relativos al descubrimiento, conquista y organización de las antiguas posesiones españolas de América y Oceanía, sacados de los Archivos del Reino, y muy especialmente del de Indias. Madrid. Real Academia de la Historia. *Primera serie,* 1864-84, 42 vols. *Segunda serie,* 1885-1926, 19 vols.

To find one's way through the sixty-one volumes without a guide is as bewildering as trying to in the Archivo de Indias itself. The indexes made by SCHAFER, see below, or ALTOLAGUIRRE, above, are most useful tools in searching for documentary materials published in these volumes. Abbreviation: *CODI.*

1385 PARDO GALLARDO, JOSE JOAQUIN. 1932-33-1951.

Efemérides para escribir la historia de la muy noble y muy leal ciudad de Santiago de los Caballeros de Guatemala. ASGH, 9, 11, 13, 17, 18, 21, 22, 23, 24, 25.

A random selection of documents, some of which appear in PARDO, 1944 below.

1386 PARDO GALLARDO, JOSE JOAQUIN. 1941.

Prontuario de reales cédulas, 1529-1599. Guatemala: Unión Tipográfica.

LC/CD3766.1941   DUL/972.81 P226P

A check list of *reales cédulas,* titles and call numbers in *AGG* given, pertaining to the Reino de Guatemala.

1387 PARDO GALLARDO, JOSE JOAQUIN. 1944.

Efemérides para escribir la historia de la muy noble y muy leal ciudad de Santiago de los Caballeros del Reino de Guatemala. Guatemala: Tipografía Nacional.

LC/F1476.A5P3   DUL/972.81 qP226E

A checklist of documents, titles given, arranged in chronological order. *AGG* numbers not given, but are all available in a copy kept in the Archivo. Miscellany of subjects.

1388 PARDO GALLARDO, JOSE JOAQUIN. 1945.

Indice de los documentos existentes en el Archivo General De Gobierno. Guatemala: Tipografía Nacional.

The same as Archivo General de Gobierno. 1936, above. A pamphlet.

1389 PARDO GALLARDO, J. JOAQUIN. 1958.

Catálogo de los manuscritos existentes en la colección latino americana de la Biblioteca de la Universidad de Texas relativos a la historia de Centro América. Guatemala: Universidad de San Carlos, Facultad de Humanidades.

LC/Z6621.T35L3

1390 PASO Y TRONCOSO, FRANCISCO DE (1842-1916). 1939.

Espistolario de Nueva España, 1505-1818. México: Antigua Librería Robredo, de J. Porrúa e hijos.

LC/F1229.P27   DUL/972 B582A no.1

V. 1. Documentary material compiled and paleographed by the author. Some items of interest for Central America.

1391 PERALTA, MANUEL MARIA. 1883.

Costa Rica, Nicaragua y Panamá en el siglo XVI. Madrid: M. Murillo.

LC/F1437.P42

Eranscription of documents in the Archivo de Indias, Sevilla and in the Archivo de Simancas, dealing mainly with boundary questions.

1392 PORRAS BARRENECHEA, RAUL. 1959.

Cartas del Perú, 1524-1543. Lima: Sociedad de Bibliófilos Peruanos.

LC/F3442.P83   DUL/985.qC691 t.3

Some three hundred letters dated 1524-1543, some of which are related to events and personages in contemporary Central America.

1393 REPORTS OF 1765.

Año de 1763. Autos formados sobre la Real Cédula para que esta Real Audiencia con la brevedad y reserva possible remita una relación individual de los corregimientos y Alcaldías Mayores de este Reyno. *BAGG,* 2(1936-1937): 274-329, 448-486.

Very interesting and informative *relaciones geográficas* of various regions in Chiapas, Guatemala, Hondures, El Salvador and Costa Rica. Rendered mainly in 1765 in compliance with the *Cédula* of 1763.

1394 RIVERA, FRAY JUAN DE. 1650.

Visión de Paz. Nueva Jerusalén construida y figurada en los primitivos héroes de la fundación de esta provincia, antes Tierra de Guerra, hoy Verapaz. Breve narrativa de sus vidas. Noticia de su Reducción y otras que conducen al mayor lustre de ella, etc. Por Fr. Juan de Rivera. *AGG:* A 1. 18.4(1650)38.300–4501.

See Section I above, CEVALLOS, *Visión de paz* for a transcription of the text, *ASGH,* 12(1935–36):463–485. Missionary activity in mid-sixteenth century Verapaz, Guatemala.

1395 RUBIO MORENO, LUIS. 1930.

Pasajeros a Indias. Madrid: Compañía Ibero-americana de Publicaciones. 2 vols.

A systematic catalogue of the documents dealing with immigration to the New World, 1492–1592. Also some extracts from VEITIA LINAJE, 1672, 1:265–287; 2:265–83. See Section I, above.

1396 SAN JUAN DE DIOS, ORDEN DE.

Relaciones históricas.

AGG: A1.18.3(1740)8271–396 en Granada, Nicaragua.
A1.18.3(1740)5024–211 en Leon Nicaragua.
A1.18.3(1763)14002–2021 en Guatemala.

Historical reports on order of San Juan de Díos, hospitallers, for 1740 and 1763.

See Section VIII for complete titles.

1397 SCHAFER, ERNST. 1946–47.

Indice de la colección de documentos Inéditos de Indias. Madrid: Consejo Superior de Investigaciones Científicas. 2 vols.

LC/E123.C701   DUL/970 C97C

An invaluable aid in the use of *CODI,* See PACHECO, 1864–1926, above.

1398 SERRANO Y SANZ, MANUEL, editor. 1908.

Colección de libros y documentos referentes á la historia de América. Madrid. v. 8, Relaciones históricas y geográficas de América Central. Madrid: V. Suárez.

Abbreviation *COLD.*

LC/F1401.C68 vol. 8   DUL/980.C697C

Documents in *AGI* pertinent to Central America.

1399 SIMPSON, LESLEY BYRD. 1936.

The Colonial Archives of Guatemala. *HLAS*. 1:232–234.

Description of the colonial archives in Guatemala City. Description of contents of *AGG*, the Archivo Colonial and the Archivo Municipal, also Archivo de la Municipalidad de Antigua.

Cathedral library wrecked in earthquake of 1917.

1400 SOCIEDAD DE BIBLIOGRAFOS ESPANOLES. 1916.

Relaciones históricas de América. Primera mitad del siglo XVI. Manuel Serrano y Sanz, editor. Madrid: "Imprenta Ibérica" de E. Maestro.

LC/F1411.S48

Has some material on Cristóbal PEDRAZA, Section I, No. 240.

1401 SPAIN. CONSEJO SUPERIOR DE INVESTIGACIONES CIENTIFICAS. INSTITUTO HISTORICO DE MARINA.

Colección de diarios y relaciones para la história de los viajes y descubrimientos. Madrid. 5 vols.

1402 SPAIN. MINISTERIO DE FOMENTO. 1877.

Cartas de Indias. Madrid: Hernandez.

DUL/980.7 fS733C

Various contemporary letters, reports and other works published for the first time. Has some maps. Some Central American matters included.

1403 SQUIER, EPHRAIM GEORGE, editor. 1860.

Collection of Rare and Original Documents and Relations, Albany, N.Y.: J. Munsell. Reprinted, New York: Charles B. Norton, 1890.

LC/F1411.S77

Has the text of GARCIA PALACIO, see Section I above.

1404 TEXAS, UNIVERSITY OF. 1939.

Guide to Latin American manuscripts in the University of Texas Library. Cambridge, Mass.: Harvard University Press.

DUL/R016.09 T355G

Over one million pages of original MSS, transcripts, typed copies and photostats of documents pertinent to Spanish America. Includes material on Guatemala. See PARDO, 1958, above for MSS directly related to colonial Central America.

1405 TORRES DE MENDOZA, LUIS, *et al.,* editors. 1864–1884.

Colección de documentos inéditos relativos al descubrimiento conquista y organización de las antiguas posesiones de América y Oceanía. Madrid: 42 vols. 2a. serie, Madrid: 1885–1926. 19 vols.

The same as CODI. See above. PACHECO, 1864–1926. Vols. 1–3 are titled *Colección de documentos ineditos relativos al descubrimiento, conquista y colonización de las posesiones espãnolas en Indias.*

1406 TORRES LANZAS, PEDRO. 1919.

Catálogo de legajos del Archivo General de Indias. Sevilla: Patronato y Contaduría General del Consejo de Indias.

DUL/972.9 qS733C

Covers but a fraction of the MSS held in *AI.*

1407 TUDELA DE LA ORDEN, JOSE. 1954.

Los manuscritos de América en las bibliotecas de España. Madrid: Ediciones Cultura Hispánica.

LC/Z6601.T8   DUL/z091 T899M

Documentary historical sources ranging over all of Hispano-America. Some related to Central America.

1408 VEGA BOLANOS, ANDRES editor. 1954–1955, 1956.

Colección Somoza. Documentos para la historia de Nicaragua. Madrid: Imprenta Juan Bravo. 17 vols.

LC/F1521.V39

Transcription of sixteenth-century documents in the Archivo de Indias, Sevilla, dealing with Nicaragua. Includes royal *cédulas,* letters, reports, memorials, etc. Documents are arranged in chronological order. Indices of persons and places included.

1409 VEDIA, ENRIQUE DE. 1852–53.

Historiadores primitivos de Indias. Madrid: Imprenta de M. Rivadeneyra. 2 vols.

DUL/860 B582B t. 22,26

Contains various contemporary accounts including notices, biographical notes of LOPEZ DE GOMERA, CORTES, ALVARADO, OVIEDO, DIAZ DEL CASTILLO, and others. See Section I.

1410 ZAMORA, JOSE MARIA. 1807.

Recopilación sumaria etc. Nueva Guatemala.

See Section I, ZAMORA, for complete title.

A document in *AGG.*

Section VII

MAPS AND PLANS

Published collections of maps of Central America as well as of cities and also plans of buildings.

1411 ANGULO INIGUEZ, DIEGO. 1933–1940.

Planos de monumentos arquitectónicos de América y Filipinas existentes en el Archivo de Indias. Sevilla: Laboratorio del Arte, Universidad de Sevilla. 5 vols.

LC/NA702.A6

The fifth volume consists of three portfolios with facsimile reproductions of plans. Many of Central America.

1412 ANTIGUA GUATEMALA. 1849.

Plano de la Antigua ciudad de Guatemala, como era antes de la ruina acae-cida el 29 de julio de 1773 de un plano antiguo, cuyo autor ignornan ha sido copiado al presente por Delfina(?)Luna. Año 1849. Origin: A photocopy in the Bibliotheque National, Paris.

1413 ARMY MAP SERVICE.

Geographic Branch, Military Intelligence Division (G-2) General Staff, U.S.A. Army Map Service Corps of Engineers, War Department, Washington, D.C.

Central America. 1:250,000. Published, various dates 1930's and 1940's.

Excellent maps made by aerial and ground surveys. Includes many plans of towns, some in detail and location of churches and public buildings.

1414 *Atlas del Estado de Guatemala.* Guatemala. 1835.

Some plates from this atlas are reproduced in the transcription of PINEDA, 1924. See Section I above. It may be the same atlas of maps published by MARURE, 1837, *Bosquejo* etc. See Section II above and also MARURE, 1832, below.

1415 BAILY, JOHN. 1850.

Map of Central America, including the States of Guatemala, Honduras, San Salvador, Nicaragua and Costa Rica, etc. London: T. Saunders.

According to SQUIER . . . 1855 *Notes* xxii, is only partially accurate. Gives wrong boundaries for sinister purposes *in re* Belize an indication of English territorial pretensions. Shows half of Verapaz as part of Belize. See also CALDERON QUIJANO . . . 1944. *Belice*, Section II, above.

Another edition, London: E. Stanford, 1856.

1416 BERWICK, JACOB MARIA DEL PILAR CARLOS MANUEL STUART FITZ-JAMES, DUQUE DE ALBA. 1951.

Mapas españoles de América, siglos XV-XVII. Madrid.

LC/G1100.B4 1951 copy 3

From his personal collection. Privately printed. Limited edition of 312 copies.

1417 CALIFORNIA. UNIVERSITY. BERKELEY. BANCROFT LIBRARY. 1964.

Index of Printed Maps. Boston: G.K. Hall.

Maps dating from the sixteenth to the twentieth centuries. Mainly western North America and Mexico. Also some of Central America. Many old and rare maps.

1417a CALDERON QUIJANO, JOSE ANTONIO and LUIS NAVARRO GARCIA. 1961.

Guía de los documentos, mapas y planos sobre la historia de América y España moderna en la Biblioteca Nacional de París, Museo Británico y Public Record Office. Sevilla: Escuela de Estudios Hispano Americanos. Also, *Anuario EA, 18.*

General materials including some pertinent to colonial Central America, including contemporary maps.

1418 CENTRAL AMERICA-MAP. 1856.

Map of Central America Completed from Materials Furnished by the Committee on Foreign Relations of the Senate of the United States, March, 1856. Washington, D.C.

Has inserts on Nicaragua from San Juan to bay of Fonseca, also port of San Juan, Nicaragua as well as data on Belize and the Mosquito coast.

1419 CHUECA GOITIA, FERNANDO, LEOPOLDO TORRES BALBAS and JULIO GONZALEZ Y GONZALEZ. 1951.

Planos de ciudades Iberoamericanas y Filipinas existentes en el Archivo de Indias. Madrid: Instituto de Estudios de Administración Local Seminario de Urbanismo. 2 vols.

DUL/711.4 q5733P

Facsimile reproductions of town plans. Indispensable for studies in urbanization.

1420 COSA, JUAN DE LA (fl. 1460?–1510). 1892.

Reproducción en facsímil del célebre mapamundi de Juan de la Cosa. Madrid.

DUL/Map Collection

Facsimile reproduction of Cosa's map based on the voyages he made with Columbus. Six sheets. Legend on map reads, "Juan de la Cosa la fizo en el puerto de S. Ma. en el año de 1500."

1421 COSA, JUAN DE LA. 1950.

Mapa de Juan de la Cosa. Madrid: Ediciones Cultura Hispánica.

A modern facsimile in colors of the foregoing item.

1422 DIEZ DE NAVARRO, LUIS.

Valle de Goathemala (Antigua), dated 25 September 1774. *AGI,* estante 101, cajón 2, legajo 4(2).

Cited by TORRES LANZAS, 1903b, 1906, below.

1423 GUATEMALA. COMISION DE LIMITES. 1929.

Cartografía de la América Central. Guatemala: Tipografía Nacional.

Facsimile reproductions of old and modern maps of Central America, particularly of Guatemala relative to the boundary dispute between Guatemala and Honduras. 125 maps ranging in date from 1527 to 1924.

1424 GUATEMALA. DIRECCION GENERAL DE CARTOGRAFIA. 1961–62.

Diccionario geográfico de Guatemala. Guatemala: Tipografía Nacional. 2 vols.

DUL/917.281 qG918D

A listing of all urban centers in Guatemala, the majority of which are of colonial origin.

A supplement has appeared, Guatemala: Instituto Geográfico Nacional, 1968. 2 vols.

1424a GUATEMALA. DIRECCION GENERAL DE CARTOGRAFIA. 1962 and later.

Guatemala, 1:50,000. Guatemala: Ministerio de Comunicaciones y Obras Públicas, Instituto Geográfico Nacional. 225 sheets.

Excellent maps with many details not normally seen on maps of larger scale: hamlets with houses, street plans of villages, scattered settlements, etc. These maps were prepared through the collaboration of the DGC, the Inter-American Geodesic Survey, and the U.S. Army Map Service. Based on aerial photographs with horizontal and vertical control.

1425 GUATEMALA. DIRECCION GENERAL DE ESTADISTICA. 1953.

Departamentos, municipios, ciudades, villas, pueblos, aldeas, y caseríos de la República de Guatemala. Guatemala.

22 sheets, maps of all departamentos ranging in scale from 1:100,000 to 1:400,000. Petén is 1:800,000. Lists all towns, villages, settlements in a gazeteer with data derived from census of 1950.

1425a GUATEMALA. INSTITUTO GEOGRAFICO NACIONAL. 1959.

América Central, 1:250,000. Guatemala. Washington, D.C.: Army Map Service, Corps of Engineers.

Large scale maps for general use.

1425b GUATEMALA. INSTITUTO GEOGRAFICO NACIONAL. 1972.

Atlas nacional de Guatemala. Guatemala: Tipografía Nacional.

A large folio volume of maps of contemporary Guatemala dealing with economic matters and sundry subjects which are also discussed in a brief text.

1425c GUATEMALA. SEMINARIO DE INTEGRACION SOCIAL. 1964.

Planos de la ciudad de Guatemala. Guatemala: Tipografía Nacional.

A collection of maps of Guatemala City from the time of its founding after the earthquake of 1773 that destroyed the former capital of the Reino de Guatemala, now Antigua Guatemala, through the nineteenth century to the present. Invaluable for urban studies.

1426 LATORRE, GERMAN. 1916.

La cartografía colonial americana. Sevilla: Establecimiento Tipográfico de la Guía Oficial.

See Chp. IV, 56–57 for maps made by Bautista Antonelli and Pedro Ochoa de Leguizamón.

1427 LOPEZ DE VELASCO, JUAN (fl. 16th century).

Descripción de la Audiencia de Guatemala. In BERWICK, 1951, above, pl. 57, p. 241.

A rare sixteenth-century map. See LOPEZ DE VELASCO, 1894, Section I, above.

1428 MARURE, ALEJANDRO. 1832.

Atlas Guatemalteco, en ocho cartas, formadas y grabadas en Guatemala, de orden del Gefe del Estado, L. Doctor Mariano Galvez, año 1832.

Mentioned by SQUIER, 1855, *Notes,* vii ff., see Section II above. Does not say it was good or bad, but that it was the only map published up to 1855.

Batres Jáuregui, *ASGH,* 4(1927–28):225 says it was published in 1832, and that Marure published a report on this atlas. Batres includes the eight maps by way of illustrations on pages 226, 233.

See *Atlas del Estado* . . . 1835, above. These maps may be the very ones that Marure published in his *Bosquejo histórico,* 1837, see Section II.

1429   MONTEIRO, PALMYRA V.M. 1967.

A Catalogue of Latin American Flat Maps, 1926–1964. Austin, Texas: University of Texas Press. 2 vols. Vol. 1: Mexico, Central America, West Indies Vol. II: South America, Falkland (Malvinas) Islands and the Guianas.

LC/Z6027.S72M6   DUL/RZ912.8 M775C

1430   MORALES PADRON, FRANCISCO, and J. LLAVADOR MIRA. 1964–65.

Mapas, planos y dibujos existentes en el Archivo General de Indias. Sevilla: Escuela de Estudios Hispanoamericanos. 2 vols.

DUL/911.87 M828M

Some new material not in TORRES LANZAS below.

1431   NORIEGA, FELIX F. 1904.

Diccionario geográfico de Costa Rica. San José, C.R.: Imprenta de A. Alsina.

LC/F1542.N84   DUL/917.286 N841D

1432   OUTES, FELIX F. 1930.

Cartas y planos inéditos de los siglos XVII y XVIII y primer decenio de XIX. Buenos Aires: "Coni."

Has various town plans.

1433   PALMERLEE, ALBERT E. 1965.

Maps of Costa Rica. An Annotated Bibliography. Lawrence, Kansas: University of Kansas Library.

LC/Z6027.C83P33

A bibliography of published and unpublished maps of Costa Rica including information where they may be located. Well indexed.

1434   RIVERA MAESTRE, MIGUEL. 1838.

El atlas guatemalteco.

Published in 1838 according to Batres Jáuregui, *ASGH,* 5 (1928–29):385. Also mentions it or another as *Atlas del Estado de Guatemala,* above. May have confused this item with MARURE, above.

1435   SALAZAR, CARLOS. 1929.

Cartografía de la América Central. Guatemala.

Could not be located in LC or Biblioteca Nacional, Guatemala. Probably contains same materials as GUATEMALA, COMISION DE LIMITES, 1929, above.

1436 SPAIN. SERVICIOS GEOGRAFICO E HISTORICO DEL EJERCITO. 1957.

Cartografía de Ultramar: carpeta IV; America Central. Toponimia de los mapas que la integran y relaciones históricas de ultramar. Madrid. 2 vols.

A beautiful book with facsimile reproductions in color. Vol. 1 transcribes all the verbal annotations and gives other details; vol. 2, maps.

Most maps date from the eighteenth century.

1437 STEVENSON, EDWARD LUTHER, editor. 1903.

Maps illustrating early discovery and exploration in America, 1502–30. New Brunswick, N.J.: 2 vols.

Facsimile reproductions of the first maps of America.

1438 SUCHITEPEQUEZ and ZAPOTITLAN. 1579.

Mapa de la costa de Suchitepéquez y Zapotitlán, 1579. *ASGH,* 39, (1966): 96–99.

Part of a relación geográfica of a region in Guatemala in the sixteenth century. Previously published but without a reproduction of the accompanying map. See ESTRADA, 1955, Section I, above.

Paleography of the legends are included.

1439 TOOLEY, R.V. 1952(1962).

Maps and Map-Makers. 2nd edition (4th impression). New York: Bonanza Books.

First published in London, by B.T. Batsford in 1949.

A well-written and concise survey of the history of maps. Ch. XII deals with the history of maps of the New World especially of Latin America including maps where Mexico and Central America are indicated. Has an excellent bibliography appended to this chapter.

A reproduction of M. Talton's map of California and Central America, dated 1616, fig. 81.

1440 TORRES LANZAS, PEDRO. 1903a.

Relación descriptiva de los mapas, planos, etc. de la Audiencia y Capitanía General de Guatemala (Guatemala, San Salvador, Honduras, Nicaragua y Costa Rica) existentes en el Archivo General de Indias. *Revista de Archivos, Bibliotecas y Museos,* 3a época, 8:20–35, 203–214, 279–290; 9:109–124.

LC/Z6027.G9T7

Also published as an off-print, 214 pp., 4 illus. See item immediately below.

A check list with call numbers of the documents where these maps and plans are located in *AI.*

1441 TORRES LANZAS, PEDRO. 1903b, 1906.

Relación descriptiva de los mapas, planos, etc. de la Audiencia y Capitanía General de Guatemala (Guatemala, San Salvador, Honduras, Nicaragua, y Costa Rica) existentes en el archivo general de Indias. Madrid: Tipografía de la Revista de Archivos, Bibliotecas, y Museos.

Catalogue of plans and maps of colonial Central America. See foregoing item.

1442 TORROELLA, F.P. DE. 1948.

Mapa de la República de Guatemala. Guatemala: Litografía Arimany.

A large modern wall map, scale 1:600,000.

1443 URICOECHEA, EZEQUIEL (fl. 1834–1880). 1860.

Mapoteca colombiana. Colección de los títulos de todos los mapas, planos, vistas, etc. relativos á la América española, Brasil é islas adyacentes. Arreglada cronológicamente i precedida de una introducción sobre la historia cartográfica de América. London: Trubner and Co. (Londres: Trubner y Cía.). Reprinted. New York: Lenox Hill Publishing Co., 1972.

LC/Z6027.A5U45

1444 VINDEL, FRANCISCO. 1955.

Mapas de América en los libros españoles de los siglos XVI al XVII (1503–1798). Madrid.

LC/G1100.V5 1955   DUL/912.8 fV779M

An anthology of maps extracted from printed books.

1445 VINDEL, FRANCISCO. 1959.

Mapas de América y Filipinas en los libros españoles de los siglos XVI al XVIII: Apéndice a los de América; Adición de los de Filipinas. Madrid.

DUL/912.8 fV779 App.

The same as the foregoing item with a section on the Philippine islands.

1446 WAIBEL, LEO HEINRICH. 1933.

Die Sierra Madre de Chiapas. *Mitteilungen Geographische Gesellschaft in Hamburg,* 43:12–162.

For the same map, see *La Sierra Madre de Chiapas* (México: Sociedad Mexicana de Geografía Estadística, 1946).

Section VIII

CATALOGUE OF DOCUMENTS

Culled from *AGG* and pertinent to the history, art and architecture as well as the subjects covered in Sections I, II and IV. Call numbers and descriptive titles of documents transcribed from the card index in *AGG*, Guatemala City. Descriptive titles in English by the compiler of this bibliography.

For published transcriptions see citations given in *BAGG*.

1447 A 1 (1687) 1–23

El obispo de Guatemala, Fr. Andrés de las Navas y Quevedo, solicita la ayuda del brazo civil, para reducir al orden a los indios del Valle de Goathemala, quienes se negaban a asistir a misa.

1448 A 1.1 (1607) 1–1

Providencia ordenando que ciertos pueblos de la region occidental, proporcionen indios para trabajar en las obras de la ciudad, con motivo de la ruina de 9 de octubre de 1607.

1449 A 1.1 (1726) 52426–5970

Nicolás Estevan, maestro albañil, vecino d Chiquimula de la Sierra, solicita se le extienda título de 10 caballerías de tierra, situadas en el paraje Sitio Viejo o del Carmen y quebrada de Ticchicguante, en pago del valor de la obra del templo parroquial de aquella población.

1450 A 1.1 (1740) 8271–396

Relación histórica del Convento y Hospital de San Juan de Dios, de la ciudad de Granada (Nicaragua).

text, *BAGG*, 1 (1935–36):148ff.

1451 A 1.1 (1749) 28865–2817

Real provisión para que don Basilio Vicente Romá, regidor de Guatemala, reconozca la inundación de las avenidas que descendieron del Volcán de Agua.

1452 A 1.1 (1751) 4215–32

El cabildo Eclesiástico suplica que se eleve informe a S.M. detallando el estado en que quedó la catedral con motivo de los temblores de 4 de Marzo de 1751.

1453   A 1.1 (1758) 3–156

Cédula de 3 de Julio de 1753, acerca de que el Ing. Luis Diez de Navarro le sea restituídos 700 pesos que gastó en la Provincia de Costa Rica en el tiempo que fué gobernador de ella.

1454   A 1.1 (1760) 3–163

Queja presentada por Ignacio Salazar, cura de Retalhuleu, contra el Alcalde porque este no castiga a los indios remisos en asistir a misa.

1455   A 1.1 (1760) 24871–2817

Don Pedro de Sala y Uruena, informa de las medidas que el ingeniero Luis Diez de Navarro, usó en el mapa del valle de Guatemala.

1456   A 1.1 (1778) 24886–2817

Se permite al Ayuntamiento de la Villa de San Vicente, que pueda gastar cierta suma en reparar la iglesia.

1457   A 1.1 (1780) 17990–2374

José Ramírez, maestro de albañilería, rinde su informe acerca del valor de un predio de Nicolás Cervantes. Agregado un plano.

1458   A 1.1. (1781) 219–9, fol. 71

Plano de la casa de don Nicolás Ortiz de Letona, en la Nueva Guatemala, levantada por el Maestro Mayor de Obras, Bernardo Ramírez.

1459   A 1.1 (1796) 4294–35

Don José María Espinosa, presenta las planillas y comprobantes de los gastos del Colegio de Niñas de la Asunción.

1460   A 1.1 (1796) 4297–35

Don José María Espinosa, presenta los comprobantes de los gastos hechos en el Colegio de Niñas.

1461   A 1.1 (1796) 24902–2817

Reglamento general para el establecimiento de la Escuela de Dibujo, adscrita a la Sociedad Económica.

1462   A 1.1 (1797) 24904–2817

Bando dando a conocer las nuevas rutas de los correos.

1463   A 1.1 (1798) 514–18

El Ingeniero José Sierra, pide que le sean cancelados los emoluciones que devengó en la reconstrucción del edifício de la fábrica de pólvora de la Antigua Guatemala.

1464   A 1.1 (1802) 660–22

Providencia ordenando que ningún edifício público se inicie en su construcción sin haber sido aprobado el plano respectivo.

1465 A 1.1 (1806) 702–23

Don Santiago Marquí, arquitecto, siguió autos para probar que no se retardó más de lo necesario, de España a Guatemala . . .

1466 A 1.1 (1810) 5212–221

El arquitecto Santiago Marquí, solicitando cierta suma del Fondo de Comunidades, para cubrir parte del edificio del Educatorio de Indias.

1467 A 1.1 (1810) 5213–221

El arquitecto Santiago Marquí, solicitando cierta suma de gratificación por los trabajos que ha hecho en el Educatorio de Indias.

1468 A 1.1 (1810) 18009–2377

El maestro de carpintería, Diego de Nájera, da un informe acerca del valor de la fábrica (obras) de carpintería, de la casa que fué de don Juan Ramírez.

1469 A 1.1 (1811) 5744–261

Planilla del material que ha sido comprado de don Gregorio de Urruela, comisionado del Ayuntamiento, para la construcción de varias tiendas en la plaza mayor de la ciudad de Guatemala.

1470 A 1.1 (1812) 56.940–6922

El ayuntamiento del pueblo de Machaloa, ante el subdelegado del partido de Tencoa, pide autorización para erogar de sus fondos para la reedificación de la iglesia parroquial, construida de adobe y con techo de palma, destruido por un incendio en 1810.

1471 A 1.1 (1820) 922–30

El Arquitecto Santiago Marquí, solicita la devolución de la tercera parte de su sueldo que está embargada, por tener que cancelar cierta suma a doña Francisca Ferrer.

1472 A 1.1 (1821) 24942–2819

Informa el Ayuntamiento de Chimaltenango y el de Tecpán Guatemala, el estado lamentable de sus casas consistoriales.

1473 A 1.1 (1821) 50526–5910

Ayuntamiento of San Andrés Izapa asks government for funds to reconstruct church.

1474 A 1.2 (1565) 2196, fol. 140

30 de junio de 1565.-R.P. La audiencia prohibe a las autoridades civiles y eclesiásticas, otorguen licencias para la construcción y reparación de templos.

Declara la audiencia que solo con licencia previa de su majestad, podrían ser construidos templos.

1475   A 1.2 (1565) 2196–140

30 de junio de 1565. R.P. Declara la audiencia que solo con licencia previa de su majestad, podrían ser construidos conventos y monasterios.

1476   A 1.2 (1567) 24947–2820

Memoria de lo que han de dar los vecinos de la ciudad de Guatemala, para el arreglo del cauce del río Pensativo.

1477   A 1.2 (1663) 951–39

El Síndico del Ayuntamiento, don Luis Abarca Paniagua, solicita autorización para el gasto de la construcción de dos puentes: uno de San Lázaro y otro en Santa Lucía.

1478   A 1.2 (1696) 952–39

El Síndico del Ayuntamiento, don Francisco Xavier Folgar, pide autorización para gastar cuatrocientos pesos, con el fin de concluir la construcción de las Casas Consistoriales.

1479   A 1.2 (1697) 15793–2211

El Fiel Ejecutor, Capitán don Francisco Antonio Fuentes y Guzmán, informa del estado de los cajones de la plaza y pulperías de la ciudad de Guatemala.

1480   A 1.2 (1723) 15806–2212

Instancia del Síndico de la ciudad de Guatemala, acerca de que no sean arrastradas por las calles las maderas.

1481   A 1.2 (1732) 15808–2212

Autos relativos a ceder varias pajas de agua, por parte del Ayuntamiento, al Beaterio de Santa Rosa.

1482   A 1.2 (1749) 15815–2212

Testimonio de la inspección efectuado por los regidores, en el río Pensativo.

1483   A 1.2 (1762) 15824–2213

Cuaderno de las providencias dictadas por el Ayuntamiento, relativas a la limpia del río Pensativo.

1484   A 1.2 (1768) 13513–1980

Cuenta de lo gastado en la construcción de la zanja de la Calle de Santa Lucía.

1485   A 1.2 (1774) 15828–2213

Instancia de los cajoneros de la plaza de la Antigua Guatemala, para que no se les cobre la misma tarifa de antes del terremoto.

1486 A 1.2 (1790) 15833–2213

Renuncia presentada por el Maestro Mayor de Obras Públicas, don Bernardo Ramírez.

1487 A 1.2 (1803) 15857–2214

El maestro Bernardo Ramírez cobra la suma de 40 pesos. (from Ayuntamiento)

1488 A 1.2 (1813) 11.815–1805

Acerca de ocupar la catedral para asiento de la Parroquia de San José.

text, *BAGG,* 8 (1943):199ff.

See also 11.818–1805; 11.819–1805; 11.820–1805; 11.821–1805.

1489 A 1.2 (1815) 25032–2822

Providencia del Ayuntamiento mandando despejar la plaza de cajones frente a las puertas de la Catedral.

1490 A 1.2.1 (1661) 25063–2824

Cuenta de lo gastado por el alcalde Capitán Martín de Alvarado Villacreces Cueva y Guzmán, en el arreglo de la calle de la Joya.

1491 A 1.2.1 (1684) 25064–2824

Instancia del Capitán Cristóbal Fernández de Rivera, sobre que se le paguen los gastos hechos en las reparaciones de los puentes, edificio del matadero y calles.

1492 A 1.2.1 (1751) 15951–2226

Pago de la reconstrucción de una casa situada sobre el camino de Animas.

1493 A 1.2.1 (1795) 635–57

El Ayuntamiento de Ciudad Real pide autorización para que de los fondos de propios y arbitrios se costee la obra de puente situado sobre el río que corre al sur de la ciudad.

1494 A 1.2.2 (1611) 11.766–1772

El Alcalde don García de Castellanos opina que no es conveniente la fundación del Monasterio de San Agustín.

text, *BAGG,* 8 (1943):27.

1495 A 1.2.2 (1668) 11.774–1780

A moción del Alcalde José de Aguilar Revolledo, el Ayuntamiento acuerda informar a su Majestad, ser conveniente la fundación del Convento de Santa Teresa.

1496   A 1.2.2 (1669) 11.774–1780

El Ayuntamiento acuerda contribuir con doscientos pesos anuales para los gastos de la obra de la Catedral.

text, *BAGG*, 8 (1943):29ff.

1497   A 1.2.2 (1668) 11.775–1781

El Ayuntamiento es informado acerca de la próxima llegada de las monjas fundadoras del convento de Santa Teresa de Jesús con procedencia de la ciudad de Lima, Virreynato del Perú.

text, *BAGG*, 8 (1943):31ff.

1498   A 1.2.2 (1668) 11.775–1781

El Ayuntamiento acuerda celebrar fiestas de plaza, conmemorando el estreno de la iglesia de Belén y Hospital de convalecientes.

text, *BAGG*, 8 (1943):33ff.

1499   A 1.2.2 (1674) 11.774–1780

Cabildo dated 24 April 1674. Ayuntamiento agrees to inform the king that they are not opposed to founding the convento of Santa Teresa. Houses and a site are ready for the nuns, given by Maestro don Bernardino de Obando, presbítero, etc. He is the one proposing the establishment of this convento.

1500   A 1.2.2 (1677) 11.775–1781

El Ayuntamiento acuerda asistir al acto inaugural del convento de Santa Teresa de Jesús.

text, *BAGG*, 8 (1943):32ff.

1501   A 1.2.2 (1679) 11.776–1782

Introducción del agua de Santa Ana y construcción de la pila de la Alameda del Calvario:

text, *BAGG*, 8 (1943):36ff.

1502   A 1.2.2 (1683) 11.776–1782

Pretención del convento de Santa Catalina Mártir, acerca de que se le ceda una calle, cerrándola e incorporándola a dicho convento.

text, *BAGG*, 8 (1943):45ff.

1503   A 1.2.2 (1687) 11777–1783

Acuerda el ayuntamiento hacer festividades con motivo del estreno de la iglesia y convento de Santa Teresa, agradeciendo a don José de Aguilar y Rebolledo, haber costeado dicha obra.

text, *BAGG*, 10 (1945): 248ff.

1504   A 1.2.2 (1689) 11.778–1784

Providencias dictadas por el Ayuntamiento, con motivo de la ruina ocasionada por los temblores de 12 de Febrero.

text, *BAGG*, 8 (1943):56ff.

1505   A 1.2.2 (1689) 11.778–1784

El Ayuntamiento acuerda reconstruir las casas consistoriales.

text, *BAGG*, 8 (1943):57ff.

1506   A 1.2.2 (1689) 11.778–1784–14

El Ayuntamiento nombra comisionados para que señalen los predios en que deben ser construidas las capillas de los pasos.

text, *BAGG*, 8 (1943):58.

1507   A 1.2.2 (1691) 11.778–1784

Acuerdos y determinaciones del Ayuntamiento acerca de la fundación del colegio de misioneros de Propaganda Fide de Cristo Crucificado.

text, *BAGG*, 8 (1943):62ff.

1508   A 1.2.2 (1693) 11.778–1784

El Convento de Santa Catalina Mártir solicita del Ayuntamiento licencia para hacer construir un arco, sobre la calle que conduce de la plaza mayor a la iglesia de Nuestra Señora de las Mercedes.

text, *BAGG*, 8 (1943):77ff.

1509   A 1.2.2 (1695) 11.779–1785

El Síndico del Ayuntamiento presenta la licencia otorgada por la Audiencia, para la reconstrucción de las casas consistoriales.

text, *BAGG*, 8 (1943):81ff.

1510   A 1.2.2 (1696) 11.779–1785

El Mayordomo de los propios, pide licencia para iniciar la obra de las casas consistoriales.

text, *BAGG*, 8 (1943):82ff.

1511   A 1.2.2 (1696) 11.779–1785

El Ayuntamiento dispone contribuir en las festividades preparadas por la religión Belemítica, con motivo de su erección.

text, *BAGG*, 8 (1943):86ff.

1512   A 1.2.2 (1698) 11.779–1785

Cabildo dated Tuesday, 21 October 1698. Cabildo for December 5 omitted because of the festivities planned for the dedication of the new church of the Compañía de Jesús, ". . . el nuevo templo tan costoso como oseado y curioso."

1513   A 1.2.2 (1698) 11.779–1785

El Ayuntamiento acuerda asistir a la festividad de la dedicación de la iglesia del colegio de la Compañía de Jesús.

text, *BAGG,* 10 (1945):193.

1514   A 1.2.2 (1699) 11.776–1782

El Ayuntamiento acuerda nombrar comisionados para que atiendan y reciban a las monjas que han de fundar el convento de Santa Clara.

text, *BAGG,* 8 (1943):92ff.

1515   A 1.2.2 (1701) 11.780–1786

Recolección ". . . licencia para fundarse en el Barrio de Sn. Jerónimo . . ." 30 de Mayo 1701.

text, *BAGG,* 8 (1943):71.

1516   A 1.2.2 (1701) 11.780–1786

Cabildo dated 4 February 1701 agrees to help in the expense of bringing an oil painting of Christ from Esquipulas for the Iglesia del Carmen.

1517   A 1.2.2 (1702) 11.780–1786

El Ayuntamiento cede tres mil maravedis para la reedificación de la iglesia de las Benditas Animas.

text, *BAGG,* 8 (1943):105.

1518   A 1.2.2 (1703) 11.780–1786

License granted to enlarge "la Hermita de la Cruz del Milagro." Cabildo dated 8 June 1703.

text, *BAGG,* 8 (1943):107.

1519   A 1.2.2 (1703) 11.780–1786

Vecinos of barrio of Chipilapa ask for a sitio to build "una Hermita para la Santa Cruz" in cabildo 8 May 1703.

text, *BAGG,* 8 (1943):107.

1520   A 1.2.2 (1703) 11.780–1786

Es presentada al Ayuntamiento una solicitud acerca de la construcción de la Ermita de Nuestra Señora de los Dolores.

text, *BAGG,* 8 (1943):108.

1521   A 1.2.2 (1704) 11.780–1786

Speak of the oil painting now located in the church of El Carmen—cabildo dated 29 January 1704.

1522 A 1.2.2 (1704) 11.780–1786

Accounts of paving the plaza presented to Ayuntamiento—totals 600 pesos.

text, *BAGG*, 8 (1943):111.

1523 A 1.2.2 (1705) 11.780–1786

Ayuntamiento makes public rogations because of eruption of Volcán de Fuego.

1524 A 1.2.2 (1711) 11.781–1787

Cabildo dated 18 August 1711. Neighbors of barrio of Espíritu Santo ask for 50 varas and get them to build an ermita to Nuestra Señora de Guadalupe.

text, *BAGG*, 8 (1943):122.

1525 A 1.2.2 (1743) 11.787–1793

El Alcalde don Juan González Batres, informa estar terminada la obra de las casas consistoriales.

text, *BAGG*, 8 (1943):131ff.

1526 A 1.2.2 (1743) 11.787–1.7 93

Inauguración de las nuevas casas consistoriales de la ciudad de Santiago de los Caballeros.

text, *BAGG*, 8 (1943):132ff.

1527 A 1.2.4 (1533) 15.752–9 v.

19 de diciembre de 1533.—Ordénase que los vecinos de la provincia de Guatemala, que tienen sus esposas en Castilla vayan por ellas, so pena de perder toda merced que disfruten.

1528 A 1.2.4 (1536) 15.752–42

9 de septiembre de 1536.—Ordena su majestad que los encomenderos deben contraer matrimonio.

1529 A 1.2.4 (1536) 15.752–43

30 de marzo de 1536.—Dispone su majestad que el gobernador de la provincia de Guatemala, el obispo de ella y los provinciales de las órdenes de religiosos celebren juntas para formular un plan, con objeto de convertir a los indios.

1530 A 1.2.4 (1538) 15.752–41

25 de febrero de 1538.—Recomendando al gobernador de la provincia de Guatemala, que intervenga ante las órdenes religiosas que hagan construir monasterios en los pueblos de indios o en sus inmediaciones.

1531 A 1.2.4 (1538) 15.752–44 v.

20 de diciembre de 1538.—Ordena su majestad que a los seis meses de promulgarse en la ciudad de Santiago, esta cédula, todos los vecinos hagan construir sus viviendas de piedra, ladrillo y teja.

1532 A 1.2.4 (1538) 2196–138

20 de diciembre de 1538.—Dispónese que en la construcción de las casas, solamente sea empleada la piedra y el ladrillo y que los techos sean de teja; las salas amplias y los patios con sol.

1533 A 1.2.4 (1540) 15.752–54 v.

10 de junio de 1540.—Ordena su majestad que con los indios que viven dispersos en los montes de la provincia de Guatemala, reduciéndolos, se formen pueblos.

1534 A 1.2.4 (1540) 15.752–54

9 de noviembre de 1540.—Dando instrucciones al obispo de la provincia de Guatemala, que reúna a los indios principales, a los caciques y al resto de naturales, para instruirlos en las cosas de la fe católica, en industrias 'e otras cosas de policía'.

1535 A 1.2.4 (1541) 15.752–52

20 de enero de 1541.—Ordénase a los ayuntamientos que tengan bajo su cuidado la construcción y conservación de los caminos.

1536 A 1.2.4 (1544) 2196–168

11 de agosto de 1544.—Ordenando a las justicias de los pueblos de la jurisdicción de la Audiencia de los Confines, que sigan informaciones secretas para establecer el número de esclavos existentes en sus límites y el trato que reciben de parte de sus amos.

1537 A 1.2.4 (1547) 2196–153

20 de junio de 1547.—Que la administración de los fondos, provinientes de las encomiendas que fueron de doña Beatriz de la Cueva y de su esposo don Pedro de Alvarado, y destinados para la obra de la Catedral de Guatemala, le sea a cargo de Juan Pérez Dardón.

1538 A 1.2.4 (1548) 2196–122

25 de julio de 1548.—Ordenando al ayuntamiento de la ciudad de Santiago de la provincia de Guatemala, que formule un reglamento para el pago de los jornales que devenguen los oficiales mecánicos.

1539 A 1.2.4 (1556) 2196–127

18 de julio de 1556.—Que el ayuntamiento de la ciudad de Santiago de la provincia de Guatemala, pueda establecer dos barreros (obrajes) para labrar teja y ladrillo.

1540   A 1.2.4 (1587) 2195–247

20 de julio de 1587.—Su majestad ordena a la Real Audiencia, que dé toda su ayuda económica a los que se están encargando de la construcción y dotación de la ermita de Nuestra Señora de los Remedios, en la capital.

1541   A 1.2.4 (1723) 16.192–2245

Información acerca del patronato que goza el ayuntamiento en el convento de nuestra Señora de la Limpia Concepción de Maria.

text, *BAGG*, 10 (1945):210ff.

1541a   A 1.2.5 (1534) 15.760–2202

Libro rotulado: "Cartas Barias—antiguas". Este volumen contiene: cartas del Adelantado don Pedro de Alvarado, del Obispo Francisco Marroquín, del Obispo Fr. Bartolomé de las Casas y otras personas.

1542   A 1.2.5 (1564) 15.766–2207–36

"Gran inconveniente es para lo que toca, al servicio de V.M., y bien desta República, así de Españoles como de naturales, sea gobernada de jueces nuevos, que vengan desos reinos sin haber estado en las indias; porque primero que entienden lo que conviene a la buena gobernación se pierde mucho, y siempre vienen con criados y paniaguados y debdos y los prefieren a los que acá están."

text, *BAGG*, 8 (1943):23ff.

1543   A 1.2.5 (1709) 15.766–2207–33

El Cabildo, Justicia y Reximiento de la ciudad de Guatemala expresa la extrema pobreza de los pobladores del reino y las causas de ella.

text, *BAGG*, 8 (1943):114ff.

1544   A 1.2.5. (c. 1717) 15.777–2207–69

El Cabildo hace presente los lamentables estragos, que causaron los terremotos habidos en esta ciudad.

text, *BAGG*, 8 (1943):123ff.

1545   A 1.2.5 (1718) 15.766–2207–16

El Cabildo, habiendo informado al Rey el general estrago de esta ciudad con los terremotos del año de diez y siete, lo hace en particular de la iglesia y convento de Nuestra Señora de la Merced.

text, *BAGG*, 10 (1945):161ff.

1546   A 1.2.5 (1719) 15.776–2207–71

El cabildo informa haber reparado la ciudad, de las ruinas, que padeció con los terremotos de 1717.

text, *BAGG*, 8 (1943):125ff.

1546a   A 1.2.6 (1604) 11.810–1804

Becerro del asiento general y particular de las cuadras, casas y vecinos que hay en ellas de la ciudad de Santiago de los Caballeros de la Provincia de Guatemala, en que se ha de repartir la alcabala que está obligada a pagar a su Magestad . . .

1547   A 1.2.6 (1699) 16.577–2283

El Ayuntamiento cede cierta porción de agua a favor del nuevo Monasterio de Santa Clara.

1548   A 1.2.6 (1703) 25.573–2848

Ask Ayuntamiento for more water. Santa Clara.

1549   A 1.2.6 (1703) 29.978–4000

Juan Antonio de Ursilla en nombre de los religiosos del convento de Santa Clara, sobre que se asiente la partida a su favor, antes a nombre de comisario general Pedro de Gastañaza y del maestro Jerónimo de Barabona en cuyas casas se fundó dicho convento.

1550   A 1.2.6 (1716) 29.993–4000

El Hermano Tomás García, en nombre de la Tercera Orden de San Francisco pide tributo de agua de goza para la casa y templo del Calvario.

1551   A 1.2.7 (1751) 30.341–4004

Fr. Pedro de San Francisco, pide que el Ayuntamiento ayude para la reedificación del templo y convento de Belén.

1552   A 1.2.9 (1698) 25.348–2840

El Ayuntamiento de Guatemala, da 150 pesos para celebrar el estreno de la iglesia de la Compañía de Jesús.

1553   A 1.3 (1680) 12.245–1885

Autos sobre la posesión de las Cátedras de la Real Universidad de San Carlos, asignación de materias e inauguración de los cursos.

text, *BAGG,* 9 (1944):119ff.

1554   A 1.3 (1760) 13.769–2003

Representación del Tesorero de la Universidad, relativo al traslado de la Universidad y que los frailes dominicos alegan ser dueños del solar en que estaba (éste se encontraba inmediato al templo de Santo Domingo).

1555   A 1.3 (1763) 1157–45

Autos acerca de que la Universidad sea trasladada a la casa que había ocupado don José de Alcantará, ubicada al sur de la catedral.

1556   A 1.3 (1782) 1163–45

Instancia del señor Dr. Don Felipe Romana y Herrera, Fiscal de esta Real

Audiencia en razón de haberse puesto en las paredes públicas de la Real Universidad el blasón de la Silla Apostólica alternando con las armas reales de Su Majestad.

1557 A 1.3.1 (1676) 12.235–1882

Autos de la merced y fundación de la Real Universidad de San Carlos de esta ciudad de Santiago de Guatemala. Cédula de la erección de 31 de enero de 1676.

text, *BAGG,* 9(1944):55ff.

1558 A 1.3.3 (1683) 12.388–1896

Agustín Núñez, maestro ensamblador, enters a bid of 600 pesos to construct a retablo for the university, according to the plan and design he submits, 6 varas wide by 5 varas high, including various sculptures.

1559 A 1.3.4 (1760) 12.328–1890

Acta del Claustro (pleno) celebrado el 20 de Agosto de 1760. Se trató de la rendición de cuentas, de la compra de las casas pertenecientes a don Agustín de la Cagiga, para dotación del edificio de la Universidad.

1560 A 1.3.4 (1782) 4410–49

Autos acerca de la petición del Fiscal de la Audiencia y contra dichos por el Rector Dr. Juan Antonio Dighero relativos a los blasones en la Universidad.

1561 A 1.3.8 (1681) 12.445–1899

University. Problem of class attendance. Theological students worst offenders.

1562 A 1.3.20 (1681) 13.145–1956

Contra el Doctor Juan Bautista de Urquiola, por ciertos gastos hechos en la construcción de la capilla y otras dependencias del edificio de la Universidad.

1563 A 1.3.21 (1751) 13.160–1957

Autos del reconocimiento del estado del edificio de la Universidad, debido a los temblores del día 4 de marzo.

1564 A 1.3.21 (1751) 13.161–1957

Copia del informe rendido a S.M. del estado ruinoso en que quedó el edificio de la Universidad, debido a los temblores de 4 de marzo.

1565 A 1.3.21 (1764) 13.162–1957

Avalúo y remate del sitio y edificio que ocupó la Universidad en las inmediaciones de Santo Domingo.

1566 A 1.3.21 (1773) 13.163–1957

Reconocimiento del estado en que quedó el edificio de la Universidad, debido al terremoto de Santa Marta (29 de Julio).

1567   A 1.3.21 (1788) 13.164–1957

Nicolás Monzón informa de que el techo de la biblioteca de la Universidad está ruinoso.

1568   A 1.3.21 (1790) 13.165–1957

Borrador del costo que tuvo el edificio de la Universidad de la Antigua Guatemala.

1569   A 1.3.21 (1790) 13.166–1957

Instancia del Claustro y Rector de la Universidad para que el Superior Gobierno le ayude en la construcción del nuevo edificio.

1570   A 1.3.21 (1809) 13.168–1957

Cuentos del producto de la suscripción para terminar la construcción del edificio de la Universidad. Fueron recogidos 28 pesos.

1571   A 1.3.21 (1815) 13.170–1957

Relación de los gastos y arbitrios invertidos en la construcción del edificio de la Universidad.

1572   A 1.3.25 (1773) 13.252–1961

El Capitán General, expone la necesidad de la traslación de la ciudad a otro sitio por los terremotos de San Miguel.

1573   A 1.3.25 (1775) 13.253–1961

Acerca de la traslación de la Universidad al Llano de la Virgen.

1574   A 1.7 (1614) 12.006–1813

Libro de asiento del costo de reparaciones hechas al edificio que ocupa el Hospital Real de Santiago.

1575   A 1.7 (1661) 1283–52

Autos para determinar el estado ruinoso en que se encuentra el edificio que ocupa el Hospital de San Alejo. La visita fué hecha por el Oidor Lic. Juan Francisco Esquivel.

1576   A 1.7 (1663) 14.263–2051

Informe rendido por el Prior del hospital de Granada acerca de que él fundó un hospital en la Villa y Puerto de Realejo.

1577   A 1.7 (1715) 5873–268

Autos sobre la erección y traslación del Hospital de San Alejo, para la curación de los indios e indias que pretende hacer el Ilmo. Obispo Fr. Juan Bautista Alvarez de Toledo. Esta traslación no era más que la "separación" del Hospital de San Alejo del Real y pasarlo a ciertas casas, bajo la advocación de Santa Ana.

1578 A 1.7 (1745) 1294–52

Autos para conceder a doña Juana Ortiz y Núñez la casa de altos, propiedad del Hospital, situada en las inmediaciones de la plaza mayor.

1579 A 1.7 (1752) 1296–52

El maestro Juan de Dios Estrada, quien había rematado la obra de albañilería del Hospital, se queja por no habérsele admitido la fianza.

1580 A 1.7 (1754) 1297–52

Fr. Joaquín Vargas, administrador del Hospital, rinde cuentas.

1581 A 1.7 (1784) 14.436–2062

Planos del edificio del hospital de San Juan de Dios, de la ciudad de Guatemala.

1582 A 1.7 (1785) 14.436–2062, fol. 54

Plano y anteproyecto para la construcción del Hospital de San Pedro, en la Nueva Guatemala de la Asunción. Autor: Bernardo Ramírez.

1583 A 1.7 (1815) 54.236–6067, fol. 4

Plano del area que ocupó el Hospital de San Juan de Dios en la Antigua Guatemala.

1584 A 1.9 (1731) 1380–54

Permuta de la casa e iglesia de Capuchinas por la casa del Colegio de Niñas, en tanto es concluída la obra del monasterio de las capuchinas.

1585 A 1.10 (1717) 1528–55

Autos ordenando el reconocimiento de algunos valles (el de Las Vacas, Chimaltenango, etc.) para trasladar la ciudad con motivo de los terremotos de San Miguel (Septiembre 27 de 1717). Estos autos fueron revisados con motivo del terremoto de Santa María (29 de Julio de 1773).

1586 A 1.10 (1773) 1535–55

Padrón que determina, por parroquias, la población existente en la antigua Guatemala.

1587 A 1.10 (1773) 4462–62

Padrón de los pueblos de Mixco, San Miguel Petapa y Villa Nueva para determinar el número de indios que deben dar como repartimiento para las obras de la nueva ciudad.

1588 A 1.10 (1773) 18.773–2444

Carta del 31 de Agosto de 1773, dirigida por el Ayuntamiento a su Majestad, informándole de la ruina acaecida el 29 de julio y solicitando algunas providencias en favor del vecindario.

text, *BAGG*, 8 (1943):152ff.

1589 A 1.10 (1775) 1543–56

El Maestro Fr. Simón Reina, presenta su informe acerca del estado de algunos materiales que existen aprovechables de los edificios de la antigua Guatemala.

1590 A 1.10 (1775) 1544–56

Autos enviados por el Alcalde de Primer Voto de la antigua Guatemala, relativos a la reconstrucción que ha iniciado el Pbro. Carlos Sunsín.

1591 A 1.10 (1775) 1700–72, fol. 13

Plano del Convento de San Agustín, en proceso de construcción en la Nueva Guatemala. Autor: José María Alejandre.

1592 A 1.10 (1776) 1548–56

Providencias reglamentando la elevación, terraplenes y materiales de construcción que debían ser empleados en la Nueva Guatemala.

1593 A 1.10 (1776) 1549–56

El Justicia Mayor de la antigua Guatemala, rinde información acerca de la obra que ha emprendido el Pbro. Carlos Sunsín en cierta casa.

1594 A 1.10 (1776) 1563–58

Bando disponiendo que la carga de cal (cinco arrobas) valga real y medio y cuando sea de diez arrobas, tres reales.

1595 A 1.10 (1776) 1567–58

Sumaria instruída a los Justicias de Santa Catarina Pinula, por no haber acatado la orden en enviar un repartimiento de indios que debían trabajar en las obras de la ciudad.

1596 A 1.10 (1776) 1568–58

Providencia acerca del repartimiento de indios entre los vecinos de la nueva Guatemala.

1597 A 1.10 (1776) 1569–59

Providencia a fin que el Alcalde Mayor de Verapaz remita cierta cantidad de indios con destino a los trabajos de la nueva Guatemala.

1598 A 1.10 (1776) 1684–71, fol. 22

Plano de la iglesia y convento de Ntra. Sra. del Pilar de Zaragoza (Capuchinas). Autor: Bernardo Ramírez. Ciudad de Nueva Guatemala.

1599 A 1.10 (1776) 4466–62

Autos de las medidas que debían ser tomadas con motivo de la ruina de San Salvador (30 y 31 de Marzo 1776). Estos temblores fueron sentidos en Guatemala.

1600 A 1.10 (1776) 4470–62

El Justicia Mayor de Sacatepéquez expone que varios indios han solicitado que se les dispense del trabajo en las obras de la nueva ciudad por tener que dedicarse a sus siembras.

1601 A 1.10 (1776) 18.753–2445 fol. 26

Plano (cuadro) de las areas que comprenden los pueblos situados en las inmediaciones de Guatemala.

1602 A 1.10 (1776) 31.361–4049

Método regular en formación de los cimientos. Sobre colocación de horcones.

1603 A 1.10 (1777) 1571–59

Los indios de Chimaltenango solicitan no venir a los trabajos de Guatemala por estar ocupados en sus siembras.

1604 A 1.10 (1777) 1572–59

Igual solicitud presentada por los de Rabinal.

1605 A 1.10 (1777) 1575–59

Autos ordenando la cancelación de los gastos que hicieron don Marcos Ibañez (arquitecto) y don Antonio Bernasconi (dibujante) para su venida.

1606 A 1.10 (1777) 1578–59

El Arzobispo Larraz solicita ayuda para reconstruir ciertas iglesias de algunos pueblos comarcanos.

1607 A 1.10 (1777) 1586–59

Providencia nombrando dos aparejadores: uno para la obra de albañilería y otro para la de carpintería en el Palacio Real.

1608 A 1.10 (1777) 4473–62

Los indios de varios pueblos de la Alcaldía Mayor de Sololá solicitan la dispensa en las obras de la nueva Guatemala, por tener que dedicarse a sus siembras.

1609 A 1.10 (1777) 4474–62 and following

The following documents contain petitions on the indios of the towns indicated below asking to be exempted from working on the construction of Nueva Guatemala.
       4474–62 – Quetzaltenango
       4475–62 – Patzún
       4476–63 – San Pedro Las Huertas
       4477–63 – San Andrés Izapa
       4478–63 – Ciudad Vieja (Antigua)

4479–63 – Izapa
4480–63 – Santiago Mataescuintla
4481–63 – San Pedro Pinula
4482–63 – Santa Apolonia (Chim.)
4483–63 – San Raymundo de las Casillas (Sac.)
4485–63 – Petapa
4486–63 – Chimaltenango
4487–63 – Chimaltenango, order to capture indios who refuse
(1788)   4488–63 – Sololá
4489–63 – Sololá
4490–63 – Cubulco

1610   A 1.10 (1777) 4484–63

Informe del corregidor de Quetzaltenango, acerca del número de oficiales de carpintería que hay en su jurisdicción.

1611   A 1.10 (1777) 4524–69

Autos llevados a cabo por el oidor don Manuel Antonio de Arredondo acerca de que sean trasladados de la Antigua Guatemala, los escombros de los edificios reales.

1612   A 1.10 (1778) 1656–67, fol. 31

Plano de una de las casas construidas para residencia de uno de los Oidores de la Audiencia.

1613   A 1.10 (1778) 1694–72, fol. 3

Plano del convento e iglesia de Santo Domingo. Autor: Francisco Carbonel.

1614   A 1.10 (1779) 1665–68, fol. 7

Plano de la manzana no. 79 del Plano General de la Nueva Guatemala, detallando los sectores destinados para la obra de la Universidad de San Carlos y Colegio Tridentino.

1615   A 1.10 (1779) 4500–63

Ponce de León, avisa que comunicó a los oficiales de carpintería residentes en Tecpán, que estaban revelados de trabajar en la nueva Guatemala.

1616   A 1.10 (1779) 4501–63

Providencia que los capataces y alcaides usen armas.

1617   A 1.10 (1783) 6445–305

Comprobante de ciertos gastos de la reparación del puente de Los Esclavos.

1618   A 1.10 (1784) 6446–306

Planilla de los gastos efectuados en la reparación del puente de Los Esclavos.

1619   A 1.10 (1784) 6447–306

Planilla de la obra del puente de Los Esclavos.

1620   A 1.10 (1786) 1614–61

Providencia de la Real Audiencia acerca de que los Oficiales de la Real Hacienda, sean los encargados de cancelar los trabajos de la pila de la Plaza Mayor. Asimismo los relativos a empedrados.

1621   A 1.10 (1787) 4591–76, fol. 3

Plano de la iglesia de Ciudad Vieja trasladado a las inmediaciones de la Nueva Guatemala. Autor: Bernardo Ramírez.

1622   A 1.10 (1788) 6575–317, fol. 13

Plano del Colegio de Cristo Crucificado de la Nueva Guatemala. Autor: Bernardo Ramírez.

1623   A 1.10 (1796) 4596–76, fol. 2

Plano de la iglesia de Colegio de Cristo Crucificado de Misioneros de Propaganda Fide, de la ciudad de Nueva Guatemala. Autor: Pedro de Garci Aguirre.

1624   A 1.10.1 (1676) 1418–64

El tesorero de la Real Caja solicita que se autorice la reparación de la casa que habita.

1625   A 1.10.1 (1711) 14.902–2101

Cuenta de lo gastado en la reconstrucción del Palacio.

1626   A 1.10.1 (1736) 14.903–2101

Accounts of money spent on Palacio de los Capitanes.

1627   A 1.10.1 (1736) 14.904–2101

Account of money spent on Palacio de los Capitanes.

1628   A 1.10.1 (1740) 14.905–2101

Account of money spent for building some rooms in Palacio de los Capitanes.

1629   A 1.10.1 (1746) 14.906–2101

Planillas de gastos. Reconstrucción del Palacio Real.

1630   A 1.10.1 (1760) 1421–64

Providencia ordenando que se reconozca el estado que tiene el Palacio.

1631   A 1.10.1 (1761) 1422–64

Providencia autorizando el gasto de la reparación de la portada de Palacio. Este trabajo lo dirigió Diez de Navarro.

1632   A 1.10.1 (1766) 17.907–2101

Informe sobre la cantidad de piedra extraída en la cantera de Cabrejo para la obra del nuevo Palacio Real.

1633   A 1.10.1 (1768) 1498–2101

Cuenta de lo gastado en reconstruir las defensas del puerto de Omoa.

1634   A 1.10.1 (1768) 31.220–4044

Acerca de que sea desocupada la pieza destinada a la oficina de almonedas, en vista de la reedificación del Palacio Real.

1635   A 1.10.1 (1768) 31.222–4044

Por haber quedado terminada la reedificación del Real Palacio, dispónese el traslado del Real Tribunal, de las habitaciones de la casa de moneda a sus dependencias permanentes.

1636   A 1.10.1 (1768) 31.223–4044

Comprobante de haber recibido el Ayuntamiento de Guatemala los comprobantes a las cuentas de la construcción del Real Palacio.

1637   A 1.10.1 (1769) 184–8

Testimonio de la cédula de 8 de enero de 1763 acerca de otorgar licencia para el gasto de 65,183 pesos en la construcción del Palacio de los Capitanes Generales.

1638   A 1.10.1 (1769) 1423–64

Autos hechos en razón de lo ordenado en cédula de 8 de enero de 1763, autorizando el gasto para la reparación de Palacio de los Capitanes Generales. (65,183 pesos).

1639   A 1.10.1 (1779) 6458–307

Libro en que consta la cantidad de escombros traídos de la Antigua Guatemala, para ser empleados en la obra de ciertos edificios reales.

1640   A 1.10.1 (1779) 6458–307

A ledger with accounts of materials from Antigua, Guatemala for construction of the new capital.

1641   A 1.10.1 (1783) 916–119

Los alcaldes y regidores del barrio del Cerrillo, Ciudad Real, piden medios para la reedificación de sus casas consistoriales. (In Archivo General del Estado de Chiapas, R7-SE-3).

1642   A 1.10.1 (1785) 6491–309

Libro de planillas (semanales) de los empleados en la construcción de la pila de la Plaza Mayor.

1643   A 1.10.1 (1785) 6499–309

Legajo de planillas (desde 66 a la 61) de los sueldos devengados por los trabajadores empleados en la obra del Real Palacio.

1644   A 1.10.1 (1795) 1441–64

Autos hechos en razón de la Real Orden relativa a la forma que debe seguirse en las construcciones de fortaleza.

1645   A 1.10.1 (1804) 1484–65

El Arquitecto Pedro Garci-Aguirre, solicita que le sean cancelados los sueldos que devengó en carácter de dirigente de los trabajos de reparación de la casa que habita el Oider Francisco Camacho.

1646   A 1.10.2 (1751) 18.769–2447

Juan de Dios Estrada, Maestro Mayor de Obras del Ayuntamiento de Guatemala, pide se controle la edifcación de casas de particulares.

1647   A 1.10.2 (1766) 973–39

Proyecto formulado por el ayuntamiento de la ciudad de Guatemala, para la construcción del edificio de las casas consistoriales en el lado norte de la plaza.

1648   A 1.10.2 (1766) 18.771–2447

El maestro de Obras del Ayuntamiento de Guatemala Francisco de Castro, presenta el proyecto sobre construir de arcadas el portal del cabildo en su extremo poniente.

1649   A 1.10.2 (1767) 14.978–2108

Cuenta de la reparación del edificio del ayuntamiento de la ciudad de Guatemala.

1650   A 1.10.2 (1774) 1642–66

Providencia acerca de que los escombros del Palacio y Real Aduana y Hospital, sean conservados para ser empleados en la construcción de edificios en la nueva Guatemala.

1651   A 1.10.2 (1777) 1650–67

Juan Medina, solicita que se le dé alguna gratificación por los trabajos que efectuó con el objeto de acopiar materiales.

1652   A 1.10.2 (1777) 4523–69

Legajo de la correspondencia cruzada entre don Manuel de Arredondo y don José Manuel de Barroetea, acerca de la conducción de escombros, maderas, puertas, etc. de la Antigua Guatemala.

1653   A 1.10.2 (1777) 4524–69

Autos llevados a cabo por el Oidor don Manuel Antonio de Arredondo acerca de que sean trasladados de la Antigua Guatemala, los escombros de los edificios reales.

1654   A 1.10.2 (1783) 1660–68

El Maestro Bernardo Ramírez, propone que el portal de las casas consistoriales, sea fabricado siguiendo el mismo estilo que el que tiene el de la Real Aduana.

1655   A 1.10.2 (1786) 14.986–2108

Cuenta del costo de la pila de la plaza central de Guatemala.

1656   A 1.10.2 (1786) 14.987–2108

Cuenta del costo de la piedra empleada en la pila de la plaza central de Guatemala.

1657   A 1.10.2 (1786) 1669–68

Don Manuel de la Bodega, es nombrado Superintendente de la obra de la Catedral.

1658   A 1.10.2 (1788) 20–2

Sobre la reedificación del Ayuntamiento y Mesón del pueblo de Zinacantán.

1659   A 1.10.2 (1788) 1670–68

Por fallecimiento de don Sebastián Gamundi, Director Interino de la obra de la Catedral, es nombrado el Ing. José Sierra. En este cuaderno está el proyecto general de la obra, debido al maestro José Arroyo.

1660   A 1.10.2 (1792) 4529–69

Indians of Santa Catarina Pinula ask for help of the Alcalde of Sacatepéquez to intercede for them since they did not come to work in Nueva Guatemala.

1661   A 1.10.2 (1797) 1672–68

Don Manuel del Campo y Rivas, solicita que él es el llamado a ser el Superintendente de la obra de la Catedral.

1662   A 1.10.2 (1798) 1673–68

Providencia nombrando el maestro Bernardo Ramírez, para que dirija la obra de la catedral.

1663   A 1.10.2 (1800) 1674–68

Habiéndose enfermado el Ing. Antonio Porta, quien había sido comisionado para ir a Granada y revisar la catedral de aquella ciudad, fué nombrado el Ing. José Sierra.

1664   A 1.10.2 (1801) 1675–68

Autos acerca de la construcción de catedral.

1665   A 1.10.2 (1802) 2677–68

El Ing. José Sierra, solicita que le sean cancelados los sueldos que devengó como Director de la obra de la Catedral, Sierra pensaba marcharse a España.

1666   A 1.10.2 (1802) 1678–68

El Ing. Pedro Garci-Aguirre, uno de los encargados de la obra de la Catedral, solicita que ya no se explote la cantera de Arrivillaga sino que la de El Naranjo.

1667   A 1.10.2 (1806) 1679–68

Providencia acerca de que en la obra de la Catedral, para mayor seguridad y solidez, sean colocados tirantes de hierro.

1668   A 1.10.2 (1817) 7713–373

Sobre la reedificación de la casa consistorial de San Cristóbal Amatitlán.

1669   A 1.10.3 (1597) 31.246–4086

Pedro Valle de Quejo, pide que el Ayuntamiento le cubra el valor de su casa, tomada para la construcción de la Capilla de San Sebastián.

1670   A 1.10.3 (1630) 31.247–4046

Varios indígenas de San Francisco Motozintla, partido de Totonicapán ask to be relieved of tributación since they are reconstructing their church destroyed by fire.

1671   A 1.10.3 (1639) 31.248–4046

Diego Quiñónez, Gobernador del pueblo de San Antonio Suchitépequez, y los componentes del Ayuntamiento solicitan no sean ocupados los indígenas, por estar trabajando en la construcción de su iglesia.

1672   A 1.10.3 (1644) 31.249–4046

Aid to help build church. Santiago El Sambo.

1673   A 1.10.3 (1644) 31.250–4046

Alcaldes give licence to raise money to build church. Santiago el Sambo.

1674   A 1.10.3 (1644) 31.265–4046

Comalapa—temple and convento in bad condition.

1675   A 1.10.3 (1645) 31.251–4046

Apoderado of the indios asks help to build church—Santiago el Sambo.

1676   A 1.10.3 (1647) 31.252–4046

San Antonio Nejapa—ask part of tribute for rebuilding of church.

1677   A 1.10.3 (1667) 31.253–4046

Los alcaldes y regidores del pueblo de San Agustín de la Real Corona, del corregimiento de Acasaguastlán, piden parte de sus tributos para edificar su iglesia de artezón y no de paja como es.

1678   A 1.10.3 (1671) 31.394–4053

Asunción Mita—ask help to build church "con mayores seguridades."

1679   A 1.10.3 (1672) 31.254–4046

El común de Santiago de Tepesmoto (Segovia, Nicaragua) piden fondos para reedificar su iglesia.

1680   A 1.10.3 (1672) 31.255–4046

Informe acerca del estado de la edificación de la nueva catedral de Guatemala.

1681   A 1.10.3 (1672) 31.257–4046

Los indígenas de Quetzaltenango piden ser exonerados de trabajos por estar dedicados a la reconstrucción de su iglesia.

1682   A 1.10.3 (1672) 31.258–4046

El maestro de albañilería José de Porras, director de la obra de la catedral de Guatemala, pide aumento de sueldo.

1683   A 1.10.3 (1673) 31.259–4046

El común del pueblo de San Agustín del corregimiento de Acasaguastlán, pide ayuda para reedificar su iglesia.

1684   A 1.10.3 (1677) 31.260–4046

Los indígenas del pueblo de San Juan del Obispo, del valle de Guatemala, sobre que se les ayude con 800 pesos para reedificar su iglesia.

1685   A 1.10.3 (1677) 31.261–4046

Los indígenas del pueblo de Santa Barbara, del corregimiento de Totonicapán piden ayuda de tributos para reedificar su iglesia.

1686   A 1.10.3 (1677) 31.262–4046

Los indígenas de San Lucas Sacatepéquez, piden ayuda para reedificar la capilla mayor de su iglesia.

1687   A 1.10.3 (1679) 31.263–4046

San Dionisio de los Pastores—*in re* rebuilding of church.

1688   A 1.10.3 (1679) 31.264–4046

Cura of Pastores—asks indios be relieved of repartimiento—working on church.

1689 A 1.10.3 (1679) 31.265–4046

Fr. Pedro de Estrada (O.F.M.) guardián del convento de Comalapa, certifica estar en mal estado dicho convento y templo.

1690 A 1.10.3 (1679) 31.266–4046

Los alcaldes y regidores del pueblo de San Francisco Zapotitlán piden real provisión para durante el tiempo que estén ocupados en la construcción de la iglesia, no sean repartidos.

1691 A 1.10.3 (1679) 31.267–4046

El Capitán José de Aguilar de Revolledo, alcalde de la ciudad de Guatemala, expone que se le notificó un auto para que en unión del Cap. Francisco Antonio de Fuentes y Guzmán, colecten limosnas para sufragar los gastos de la edificación del templo de Ntra. Sra. de los Remedios.

1692 A 1.10.3 (1679) 31.268–4046

Instancia del común de Petapa sobre la reedificación del templo de dicho pueblo.

1693 A 1.10.3 (Siglo XVII) 31.386–4051

Cuenta de lo invertido en la obra de la catedral de Guatemala.

1694 A 1.10.3 (1685) 18.801–2448

Instancia de los Pbros. Manuel de Ocampo, Francisco de Rosas, Francisco de Espinosa, y Matías de Acuña, para que se les permita construir una Ermita, en las cercanías del murallón de Santa Lucía, en la ciudad de Guatemala.

1695 A 1.10.3 (1685) 31.269–4046

Priest asks ayuntamiento for "un solar para hacer construir una ermita en la Sabana de Santa Lucía dedicada a la Virgen de la Concepción."

1696 A 1.10.3 (1689) 31.270–4046

Los alcaldes del pueblo de San Pedro de los Hortelanos (hoy las Huertas) indican que con el temblor del 12 de Febrero, quedó arruinado el templo y piden ayuda para reconstruirlo.

1697 A 1.10.3 (1691) 31.271–4046

El Pbro. Nicolás Díaz, solicita al ayuntamiento de Guatemala, cierta cantidad de madera (limosna) para el techo de Santa Lucía.

1698 A 1.10.3 (1693) 31.272–4046

El procurador del convento de San Francisco de Guatemala, pide dos canteros del pueblo de Santa María de Jesús, para la obra del templo.

1699 A 1.10.3 (1693) 31.273–4046

El apoderado de Fr. Felipe de Pantaza, O.F.M., pide ayuda económica para la construcción del Calvario del pueblo de Santiago Cotzomalguapa.

1700 A 1.10.3 (1693) 31.274–4046

El apoderado de Fr. Pedro Chavarría, O.F.M., pide ayuda económica para reedificar el Calvario del pueblo de Patulul.

1701 A 1.10.3 (1695) 31.275–4046

El Capitán José Domínguez, mayordomo de la ermita de Santa Lucía, a cuyo cargo corre la obra, pide licencia para pedir limosna y finalizar la construcción.

1702 A 1.10.3 (1698) 31.276–4046

Autos sobre la asignación de fondos para la construcción del templo parroquial de San Francisco Quetzaltepeque.

1703 A 1.10.3 (1699) 31.277–4046

Instancia de los indígenas del pueblo de Santo Domingo Xenacoj, sobre que se les den de sus tributos los dineros para reedificar el templo parroquial.

1704 A 1.10.3 (1702) 31.278–4047

Los indígenas del barrio del Espíritu Santo, de la ciudad de Guatemala, sobre que se les conceda la cuarta parte de sus tributos para edificar su templo.

1705 A 1.10.3 (1703) 31.279–4047

Juan Antonio Barahona, Felipe de Herrera, Benito de Santa María y Juan Ventura, vecinos de Guatemala, piden al ayuntamiento la cantidad de 10 varas más de tierra, para ampliar la ermita de la Santa Cruz a espaldas, del convento de Concepción.

1706 A 1.10.3 (1705) 6778–328

Autos acerca de la reedificación de la iglesia Catedral de Comayagua.

1707 A 1.10.3 (1705) 31.280–4047

José de Santa María y Maria de Loaiza, ambos pardos libres, piden licencia para recaudar limosnas con destino a la construcción del templo de Mazagua.

1708 A 1.10.3 (1706) 31.281–4047

(San Jorge in Sololá)

El común del pueblo de San JARGO, jurisdicción de la Alcaldía Mayor de Tecpanatitlán, piden fondos de sus caudales, para hacer una campana.

1709 A 1.10.3 (1710) 31.282–4047

San Lorenzo Suchitepéquez—necessary to rebuild church.

1710 A 1.10.3 (1711) 31.283–4047

Fr. José Romero Tamariz, O.F.M., certifica el mal estado del templo del pueblo de Santa María de Jesús, etc.

1711 A 1.10.3 (1712) 16.543–2280

El ayuntamiento cede a favor del templo de Santa Lucía en la ciudad de Guatemala un predio para lonja.

1712 A 1.10.3 (1716) 39.690–4649

Otorgando la cuarta parte de tributos a favor de los indígenas del pueblo de Naulingo, para la reedificación del templo parroquial. (El Salvador)

1713 A 1.10.3 (1717) 31.284–4047

Santiago Zamora, Valle de Guatemala, asks help to rebuild temple destroyed in September.

1714 A 1.10.3 (1717) 31.285–4047

Acerca de la reedificación del templo y cabildo de San Agustín Sumpango.

1715 A 1.10.3 (1717) 31.286–4047

Instancia del común de Tecpán Guatemala sobre la reedificación del Cabildo.

1716 A 1.10.3 (1717) 31.294–4047

Santa Catalina Siquinalá asks permission to rebuild church.

1717 A 1.10.3 (1717) 31.396–4047

Santa Apolonia asks permission to rebuild church.

1718 A 1.10.3 (1718) 31.287–4047

El cura doctrinero de San Andrés Izapa, indica que el templo de dicho pueblo quedó arruinado con los temblores del 29 de Septiembre.

1719 A 1.10.3 (1718) 31.288–4047

El apoderado del común del pueblo de San Cristóbal Amatitlán pide ayuda para reedificar el templo de dicho pueblo.

1720 A 1.10.3 (1718) 31.289–4047

Fr. Ignacio Caballero, O.P., certifica el mal estado en que quedó el templo del pueblo de San Cristóbal Amatitlán con los temblores de Septiembre de 1717.

1721 A 1.10.3 (1718) 31.290–4047

Ask part of tribute to reconstruct temple—Guazacapán.

1722 A 1.10.3 (1720) 18.803–2448

Sobre la construcción del templo de San Lázaro (Antigua).

1723 A 1.10.3 (1720) 31.291–4047

Bernardo Manuel y José de Larios, vecinos de la ciudad de Guatemala, piden ayuda para reedificar la ermita de Santa Lucía, arruinada en Septiembre de 1717.

1724 A 1.10.3 (1720) 31.297–4047

Acerca la reedificación de la ermita del Calvario de la ciudad de Guatemala.

1725 A 1.10.3 (1722) 31.292–4047

El común del pueblo de San Mateo, jurisdicción de Quetzaltenango, pide licencia para la construcción de un templo.

1726 A 1.10.3 (1723) 31.293–4047

Acerca de la reedificación del templo de San Agustín Sumpango.

1727 A 1.10.3 (1723) 31.396–4053

Santa Apolonia Tecpán—asks help to reconstruct temple.

1728 A 1.10.2 (1725) 16.544–2280

El Pbro. Manuel de Morga, solicita al ayuntamiento la limosna de agua con destino al templo de Nuestra Señora del Carmen.

1729 A 1.10.3 (1725) 31.295–4047

Santiago Jocotán—asks permission to rebuild church.

1730 A 1.10.3 (1726) 31.296–4047

Jacaltenango en Huehuetenango—licencia para reedificar y ampliar su iglesia.

1731 A 1.10.3 (1726) 31.298–4047

Jacaltenango en Huehuetenango. Report on cost of rebuilding and enlarging church.

1732 A 1.10.3 (1727) 18.804–2448

Sobre la reconstrucción del templo de la Cruz del Milagro. (Antigua).

1733 A 1.10.3 (1728) 18.805–2448, fol. 2

23 de Julio de 1728—Cédese a favor de la Ermita de Nta. Sra. de los Dolores (Cruz del Milagro) dos varas de terreno y una más sobre la banda donde corre el río Pensativo, obligándose el Prioste y Cofrades de esta ermita, según disposición del Ayuntamiento, a hacer construir una calzada en la margen derecha del citado río.

1734 A 1.10.3 (1728) 18.805–2448

Reconstrucción de la ermita de Los Dolores (a) de la Cruz que tembló. (Antigua).

1735 A 1.10.3 (1729) 6836–329

Instancia de los Indios de Santa María Tactic, de que estando la iglesia de su pueblo en ruinas, se les ayude.

1736 A 1.10.3 (1729) 13.407–1975

Instancia del común del pueblo de San Francisco, jurisdicción de San Miguel, acerca de que se les ayude para recontruir su iglesia.

1737 A 1.10.3 (1729) 31.299–4047

El común de San Gaspar Vivar, pide fondos para reedificar el templo. (Antigua).

1738 A 1.10.3 (1730) 39.703–4650

Comisión al Alcalde Mayor de Suchitepéquez, para que ordene visita de ojos para determinar el estado y cuantia de la reparación del templo parroquial del pueblo de San Sebastián Quetzaltenango.

1739 A 1.10.3 (1733) 31.300–4047

Los alcaldes y regidores del pueblo de San Francisco Quetzaltepeque solicitan parte de sus tributos para la reedificación del templo.

1740 A 1.10.3 (1733) 31.301–4047

Los alcaldes y regidores de San Juan Amatitlán, piden que los vecinos no den servicios (repartimientos) por estar ocupados en la reedificación del templo.

1741 A 1.10.3 (1733) 31.302–4047

Fr. José Vásquez, O.P., cura doctrinero del pueblo de San Gaspar Vivar, indica que faltan fondos para terminar el templo.

1742 A 1.10.3 (1733) 31.303–4047

Alotenango, Guatemala. Church damaged by earthquake on San Joaquin's day.

1743 A 1.10.3 (1734) 31.304–4047

Santa Cruz, jurisdicción de Verapaz, asks part of tribute to build a church.

1744 A 1.10.3 (1734) 31.305–4047

San Andrés Deán—asks help to rebuild church.

1745 A 1.10.3 (1735) 31.306–4047

Santos Inocentes Parramos, Guatemala, asks help to rebuild the church.

1746 A 1.10.3 (1735) 31.307–4047

Sobre reedificar el templo del pueblo de Santo Domingo Xenacoj.

1747 A 1.10.3 (1735) 31.308–4047

El común del pueblo de Santiago Atitlán pide parte de sus tributos para reedificar el templo.

1748   A 1.10.3 (1735) 31.310–4047

El común del pueblo de Santiago Atitlán, presenta el costo que tendrá la reedificación del templo.

1749   A 1.10.3 (1736) 31.311–4047

Los alcaldes del pueblo de San Sebastián y San Miguel El Tejar, piden fondos para reedificar el templo.

1750   A 1.10.3 (1736) 31.311–4047

Ante la Audiencia los justicios del pueblo de San Miguel El Tejar, solicitan parte de sus tributos para la reconstrucción del templo parroquial.

1751   A 1.10.3 (1736) 31.312–4047

Los alcaldes de San Sebastián y San Miguel el Tejar, piden parte de sus tributos para reedificar su templo.

1752   A 1.10.3 (1736) 31.312–4047

Los alcaldes y justicia del pueblo de San Sebastián El Tejar, ante la Audiencia, solicitan fondos para reconstruir el templo parroquial.

1753   A 1.10.3 (1738) 31.313–4047

El P. Manuel de Herrera, rector del Colegio de la Compañía de Jesús, pide al Ayuntamiento ayuda económica para reconstruir este centro de estudios.

1754   A 1.10.3 (1738) 31.314–4047

El vecindario de Santa Lucía, jurisdicción de Escuintla, pide ayuda para reedificar el templo.

1755   A 1.10.3 (1738) 31.315–4047

Jocotán—asks part of tributo to help rebuild church.

1756   A 1.10.3 (1738) 31.316–4047

San Antonio Suchitepéquez asks help to "edificar y ampliar" church.

1757   A 1.10.3 (1739) 18.806–2448

El Ayuntamiento recibe la cédula por la cual se le ordena ayude a la reconstrucción del convento y monasterio de San Agustín.

1758   A 1.10.3 (1739) 31.317–4047

Jocotán again asks help to rebuild church.

1759   A 1.10.3 (1739) 31.318–4047

Acerca de ceder la cuarta parte de tributos para reconstruir el templo de Santa Ana. (Antigua).

1760 A 1.10.3 (1741) 31.319–4048

El común del pueblo de Cobán piden parte de sus tributos para la reedificación del templo.

1761 A 1.10.3 (1742) 31.320–4048

Los alcaldes y regidores del pueblo de San Antonio Retalhuleu exponen no tener fondos para terminar la obra del templo parroquial.

1762 A 1.10.3 (1743) 31.321–4048

El Lic. Roque Ivarrueta, mayordomo de la imagen de Esquipulas, pide no sea suspendida la licencia para recolectar limosnas, destinadas a la obra del templo de Santiago Esquipulas.

1763 A 1.10.3 (1743) 31.322–4048

Visita de ojos para determinar el estado del templo de Santa Ana, extramuros de la ciudad de Guatemala.

1764 A 1.10.3 (1743) 31.323–4048

Tacuilula, jurisdicción de Guazacapán—needs help to rebuild church.

1765 A 1.10.3 (1743) 31.324–4048

El común de San Sebastián Quetzaltenango pide parte de sus tributos para la edificación del templo parroquial.

1766 A 1.10.3 (1743) 31.325–4048

San Martín Perulapán, El Salvador, on rebuilding of church.

1767 A 1.10.3 (1743) 31.326–4048

El Común del pueblo de Sto. Domingo Mixco, pide fondos para reedificar el templo parroquial.

1768 A 1.10.3 (1743) 31.327–4048

Santa María Magdalena Milpas Altas asks help to rebuild church.

1769 A 1.10.3 (1743) 31.328–4048

San Antonio Mazatenango asks help to rebuild church.

1770 A 1.10.3 (1743) 31.329–4048

El Lic. Roque Ivarrueta, mayordomo de la imagen de Esquipulas, pide no sea suspendida la licencia para recolectar limosnas, destinadas a la obra del templo de Santiago Esquipulas.

1771 A 1.10.3 (1743) 39.740–4651

San Estevan Texistepeque—that alcalde mayor of Santa Ana, El Salvador, inspect temple and calculate repairs needed.

1772   A 1.10.3 (1743) 39.741–4651

Comisión al alcalde mayor de Chiapas para que en unión de alarifes calculen el gasto de la reparación del templo parroquial del pueblo de Sinacantan.

1773   A 1.10.3 (1743) 39.742–4651

Comisión al gobernador de Honduras, para que por medio de alarifes calcule el gasto de la reparación del templo del pueblo de Santa María Magdalena Maxolea.

1774   A 1.10.3 (1744) 31.329–4048

El cura doctrinero del pueblo de San Agustín Sumpango, pide sean suspendidos los repartimientos de indios por estar ocupados en la reedificación del templo.

1775   A 1.10.3 (1744) 31.331–4048

Zacapa—rebuilding of church.

1775a   A 1.10.3 (1744) 31.332–4048

Concerning the rebuilding of the church of San Francisco Zapotitlán.

1776   A 1.10.3 (1744) 39.747–4652

Sobre el reconocimiento y avaluo de la reconstrucción del templo del pueblo de San Pedro Cururén, jurisdicción de Honduras.

1777   A 1.10.3 (1744) 39.750–4652

Sobre que el Alcalde Mayor de Escuintla, informe sobre el costo que tendría la reconstrucción del templo parroquial de Escuintla.

1778   A 1.10.3 (1745) 16.545–2280

Instancia de los vecinos de la Calle Ancha ante el Ayuntamiento de Guatemala sobre que se permita cubrir la Cruz de Piedra. Hay un plano.

See also A 1.11 (1753) 2091–98

1779   A 1.10.3 (1745) 31.333–4048

Sobre reedificar la iglesia del pueblo de Tamahú.

1780   A 1.10.3 (1745) 31.334–4048

Fr. Juan de San Mateo, Prior del Convento y hospital de Ntra. Sra. de Belén, indica que para perpetuar la memoria del Hermano Pedro, han dispuesto la reedificación de la ermita de las Animas.

1781   A 1.10.3 (1745) 31.335–4048

Fr. Juan de San Mateo, Prior del convento y hospital de Ntr. Sra. de Belén, pide ayuda al Ayuntamiento para la reedificación de la ermita de las Animas.

1782 A 1.10.3 (1745) 31.336–4048

Concerning the reconstruction of church. Cubulco in Verapaz.

1783 A 1.10.3 (1745) 31.337–4048

Concerning the rebuilding of church Teometapa, Santa Catalina jurisdicción of Chiquimula.

1784 A 1.10.3 (1745) 39.753–4652

Para que el Alcalde Mayor de Verapaz, informe sobre el costo de la reedificación del templo del pueblo de San Pablo Tamahú.

1785 A 1.10.3 (1747) 31.338–4048

San Bernardino Tzamut—rebuilding of church.

1786 A 1.10.3 (1747) 39.758–4652

San Bartolomé Mazatenango—cost of rebuilding church, after the earthquake of 13 October 1747.

1787 A 1.10.3 (1747) 39.761–4652

Order to inspect church and estimate cost of repairs. Cuyotenango, San Gaspar.

1788 A 1.10.3 (1748) 31.340–4048

Real provisión asignando fondos para la reconstrucción de las iglesias de los pueblos de San Sebastián Quetzaltenango y San Antonio Retalhuleu.

1789 A 1.10.3 (1748) 31.341–4048

Money to finish work of reconstruction of church at San Sebastián Quetzaltenango.

1790 A 1.10.3 (1748) 31.342–4048

San Gaspar Cuyotenango, asks help to rebuild parrish church.

1791 A 1.10.3 (1750) 2079–97

El fiscal de la Audiencia expone que cuando a los pueblos se les ayuda de costa para construir iglesias, los fondos los proporcione la Real Caja.

1792 A 1.10.3 (1750) 31.343–4049

Instancia de los indígenas de Sumpango, acerca ayuda económica para reedificar la casa conventual.

1793 A 1.10.3 (1751) 127–8, fol. 72

Order to estimate cost of repairs to cathedral ruined in earthquake of March 4, 1751.

1794 A 1.10.3 (1751) 4215–33

Sobre informar a su Magestad sobre el estado en que quedó la catedral metropolitana con los terremotos de 4 de Marzo de 1751.

1795   A 1.10.3 (1751) 18.807–2448

Instancia del P. Miguel de los Ríos, prepósito de la congregación de San Felipe Nerí, sobre que el ayuntamiento ayude para la reconstrucción del templo.

1796   A 1.10.3 (1751) 31.344–4049

Acerca la redificación de la iglesia del pueblo de San Pedro de las Huertas.

1797   A 1.10.3 (1751) 31.345–4049

Santa María Magdalena Milpas Altas asks help to reconstruct church.

1798   A 1.10.3 (1751) 31.346–4049

Sor Josefa María de Santa Gertrudis, priora del convento de Carmelitas Descalzas (Sta. Teresa) pide ayuda para reconstruir el templo arruinado con los terretmotos del 4 de Febrero de 1751.

1799   A 1.10.3 (1751) 31.347–4049

Ask help to reconstruct ermita de Santa Lucía.

1800   A 1.10.3 (1751) 31.348–4049

in re rebuilding of Church of San Dionisio—Pastores.

1801   A 1.10.3 (1751) 31.349–4049

Informes acerca del estado en que quedó la catedral con motivo del terremoto del 4 de Febrero de 1751.

1802   A 1.10.3 (1751) 31.350–4049

Auto de Arzobispo Fr. Pedro Pardo de Figueroa, por el cual nombre al regidor Cap. José Delgado de Nájera, depositario de las limosnas y bienes destinados a la obra del templo de Esquipulas.

1803   A 1.10.3 (1753) 18.808–2448

Ask help to reconstruct church of San Felipe Neri. (Antigua).

1804   A 1.10.3 (1753) 31.351–4049

Real provisión otorgando licencia a Fr. Diego de Iruve, O.P., cura del templo de Candelaria, de la ciudad de Guatemala, para que pueda pedir limosna y reconstruir el templo.

1805   A 1.10.3 (1753) 31.352–4049

Rebuilding of church of Retalhuleu.

1806   A 1.10.3 (1753) 31.353–4049

Concerning the rebuilding of the church of San Felipe de Jesús, Valle de Guatemala.

1807   A 1.10.3 (1757) 31.355–4049

No funds to rebuild church of Cuyotenango.

1808   A 1.10.3 (1758) 2971–151

El Ayuntamiento de San Juan Alotenango, solicita cierta suma para la reedificación del templo parroquial.

1809   A 1.10.3 (1759) 31.356–4049

Concerning the rebuilding of church of Santa Elena. Near Chiquimula.

1810   A 1.10.3 (1761) 4679–236, fol. 1

Indios of Jocotenango ask to be relieved of extraordinary contributions —are engaged in the construction of the parish church.

1811   A 1.10.3 (1769) 31.357–4049

Cura asks for renewal of license to say mass in an *oratorio* located in Titiguapa, Salvador.

1812   A 1.10.3 (1771) 18.809–2448

Concerning the rebuilding of the church in San Miguel Coxolá (in jurisdiction of Quetzaltenango).

1813   A 1.10.3 (1773) 31.358–4049

Sobre finalizar la construcción del templo de Jocotenango. (Antigua).

1814   A 1.10.3 (1774) 1720–73

Providencia prohibiendo la reconstrucción de la iglesia de Ciudad Vieja. Nicolás, Jacinto y Lucas Quiñónez y José Carrillo, habían donado cierta suma de dinero.

1815   A 1.10.3 (1774) 31.359–4049

El alcalde ordinario de segundo voto de la ciudad de Guatemala (la Antigua) consulta si es permitido reedificar el Templo del pueblo de San Miguel Dueñas.

1816   A 1.10.3 (1775) 4536–74

Carta del Ingeniero Diez de Navarro, solicitando los implementos necesarios para el delineamiento de la nueva ciudad.

1817   A 1.10.3 (1776) 4544–75

Los fabricantes de teja y ladrillo, solicitan mejor paga por el millar de estos productos.

1818   A 1.10.3 (1776) 16.546–2280

Reconstruction of parish church—San Antonio Suchitepéquez.

1819   A 1.10.3 (1776) 31.360–4049

José Bercián, mayordomo del Santuario del Niño de Belén (Amatitlán) solicita licencia para colectar limosnas y reedificar el templo.

1820   A 1.10.3 (1776) 31.361–4049

Metodo regular en formación de los cimientos.—Sobre colocación de horcones.—Instrucciones para construir.

1821   A 1.10.3 (1777) 1716–73

El Alcalde de Sacatepéquez, consulta las medidas para llevar a cabo la
traslación de los pueblos de Ciudad Vieja y de San Pedro de las Huertas.

1822   A 1.10.3 (1777) 1717–73

Providencia para que los indios jocotecos, que están dedicados a los trabajos de la ciudad, cumplan con los conceptos pascuales.

1823   A 1.10.3 (1777) 4571–76

Don Benito Matute escribe desde la Antigua Guatemala, que una parte del
ex-Palacio se había hundido por el excesivo peso de los materiales guar-
dados en él.

1824   A 1.10.3 (1778) 1695–72

Los nativos de Ciudad Vieja, en las inmediaciones de la Antigua
Guatemala, se quejan de que el Alcalde Mayor no los deja reconstruir su
iglesia y los quiere obligar a trasladarse.

1825   A 1.10.3 (1778) 1707–72

Autos ordenando la traslación de los nativos de Ciudad Vieja a las inmediaciones de la nueva Guatemala.

1826   A 1.10.3 (1778) 24.886–2817

Se permite al ayuntamiento de la villa de San Vicente, que pueda gastar
cierta suma en reparar la iglesia.

1827   A 1.10.3 (1779) 1709–73

Autos acerca de que los nativos de Ciudad Vieja, se trasladen a las inmediaciones de la nueva Capital.

1828   A 1.10.3 (1780) 4576–76

Las autoridades de Ciudad Vieja—en las inmediaciones de la antigua
Guatemala—solicitan ayuda pecuniaria para llevar a cabo la reconstrucción de su templo parroquial.

1829   A 1.10.3 (1780) 18.818–2448

Sobre la reconstrucción del templo parroquial del pueblo de Sumpango.

1830   A 1.10.3 (1780) 31.365–4049

Concerning the reconstruction of the church of Santa Apolonia, near Tecpán.

1831   A 1.10.3 (1781) 1722–73

El cura de la iglesia de Nuestra Señora de la Asunción de Jocotenango, solicita ayuda para amueblar la casa conventual.

1832   A 1.10.3 (1781) 4579–76

Los indios de San Pedro las Huertas, situado en las afueras de la nueva capital, solicitan ayuda para construir sus casas consistoriales e iglesias.

1833   A 1.10.3 (1782) 4581–76

Las autoridades del pueblo de Ciudad Vieja, situado en las goteras de la nueva capital, dan parte que muchas familias se han escapado transladándose a su antiguo poblado.

1834   A 1.10.3 (1782) 4582–76

Las justicias de Ciudad Vieja solicitan ayuda para construir su iglesia. Asimismo para traer de su antiguo pueblo los ornamentos y campanas.

1835   A 1.10.3 (1782) 25.545–2847

Instancia de los indígenas de Santiago Conchagua, sobre la reedificación del templo parroquial.

1836   A 1.10.3 (1782) 31.368–4049

Request for funds to rebuild church of Santiago Sacatepéquez.

1837   A 1.10.3 (1784) 15.091–2123

Acerca de la zona que corresponde al Sagrario. Hay un anteproyecto de la fachada de la Catedral de Antigua Guatemala.

1838   A 1.10.3 (1788) 1728–73

Los milicianos de la compañía de pardos, residentes en el barrio de la Hermita, solicitan tierras.

1839   A 1.10.3 (1788) 18.820–2448

Licencia otorgada a la orden de San Francisco de Guatemala, para que pueda recolectar limosna en León (Nicaragua) para sufragar los gastos de la obra del templo y convento.

1840   A 1.10.3 (1790) 1729–73

El cura de Jocotenango, Juan Goya, solicita providencia acerca de la formal traslación del pueblo, éste estaba en las inmediaciones de la Antigua Guatemala.

1841   A 1.10.3 (1790) 18.823–2448

El Pbro. Antonio García Redondo, pide se le permita traslader de la ermita de Sta. Lucía (de Antigua) las imágenes con destino al templo de San Sebastián.

1842 A 1.10.3 (1790) 18.824–2448

Ask permission to turn over some of the ornaments from church of Sta. Lucía in Antigua to church of San Sebastián in Nueva Guatemala.

1843 A 1.10.3 (1790) 31.369–4050

Nuevo pueblo de San Pedro de las Huertas, en las goteras de la Nueva Guatemala, pide licencia para la construcción de su templo.

1844 A 1.10.3 (1791) 8395–398

Oficio de don Bernardo Troncoso, Capitán General, enviando el 99 expediente seguido sobre la necesidad de construir una iglesia en Sonsonate.

1845 A 1.10.3 (1793) 4591–76

Need money to build church in new town of Ciudad Vieja near Nueva Guatemala.

1846 A 1.10.3 (1794) 8616–41

Oficio of don Bernardo Troncoso, capitán general, *in re* rebuilding of church of Jacaltenango.

1847 A 1.10.3 (1794) 8617–410

Oficio de don Bernardo Troncoso, capitán general, *in re* rebuilding of church San Jacinto Jilotepeque.

1848 A 1.10.3 (1794) 22.067–2643

Carta de Dean y Cabildo Eclesiástico del obispado de Nicaragua, sobre la reconstrucción de la Casa Episcopal. (León, Nicaragua)

1849 A 1.10.3 (1794) 18.826–2448

Complaint against priest for not returning a certain sum of money for the rebuilding of the parish church. (Jocotán)

1850 A 1.10.3 (1797) 18.827–2448

Nicolás Monzón pide se le paguen sus honorarios devengados por dirigir la obra del templo de Santo Domingo Xenacoj.

1851 A 1.10.3 (1798) 2293–106

Cédula y autos hechos en razón de ella, ordenando y reglamentando la forma en que debían ser administrados los fondos destinados a cubrir los gastos de construcción de iglesias, monasterios, y beaterios.

1852 A 1.10.3 (1801) 18.828–2448

Concerning the rebuilding of the parish church of San Pedro Sacatepéquez.

1853 A 1.10.3 (1803) 2356–109

Autos para llevar a cabo la creación (construcción) del Beaterio de Indias. Hay un plano.

1854 A 1.10.3 (1803) 4784–113

Cuaderno de las cuentas de los gastos verificados en la construcción de la iglesia parroquial de Chiquimula.

1855 A 1.10.3 (1805) 6621–322

Cuenta del costo de la construcción de la iglesia y casa parroquial de Ciudad Vieja (Almolonga).

1856 A 1.10.3 (1807) 2378–109

Account of building costs for church construction for year of 1807. Jutiapa

1857 A 1.10.3 (1810) 31.383–4051

Acerca de reconstruir parte del templo de Santiago Esquipulas.

1858 A 1.10.3 (1820) 8630–410

Receipts for expenditures in reconstruction of church. Santa María de Jesús—Quetzaltenango.

1859 A 1.10.3 (1820) 18.831–2448

Cabildo Ecclesiástico of Nueva Guatemala grants Ayuntamiento of Antigua permission to reconstruct the ex-cathedral.

1860 A 1.10.4 (1679) 31.263–4046

On construction of church of San Dionisio Pastores.

1861 A 1.10.25 (1758) 3284–163

Información para establecer cuales son los trabajos que hay que hacer en el templo parroquial de San Juan Comalapa, para su reedificación en el año 1758.

1862 A 1.11 (1634) 2026–94

Fray Lucas González (O.P.), informa de las reducciones del Manché.

text, *BAGG,* 5(1939–40): 175ff.

1863 A 1.11 (1634) 4727–104

Carta de Fr. Juan de Ochoa, acerca de la reducción del Manché, Mopán y Lacandón.

1864 A 1.11 (1664) 6747–328

Certificación del escribano Antonio Martínez de Ferrera, de la vacante de la doctrina de los pueblos Bachajón, Guayttenoa, Sinacantán e Izttapa de la provincia de Chiapa.

1865 A 1.11 (1688) 6756–328

Instancia de Fr. Pedro Morán (O.P.) cobrando la limosna de aceite que S. M. asignó a los conventos de dominicos en el reino de Guatemala. En este expediente hay una lista de los frailes que vivían en cada uno de los 16 conventos.

1866   A 1.11 (1695) 8538–409

El Capitán General don Jacinto de Barrios Leal, informa de su llegada al pueblo de Ntra. Sra. de los Dolores del Lacandón.

text, *BAGG,* 5 (1939–40): 177ff.

1867   A 1.11 (1700) 6762–328

Autos acerca de la capellanía de Gaspar Rodríguez, fundada en el convento de Santa Teresa de Jesús.

1868   A 1.11 (1696) 2031–91

Govierno 1696. Quaderno de diferentes cartas y papeles pertenecientes a la reducción de los yndios ynfieles assi por lo que toca a El Mopán como al pueblo de Ntra. Sra. de los Dolores.

text, *BAGG,* 5 (1939–40): 149ff.

1869   A 1.11 (1705) 6778–328

Autos acerca la reedificación de la iglesia Catedral de Comayagua.

1870   A 1.11 (1707) 10.220–1576, fol. 183

15 de junio de 1707. R. P. Son cedidos los tributos, en su cuarta parte y por dos años, a favor del común del pueblo de San Juan Chinameca, jurisdicción de la ciudad de San Miguel, para cubrir los gastos de reedificación del templo parroquial.

1871   A 1.11 (1709) 4730–104

Carta de Tomás del Castillo, acerca de la reducción de los indios de Verapaz.

1872   A 1.11 (1710) 2043–94

Demanda entablada por el Dean y Cabildo Ecclesiástico contra los religiosos mercedarios, dominicos y franciscanos para que estos enteren el 3% del fruto de sus curatos, para la substancia del Seminario Tridentino.

1873   A 1.11 (1710) 2044–94

Autos hechos a pedimento de Andrés Ruiz de la Cota, mayordomo de la obra de la iglesia de Remedios, contra el fundidor José de Arria. Este no había cumplido con la entrega de una campana.

1874   A 1.11 (1712) 4724–96

Informes de la reducción de indios lacandones al paraje nombrado Ypchia.

text, *BAGG,* 5(1939–40):180ff.

1875   A 1.11 (1713) 2049–95

Autos acerca de que los curas doctrineros enteren el 3% de sus rentas para subvenir los gastos del Seminario Tridentino.

1876   A 1.11 (1720) 16.779–2292

Informe del Ayuntamiento acerca de la fundación del convento de Capuchinas.

This document also has data on the income and endowments of other ecclesiastical communities in Antigua Guatemala: Escuela de Cristo, San Agustín, etc.

text, *BAGG*, 8 (1943):127ff.

1877   A 1.11 (1729) 6836–329

Instancia de los indios de Santa María Tactic, de que estando la iglesia de su pueblo en ruinas, se les ayude.

1878   A 1.11 (1736) 8544–409

Certificación acerca de la instancia de los indios de Tecpán Guatemala, quienes solicitan que de los fondos prometidos de carnicerías—deposita-dos en el ayuntamiento de Guatemala se les dé lo necesario para hacer los retablos de su iglesia.

1879   A 1.11 (1736) 45.427–5369

Se ordena se proceda a revisar el estado del templo de San Miguel El Tejar, para la fijación de fondos para su reconstrucción.

1880   A 1.11 (1741) 5025–211

Relación histórica de la provincia de nuestra Señora de la Merced, reden-ción de cautivos de la presentación de Guatemala.

text, *BAGG* 10 (1945):162ff.

1881   A 1.11 (1752) 2082–97

El rector del colegio de la Compañía de Jesús (Colegio de San Lucas) solicita cierta ayuda para reconstruir el edificio que ocupa dicho centro, arruinado con motivo de los temblores de San Casimiro (4 Marzo 1751).

1882   A 1.11 (1752) 2087–97

El cabildo eclesiástico solicita que los oficiales reales sean los que descuen-ten el 3% de los sínodos dados a los curas, para que así se cumpla con la dádiva destinada al Seminario Tridentino.

1883   A 1.11 (1753) 2091–98

Varios vecinos de la Calle Ancha de Herreros solicita construir de bóveda la ermita de Santa Cruz (Cruz de Piedra).

See also A 1.10.3 (1745) 16.545–2280.

1884   A 1.11 (1763) 2113–98

Instancia seguida en el Superior Gobierno por el Real Fisco, con la Provin-cia de Nuestra Señora de La Merced sobre la exivición de la Real Licencia de su Mag. para la fundación del Colegio de San Gerónimo que por este defecto se declaró extinto.

text, *BAGG*, 8 (1943):414ff.

1885 A 1.11 (1770) 4743–104

Promulgación de la cédula de 23 de mayo de 1769, reglamentando los gastos en las iglesias.

1886 A 1.11 (1771) 2117–98–9

Queda establecida la clausura perpetua en el beaterio de Nuestra Señora del Rosario, de la Tercera orden de Santo Domingo. (Antigua).

text, *BAGG*, 10 (1945):262ff.

1887 A 1.11 (1772) 2117–98–7

Construcción y bendición del beaterio de Nuestra Señora del Rosario de la ciudad de Guatemala, de la tercera orden de Santo Domingo.

text, *BAGG*, 10 (1945):261ff.

1888 A 1.11 (1774) 2117–98–13 v.

Destrucción del edificio del beaterio de Nuestra Señora del Rosario, de la tercera orden de Santo Domingo.

text, *BAGG*, 10 (1945):263ff.

1889 A 1.11 (1779) 2117–98–9

Traslación de las beatas indias a la nueva Guatemala de la Asunción.

text, *BAGG*, 10 (1945):264.

1890 A 1.11 (1780) 2178–101, fol. 12

Plano de la ermita de San José y de las demás construcciones hechas y por haber en la manzana donde está dicha ermita. (Antigua).

1891 A 1.11 (1782) 2194–102

Cuaderno que contiene las nóminas de provisión de curatos 1770–1782.

1892 A 1.11 (1783) 2196–103

Autos acerca del cumplimiento de lo ordenado en cédula para que se determine el estado presente de los franciscanos, determinando si hay necesidad de que vengan religiosos.

1893 A 1.11 (1783) 4764–104

Nóminas de provisión de curatos.

1894 A 1.11 (1784) 2356–109, fol. 57

Plano del convento de las Beatas Indias de esta Nueva Ciudad de Goatemala de la Asunción.

1895 A 1.11 (1785) 2200–103

Autos para llevar a cabo la reedificación de la iglesia del Beaterio de Indias.

1896 A 1.11(1789) 2195–103

Detalle del nombramiento de curas (dominicos) 1770–1789.

See also A 1.11 (1782) 2194–102 and A 1.11 (1783) 4764–104, dealing with curatos 1770–1782, and 1783.

1897 A 1.11 (1789) 2197–103

Libro de nóminas de provisión de curas. 1783–1789.

1898 A 1.11 (1792) 2231–105

El Pbro. José Zomoza, Prioste de la iglesia de Nuestra Señora del Carmen, solicita licencia para la construcción del templo.

1899 A 1.11 (1797) 464–48

Gobierno.—Comayagua.—1797. Sobre reducir a poblado a los del partido de Olancho.

text, *BAGG,* 6 (1940–41):290ff.

1900 A 1.11 (1803) 4784–113

Cuaderno de las cuentas de los gastos verificados en la construcción de la iglesia parroquial de Chiquimula, iniciada en 1803.

1901 A 1.11 (1807) 2378–109

El mayordomo encargado de la obra de la iglesia de Jutiapa, rinde las cuentas correspondientes al año de la fecha.

1902 A 1.11 (1813) 2405–110

Cédula concediendo merced a los cuatro curatos del Quiché para que no sean secularizados.

1903 A 1.11.3 (1820) 8630–410

Receipts for money spent on reconstruction of church of Santa María de Jesús.

1904 A 1.11.25 (1678) 5405

Informe acerca de que no es cierto que el Pbro. Agustín Ortiz de Almonte, cobre tributos con destino a la reedificación del templo parroquial de Izapa.

1905 A 1.11.25 (1734) 46.568–5438

Instancia del común del pueblo de Chiquimula, sobre que del fondo de Tributos, se les de lo necesario para la construcción del templo parroquial y adquisición de ornamentos.

1906 A 1.11.25 (1736) 45.427–5369

Se ordena la revisión del templo del pueblo de San Sebastián el Tejar, para calcular el costo de reedificación.

1907 A 1.11.25 (1737) 46.059–5405

Cuenta y avalúo del costo de la reedificación del templo parroquial de Escuintla.

1908 A 1.11.25 (1743) 46.473–5439

Instancia del común de Chiquimula sobre que se les de fondos para reedificar el templo arruinado con los temblores del año de 1743.

1909 A 1.11.25 (1752) 3538–175

Acerca de la reconstrucción del templo del pueblo de San Cristóbal Acasahuastlán.

1910 A 1.11.25 (1757) 2970–151

San Pedro Huertas—Permission given to use community funds to reconstruct church.

1911 A 1.11.25 (1776) 39.821–4656

Real provisión poniendo en conocimiento la cédula por la cual queda prohibida la construcción de monasterios, templos, hospicios y hospitales sin real permiso.

1912 A 1.11.25 (1777) 3296–163

Reconstruction of templo—Patzicía.

1913 A 1.11.25 (1779) 3302–163

El común de San Miguelito de El Tejar, de la jurisdicción de la Alcaldía Mayor de Chimaltenango, solicita licencia para la construcción de un templo.

1914 A 1.11.25 (1779) 3400–169

Informa el alcalde mayor de Escuintla, que un incendio destruyó en gran parte el templo parroquial de la cabecera.

1915 A 1.11.25 (1784) 3570–176

Licencia para solicitar limosna con destino a la construcción del templo parroquial de Ntra. Sra. de la Asunción de Chiquimula.

1916 A 1.11.25 (1784) 3964–195

Quetzaltenango—parish church in ruinous state.

1917 A 1.11.25 (1780) 15.283–2144

Patzicía—reconstruction of church.

1918 A 1.11.25 (1784) 15.291–2144

Accounts of cost of reconstruction of church of Patzicía.

1919 A 1.11.25 (1790) 7857–379

El corregidor de Chiquimula solicita fondos de la Real Hacienda para sufragar los gastos de la obra del templo parroquial de la cabecera de dicho corregimiento.

1920 A 1.11.25 (1792) 3723–181

Autos sobre las reparaciones que son necesarias hacer en el templo parroquial de Cobán.

1921 A 1.11.25 (1794) 3728–181

El común de Santo Domingo Cobán solicita ayuda para la reedificación del templo de San Sebastián.

1922 A 1.11.25 (1797) 3059–154

El Padre Cura de San Sebastián El Tejar, solicita permiso para efectuar la reconstrucción de la iglesia.

1923 A 1.11.25 (1797) 3415–169

El común del pueblo de Nuestra Señora de la Concepción de Escuintla, solicita sea autorizada la construcción de un templo provisional, en tanto es construido el definitivo.

1924 A 1.11.25 (1800) 7783–377

Informa el parroco del pueblo de Escuintla ser necesario reedificar el templo parroquial.

1925 A 1.11.25 (1811) 3658–179

El parroco de Santiago Esquipulas solicita autorización para pedir limosnas con destino a la reconstrucción del Santuario.

1926 A 1.11.25 (1815) 7974–383

Fr. Buenaventura Santa Cruz, parroco de San Sebastián, ciudad de Cobán, solicita fondos para reedificar dicho templo.

1927 A 1.11.25 (1817) 7727–373

Sobre la reparación de la iglesia de Santa María de Jesús.

1928 A 1.11.25 (1818) 3236–160

Autos para llevar a cabo la reconstrucción de la iglesia de San Juan del Obispo.

1929 A 1.11.25 (1818) 8198–393

San Andrés Semetabaj—*in re* reconstruction of church.

1930 A 1.11.25 (1820) 8152-391

Sobre la reedificación de la iglesia de Almolonga, jurisdicción de Quetzaltenango.

1931 A 1.11.25 (1821) 8159-391

El cura de Almolonga, sobre la necesidad de reedificar la iglesia.

1932 A 1.11.25 (1821) 8210-393

Panajachel—ayuntamiento asks money to reconstruct church.

1933 A 1.11.25 (1821) 24.354-2782

Patzicía—asks funds for reconstruction of church.

1934 A 1.11.25 (1821) 24.361-2782

San Andrés Izapa—asks authorization to reconstruct church.

1935 A 1.11.30 (1786) 3751-183

Quinze inbentarios de las alaxas de oro y plata de las iglesias de la provincia de Verapaz.

1936 A 1.12 (1685) 13.934-2013

En Junta de Real Hacienda, se autoriza lo necesario para continuar las reducciones de infieles de la Provincia de Honduras.

text, *BAGG,* 5 (1939–40):153ff.

1937 A 1.12 (1687) 7012-333

Testimonio de la Cédula por lo cual se otorga licencia al Pbro. Francisco Gonzalez de Castro, para que pase a misiones de los indios xicaques.

text, *BAGG,* 5 (1939–40):24ff.

1938 A 1.12 (1690) 7013-333

Testimonio de la Junta de Real Hacienda celebrada por el Capitán don Jacinto de Barrios Leal, para dar ayuda económica a los vecinos de la Villa de Santa Cruz de Yoro, para la conquista de los indios payas, leanes y mulias.

text, *BAGG,* 5 (1939–40):27ff.

1939 A 1.12 (1695) 16.795-2294

Cabildo.—Año de 1695.—Sobre la fundación de los Rdos. Ppes. Misioneros en esta ziudad.

text, *BAGG,* 5, (1939–40):158ff.

1940 A 1.12 (1709) 7024-333

El Capitán Gaspar Raymundo de Vagara, informa del estado de las milicias encargadas de las reducciones de los socmoes y lacandones.

text, *BAGG,* 5 (1939–40):178ff.

1941 A 1.12 (1716) 494–50

Informe rendido ante el Gobernador de la Provincia de Honduras acerca de la invasión que indios payas pretendían hacer al pubelo de Catacamas.

text, *BAGG*, 5 (1939–40):187ff.

1942 A 1.12 (1727) 7049–334

Carta de don Juan de Oseguera y Quevedo, acerca del Estado, gastos, etc. que tiene la misión de Lean y Mulia.

text, *BAGG*, 5 (1939–40):48ff.

1943 A 1.12 (1733) 497–50

Autos fechos por su Señoría Ilustrísima mi Señor en virtud de consulta del Visitador General para remediar la mala administración de algunos curatos y doctrinas de este Obispado de Honduras.

text, *BAGG*, 7 (1941–42):45ff. and 63ff.

1944 A 1.12 (1740) 498–50

Autos sobre haberse reducido a nuestra santa fe catholica varias familias que salieron de las montañas de la provincia de Comayagua y diligencias practicadas para su conservación.

text, *BAGG*, 5 (1939–40):191ff.

1945 A 1.12 (1745) 7056–334

Libranza de pago por sínodos y doctrinas a favor de varios misioneros que trabajan en la reducción de indios jicaques.

text, *BAGG*, 5 (1939–40):50ff.

1946 A 1.12 (1747) 7057–334

Instancia del Síndico General del Colegio de Misioneros, Sargento don Cristóbal de Gálvez Corral, solicitando los sínodos para los misioneros que han de marchar a Tologalpa.

text, *BAGG*, 5 (1939–40):51ff.

1947 A 1.12 (1752) 7058–334

Testimonio del cuaderno y diligencias originales practicadas a la saca y población de varios indios jicaques en el Valle de San Juan, jurisdicción de la misión de Cataguna, del P. misionero Juan José Saldaña.

text, *BAGG*, 5 (1939–40):76ff.

1948 A 1.12 (1752) 7060–334

Testimonio del cuaderno de donde constan los autos hechos en la misión y conquista de los indios jicaques en las montañas de León y Yoro, por los PP. Misioneros Apostólicos.

text, *BAGG*, 5 (1939–40):87ff.

1949   A 1.12 (1752) 7061–334

Testimonio del cuaderno de diligencias e instrumentos de los gastos hechos en la conquista y misión de los indios jicaques, en las montañas de Lean y Yoro.

text, *BAGG,* 5 (1939–40):59ff.

1950   A 1.12 (1757) 2479–117

Informes acerca de las misiones de Lean y Mulia de la Provincia de Honduras.

text, *BAGG,* 6 (1940–41):83ff., 159ff., 255ff.; 7 (1941–42):80ff.

1951   A.12 (1768) 506–50

Acerca del pago de la doctrina asignada a los misioneros que radican en la reducción de San Buena Ventura, poblado de indios batucos.

text, *BAGG,* 5 (1939–40):283ff.

1952   A 1.12 (1768) 2472–117

Año de 1768.—Testimonio de la consulta hecha al Superior Gobierno de Guathemala por el R.P. Francisco Javier Ortiz, Comisario Apostólico de los colegios de Propagande Fide, y el estado y sucesos de las tres conquistas que tiene a su cargo en las provincias de Comayagua, Matagalpa y Thalamanca, Providencias que se dieron en junta de Real Hacienda para su consecución y aumento.

text, *BAGG,* 3 (1937–38):241; 5 (1939–40):236.

1953   A 1.12 (1768) 4826–119

Informe relativo a que cuarentaicinco indios caribes de la Provincia de Matagalpa, habían sido bautizados, corre agregado el que se refiere a que ciertos pueblos de caribes se resisten a someterse al cristianismo.

text, *BAGG,* 5 (1939–40):214ff.

1954   A 1.12 (1768) 4826–129

Informes de los Gobernadores de Comayagua y Costarrica sobre el proyecto de desvelar a los mosquitos.

text, *BAGG,* 5 (1939–40):311ff.

1955   A 1.12 (1769) 2474–117

Autos relativos a las misiones de Parac y Pantasma.

text, *BAGG,* 6 (1940–41):3ff.

1956   A 1.12 (1769) 2475–117

Autos de la consulta que elevó el Capitán Gobernador de la Provincia de Costa Rica, acerca de que varios indios Moscos al mando de Yasparal, Yani y Versa, intentan su reducción.

text, *BAGG,* 5 (1939–40):336ff.

1957 A 1.12 (1771) 4831–119

Autos acerca de determinar la forma de llevar a cabo la reducción de los indios moscos (estos se consideraban, por los ingleses, como dependientes de la autoridad británica).

text, *BAGG*, 6 (1940–41):15ff.

1958 A 1.12 (1775) 2477–117

El Gobernador de Veragua informa al Ayuntamiento de la ciudad de Guatemala la marcha de la reducción de talamancas.

text, *BAGG*, 6 (1940–41):33ff.

1959 A 1.12 (1785) 514–50

Sobre la traslación de los Yndios Payas de la ciudad de Comayagua (que hicieron fuga del pueblo de San Matías) al pueblo de Sensenti jurisdicción de Gracias a Dios, o a otra parte.

text, *BAGG*, 6 (1940–41):115ff.

1960 A 1.12 (1788) 2482–118

Consulta del Obispo de Nicaragua acerca de la forma de llevar a cabo la reducción de los indios caribes que habitan en las montañas de Matagalpa.

text, *BAGG*, 6 (1940–41):193ff.

1961 A 1.12 (1795) 2486–118

Fr. Mariano Borya informa que los indios Tzendales están prestos a someterse a prácticas cristianas.

1962 A 1.12 (1813) 2489–118

Instancia presentada por el Fiscal de la Real Audiencia para que las misiones sean más activas.

text, *BAGG*, 7 (1941–42):119ff.

1963 A 1.15 (1591) 1751, fol. 26 v.

Auto de 14 de octobre de 1591, por el cual queda prohibido que indígenas contraten a oficiales plateros, etc., para hacer obras en sus iglesias y casas de comunidad, las cuales "son impertinentes y no necesarias: que ningún oficial platero, bordador, albañil, carpintero . . . ni otro ningún oficial . . . puedan hacer ni hagan ninguna obra a pueblo de indios . . . sin previa licencia de la Audiencia."

1964 A 1.15 (1609) 8633–411

De oficio. Por querella de Juana Gutiérrez Torres, viuda, contra el maestro de pintura Pedro de Aliendo, por malos tratos a Agustín Vargas, hijo de Juana, aprendiz del pintor Pedro de Aliendo.

1965 A 1.16 (1591) A I–39–1751, fol. 26 v.

Auto de 14 de octubre de 1591, por el cual queda prohibido que indígenas contraten a oficiales plateros, etc., para hacer obras en sus iglesias y casas de comunidad, las cuales "son impertinentes y no necesarias: que ningún oficial platero, bordador, albañil, carpintero . . . ni otro ningún oficial . . . pueda hacer ni hagan obra a pueblo de indios sin previa licencia de la Audiencia."

1966 A 1.16 (1747) 2811–148

El Hermano (de la Tercera Orden Franciscana) Tomás de Morales, Maestro Fundidor de campanas y cañones, pide que nadie en Guatemala pueda ejercer su oficio.

See also A 1.16.4 (1747) 2811–148.

1967 A 1.16 (1758) 2809–148

Don Diego Gameros, Maestro de Ensayador, Marcador, Fundidor y Balanzario del Reino, solicita la aprobación de las ordenanzas que ha hecho para el Gremio de platería. Las ordenanzas aludidas no están, porque el expediente está mutilado.

1968 A 1.16 (1759) 2814–148

Autos del examen que hizo José de Montalva para adquirir el título de maestro de platería.

1969 A 1.16 (1762) 2817–148

Manuel Antonio Victoria recibe el título de maestro de platería.

1970 A 1.16 (1771) 2818–148

Pedro de Valenzuela recibe el título de maestro de platería.

1971 A 1.16 (1772) 2819–148

Juan Paz y Paredes recibe el título de maestro de platería.

1972 A 1.16 (1772) 2821–148

Don Pedro Rubio recibe el título de maestro de platería.

1973 A 1.16 (1772) 2822–148

Juan Rios recibe el título de maestro de platería.

1974 A 1.16 (1772) 2823–148

Francisco de Avila recibe el título de maestro de platería.

1975 A 1.16 (1772) 2824–148

Juan Miguel Espinosa recibe el título de maestro de platería.

1976 A 1.16 (1772) 2825–148

Gregorio Avila recibe el título de maestro de platería.

1977 A 1.16 (1772) 2826–148

José Antonio de Paz de Avila recibe el título de maestro de platería.

1978   A 1.16 (1772) 2828–148

Pedro José Carillo recibe el título de maestro de platería.

1979   A 1.16 (1772) 2820–148

Informe que presentó el Maestro Ensayador de la Casa de Moneda, de su visita a las tiendas de plateros.

1980   A 1.16 (1773) 2830–148

El Maestro de Arquitectura, don Bernardo Ramírez, expone la necesidad de arreglar la Oficina de Albañilería.

1981   A 1.16 (1798) 2905–149

Fr. Antonio de San José Munoz solicita la impresión de una memoria acerca de las ventajas que resultan a los indios y ladinos de que se calcen.

1982   A 1.16.1 (1761) 17.133–2312

Solicitan los Ermitaños de la orden de San Agustín, sobre que los albañiles presten su cooperación en la reconstrucción del templo.

1983   A 1.16.4 (1747) 2811–148

El Hermano de la Tercera Orden Franciscana, Tomás de Morales, Maestro Fundidor de Campanas y cañones, pide que nadie en Guatemala pueda ejercer su oficio.

1984   A 1.16.22 (1641) 38.298–4500

Salvador García, oficial carpintero, pide examen para el grado de maestro.

1985   A 1.17. Relaciones Geográficas.

See *BAGG,* 4 (1938–39):267ff., for a complete list of titles and catalogue numbers.

1985a   A 1.17 (1740) 112–6

Real provisión circulada a las autoridades del Reino y RR. PP. de las órdenes religiosas, para que formulen descripciones geográficas e históricas.

1986   A 1.17 (1740) 5012–210

Relación Geográfica de la Provincia de San Salvador, por don Manuel de Gálvez, Alcalde Mayor de ella.

text, *BAGG,* 2 (1936–37):20ff.; 4 (1938–39):268

1987   A 1.17 (1741) 5009–210

Relación Geográfica del Corregimiento o Alcaldía Mayor de Quetzaltenango, por don Francisco López Marchán.

1987a   A 1.17 (1765) 13.999–1840

Año de 1763. Autos formados sobre la Real Cédula para que esta Real Audiencia con la brevedad y reserva posible remita una relación individual de los Corregimientos y Alcaldías Mayores de este Reyno.

text, *BAGG,* 7 (1941–42):210ff.

See also, 2 (1936–37):274–329 and 448–486, for reports rendered in 1765 in compliance with the cédula of 1763.

1988   A 1.17 (1765) 13.999–1840

Tegucigalpa. See Report of 1765, below. In 1765 curates are very large in extention, majority of them are more than 30 leguas in length and 20 in width.

text, *BAGG,* 7 (1941–42):214ff.

1989   A 1.17 (1765) 13.999–1840 (Report of 1765)

"Año de 1763.—Autos formados sobre la Real Cédula para que esta Real Audiencia con la brevedad y reserva possible remita una relación individual de los Corregimientos y Alcaldías Mayores de este Reyno."

text, *BAGG,* 2 (1936–37):274–329; 448–486.

See also item nos. 1393 and 1987a.

1990   A 1.17 (1790) 4730–238, fol. 6

Quetzaltenango. Descripción Geográfica.

1991   A 1.17.1 (1720) 38.301–4501

Relación Geográfica del corregimiento de Suchitepéquez.

1992   A 1.17.1 (1740) 5002–210

Relación Geográfica del Valle de Goathemala, por Guillermo Martínez de Pereda, corregidor y Alcalde Mayor de dicho Valle.

text, *BAGG,* 1 (1935): 5ff.

1993   A 1.17.1 (1740) 5003–210

Relación Geográfica de la Alcaldía Mayor de Escuintla y Guazacapán, por Alonso Crespo.

text, *BAGG,* 4 (1938–39):267.

1994   A 1.17.1 (1740) 5004–210

Relación Geográfica del corregimiento de Chiquimula de la Sierra, por José González Rancaño.

1995   A 1.17.1 (1740) 5005–210

Relación Geográfica de la Alcaldía Mayor de Verapaz, por José Antonio de Aldama.

1996   A 1.17.1 (1740) 5006–210

Relación Geográfica de Verapaz. Esta contiene los datos relativos a San Mateo Salamá, por Pedro Antonio Luxán.

1997 A 1.17.1 (1740) 5008–210

Relación Geográfica de la Alcaldía Mayor de Totonicapán y Huehuetenango, por José Pedro Olavarreta.

text, *BAGG*, 1 (1935):16ff.

1998 A 1.17.1 (1740) 5010–210

Relación Geográfica de Sololá, por don Felipe Manrique de Guzmán.

1999 A 1.17.1 (1740) 5014–210

Relación Geográfica de la Villa y Puerto de Realexo, por Felipe Gómez y Messia.

2000 A 1.17.1 (1740) 5015–210

Relación Geográfica de Matagalpa, por Francisco de Posada.

2001 A 1.17.1 (1640) 5018–210

Relación Geográfica del partido de Sébaco y Chontales, por don Francisco de Mora y Pacheco.

2002 A 1.17.1 (1740) 5017–210

Relación Geográfica de Soconusco, por don Antonio de Castellanos.

2003 A 1.17.1 (1741) 5009–210

Relación Geográfica del Corregimiento o Alcadía Mayor de Quetzaltenango, por don Francisco López Marchán.

2004 A 1.17.1 (1743) 5013–210

Relación Geográfica de Subtiava, por Juan Salgado y Artunchiaga.

2005 A 1.17.1 (1741) 5016–210

Relación Geográfica de la Provincia de Costa Rica, por don Juan Gemmir Lleonatta.

text, *BAGG*, 1 (1935):40ff.

2006 A 1.17.1 (1743) 5007–210

Relación Geográfica de la Alcaldía Mayor de Totonicapán. (esta contiene los datos relativos al partido de Huehuetenango) por José Antonio de Aldama.

text, *BAGG*, 1 (1935):25ff.

2007 A 1.17.1 (1743) 5011–211

Relación Geográfica de la Alcaldía Mayor de Tegucigalpa, por don Juan Bautista Ortiz de Letona.

text, *BAGG*, 1 (1935):29ff.

2008 A 1.17.1 (1790) A 3.16/4728–238, fol. 10

Relación geográfica del Corregimiento de Escuintla.

2009 A 1.17.1 (1790) 4730–238, fol. 6

Relación Geográfica del corrégimiento de Quezaltenango.

2010 A 1.17.1 (c.1791) A 3.16/4701–236, fol. 14

Relación de las distancias que medían desde la cabecera de la Alcaldía Mayor de Sololá a los pueblos de su jurisdicción.

2011 A 1.17.1 (1791) A 3.16–4732–239, fol. 1

Relación Geográfica de Chiquimula.

2011a A 1.17.1 (1792) 38.305–4501

Relación Geográfica de Verapaz—Corregimiento, pueblos, etc.

2012 A 1.17.1 (no date) 38.312–4502

Relación e informe descriptivo de las plantas, animales y minerales en el pueblo de San Pedro Carchá, alcaldía de Verapaz.

2013 A 1.17.1 (1804) 17.516–2335

Oficio de gobernador de Costa Rica evacuando el informe acerca del puerto de Caldera. Hay un mapa.

2014 A 1.17.2 (1741) 5016–210

Relación Geográfica de la Provincia de Costa Rica.

2015 A 1.17.2 (1795) A 3.27–28.215–1756, fol. 2

Nomenclatura de los pueblos que integran la Intendencia de San Salvador.

2015a A 1.17.2 (1798) 17.514–2335

Informe rendido por Ramón de Anguiano, gobernador intendente de la provincia de Honduras, de las zonas geográficas. Hay un mapa a colores.

2016 A 1.17.2 (1802) A.16–4856–243, fol. 4

Número de tributarios en las cuatro intendencias, en los tres corregimientos y siete alcaldías mayores de la Gobernación de Guatemala.

2017 A 1.17.2 (1813) 26.356–2975

Relación Geográfica de la Intendencia de Honduras, formado por Ramón de Anguiano.

2017a A 1.17.3 (1744) 17.508–2335

Información rendida por el Ing. Luis Diez de Navarro de su viaje por las provincias de Guatemala. Año de 1744.

2017b A 1.17.3 (1756) 38.302–4501

Relación e informe sobre el camino que de la capital al puerto de San Fernando Omoa, puede servir para el comercio y defensa del Reino. Por el Ing. Luis Diez de Navarro.

2018 A 1.17.3 (1793) A 1.25–21.389–2603, fol. 4

Estado a Razón de las distancias que hay desde la capital a las demás cuidades de este Reino y cabezas de Partidos: días en que entran y salen los correos en ellas y leguas que cruzan a las poblaciones por donde transitan los correos de a caballo y a pie.

2019 A 1.18 (1718) 1400–2021

Breve y Verdadera Historia del Incendio del Volcán . . . y terremotos de la ciudad . . . 27 de Septiembre de 1717.

2020 A 1.18 (1740) 5021–211

Cuenta y detalles de las rentas del obispado de Guatemala.

2021 A 1.18 (1740) 5022–211

Testimonio de las diligencias hechas en la Curia Eclesiástica de Guatemala en orden a las relaciones de los 4 Conventos de Religiosas sugetos al ordinario, sus erecciones, órdenes a que pertenecen, número de Religiosas de que se componen y sus rentas con la comprobación de dichas relaciones.

2022 A 1.18 (1740) 07/5022–211

Relación del administrador de Santa Cathalina.

text, *BAGG,* 10 (1945):225ff.

2023 A 1.18 (1740) 1740–5022–211

Relación del Convento de religiosas Capuchinas.

text, *BAGG,* 10 (1945):260ff.

2024 A 1.18 (1740) 1740–5022–211

Relación del administrador de Santa Teresa.

text, *BAGG,* 10 (1945):249ff.

2025 A 1.18 (1740) 5022–211

Relación del administrador de nuestra Señora de la Concepción.

text, *BAGG,* 10 (1945):217ff.

2026 A 1.18 (1740) 5023–211

Relación histórica del obispado de Guatemala.

2027 A 1.18 (1740) 5025–211

Relación histórica de la Orden de Nuestra Señora Redención de Cautivos (mercedarios).

2028   A 1.18 (1740) 5026–211

Relación histórica de los monasterios de la provincia del dulce nombre de Jesús de Guatemala (San Francisco) y del convento de Santa Clara.

text, *BAGG*, 10 (1945):134ff.

2029   A 1.18 (1740) 5027–211

Relación histórica del colegio de misioneros de Cristo Crucificado de la ciudad de Guatemala. Por Fr. Antonio de Andrade.

text, *BAGG*, 10 (1945):200ff.

2030   A 1.18 (1740) 5031–211

Relación histórica del Colegio de la Compañía de Jesús, por el P. Manuel Herrera.

text, *BAGG*, 10 (1945):194ff.

2031   A 1.18 (1740) 5034–211

Relación Histórica del Convento y Hospital de convalecientes de Nuestra Señora de Bethlen de Guatemala.

text, *BAGG*, 10 (1945):197ff.

2032   A 1.18 (1741) 5028–211

Relación histórica de los monasterios de la provincia de San Vicente de Chiapa y Guatemala. (O.P.).

text, *BAGG*, 10 (1945):104ff.

2033   A 1.18 (1741) 5029–211

Relación Histórica del Convento de San Felipe Neri de la Ciudad de Santiago de Guatemala. Por el Pbro. Pedro Martínez de Molina.

text, *BAGG* 1 (1935–36):136ff.

2034   A 1.18 (1742) 5032–211

Información presentada por el P. Provincial de la Seráfica Religión de San Francisco, del estado de sus conventos.

2035   A 1.18.3 (1740) 5024–211

Relación histórica del Hospital de San Juan de Dios de la ciudad de León (Nicaragua).

2036   A 1.18.3 (1740) 5024–211

Relación Histórica del Convento de Nuestra Señora de Santa Catalina Mártir de la Ciudad de León Nicaragua, escrita por Fray Juan de Ledesma, Prior de dicho Hospital.

text, *BAGG*, 1 (1935–36):148ff.

2037 A 1.18.3 (1740) 8271–396

Relación histórica del convento y hospital de San Juan de Dios de la Ciudad de Granada (Nicaragua).

2038 A 1.18.3 (1763) 14.002–2021

Relación Histórica del Convento y Hospital de Sn Juan de Dios de Guatemala.

2038a A 1.18.4 (1650) 38.300–4501

Visión de Paz, etc., de VeraPaz, por Fr. Juan de Rivera.

See Rivera, 1650, Section VI, above, for complete title.

2039 A 1.18.6 (1718) 1400–2021

Breve y Verdadera Historia del Incendio del Volcán (de Fuego) y terremotos de la ciudad (de Guatemala) 27 de Septiembre de 1717.

2040 A 1.18.6 (1774) 38.306–4502

GONZALEZ BUSTILLO, JUAN.

Razon Particular de los Templos, Casas de Comunidades, y Edificios Públicos y por mayor del número de los vecinos de la capital de Guatemala; y del deplorable estado a que se hallan reducidos por los terremotos de la tarde del veinte y nueve de Julio, trese y catorce de diciembre del año próximo pasado de setenta y tres. Por Juan Gonzalez Bustillo, Año 1774.

2041 A 1.18.16 (1904) 14.001–2021

A modern copy of A 1.18.6 (1774) 38.306–4502, immediately above, transcribed by José Neri González Poza en 1904.

2042 A 1.20 (1591) 9825–428

13 de julio de 1591. Gaspar Pérez, indio natural de San Juan Comalapa, estante en la ciudad de Guatemala ingresa como aprendiz del maestro albañil Blas de la Cruz.

2043 A 1.20 (1591) 10.000–428

13 de febrero de 1591. Diego López, vecino de la ciudad de Guatemala, es recibido en calidad de aprendiz de albañilería con el maestro Juan Garnica.

2044 A 1.20 (1593) 10.147–429

20 de diciembre de 1593. Pedro de León y Francisco Pérez, indígenas, oficiales de cantería vecinos (?) de la ciudad de Guatemala, se obligan la hechura de una portada de piedra, con sus molduras y remate, para la casa del contador Gregorio de Polanco.

2045 A 1.20 (1602) 10.171 – 16 v.

Escritura de la toma de posesión del pueblo de Jocotenango por parte de los frailes de Santo Domingo, para la fundación de un convento y vicaria, otorgada el 21 de enero de 1602.

text, *BAGG,* 10 (1945):95ff.

2046 A 1.20 (1626) 757

Escritura de concierto para la edificación del templo de Santa Catalina.

text, *BAGG,* 10 (1945):221ff.

2047 A 1.20 (1636) 690–53

El maestro pintor Pedro de Liendo se obliga a hacer el retablo de la capilla de Nuestra Señora La Antigua, en la iglesia de Santo Domingo. 30 de Mayo de 1636.

text, *BAGG,* 10 (1945):99ff.

2048 A 1.20 (1636) 690–69

Escritura otorgada el 18 de junio de 1636 por los canteros Juan Bautista del Vallejo y Martín de Autillo, obligándose a hacer la obra de cantería del altar mayor de la iglesia de Santo Domingo.

text, *BAGG,* 10 (1945):101ff.

2049 A 1.20 (1643) leg. 1053, fol. 69

9 de marzo de 1643. Juan de Santa Cruz, maestro de oficio de albañilería, recibe en calidad de aprendiz a Diego de Zaldaña.

2050 A 1.20 (1648) 694–668

Escritura de concierto otorgada por Martín de Ugalde el 14 de octubre de 1648, a favor del convento de Santo Domingo, comprometiendose a terminar la obra de la capilla mayor de la iglesia de dicho convento.

text, *BAGG,* 10 (1945):102ff.

2051 A 1.20 (1649) 1055, fol. 50

Juan Pascual, se obliga a la construcción de la capilla mayor del templo del pueblo de Escuintla.

2052 A 1.20 (1668) 1480 –14 v.

Poder general de la tercera orden de San Francisco, otorgado a favor de Antonio de la Cruz, para que gestione en el real consejo de Indias, la aprobación de la possesión sobre el templo del Calvario.

text, *BAGG,* 10 (1945):202ff.

2053 A 1.20 (1668) 14/1480–28

Poder otorgado por el Pbro. Bernardino de Ovando para la fundación del Convento de Santa Theressa.

text, *BAGG,* 10 (1945):229ff.

2054   A 1.20 (1668) 1480–35

El Pbro. Antonio de Salazar dona mil pesos para la fundación del convento de Religiosas Monjas de Carmelitas Descalzas.

text, *BAGG,* 10 (1945):232ff.

2055   A 1.20 (1668) 1480 – 40 v.

Manda el maestro don Esteban de Salazar a favor de la fundación del convento de Santa Teresa.

text, *BAGG,* 10 (1945):234ff.

2056   A 1.20 (1669) 683–191

Escritura de dotación ... a favor de la fundación del convento de Carmelitas Descalzas, bajo la advocación de Santa Teresa de Jesús.

text, *BAGG,* 10 (1945):235ff.

2057   A 1.20 (1672) 784, fol. 37

20 de julio de 1672.- Obligación otorgada por Sebastián Solís, mulato libre y maestro carpintero. Se obligaba a la hechura de la capilla mayor del templo parroquial del pueblo de San Juan Amatitlán. Semejante a la sacristia mayor del convento de Santo Domingo de la capital.

2058   A 1.20 (1673) 476–10

Los carpinteros Nicolás y Juan López, se obligan. . . . de hacer de nuevo el techo de la iglesia del convento de San Francisco de la ciudad de Santiago de Guatemala.

text, *BAGG,* 10 (1945):131ff.

See also VASQUEZ, 1937–44, 4:67ff., Section I, for the text transcribed by the editor of the edition.

2059   A 1.20 (1675) 477–32

Escritura de concierto de la obra de la portada de la iglesia del convento de San Francisco de la ciudad de Santiago de Guatemala.

text, *BAGG,* 10 (1945):133ff.

See also VASQUEZ, 1937–44, 4:71ff., section I above, for text transcribed by the editor of the edition.

2060   A 1.20 (1675) 1322–803

Fernando de Cuellas dona cierta suma para la fundación del convento de Santa Teresa. (Antigua).

text, *BAGG,* 10 (1945):245ff.

2061   A 1.20 (1675) 9093–600

Poder otorgado por el Maestro don Bernardino de Obando, Clérigo Presbitero, para la fundación del convento de Santa Teresa de Jesús.

text, *BAGG,* 10 (1945):243ff.

2062 A 1.20 (1678) 14.480–28

Dated 23 April 1678. Says there has been agitation for such a convent for the last 50 years—Santa Teresa.

text, *BAGG*, 10 (1945):229ff.

2063 A 1.20 (1678) 1480–35

Pbro. Antonio de Salazar donates 1000 pesos for the founding of the convent of Sta. Teresa.—30 April 1678.

text, *BAGG*, 10 (1945):232ff.

2064 A 1.20 (1678) 1480 – 40 v.

May 1, 1678. Another testimonial in favor of founding the convent of Sta. Teresa.

text, *BAGG*, 10 (1945):234ff.

2065 A 1.20 (1679) 683–191

Escritura de dotación otorgada por dn. Sevastián Alvarez Alfonso Rosica de Caldas, presidente de la real audiencia y otros vecinos, a favor de la fundación del convento de Carmelitas Descalzas, bajo la advocación de Santa Teresa de Jesús.

text, *BAGG*, 10 (1945):234ff.

2066 A 1.20 (1690) 641, fol. 53

18 de julio de 1690. El maestro albañil Diego Barrientos, se obliga la construción del templo parroquial del pueblo de Atquizaya, partido de Chalchuapa.

2067 A 1.20 (1690) 695 – 26

Tomás de la Vega, maestro pintor, se compromete a hacer diez y ocho lienzos de santos de la tercera orden, con insignias de la pasión de Cristo.

text, *BAGG*, 10 (1945):204ff.

2068 A 1.20 (1690) 695 – 119

Escritura otorgada el 13 de octubre de 1690 por el maestro ensamblador Vicente de la Parra . . . obligándose a hacer el retablo de nuestra señora de la Natividad de la iglesia de Santa Catalina Mártir.

text, *BAGG*, 10 (1945):224ff.

2069 A 1.20 (1691) 1189 – 120 v.

El alférez Ramón de Molina, se obliga hacer el retablo de la capilla del Santo Cristo, de la iglesia de Nuestra Señora de las Mercedes.

text, *BAGG*, 10 (1945):158ff.

2070 A 1.20 (1692) 643, fol. 54

26 de Julio de 1692. En una escritura de venta de unas casas situadas al

norte de las Casas Episcopales de la ciudad de Guatemala, consta que estas Casas estaban siendo edificadas.

2071 A 1.20 (1692) 696–23

Poder otorgado por el difinitorio de la provincia del Santísimo nombre de Jesús de la regular observancia del Señor San Francisco, el 29 de enero de 1692, para el cobro de las asignaciones destinadas a la fundación del convento de Santa Clara.

text, *BAGG*, 10 (1945):253ff.

2072 A 1.20 (1692) 29.330–147 (?)

Tomás de los Reyes, vecino de Oaxaca y Juan de los Reyes, vecino de Totonicapán, se obligan para hacer la construcción del templo del Calvario del pueblo de Quetzaltenango. Este templo sería de cantería.

2073 A 1.20 (1696) 757

Francisco Hernández de Fuentes, maestro del arte de cantería, se obliga construir una nueva iglesia para el convento de Sta. Catalina.

text, *BAGG*, 10 (1945):221ff.

2074 A 1.20 (1699) 466

Diego Martín, maestro de ensambladuría, se obliga hacer el retablo para el altar de Ntra. Sra. de los Remedios del templo de Santa Catalina Mártir.

2075 A 1.20 (1703) 738—24 v.

Agustina Ramona, india, cede un sitio al Colegio de Cristo Crucificado.

text, *BAGG*, 10 (1945):199.

2076 A 1.20 (1704) 739—183 v.

Pedro Lorenzo y José Veles, se obligan a dorar el altar mayor de la iglesia de nuestra Señora de las Mercedes.

text, *BAGG*, 10 (1945):160ff.

2077 A 1.20 (1770) 1120, fol. 215

29 de diciembre de 1770. En el testamento otorgado en la ciudad de Guatemala por Antonio de Molina, natural y vecino de la Villa de San Vicente de Austria consta la donación de 2000 pesos, para la fundación de un convento de San Francisco en dicha Villa y si dentro de 6 años no había tenido lugar, se tomen 500 pesos de los 2000 para hacer un retablo a San Francisco en la iglesia parroquial.

2078 A 1.20 (1770) 1120, fol. 215

29 de diciembre de 1770. Consta en el testamento que Antonio de Molina, vecino y natural de la Villa de San Vicente de Austria, otorgó en la ciudad de Guatemala, la donación de 200 pesos, a favor de la obra del templo de Ntra. Sra. de los Dolores del Cerro.

2079   A 1.21 (1772) 24.691–2807

Plano para la construcción de las Casas Consistoriales y carcel del pueblo de Quetzaltenango.

2080   A 1.21 (1794) 7558–368, fol. 45

Vista del trazo de la iglesia del pueblo de Jocotenango, situado al norte de la Nueva Guatemala. Autor: José Sierra.

2081   A 1.21 (1796) 24.276–2778, fol. 5

Perfil y plano para la construcción del acueducto a ser construido para la introducción de agua a la plaza pública del pueblo de San Juan Comalapa.

2082   A 1.21 (1796) 8014–385, fol. 5

Plano que demarca la Iglesia, Convento, Residencia del alcalde mayor, cárcel y plaza del pueblo de San Miguel Totonicapán.

2083   A 1.21 (1800) 3989–197, fol. 52

Plano de la iglesia del Barrio de San Marcos, corregimiento de Quetzaltenango. Autor: José Domingo Hidalgo.

2084   A 1.21 (1807) 4013–198, fol. 14

Plano de la iglesia del Barrio de San Marcos, corregimiento de Quezaltenango.

2085   A 1.21 (1808) 4019–198, fol. 25

Vista exterior de la iglesia del convento de San Francisco del pueblo de Quetzaltenango.

2086   A 1.21.3 (1797) 24.276–2778, fol. 40

Plano que demuestra la idea de la introducción de agua que proyecta hacer en el pueblo de San Juan Comalapan. Autor: Bernardo Ramírez.

2087   A 1.21.6 (1789) 3720–181

Sobre la reedificación de las Casas Reales de Santo Domingo Cobán.

2088   A 1.23 (1540) 1511–10

10 de junio de 1540.—Para la mejor conservación y educación de los indios de las poblaciones de la provincia de Guatemala, su majestad ordéna que con los indios que están dispersos en los montes, se funden pueblos.

2089   A 1.23 (1546) 1511–32

25 de marzo de 1546.—So pena de perder sus encomiendas, los encomenderos contraigan matrimonio dentro de tres años.

2090   A 1.23 (1546) 1511–33

26 de marzo de 1546.—Dispone su majestad que los caminos de las provincias de Guatemala y Honduras "se aderezen dos vezes al año".

2091 A 1.23 (1548) 1511–72

25 de junio de 1548.—Real cédula ordenando la libertad de los esclavos existentes en la provincia de Nicaragua.

2092 A 1.23 (1548) 1511–74

14 de julio de 1548.—Su majestad da su aprobación al auto por el cual el Licenciado López de Cerrato declaró libres a los esclavos indios, los cuales eran vendidos ". . . como negros de Guinea . . ."

2093 A 1.23 (1548) 1511–87

27 de diciembre de 1548.—Su majestad acuerda que los encomenderos e indios libres de los pueblos de la jurisdicción del obispado de Chiapas, cooperen en la construcción de la iglesia y monasterio de los frailes dominicos.

2094 A 1.23 (1549) 1511–108

20 de abril de 1549.—Prohibiendo que los encomenderos de la provincia de Chiapas, den en alquiler a sus indios para que trabajen en los ingenios "porque diz que basta un yngenio a matar cada año dos mil de ellos . . .".

2095 A 1.23 (1549) 1511–101

29 de abril de 1549.—La Audiencia es autorizada para que reparta solares y tierras entre los vecinos de la provincia de Guatemala.

2096 A 1.23 (1549) 1511–125

16 de septiembre de 1549.—Su majestad aprueba el proyecto que el licenciado Cerrato le presentó con fecha 9 de noviembre de 1548, sobre la construcción de varios caminos en la provincia de Guatemala.

2097 A 1.23 (1549) 1511–133

31 de diciembre de 1549.—Ordenando a la Audiencia de los Confines, que extienda sus instrucciones a Juan Pérez de Cabrera, para que conquiste los pueblos de la provincia de Cartago.

2098 A 1.23 (1550) 1511–140

7 de junio de 1550.—Su majestad recomienda a los frailes franciscanos, que traten de enseñar la lengua castellana a los indígenas.

2099 A 1.23 (1549) 1511–142

13 de junio de 1549.—El Licenciado Cerrato, Presidente de la Audiencia, informa a su majestad que había iniciado la construcción de un camino que conduciría de la capital a la costa del mar del norte.

2100 A 1.23 (1550) 1511–146

20 de julio de 1550.—Real cédula anexando la provincia de Tabasco a la audiencia de Guatemala.

2101 A 1.23 (1550) 1511–148

4 de agosto de 1550.—Su majestad dispone que para finalizar la obra de la Catedral de Guatemala, su costo sea distribuido así: un tercio sea tomado de los fondos reales; un tercio de las encomiendas y tributos de la jurisdicción del obispado y el resto por los vecinos e indios (éstos estando encomendados bajo la corona real.

2102 A 1.23 (1550) 1511–153

27 de octubre de 1550.—Que para la construcción de la iglesia y monasterio de los frailes dominicos, en Ciudad Real de Chiapas, el costo total de la obra sea repartido en tres partes: una que pague la caja real; otra los encomenderos y la última los indios libres de la jurisdicción del obispado de Chiapas.

2103 A 1.23 (1553) 1511–188

20 de enero de 1553.—Real cédula anexando la provincia de Soconusco a la audiencia de Guatemala.

2104 A 1.23 (1553) 1511–193

27 de abril de 1553.—Que todo español avecindado de la provincia de Guatemala, sea obligado a ejercer su oficio o a cultivar la tierra, so pena de ser enviado a España bajo partida de registro.

2105 A 1.23 (1556) 1511–218

22 de enero de 1556.—Recomendado a los dominicos y franciscanos, que olviden su rencillas.

2106 A 1.23 (1556) 1511–223

6 de agosto de 1556.—Carta real que inserta la cédula que declara que la provincia de Soconusco depende de las autoridades de Guatemala.

2107 A 1.23 (1556) 1511–224

6 de agosto de 1556.—Su majestad confirma la anexión de la provincia de Soconusco a la audiencia de Guatemala.

2108 A 1.23 (1558) 1511–238

1 de agosto de 1558.—Ordenando que se dé ayuda económica, y no indios en repartimiento, para la construcción de los monasterios.

2109 A 1.23 (1559) 1512–262

29 de noviembre de 1559.—Su majestad dispone otorgar la cantidad de quinientos pesos de oro de minas, a favor del hospital fundado por el obispo Francisco Marroquín y donado a la real corona.

2110 A 1.23 (1559) 1512–270

18 de diciembre de 1559.—Su majestad pide informes acerca de lo proyectado por la audiencia de Guatemala, relativo al establecimiento de un obispo en la provincia de Soconusco.

2111   A 1.23 (1559) 1512-270

18 de diciembre de 1559.—La Real Audiencia con el objeto de fomentar la agricultura y evitar la holgazanería de los españoles, propone repartir tierras en el valle de Guatemala.

2112   A 1.23 (1560) 1512-275

31 de agosto de 1560.—Que los indios de la provincia de Honduras, sean reducidos a poblados.

2113   A 1.23 (1561) 1512-292

15 de septiembre de 1561.—Su majestad para evitar que los indios sean empleados en el laboreo de minas y en las obras públicas, autoriza la venta de esclavos negros.

2114   A 1.23 (1569) 1512-354

25 de enero de 1569.—En vista de haber quedado restablecida la audiencia en la ciudad de Santiago de los Caballeros, su majestad confirma la anexión de la provincia de Soconusco a Guatemala.

2115   A 1.23 (1570) 1512-368

12 de junio de 1570.—Indica su majestad que para evitar la despoblación de la tierra, se obligue a los casados que han dejado sus esposas en otros reinos, a que las hagan venir a Guatemala, o al lugar donde tienen sus casas pobladas.

2116   A 1.23 (1572) 1512-422

16 de agosto de 1572.—Su majestad solicita que la Real Audiencia, le envíe relación de las costumbres de los indigenas, relaciones históricas de sus pueblos, con objeto de escribir la Historia General de la Indias.

2117   A 1.23 (1573) 1512-443

15 de mayo de 1573.—Informa a su majestad el Presidente Licenciado Villalobos, que en la provincia de Costa Rica ha sido fundada una población con el nombre de Cartago y que está integrada por cuarenta vecinos, lo mismo que la de Nueva Aranjuez que tiene quince pobladores.

2118   A 1.23 (1574) 1512-447

27 de abril de 1574.—Ordénase que los negros, bozales, y esclavos, también paguen tributos.

2119   A 1.23 (1574) 1513-523

27 de abril de 1574.—Por carta de esta fecha su majestad recomienda lo siguiente: a) que los ayuntamientos tengan a su cargo la construcción y conservación de puentes y caminos; . . .

2120   A 1.23 (1575) 1512-462

18 de enero de 1575.—Que la laguna de Amatitlán, sea de propiedad de los indios situados en sus inmediaciones, para que (vivan de ella) y no estén obligados a dar sus productos a los frailes dominicos.

2121 A 1.23 (1575) 1512–474

31 de enero de 1575.—En vista que los franciscanos solicitaron a su majestad ayuda económica para reconstruir su iglesia y convento, se pide informes a la Real Audiencia.

2122 A 1.23 (1575) 1512–475

31 de Enero de 1575.—Su majestad pide informes acerca del estado en que se encuentra la obra de la iglesia y conventos franciscanos.

2123 A 1.23 (1575) 1513–496

19 de marzo de 1575.—El Presidente Licenciado Villalobos, con carta de esta fecha hace envío a su majestad de la crónica escrita por Bernal Díaz de Castillo.

See Section I, Nos. 83–88.

2124 A 1.23 (1576) 1513–497

21 de mayo de 1576.—Su majestad acusa recibo de la crónica escrita por Bernal Diáz del Castillo.

2125 A 1.23 (1576) 1513–510

18 de noviembre de 1576.—Que en virtud del terremoto que asoló la ciudad de San Salvador, se asigne cierta suma en calidad de ayuda a los vecinos de dicha ciudad.

2126 A 1.23 (1578) 1513–557

25 de noviembre de 1578.—En vista que los mulatos tratan mal a los indios, queda prohibido que ellos obliguen a los indios que les sirvan.

2127 A 1.23 (1579) 1513–569

11 de mayo de 1579.—Fray Lucas Ortiz, deseaba establecer un convento de franciscanos en Comayagua; su majestad le indica que solicite licencia al obispo de la provincia.

2128 A 1.23 (1580) 1513–576

3 de junio de 1580.—En vista de la población sumamente densa de la provincia de Suchitepéquez, su majestad recomienda a la audiencia que dote los curatos necesarios.

2129 A 1.23 (1580) 1513–534

15 de diciembre de 1580.—Ordena su majestad en vista del informe de fray Alonso de la Cerda, obispo de Honduras, de que los indios aún no forman pueblos, ordena su reducción.

2130 A 1.23 (1580) 1513–579

23 de septiembre de 1580.—Su majestad ordena de nuevo, que no se permita que los negros vivan en los pueblos de los indios.

2131 A 1.23 (1584) 1513–639

14 de noviembre de 1584.—Ordena su majestad que los indios de la jurisdicción de Honduras, sean reducidos a poblado.

2132 A 1.23 (1585) 1513–649

15 de noviembre de 1585.—En vista que la provincia de Soconusco se está despoblando, su majestad permite que los indios de otros pueblos se puedan trasladar a ella, quedando exonerados de tributar durante el primer año de su establecimiento.

2133 A 1.23 (1586) 1513–652

26 de enero de 1586.—Su majestad da trescientos pesos en calidad de ayuda de costa, para la construcción de la iglesia parroquial y del hospital de la Villa de la Santísima Trinidad.

2134 A 1.23 (1586) 1513–660

30 de mayo de 1586.—Baltasar Estévez de Santa María, "ermitaño de la ermita de Nuestra Señora de los Remedios" de la ciudad de Santiago de los Caballeros, informó a su majestad que a su llegada en el año 1574, inició la reconstrucción de dicha ermita, que estaba cubierta de paja, y que ahora estaba cubierta de artesón, y que para establecer la festividad de Nuestra Señora de la O, necesitaba cierta ayuda de costa. Su majestad de la otorgó.

2135 A 1.23 (1594) 5113–750

20 de mayo de 1594.—Ordénase al Presidente de la Real Audiencia y al obispado de la provincia de Guatemala, que informen sobre si es conveniente erigir en parroquia la ermita de Nuestra Señora de los Remedios.

2136 A 1.23 (1594) 1513–10.065

Que la Audiencia de Guatemala informe del estado de la conquista y reducción de la Taguzgalpa.

text, *BAGG,* 5 (1939–40):149.

2137 A 1.23 (1607) 1514–107

Su Magestad encomienda a Fr. Estevan Verdelet (O.F.M.) la conversión de los indios jicaques de Taguzgalpa.

text, *BAGG,* 5 (1939–40):5ff.

2138 A 1.23 (1609) Libro de Reales Cédulas 1600–1615, Leg. No. 1514 folio 147

Cédula Real para que el Presidente de Guatemala informe a su Magestad, de ciertos indios que Fr. Francisco de Rivera encontró en las montañas de Nicaragua.

text, *BAGG,* 5 (1939–40):8.

2139 A 1.23 (1610) Libro de Reales cédulas Leg. 1514, fol. 160

Su Magestad faculta al Gobernador de la Provincia de Honduras, cierta expedición contra los indios infieles.

text, *BAGG,* 5 (1939–40):8ff.

2140   A 1.23 (1610) 10.069–200

Cédula Real de su Magestad al Presidente de Guatemala sobre los indios de Nicaragua de que le da cuenta Fr. Francisco de Rivera, Vicario General de la Orden de Ntra. Sra. de las Mercedes.

text, *BAGG*, 5 (1939–40):9.

2141   A 1.23 (1613) 10.069–232–1514

Carta del Dr. Pedro Sánchez de Araque, acerca de la visita que efectuó a las Provincias de Costa Rica y Nicaragua.

text, *BAGG*, 5 (1939–40):10ff.

2142   A 1.23 (1643) 10.071–154–1516

El Rey ordena a la Audiencia de Guatemala que dé ayuda a don Diego de Vera Ordoñez de Villa Quirán, encargado de la conquista de el Próspero (a) el Lacandón.

text, *BAGG*, 5 (1939–40):14ff.

2143   A 1.23 (1656) 10.073–186–1518

A la Audiencia de Guatemala dándole gracias por la reducción que ha hecho de los indios choles.

text, *BAGG*, 5 (1939–40):15ff.

2144   A 1.23 (1664) 10.075–1520–137

Real Cédula dirigida a la Audiencia acerca de que informe de los servicios que don Bartolomé de Escota ha hecho en la reducción y conservación de los indios xicaques.

text, *BAGG*, 5 (1939–40):16ff.

2145   A 1.23 (1671) 10.075–1520–13

Su Magestad recomienda la reducción de los indios, antiguamente poblados en la Isla de Jaen, Provincia de Nicaragua.

text, *BAGG*, 5 (1939–40):18ff.

2146   A 1.23 (1674)

Relación verdadera de la reducción de los indios infieles de la provincia de la Taguisgalpa, Mansados xicaques. (Mercedarians)

text, *BAGG*, 5 (1939–40):289ff.

2147   A 1.23 (1675) 10.975–1520–220

Real cédula de 13 de Febrero de 1676, autorizando la fundación del convento de Carmelitas Descalzas, en vista de lo acordado de 22 de junio de 1675.

text, *BAGG*, 10 (1945):247ff.

2148 A 1.23 (1676) [dated 15 April 1676.]

Razón del estado en que se hallan las reducciones de indios infieles que están a cargo de los religiosos de N.P.S. Francisco desta santa provincia del Santíssimo nombre de Jesús de Guatemala.

text, *BAGG*, 5 (1939–40):285ff.

2149 A 1.23 (1680) 10.076–1521–213

A la Audiencia de Guatemala encargándole de la providencia que convenga acerca de lo que ha representado don Juan Bautista de Urquiola, sobre la reducción de indios.

text, *BAGG*, 5 (1939-40):20ff.

2150 A 1.23 (1680) 10.076–1521–221

Real Cédula mediante la cual Su Majestad aprueba lo determinado por la Junta de la Universidad, en lo relativo a la fábrica del edificio y creación de dos cátedras más y el escudo de la Universidad.

text, *BAGG*, 9 (1944):117ff.

2151 A 1.23 (1686) 10.077–1522–140

Para que el Virrey de Nueva España y las Audiencias de Guadalajara y Guatemala y los Gobernadores de esta Provincias, cuiden de la reducción y conversión de los indios gentiles.

text, *BAGG*, 5 (1939–40):22ff.

2152 A 1.23 (1686) 10.077–1522–189

A la Audiencia de Guatemala que dé toda la asistencia y ayuda que se le pidiere y fuere posible dar para la reducción de los indios del Chol, que están a cargo de la religión de predicadores.

text, *BAGG*, 5 (1939–40):21

2153 A 1.23 (1702) 10.079–1523–53

Real Cédula acerca de que los religiosos Dominicos empleados en la reducción del Petén Itza.

text, *BAGG*, 5 (1939–40):31ff.

2154 A 1.23 (1702) 10.079–1524–62

Su Magestad niega título de Castilla y Adelantado de las Provincias de Itzá a don Martín de Ursua y Arismendí.

text, *BAGG*, 5 (1939–40):33.

2155 A 1.23 (1703) 14.038–2025

Informe que con fecha 22 de diciembre de 1703, rindieron los oficiales reales de la Caja de Honduras, acerca de que la catedral de Comayagua, ha siete años, fue construida de madera por el Obispo Fr. Alonso de Vargas y Abarca y que en el presente año, el obispo Fr. Juan Pérez Carpintero, ha hecho llegar canteros para la obra de la capilla mayor.

2156 A 1.23 (1709) 10.080–1525–44

Dánse las gracias a Fr. José Xirón, de la Orden de Predicadores por haber reducido a poblado 43 indios de las montañas de asixsa.

text, *BAGG*, 5 (1939–40):36.

2157 A 1.23 (1709) 10.080–1525–46

A la Audiencia de Guatemala para que informe del estado de los indios de Boruca que confinan con la provincia de Costa Rica y si será conveniente reducirlos a poblaciones.

text, *BAGG*, 5 (1939–40):36ff.

2158 A 1.23 (1709) 10.080–1525–57

Su Magestad asigna cierta suma a los misioneros del pueblo de nuestra Señora de los Dolores de Lacandón.

text, *BAGG*, 5 (1939–40):41ff.

2159 A 1.23 (1709) 10.080–1525–59

Su Magestad encarga el aumento de las misiones y el buen tratamiento de los naturales.

text, *BAGG*, 5 (1939–40):39ff.

2160 A 1.23 (1713) 10.080–1525–254

Para que se observen y guarden las leyes que previenen lo que se ha de ejecutar con los indios recién convertidos para su mantención.

text, *BAGG*, 5 (1939–40):41ff.

2161 A 1.23 (1713) 10.080–1525–262

Su Magestad aprueba la mutación de indios lacandones al paraje nombrado Asantic, jurisdicción de Huehuetenango.

text *BAGG*, 5 (1939–40):42ff.

2162 A 1.23 (1714) 10.080–1525–317

Al Presidente de la Audiencia de Guatemala dándole gracias por lo que ejecuta en mayor seguridad y buen gobierno del presidio y poblaciones del Itzá y Petén y ordenándole lo conveniente sobre punto de misiones para aquel paraje.

text *BAGG*, 5 (1939–40):43ff.

2163 A 1.23 (1715) 10.081–1526–15

Su Magestad aprueba el traslado de indios lacandones de la reducción de Ntra. Sra. de los Delores al paraje de Asquepala, jurisdicción de la Alcaldía Mayor de Huehuetenango.

text, *BAGG*, 5 (1939–40):45ff.

2164 A 1.23 (1716) 10.081–1526–60

Su Magestad prohibe que sean extraidos los indios de las reducciones de Itzá y del Petén.

text, *BAGG*, 5 (1939–40):47.

2165 A 1.23 (1717) 10.081–1526–68

Al Presidente de la Audiencia Su Majestad le da las gracias por la pacificación y reducción de los nativos de Ytzá y Petén.

text, *BAGG*, 5 (1939–40):47ff.

2166 A 1.23 (1727) 1526–210

Su majestad aprueba la fundación del convento de religiosas de nuestra Señora del Pilar de Zaragoza (monjas Capuchinas).

text, *BAGG*, 10 (1945):256ff.

2167 A 1.23 (1733) 1526–310

Su majestad pide informes acerca de la instancia de Fr. Francisco Seco (O.F.M.) acerca de asignar fondos al convento e iglesia de Santa Clara.

text, *BAGG*, 10 (1945):255ff.

2168 A 1.23 (1759) 10.083–1528–138

A la Audiencia de Guatemala para que informe acerca del contenido de la representación del Guardián del Colegio de Cristo Crucificado, que trata del estado de las reducciones indígenas.

text, *BAGG*, 5 (1939–40):200ff.

2169 A 1.23 (1764) 10.083–1528

Real Cédula ordenando a la Audiencia que envie informes acerca del estado de las reducciones de Ntra. Sra. del Pilar y San José de Orosí.

text, *BAGG*, 5 (1939–40):210ff.

2170 A 1.23 (1799) ?

Cédula de 18 de Mayo de 1799.—De las precauciones que se han de tomar en los que se construyan en Guatemala, para que no se espongan a la ruina que causan los temblores.

2171 A 1.24 (1638) 10.202–1558, fol. 58

8 de febrero de 1638. R.P. Eróganse 300 pesos para la obra del templo del pueblo de Tuzantan de la Real Corona, jurisdicción de Soconusco.

2172 A 1.24 (1642) 10.203–1559, fol. 473

22 de diciembre de 1642. R.P. Para que el alcalde Mayor de Chiapas y los regulares doctrineros del pueblo de Soyatitán, encomienda de doña María de Villa Fuerte, de don Gregoria González de Cuenca y Contreras y del

alférez mayor don Juan de la Tovilla, rindan informes acerca del costo que tendría la construcción del templo parroquial que fuera destruido por un incendio el sabado de gloria de 1641.

2173   A 1.24 (1655) 1557–125

30 de abril de 1655. R.P. Asignación de indios en repartimiento, para que trabajen en la reconstrucción del templo parroquial de la ciudad de San Miguel, alcaldía de Salvador, y en el convento de San Francisco, destruido por un incendio.

2174   A 1.24 (1667) 10.207–1563, fol. 54

¼ of tributos ceded for 6 years so that the church of Taopac (Alcaldía Mayor de San Salvador) could be rebuilt after being destroyed in a fire (it was thatch-roofed).

2175   A 1.24 (1672) 10.208–1564, fol. 308

26 de febrero de 1672. R.P. Otorgando licencia al ayuntamiento de la Ciudad de San Salvador, para que nombre dos comisarios (sin sueldo) para que recauden limosnas, con destino a la reparación del templo parroquial el cual sufrió daños en sus bóvedas y arcos durante los temblores habidos en 1671.

2176   A 1.24 (1673) 10.208–1564, fol. 573

19 de julio de 1673. Inserto el auto por el cual la Audiencia cedió la cuarta parte de los tributos y exoneración del servicio del tostón, durante dos años, a favor de los indios de Santiago Esquipulas, para finalizar la obra del templo parroquial.

2177   A 1.24 (1681) 10.210–1566, fols. 330, 333

Church on island of Ometepe (Nic.) destroyed by pirates. ¼ of tribute ceded pueblos of Cosaliugapa, Mozogalpa, and Astagalpa—all 3 use the same church.

2178   A 1.24 (1681) 10.210–1566, fols. 482, 485

22 de diciembre de 1681. R.P. Asignando la cuarta parte de los tributos del pueblo de Chalchuapa, para cubrir el valor de la reconstrucción del templo parroquial.

2179   A 1.24 (1682) 10.211–1567, fol. 86

23 de abril de 1682. R.P. Acuerda la audiencia ceder la cuarta parte de los tributos del pueblo de Izalcos, para sufragar los gastos que ocasione la reedificación del templo.

2180   A 1.24 (1698) 10.214–1570, fol. 339

Concédese a los indigenas del pueblo de San Francisco Quetzaltepeque, corregimiento de Chiquimula, la cuarta parte de los tributos durante cuatro años, para cubrir el costo de la obra del templo parroquial que fuera destruido por incendio originado por un rayo.

2181   A 1.24 (1703) 10.217–1573, fol. 128

6 de febrero de 1703. R.P. Se concede la cuarta parte de los tributos por cuatro años, a favor de los indios del pueblo de Asunción Ahuachapa, para que construyan el templo que quedó arruinado con el terremoto habido el 14 de agosto de 1702.

2182   A 1.24 (1703) 10.217–1573, fol. 192.

28 de febrero de 1703. R.P. Concédense los tributos, en su cuarta parte, durante dos años, para sufragar la obra de la iglesia del pueblo de Santa Lucía, situada en las inmediaciones del de Santa Ana, de la alcaldía de San Salvador. Esta iglesia estaba inconclusa desde doce años.

2183   A 1.24 (1707) 10.220–1576, fol. 78

14 de abril de 1707. R.P. Concediendo a favor del común del pueblo de Ntra. Sra. de la Asunción de Ahuachapa, jurisdicción de la alcaldía de Soconusco, la cuarta parte de sus tributos, por cuatro años, para la re-edificación de la iglesia parroquial.

2184   A 1.24 (1713) 10.224–1580, fol. 220

4 de julio de 1713. R.P. Para que el Gobernador de Nicaragua proceda a revisar el estado de la iglesia del pueblo de Masaya, para cuya reconstrucción los indios solicitaron 10,000 pesos y exoneración de tributos.

2185   A 1.24 (1713) 10.224–1580, fol. 247

31 de julio de 1713. R.P. Comunicando al alcalde mayor de Sonsonate haber sido autorizado el común de naturales del pueblo de Izalco, para que de los fondos de comunidades, eroguen la cantidad de doscientos pesos para renovar el artesonado de la iglesia de dicho pueblo.

2186   A 1.24 (1714) 10.225–1581, fols. 75, 111

5 de marzo de 1714. R.P. Cediendo a favor de los naturales de Matagalpa, Solingalpa y Malaguina, en la provincia de Nicaragua, la cuarta parte de sus tributos para cubrir el valor de la edificación del templo parroquial, en Matagalpa.

2187   A 1.24 (1714) 10.225–1581, fol. 540

24 de diciembre de 1714. R.P. Para que el alcalde mayor de Chiapas, proceda inspeccionar el estado de la iglesia del pueblo de Santiago Ama-tenango, dañada con el temblor habido el 15 de mayo, calculando el presupuesto para su reedificación.

2188   A 1.24 (1719) 10.227–1583, fol. 30

19 de febrero de 1719. R.C. Asigna el noveno y medio de los diezmos, para cubrir los gastos de la construcción del templo destinado para catedral de la ciudad de Comayagua.

2189   A 1.24 (1719) 10.227–1583, fol. 120

29 de abril de 1719. R.P. Adjudicación de la cuarta parte de los tributos del

pueblo de Istapa, alcaldía de Chiapas, por un año para que se inicie la reedificación de la iglesia de dicho pueblo.

2190 A 1.24 (1719) 10.227–1583, fol. 258

8 de agosto de 1719. R.P. En que se concede por otros dos años la cuarta parte de los tributos a los indios del pueblo de Iztapa, jurisdicción de la alcaldía de Chiapas, para construir y finalizar la obra de la iglesia parroquial.

2191 A 1.24 (1724) 10.228–1584, fol. 234

16 de marzo de 1724. R.P. Para que el alcalde mayor de San Salvador haga entrega a los alcaldes del pueblo de Santiago Apostepeque de las rentas producidas por el arrendamiento de sus ejidos, suma que emplearían en la reedificación de la iglesia parroquial.

2192 A 1.24 (1728) 10.230–1586, fol. 112

16 de marzo de 1728. R.P. Se ordena al alcalde mayor de Chiapas, proceda reconocer el estado del edificio del templo parroquial del pueblo de Santa Cruz Socoltenango y formule el presupuesto para su reconstrucción.

2193 A 1.24 (1728) 10.230–1586, fol. 123

1 de marzo de 1728. R.P. Se ordena al alcalde mayor de Sonsonate, proceda a reconocer el estado del edificio del templo del Barrio de los Mexicanos y calcule el presupuesto para su reedificación.

(The Indians were exempt from *tributo* payments being descendants of the auxiliaries of Pedro de Alvarado.)

2194 A 1.24 (1728) 10.230–1586, fol. 284

24 de julio de 1728. R.P. Para que por parte del Gobernador de Nicaragua, se proceda a designar personas que pasen al pueblo de Santiago Jinotepeque a inspeccionar el estado del edificio del templo parroquial, calculando el costo de su reedificación.

2195 A 1.24 (1730) 10.231–1587, fol. 63

26 de enero de 1730. R.P. En que se concede a los naturales del pueblo de Santa Catarina Apopa, jurisdicción de la alcaldía de San Salvador, los Tributos correspondientes a cuatro años, para cubrir los gastos de la obra del templo parroquial.

2196 A 1.24 (1730) 10.231–1587, fol. 335

18 de julio de 1730. R.P. Para que don Luis Antonio Muñoz, Tesorero Juez Oficial Real de la Caja de la Villa de la Santísima Trinidad de Sonsonate, tenga a su cargo la intendencia y gastos de la obra de la iglesia del barrio de Mexicanos, contigua a dicha villa.

2197 A 1.24 (1731) 10.232–1588, fol. 249

25 de agosto de 1731. R.P. Inserta el auto proveido por la audiencia, aprobando las cuentas rendidas por el juez oficial real de la caja de la villa

de la Santísima Trinidad de Sonsonate, de lo invertido en la reconstrucción del templo del barrio de mexicanos.

2197a A 1.25 (1807) 10.357–1702, 278 folios.

Recopilación sumaria de los autos acordados de la Real Audiencia de este Reyno de Guatemala, providencias y bandos de su Superior Gobierno, que han podido recogerse desde el año de 1561 hasta el presente de 1807, dispuesta en orden alfabético por don José María Zamora, de orden del mismo tribunal de La Real Audiencia, compuesto de los SS. Ministros D. Francisco Camacho y D. Antonio Rodríguez de Cárdenas. Nueva Guatemala 1807.

See also ZAMORA, 1807, Section I, above, for the same.

2198 A 1.27 (1656) 19.418–1711

El relator don Fsco. Márquez, recusa al Oidor don Fsco. López de Solís, por haberlo insultado en cierta festividad que se celebraba en la iglesia de la Merced.

2199 A 1.37 (1627) 41.233–4777

Los PP. Curas parrocos de los templos de las ciudades de San Salvador y de San Miguel, informan a la audiencia que por falta de cooperación del vecindario, no había sido posible la construcción de un templo que fuera digno.

2200 A 1.37 (1818) 17.517–2335

El Gobernador Intendente de la provincia de Honduras, don Ramón Anguiano informa acerca dicha provincia.

text, *BAGG,* 7 (1941–42): 175ff.

2201 A 1.39 (1589) 1751, fol. 4 v.

El Presidente de la Audiencia comisiona a Francisco de Villalta Valenzuela, vecino de la ciudad de Gracias a Dios, para que tuviera cargo de repartir los indios del servicio ordinario y para labores del campo, sementeras y edificios de casas. . . . etc. en octubre 1589.

De un artículo por Zavala, Silvio en *ASGH,* 22 (1947).

2202 A 1.39 (1594) 1751, fol. 58 v.

December 29, 1594.—Person named to assign indians to come each week to work on buildings and for repair work. Audiencia.

From article by Zavala, Silvio, *ASGH,* 22 (1947).

2203 A 1.62.2 (1706) 48.139–5556

Agustín Núñez entrega dos retablos al templo de la Compañía de Jesús.

2204 A 1.69.3 (1687) 18.140–5556

Autos hechos sobre el nombramiento de maestros mayores en Agustín Núñez (del arte de arquitecto ensamblador) y en José de Porras (del arte de arquitecto de edificios). En este expediente están las ordenanzas que deben ser observadas por los habitantes de la capital.

2205 A 1.69.3 (1723) 48.141–5556

Autos acerca del examen a que deben ser sometidos los que aspiren a ser maestro en arquitectura.

2206 A 1.69.3 (1752) 48.142–5556

Juan de Dios Estrada informs the Ayuntamiento that those not examined be prohibited from directing construction.

See also A 1.10.2 (1751) 48.142–5556, above.

2207 A 1.69.3 (1789) 48.143–5556

Joaquín de Arroyo, maestro examinado y profesor de albañilería, certifica el valor y estado de la casa perteneciente a don Carlos Figueroa.

2208 A 1.80 (?) 55.040–6683

Distribución de las oficinas y dependencias establecidas en el Palacio de los Capitanes Generales de la Nueva Guatemala.

2209 A 3.1 (1779) 11.669–582, fol. 455

Instancia del obispo de Nicaragua, para que con una parte de los novenos reales cedidos a favor de la obra de la catedral de León, cuya dedicación sería en la Semana Santa del año de la fecha, se adquiera un tabernáculo que de Roma condujo a Guatemala el arcediano Dr. Francisco de la Vega y que estaba en poder de uno de sus albaceos don Antonio Carbonel.

2210 A 3.1 (1795) 22.296–1316, fol. 63

Dictamen rendido por la Contaduría Mayor de Cuentas, en el sentido que el plano y presupuesto de Trujillo, pasen en consulta al ingeniero José de Sierra, para que revise el proyecto presentado por don Manuel de Novas.

2211 A 3.1 (1797) 15.075–819

Oficio del Presidente José Domás y Valle remitiendo a la Contaduría Mayor, para su informe el expediente sobre reconstrucción de la iglesia catedral de Comayagua.

2212 A 3.1 (1797) 15.099–819

Acerca de que la Contaduría informe si se puede destinar cierta suma para entregar los gastos de la reconstrucción de la casa de la iglesia parroquial de San Salvador.

2213 A 3.1 (1806) 19.410–1072

Pedro José González, apoderado de Santiago Prado, pide los finiquitos de los caudales que manejó éste como ecónomo de la fábrica material de la catedral de la ciudad de León, en los años de 1801, 1802, y 1803.

2214 A 3.1 (1817) 22.526–1344, fol. 1

Estimate ordered made for cost of reconstruction of church of Santa María de Jesús.

2215 A 3.1 (1818) 22.543–1346, fol. 3

San Andrés Xemetabaj—concerning reconstruction, to see if there is any money available.

2216 A 3.2 (1673) 15.207–825

Memoria y Padrón de las Doctrinas y Conventos que administra la Religión de Nuestro Padre San Francisco, en Obispado de Guatemala. 24 de octubre de 1673.

text, *BAGG,* 10 (1945): 128ff.

2217 A 3.2 (1688) 13.090–706

Año de 1688. El común del pueblo de Eraguayquín, jurisdicción de la ciudad de San Miguel, solicita exoneración de tributos, debido a que los naturales estaban ocupados en la reconstrucción del templo parroquial destruido por la invasión de piratas.

2218 A 3.5 (1774) 1375–72, fol. 5

Plano del edificio para la Aduana que ha de ser construída en el establecimiento provisional de la Ermita. Autor: Bernardo Ramírez.

2219 A 3.5 (1791) 1522–77, fol. 46

Plano de la fábrica de la Real Aduana de San Salvador. Autor: José Ortiz de Letona.

2220 A 3.5 (1791) 1522–77, fols. 57–58

Plano de la fábrica de la Real Aduana de San Salvador. Autor: José Ortíz de Letona.

2221 A 3.5 (1781) 15.804–851, fol. 22

Asignación de los Tributos del pueblo de San Miguel del Tejar, para la obra del templo parroquial.

2222 A 3.10 (1790) 3670–202

Don Bernardo Ramírez, maestro mayor de las obras de la ciudad de Guatemala, propone la agremiación de los maestros de obras y cumplimiento del real decreto de 28 de febrero de 1787, por el cual se le otorgó la Medalla de Mérito de la Academia de San Fernando de Valencia.

2223 A 3.11 (1816) 3980–221, fol. 7

Plano de la planta del edificio que en la Antigua ocupó el Colegio Seminario de Nuestra Señora de la Asunción (Colegio Tridentino).

2224   A 3.12 (1778) 4069–225

Habiendo fallecido el Pbro. Juan Antonio Gallardo y Barahona, cura del pueblo de San Francisco Quetzaltepeque, sin haber terminado la obra del templo parroquial de dicho pueblo, encargó a su hermano por clausula de testamento, llevase a cabo dicha construcción y para ello solicitase indios en repartimiento.

2225   A 3.12 (1778) 4069–225

Quetzaltenango—indios assigned to work on church and convento of San Francisco.

2226   A 3.13 (1777) 29.687–1872, fol. 18

Plano del edificio que sería construido en la Nueva Guatemala de la Asunción con destino a la dirección General de Tabacos y sus dependencias. Autor: Marcos Ibáñez.

2227   A 3.16 (1731) 8941–437

El común del pueblo de Naulingo, alcaldía de Sonsonate, solicita la adjudicación de la cuarta parte de sus tributos, para reconstruir el templo parroquial.

2228   A 3.16 (1734) 17.575–942, fol. 43

Ajudicación de la cuarta parte de los tributos del pueblo de Ntra. Sra. de la Asunción de Chiquimula de la Sierra, para ser invertidos en la reconstrucción del templo parroquial por los temblores habidos en mayo del año anterior.

2229   A 3.16 (1790) 4731–238, fol. 16

Pueblos and tributarios of Alcaldía Mayor of Verapaz.

2230   A 3.16 (1791) 4727–238, fol. 1

Geographical description of Sonsonate.

2231   A 3.16 (1791) 4729–238, fol. 1

Geographical description of Suchitepéquez.

2232   A 3.16 (1804) 5171–253

El Común del pueblo de Santa María Magdalena Acasahuastlán, solicita exoneración de tributos, por estar ocupados en la reconstrucción del templo parroquial.

2233   A 3.17 (1734) 26.924–1655, fol. 32

Plano de la fábrica de la Casa de Moneda: Autor Diego de Porras.

2234   A 3.17 (1738) 26.924–1655, fol. 266

Plano de la Casa de Moneda de la Ciudad de Guatemala. Autor Diego de Porras.

2235 A 3.17 (1770) 17.802–955

Acerca de trazo del plano para la reedificación de unas salas en el edificio de la Casa de Moneda.

2236 A 3.17 (1776) 27.458–1705

Planos para la construcción de un edificio para la Casa de Moneda, en el establecimiento provisional de la Ermita.

2237 A 3.17 (1776) 27.458–1705, fol. 74

Plano de la Casa de Moneda provisional que se a construida asiento bajo como en los altos sobre la obra bieja que se hallo con lo demas que contiene la Manzana y terreno desocupado que resulta sobrante. Luis Diez de Navarro.

(Nueva Guatemala)

2238 A 3.18 (1769) 8994–440, fol. 23

Plano del ex-colegio de San Jerónimo, situado en Antigua Guatemala y que se destinó a la Aduana.

2239 A 3.27 (1787) 28.225–1757, fol. 148

Plano de la iglesia de Santa Rosa, en donde son celebradas las funciones de Catedral, en tanto es terminada la fábrica de ella en la Nueva Guatemala. Autor: Bernardo Ramírez.

2240 A 3.27 (1795) 28.217–1756

Geographical description of towns in Alcaldía Mayor of Sonsonate.

2241 A 3.27 (1808) 28.247–1758

León, Nicaragua. La Junta de la Renta Decimal, pide el cuaderno de los autos del concurso de las posturas de la obra de la Catedral, así mismo que el cuadro y plano que se habían formulado.

(Plan missing from this expediente.)

2242 B 1.13 (1821) 8432–495

Panajachel. Dispute over some funds for the reconstruction of the church.

2243 B 1.19.1 (1822) 55.501–2500, fol. 1

Patzicía—need money for repair of church.

2244 B 1.19.1 (1822) 55.519–2501, fol. 1

Patzicía—9 years before some money paid by indios to repair Capilla Mayor—still covered with thatch!

2245 B 1.19.1 (1836) 55.660–2503

Patzicía—ask approval of budget of 4000 pesos to repair church.

2246 B 1.19.1 (1836) 55.568–2503

Patzicía—work finished in reconstructing church.

2247 B 1.19.2 (1825) 56.397–2510

25 de abril de 1825. El jefe político del partido de Chiquimula, lleva a la Secretaría General del Gobierno, la solicitud de la municipalidad de la cabecera acerca de la renta de un predio invertiendo el 50% de su valor en reedificar el templo parroquial.

2248 B 1.19.1 (1840) 57.362–2526

4 de julio de 1840. Informa el corregidor de Chiquimula a la Secretaría General del Gobierno, haber sido renovado el templo parroquial de la cabecera.

2249 B 1.19.2 (1840) 57.514–2527

22 de noviembre de 1840. El corregidor de Chiquimula eleva a secretaria General del Gobierno la exposición del P. Cura parroco de la cabecera, acerca de la inversión de cierta capital de una capellanía, en la obra de la reconstrucción del templo parroquial.

2250 B 83.2 (1843) 25.235–1114

17 de agosto de 1843. Informa el provisor del arzobispado al secretario del Gobierno, que el parroco de Santa Cruz Chinautla, solicitaba autorización para colectar limosnas, destinadas a la obra de la reconstrucción del templo y de su sacristía.

INDEX
OF AUTHORS, PEOPLE, PLACES, SUBJECTS

AUTHORS are shown in all capital letters, thusly; people, places and subjects are indicated in upper and lower case letters.

Abbreviations used with   AG   Antigua Guatemala, Guatemala
place names: C   Chiapas
   CR   Costa Rica
   G   Guatemala
   H   Honduras
   N   Nicaragua
   NG   Nueva Guatemala (Guatemala City), Guatemala
   S   El Salvador